checked 18
5

Iran's Foreign Policy in the Post-Soviet Era

Iran's Foreign Policy in the Post-Soviet Era

Resisting the New International Order

SHIREEN T. HUNTER

 PRAEGER

AN IMPRINT OF ABC-CLIO, LLC
Santa Barbara, California • Denver, Colorado • Oxford, England

Library of Congress Cataloging-in-Publication Data

Hunter, Shireen.
  Iran's foreign policy in the post-Soviet era : resisting the new international
order / Shireen T. Hunter.
     p. cm.
  Includes bibliographical references and index.
  ISBN 978-0-313-38194-2 (alk. paper) — ISBN 978-0-313-38195-9 (ebook)
  1. Iran—Foreign relations—1979–1997.   2. Iran—Foreign relations—1997–
3. Iran—Foreign relations—1979–1997—Case studies.   4. Iran—Foreign
relations—1997—Case studies.   I. Title.
  DS318.83.H863   2010
  327.55—dc22   2010006658

ISBN: 978-0-313-38194-2
EISBN: 978-0-313-38195-9

14 13 12 11 10   1 2 3 4 5

This book is also available on the World Wide Web as an eBook.
Visit www.abc-clio.com for details.

Praeger
An Imprint of ABC-CLIO, LLC

ABC-CLIO, LLC
130 Cremona Drive, P.O. Box 1911
Santa Barbara, California 93116-1911

This book is printed on acid-free paper ∞

Manufactured in the United States of America

Contents

Preface

The Soviet Union's dismantlement in December 1991, as a result of its own internal developments and without any direct outside interference, was the most significant development in global politics of the second half of the 20th century. The USSR's demise fundamentally altered the character of the international political system and equations of power among its major players. However, the expectation of a post-Soviet system based on the hegemonic dominance of the United States has not been realized, although the United States still retains the greatest influence internationally.

The characteristics of the emerging international system still remain unclear and to a considerable degree undefined, although economic, political, and military trends point to a system with multiple centers of power. Similarly, despite the relative revival of socialism in parts of the world and, notwithstanding much talk of a looming clash of civilizations, the return to a sharply divided international system along ideological lines seems highly unlikely.

What has become quite clear, however, is that post-Soviet systemic developments have been detrimental to less powerful countries, albeit to varying degrees. For example, the elimination of the Cold War era zero-sum competition between the West and the Soviet bloc countries freed both sides in that conflict to intervene more boldly in other countries, including militarily. The U.S. war against Iraq in 1991, although occurring before the official end of the Soviet Union, as well as the Afghan and Iraq invasions of 2001 and 2003, respectively, would not have been possible during the height of the Cold War. Similarly, there has been a greater deal of international tolerance for turmoil in poor and powerless countries than could have been possible during the Cold War because the fear on the part of major powers that rivals might exploit that turmoil for their own ends has essentially disappeared.

While all less powerful countries have been negatively affected by the post-Soviet systemic changes, those in the proximity of the former USSR and those with hostile relations with the West have suffered most. Iran is the best example of this category of states. Even before the USSR's official demise, changes in Soviet foreign policy had led to a hardening of Western policy toward Iran. This trend has since continued and worsened. The attitude of Iran's neighbors toward it has also stiffened.

Some countries have managed to deal more effectively with the adverse consequences of post-Soviet systemic changes and adjust to them. Iran has not been one of these countries. Instead, in the last two decades Iran has resisted the emerging new international system and, at least partly as a consequence of this resistance, has incurred significant losses and setbacks.

This work will analyze the systemic changes produced by the Soviet Union's collapse. It will also demonstrate how and why Iran has failed fully to appreciate the dimensions of these systemic changes, to understand their impact on its own position and interest, and to adjust to them adequately.

This book was written in 2008–2009, during my time as a visiting professor at the Prince Alwaleed Bin Tallal Center for Muslim-Christian Understanding of Georgetown University's Edmund A. Walsh School of Foreign Service. I would therefore like to express my thanks to the School of Foreign Service and to Professor John L. Esposito, founding director of the ACMCU, for affording me this opportunity. I greatly benefited from Georgetown's valuable research facilities and its stimulating intellectual environment.

I would also like to express my thanks to my husband Robert Hunter, for his unfailing support and good advice. Ultimately, however, I am solely responsible for any errors or shortcomings of the book.

Introduction

Foreign policies of states are essentially determined by two sets of factors:

+ Those related to their internal setting, including their geopolitical situation; ethnic and religious composition; historical experience; resource base; economic, military, and technological assets and needs; the character of their political systems and elites; and ideological/ideational proclivities
+ Those related to the external milieu within which they operate—namely, the international political system and its regional subsystems

No state, no matter how big and strong, is immune from the impact of systemic factors. However, smaller and less powerful states are even more vulnerable to systemic influences. This difference in the level of states' susceptibility to systemic influences derives from the fact that large and powerful states essentially shape the basic characteristics of the international system, determine the dynamics of interstate conflict and cooperation, and set the rules that govern interstate and international relations.[1]

By contrast, historically, with few exceptions smaller and less powerful states have had minimal roles in shaping the character of the international system or determining its rules, although this has not always been for lack of trying.[2] Rather, they have had to accommodate the system as they found it as well as any changes to its character. Failure to accommodate or, worse, challenging the system and its rules, has generally entailed irrelevancy, loss of opportunity, and security and financial costs.

Among the less powerful states, those with medium power and regional ambitions occupy a special place. Quite often, such countries are not satisfied simply to observe the rules set by major international players and strive to change those rules in ways to benefit their own interests. They also tend to compete for influence with the larger and more powerful countries, albeit to a limited degree and within a relatively narrow geographical space. Consequently, there is always a degree of conflict of interest and a level of tension between powerful actors with global interests and reach and states with medium power and regional ambitions. As a general rule, when a global actor and an actual or potential regional power face a common enemy or challenge, the competitive aspects of their relationship remain dormant, only to surface if and when their common enemy disappears or when their perceptions of who and what is the enemy changes.

Generally, less powerful states and those with medium power fare better in an international system where two or several powerful states balance one another and compete with each other.[3] These less powerful states fare worse within a system either dominated by a single hegemonic power or jointly managed by a small group of key actors. This is especially true for those middle powers which, for geopolitical and economic reasons, are of particular interest to key players. These states are especially sensitive to changes in the nature of the international political system, and the character of relations among its key actors.

Iran is a typical example of a potential middle power located in a geopolitically sensitive region, stretching from the Caspian Sea to the Persian Gulf. For more than two centuries, this region has been of special interest to key international players and hence highly sensitive to changes in the nature of the international political system. As a country that straddles both bodies of water, Iran's political destiny, foreign policy choices, and margin of independence have been strongly affected by systemic factors.

IRAN AND THE BIPOLAR
INTERNATIONAL SYSTEM

Until the end of the Second World War, the modern international political system was characterized by a multiplicity of power centers, which competed with and, at least among European states, balanced one another. By contrast, between about 1948 and 1989, the international system was characterized by a fierce competition between two power blocs, gathered around the United States and the USSR, competing for global hegemony and the hearts and minds of the less developed countries—hence its appellation as bipolar.

Iran, however, had been faced with an external environment which could be called bipolar almost since the dawn of the 19th century, as a consequence of several developments:

+ The consolidation of British control in India
+ The expansion of the British military and political presence in the Persian Gulf
+ Russia's southward imperial expansion and the ensuing Russo-British competition over Iran, Afghanistan, and Central Asia known as the Great Game
+ The lack of sufficient interest and presence of other great powers in Iran's immediate environment[4]

This bipolar condition had the following disadvantages for Iran:

+ Loss of territory both to Russia and Britain
+ The gaining of discriminatory and capitulatory advantages by Russia and Britain, such as excessive concessions on trade and granting of legal immunity to their subjects
+ Growing foreign interference in its internal affairs and the thwarting by the two competing powers of Iranian efforts at economic and political development[5]

Nevertheless, this bipolar situation allowed Iran to retain most of its territory and its nominal independence. However, because, until the advent of the Bolshevik Revolution, Russo-British rivalry lacked an ideological dimension, the power equilibrium that protected Iran from the worst of imperial predatory policies was highly unstable and susceptible to the changing state of Russo-British relations. Any dilution of competition between the two potentially could lead to their making a deal at Iran's expense as they did, in fact, in 1907, when Russia and Britain signed a treaty that delineated their respective spheres of influence in Southwest and Central Asia and divided Iran into Russian and British spheres of influence.

The Russian Revolution of 1917 did not end the long-standing Russo-British rivalry because the new Russian regime continued the old imperial policies, albeit under a new ideological cover. Rather, the addition of an ideological factor intensified their rivalry. After the Second World War and the onset of the Cold War, classical strategic and economic great power rivalry was transformed into an existential battle between two diverging socioeconomic and political systems for determining the future of the world and humanity.

Within this new systemic configuration, Iran as a state with a 1,500-mile common border with the Soviet Union acquired even greater geopolitical significance. The ideological nature of the new competition also meant that, unlike in the past, competing sides offered Iran incentives, including development assistance. At the same time, the logic of the nuclear age and the balance of terror that characterized the Cold War era meant that the two competing camps had to exercise a degree of caution in dealing with strategically important countries lest their actions unleash a larger and potentially life-ending strategic nuclear war. Consequently, both camps' ability to use military force as a policy tool against countries in the vicinity of one another was severely restrained. They also often refrained from putting undue pressures on such countries, lest they turn to the competitor.[6]

SYSTEMIC RAMIFICATIONS OF THE END
OF THE COLD WAR AND THE SOVIET COLLAPSE

The Soviet Union's collapse and the end of the Cold War fundamentally transformed the character of the international political system and interstate relations. It is still unclear what kind of a system will replace that of the Cold War era, partly because, since the USSR's collapse other important events with significant systemic ramifications have occurred, notably 9/11 and the Afghan and Iraq wars. Nevertheless, the Soviet collapse has already triggered systemic changes, whose impact has been felt more strongly, and often negatively, by less powerful states, especially those located in the former USSR's proximity.

Iran is a good example of a country strongly and adversely affected by these systemic changes. Most important, post-Soviet systemic changes have rendered the external environment of Iran's foreign policy far less hospitable. They have also created new security and foreign policy dilemmas and challenges for it, requiring a higher level of flexibility, realism, and skill on the part of Iranian diplomacy that so far has been sorely lacking.

OBJECTIVES, STRUCTURE, METHODOLOGY, AND THEORETICAL FRAMEWORK

The underlying thesis of this volume is that Iran has not fully grasped the dimensions of the systemic changes caused by the USSR's collapse, and it has not sufficiently adjusted its foreign policy objectives and practices to the new international realities, and, consequently, it has incurred substantial economic, political, and strategic losses. In particular, Iran's inability or unwillingness to change its approach to relations with the United States and also Israel in a timely fashion has subjected it to severe pressures from them and their allies and even made it potentially vulnerable to military strikes. Moreover, Iran's failure to adjust to systemic changes has enabled its neighbors to manipulate its problems and force it to adopt accommodationist and even concessionary policies toward them, as will be demonstrated in the following chapters.

Iran had avoided military attack by neighbors or extraregional powers as of spring 2010, as well as total economic bankruptcy. This limited success, however, had not been due to the dexterity and wisdom of Iranian diplomacy. Rather, it had been the consequence of mistakes by regional and international players.[7] The fact that new systemic conditions have reduced the willingness of key international actors, most notably the United States, to respond positively to a number of Iranian overtures and have enhanced the influence of elements opposed to a conciliatory policy toward Iran, again especially in the United States, has greatly contributed to Iran's inability to adjust to the new systemic conditions.

However, internal factors have been mainly responsible for Iran's failure to respond appropriately to post-Soviet systemic changes. These notably include

- the structure of the Iranian political system, especially the built-in tension between its republican and Islamic dimensions, as represented by the office of the Supreme Leader on the one hand and the parliament and the office of the president on the other;
- sharp ideological differences and personal rivalries among key personalities of the regime;

◆ the continued influence of the Islamist/revolutionary ideology on foreign policy;

◆ the still close connection between the regime's ideology and its political legitimacy;

◆ the central importance of some aspects of the regime's self-image and self-appointed role, such as that of defender of the oppressed and champion of Muslim rights, and hence the importance of some of its foreign policy positions, such as its intense opposition to Israel, for its political legitimacy.

OBJECTIVES

In light of these observations, this volume's principal objectives are

◆ to describe the characteristics of the emerging international political system, the directions in which it will most likely evolve, and the consequences for Iran;

◆ to describe and analyze the domestic factors which so far have prevented Iran from making the appropriate adjustments to the new emerging system;

◆ to provide an account and assessment of Iran's relations with the outside world within these new systemic conditions. A post-Soviet account of Iran's relations with the rest of the world will be preceded by a brief historical account of these relations.

STRUCTURE

This volume is divided into two main parts, each with subdivisions:

The first section is divided into two subsections, one dealing with the external setting of Iran's foreign policy, in other words, the post-Soviet international system; and the other dealing with the internal determinants of Iran's foreign policy.

The second section deals with the evolution of Iran's relations with individual countries or groups of countries. This part will be divided into the following subparts:

1. Iran and the United States: Are They Destined to Eternal Enmity?
2. Iran and Europe: Not So Constructive Engagement
3. Iran and Russia: A Strategic Alliance or a Fool's Bargain?
4. Looking East: Iran's Relations with, India, China, and other Asian countries
5. Iran and Its Neighbors: Pakistan, Afghanistan, and Turkey
6. Iran, Central Asia, and the Caucasus: Unfulfilled Expectations
7. Iran and the Arab World: Between Conflict and Accommodation
8. Iran's Relations with Africa and Latin America: Seeking Economic Advantage or Anti-Imperialist Coalition?
9. Conclusions

THEORETICAL FRAMEWORK AND METHODOLOGY

It is the contention of this volume that no single theory of international relations—realist, neorealist (structural realist), or constructivist—can fully explain the behavior of states and less so the intricacies of their foreign policies. The realist theory, which emphasizes the pursuit of power as the main motivation behind state behavior, fails to pay adequate attention to ideational and institutional factors, such as the role of key agents' identities and interests in determining state behavior.[8] Yet even if one accepts the realist position that ultimately power is the main motivator of state behavior, the way in which states go about gaining power and the uses to which they put the acquired power is determined in significant part by their ideational propensities and proclivities. Similarly, key actors' views and interests affect their perceptions and evaluation of external developments and their assessment of the impact on a given state's interests.

By contrast, the constructivists emphasize the role of ideas and the identities and interests of purposive actors, which they claim are shaped by shared ideas, in deciding state behavior.[9] However, the constructivists' overemphasis on ideational dynamics behind state behavior tends to ignore the fact that often ideas are used to serve purposes determined by power calculations. In short, both theories tend to ignore the close relationship between power and idea dynamics in state behavior.

Furthermore, the structure of the international system, as argued by the neorealists, especially the fact that even today the international system is characterized by a lack of an efficient mechanism to prevent conflict, settle disputes, and ensure peace and, hence, is in a state of anarchy, clearly affects states' behavior.[10] It also sets certain boundaries for state behavior, overstepping of which often involves costs, especially to less powerful states. This means that in pursuance of their ambitions and goals, whether determined by power considerations or ideas, states have to consider structural factors. This also means that, in analyzing states external behavior, structural factors should be taken into account.

In view of these considerations, the methodology used in this volume will draw upon all these theories without trying to explain Iran's foreign policy within any single theoretical framework. Instead, this study will draw on the insights provided by all relevant theories and particularly of foreign policy analysis. This discipline, with its emphasis on spanning the boundaries between the internal and external environments of foreign policy—or, as noted by Margot Light, of linking "the micro level of politics with the macro level of the international system," the role of leaders, and bureaucratic politics—is particularly well-suited to a study of Iran's foreign policy.[11]

In this context, special attention is paid here to those internal political factors that are particularly influential in the case of revolutionary countries. In such regimes, legitimacy and survival are, wholly or partly, dependent on the pursuit of ideological goals in the foreign policy arena, and ideology is closely linked to power balances within the system, characteristics that make swift and timely policy adjustments in the face of substantial change difficult.

PART ONE
THEMATIC ISSUES

CHAPTER 1

The Emerging Post-Soviet International System: Implications for Iran

Two decades after the Soviet Union's dissolution and the end of the Cold War, the character of the emerging international system is still not clear. The early expectations of a unipolar system, based on a benign U.S. global hegemony, domination, or a combination of both, have not materialized.[1] Instead, the less-than-satisfactory outcomes of U.S. military engagements in Afghanistan and Iraq have raised questions about America's willingness and/or ability to perform the function of global hegemony. These doubts were intensified after the 2008–2009 financial and economic crises. Meanwhile, the emerging system, despite some efforts to develop counterweights to global U.S. power, cannot be characterized as multipolar. The reality is that the post-Soviet international system is still evolving, and the outcome of this evolution is hard to predict. The best that can be said as of this writing is what the system is and is not likely to become in the near future.

THE NEW INTERNATIONAL ORDER:
THE U.S. BID FOR GLOBAL HEGEMONY

The Soviet Union's collapse led to a fundamental shift of economic and military power in favor of the West, especially the United States, making it the most influential international player and the single most powerful country.[2] Moreover, by discrediting Communism as a viable model for the economic and political organization of societies, the Soviet collapse also shifted the balance of ideological power in the West's favor.[3] The USSR's demise seemed to validate the superiority of the Western model of economic and political liberalism and encouraged the belief in its inevitable expansion to the rest of the world. Some analysts, notably Francis Fukuyama, were so convinced of this happening that they declared the end of history.[4]

In short, the Soviet Union's collapse ended the postwar bipolar international political system, without ushering in either a unipolar or multipolar system.

The post-Soviet system cannot be characterized as unipolar because, as noted by Samuel Huntington, a unipolar system would have "one superpower, no significant major powers and many minor powers." This situation would enable the superpower to "effectively resolve important international issues alone and no combination of other states would have the power to prevent it from doing so."[5] The system could not be identified as multipolar because that would require "several major powers of comparable strength that compete and cooperate with each other in shifting patterns. A coalition of major powers is necessary to resolve important international issues."[6]

The current system, despite the rise of countries such as India and China, and the reemergence of Russia, is still characterized by a significant disparity of economic and military power among its key players. In particular, in terms of military power and the ability to project it across long distances, the United States enjoys a significant preponderance over others. This disparity in power becomes more accentuated if the Western alliance, as embodied in the North Atlantic Treaty Organization (NATO), is viewed in its entirety.

A multipolar system also requires a degree of competition and rivalry among its key members that would affect the strategic setting within which other less powerful countries operate, and thus influence their policy choices and options. Such a level of competitiveness had not emerged among key international players. For instance, China's relations with the United States had not become excessively competitive as of spring 2010, and although becoming more tense, not yet overly hostile.[7] Quite the contrary, thus far economic and political ties that bind China and the United States have proved stronger than their differences. Similarly, renewed Russian activism and the emergence of a number of disagreements between Russia and the United States do not as yet amount to the beginning of a new era of global Russo-American competition, since, despite their differences, the two agree on a number of important international issues. Furthermore, despite some increase in its international activity, Russia is still largely focused on internal stabilization and revitalization as well as the restoration and consolidation of its influence in the former Soviet space.

This is why Huntington concluded that the post-Soviet system is uni-multipolar. In this system, there is one superpower—the United States—and a number of major powers. The solution of international problems in this system requires action by the single superpower, which can veto actions by others. Nevertheless, the superpower needs the cooperation of some of the major powers in tackling major international problems.[8]

Notwithstanding the above, immediately after the Soviet collapse, many in the United States and the world predicted the emergence of a unipolar system based on a benign U.S. hegemony. In the United States, this view existed before the USSR's official end, as reflected in President George H. W. Bush's statement following the successful completion of the first U.S.-led Gulf War in March 1991. He said: "The New Order means that what America says goes." Later, Madeleine Albright, the U.S. secretary of state during the Clinton administration's second term, called the United States the "indispensable nation." Other political commentators, notably Charles Krauthammer, talked of "the unipolar moment" and the necessity of preserving it.

William Kristol and Robert Kagan openly advocated the exercise of a "benevolent U.S. hegemony" in defense of democracy and market economy and their global promotion.[9] In short, a substantial segment of the American political elite came to believe that the United States should use this unique moment in its history to reshape the world according to an economically and politically liberal model, and in ways more congenial to its own interests.

During the first decade of the post-Soviet era, the United States acted cautiously on its transformative impulses. Between 1992 and late 2001, it behaved mostly as a "conservative hegemon." It benefited from the favorable balance of power within the existing system, rather than acting as a revolutionary and change-oriented state bent on altering the system. During this period, the United States' principal systemic goal was to maintain its supremacy and to prevent the emergence of any other credible regional or global competitors.[10]

This essentially status quo–oriented and conservative objective of U.S. strategy is reflected in the 1992 draft "Defense Planning Guidance" written under the supervision of Paul Wolfowitz, then U.S. undersecretary of defense for policy. Though not formally adopted, this study stated that the post–Cold War U.S. political and military strategy's principal goal is: "to prevent the reemergence of a new rival. This is a dominant consideration underlying the new regional defense strategy and requires that we endeavor to prevent any hostile power from dominating a region whose resources would, under consolidated control, be sufficient to generate global power. These regions include Western Europe, East Asia, the territory of the former Soviet Union, and Southwest Asia."[11]

This document recognized that the United States might have to act unilaterally; it did not talk about collective action through the United Nations, and it asserted that other powers must recognize that "the world order is ultimately backed by the U.S." Nevertheless, it advised that the United States "address the sources of regional conflicts and instability in such a way as to promote increasing respect for international law, limit international violence, and encourage the spread of democratic forms of government and open economic systems." However, it did not advocate preemption, or recourse to military action unless absolutely necessary.

The Bush administration, during its last year, and the Clinton administration (1993–2000) followed a strategy similar to that advocated in the draft "Defense Planning Guidance"—that of strengthening the existing system and pursuing its transformative objectives through nonmilitary means and in limited regions. For example, the promotion of market reforms and democracy were limited to the post-Soviet space. The United States did not pursue such goals in the Middle East, except regarding states variously characterized as "rogue," "outlaw," or "backlash"—namely, Iran, Iraq, Syria, and Libya.[12] Regarding these countries, the ultimate U.S. goal was a regime change through a policy of isolation and containment, best articulated in the Clinton administration's strategy of Dual Containment of Iran and Iraq.[13] The Clinton administration did not employ military means to achieve America's transformative goals and confined its use to preventing human catastrophes (e.g., Bosnia in 1995) and enforcing preexisting rules, such as the no-fly zones in Iraq. Nevertheless, echoing the draft "Defense Guidance," President Clinton stated in a speech in 1995 that, should the need arise, the United States would not shy away from unilateral action or the use of force. He said: "When our [America's] national security interests are threatened, we will as America always has, use diplomacy when we can, *but force when we must*, we will act with others when we can, *but alone when we must*" [emphasis added].[14]

The Clinton Administration also maintained that, in cases of gross violations of human rights, entrenched international rules such as noninterference in countries' internal affairs can and should be overlooked. However, the United States should intervene militarily in such cases only if they have a direct bearing on its interests.[15]

Despite stressing the point that if, need be, the United States would act unilaterally, during the Clinton administration, in most instances, the United States used force in collaboration with multilateral institutions such as NATO and the UN in Bosnia.

Initially, principal advisors to President George W. Bush, like Condoleezza Rice, also saw the United States as a conservative hegemon. Rice believed that the United States should act on its national interests instead of pursuing transformative and revolutionary goals, especially those with an idealistic dimension such as the spread of democracy. Rice outlined this essentially conservative vision in an article published in the January 2000 issue of *Foreign Affairs*. Nevertheless, despite its realist bent, Rice's article had more than a hint of unilateralism-when-needed, and it was dismissive of the need to act in accord with international law and with the approval of international institutions. She rejected what she said was many Americans' discomfort with "notions of power politics, great powers, and power balances," which led "to a reflexive appeal to notions of international law and norms, and the belief that the support of many states—or even better, of international institutions like the United Nations—is essential to the legitimate exercise of power. The 'national interest is replaced with 'humanitarian interests' or the interests of 'the international community.'"[16] She admitted, however, that "there is nothing wrong [with] doing something that benefits all humanity," but added that that is only "a second order effect." She also echoed views first expressed by the Clinton national security advisor, Anthony Lake, that because U.S. ideals are universal, the United States' pursuit of its own interests will benefit everyone else. She claimed that America's "pursuit of its national interests after World War II led to a more prosperous and democratic world. This can happen again."[17]

This U.S. strategy changed after 9/11. Under President George W. Bush the United States pursued an idealistic and transformative policy that included the use of force, dubbed by some of its proponents "Wilsonianism on Steroids."[18] The U.S.-led wars in Afghanistan and Iraq and the contemplation of a military strike against Iran were the outcome of this change in U.S. strategic outlook.[19] The launching of the war on terror and on Islamic extremism, considered terrorism's main cause, reintroduced an ideological dimension to U.S. views of what constituted its interests and threats to them, and hence to its foreign policy goals, as some in the Bush administration came to see Islamic extremism as an "existential threat" to the United States, similar to the role that Communism played during the Cold War era.

The evolution of the military and political situations in Afghanistan and Iraq, along with economic developments, notably the financial crisis of 2008 and its economic consequences, has set in motion trends that might have significant systemic ramifications, including whether the post-Soviet system will become truly multipolar.

Thus, irrespective of the eventual shape of the post-Soviet system, the USSR's collapse has already greatly altered the character of interstate relations.

INTERSTATE RELATIONS IN THE POST-SOVIET ERA

The Soviet collapse has introduced significant changes in the nature of interstate relations at both regional and international levels, of which the following are the most important:

1. In the nonideological post-Soviet setting, there are no issues which could cause a direct conflict between two or more major powers for the sake of another country.
2. The end of all-out competition among great powers has endowed key actors, especially militarily dominant powers, with a greater degree of freedom to act in defense of their interests without much concern for other countries' reaction. This situation means that principal restraints on unilateral action by key players or a coalition of them derive mainly from resource constraints, domestic political limits, or the difficulty of the task.
3. The disparity of power among the members of the international community, along with the lack of an adequate degree of balance of power and competition among key players, has undermined established rules of international behavior, such as respect for the sovereignty of states irrespective of their size and power and noninterference in states' internal affairs. Instead, issues discussed now are about when and under what circumstances intervention within states is justified and how it should be carried out. For example, are the lack of respect for human and minority rights, pursuit of policies deemed threatening to the rest of the world (such as support for terrorist groups), or efforts to obtain nuclear weapons sufficient ground for outside intervention?[20]
4. There has been a shift in the relative strategic significance of countries and, hence, the approach of key players toward them. The Soviet Union's collapse has eroded the strategic importance of countries that lay in its proximity and that were viewed as important for preventing Soviet expansion in sensitive regions such as the Persian Gulf, South Asia, and the Middle East.
5. The end of ideological rivalry has also ended competition for hearts and minds, except in a few regions and for nonideological reasons. The main exceptions are in the Muslim world, where Islamic extremism is viewed as a rival and threat by major players.

6. The Cold War–era alliances, grouped around the two superpowers and concepts such as nonalignment, have become irrelevant.[21]
7. The competitive dimensions of relations between the great powers and middle-sized powers with the potential to become credible regional powers have become accentuated.
8. With few exceptions, notably Iran, North Korea, and to a lesser extent some Latin American countries like Cuba, Venezuela under Hugo Chavez, and Bolivia, ideological proclivities have lost their influence as a determinant of state behavior, while the impact of other classical factors—security, economic gain, political advantage—has been enhanced.

All these changes have rendered smaller and less powerful countries, especially those with no special strategic or economic value to key players, more vulnerable to actions by the more powerful states. Given Western economic and military superiority, those smaller countries with hostile relations with the West have suffered most from these systemic changes. In the case of middle-sized powers, the new systemic realities have led the great powers to weaken such countries, especially if they are not in the orbit of their influence.

The Soviet collapse has also affected the nature of interstate relations in many regions by eliminating the common fear of the Soviet Union as a mitigating factor in intraregional conflicts and rivalries. The result has been

1. the accentuation of competitive and even conflictual dimensions of regional relations, especially among countries in the proximity of the former USSR.[22] This new reality has worked against Iran as neighbors, such as Turkey and Pakistan, have come to see it more of a rival than a partner against the expansion of Soviet influence. No longer fearing Soviet inroads in Iran, they have adopted a less cooperative and at times even hostile posture toward Iran. They have further used Iran's estrangement from the West to enhance their own regional position and their value to the West. The same has been true of the Persian Gulf and other Arab states;
2. the erosion of the role of ideology in regional ties;
3. the improvement of the position of pro-Western countries and the worsening of the position of anti-Western states. This has been so because, without the Soviet counterweight and the absence of another global competitor for the West, the West has been able to act more harshly toward its opponents without fearing any negative consequences, either in terms of its relations with other countries or the risk of a global confrontation.

All countries have been affected by these changes. But countries that lie in proximity to the Soviet Union have felt their impact more strongly, either positively or negatively. Iran and Turkey present two contrasting examples of countries near the USSR that were differently affected by these changes because of the diverging character of their relations with the West. Iran's strategic importance was eroded after the Soviet collapse, as the West no longer saw it as a bulwark against Soviet ambitions in the Persian Gulf. Meanwhile, Iran's position as a potential regional power accentuated the competitive aspects of its relations with global powers. This factor, combined with Iran's anti-Western posture, made it appear as a potential threat to the West, leading to a hardening of Western, especially U.S., attitudes toward Iran.[23] By contrast, Turkey's value to the West was enhanced because of

- its position as a Western ally;
- its role as a link between the West and the newly independent Muslim Republics of the former Soviet Union;
- its position as an energy export route;
- its serving as a barrier both to Russian efforts to retain/reestablish its privileged position in these republics and potential Iranian influence in Central Asia and the Caucasus.

THE "CLASH OF CIVILIZATIONS" AS THE NEW IDEOLOGY

A cardinal principle of international relations theory is that international and regional systems abhor power vacuums, generally leading to efforts by competing powers to fill them. The post-Soviet era developments indicate that abhorrence of vacuums also applies at the ideological and paradigmatic levels. This contention is supported by Samuel P. Huntington's advancement in 1993 of his theory of the clash of civilizations between the liberal West and nearly all of the rest of the world, but more particularly the Islamic world.[24] According to this theory, in the nonideological post-Soviet world, cultural differences greatly influenced, if not determined, by religious values will shape the character of interstate relations and will mark principal international fault lines. This belief has led to a growing interest in the actual and potential role of religion in international affairs, reflecting an important, albeit unstated, assumption that religion will be the ideology of the 21st century.[25]

This emphasis on religious factors in international affairs, coupled with the perception of Islam, or at least its militant version, as the West's principal foe, has adversely affected those Muslim countries unfriendly toward the West. By the late 1990s, however, the idea of the clash of civilizations appeared to be losing some of its appeal and credibility as a paradigm capable of explaining the increasingly complex nature of global events and international relations. This was because no conflict emerged between China, with its Confucian culture, Russia with its Orthodox faith, the Muslim world with its Islamic culture, and the West, despite the fact that, according to Huntington, the first three of these creeds are culturally at odds with the liberal West.[26] On the contrary, some key Muslim governments remained either close allies of the West or in a nonconfrontational posture toward it. Exceptions to the latter rule were Iran, Iraq, Libya, Syria, and Sudan.

The situation was dramatically changed by the terrorist attacks perpetrated by Muslim extremists in the United States on September 11, 2001 (9/11). These events, followed by other terrorist attacks in Europe and Asia, triggered significant changes in U.S. policy and those of a number of European countries, thus setting in motion changes in the overall character of the international system and interstate relations, whose full implications and dimensions are not yet clear.

9/11 AND THE GLOBAL WAR ON TERROR: SYSTEMIC RAMIFICATIONS

Relevant to the discussion here, the following are the most important consequences of 9/11:

1. The thesis of a clash of civilizations was rehabilitated and a seemingly open-ended conflict with the Muslim world began, triggered by the strategy of global war on terror. This war was characterized by some observers, notably an ex-director of the Central Intelligence Agency, James Woolsey, as the fourth world war.[27]

An underlying hypothesis of the theory and strategy of the global war on terror is that the fight against Islamic extremism and what some have called Islamo-Fascism, is nothing short of an existential struggle between the forces of democracy, justice, freedom—in other words, the forces of good and light—against those of tyranny, fascism, repression: in other words, those of evil and darkness. Nothing illustrates better this Manichean vision of the world than the term "axis of evil" that President George W. Bush used in his 2002 State of the Union speech in reference to Iran, Iraq, and North Korea.[28]

Logically, therefore, the global war on terror, as envisaged by the architects of U.S. policy, such as then deputy secretary of defense Paul Wolfowitz, meant that the United States must eliminate regimes that supported terrorists and also were bent on developing weapons of mass destruction (WMDs). Indeed, early on a linkage was established between support for terrorism and the quest for WMDs.[29]

2. The attacks of 9/11 provided an opportunity for the proponents of a unilateralist and preemptive strategy on the part of the United States, for dealing not only with the challenges posed by so-called global terrorism, but also for producing fundamental change in sensitive regions, such as the Middle East. The first step in this direction was to be the elimination of regimes in Iraq, Iran, Syria, and Sudan, as indicated in an article written by two prominent and influential neoconservatives, William Kristol and Robert Kagan, in the *Weekly Standard*, the neocon flagship publication. Referring to President Bush's promise to destroy "every terrorist group of global reach," they wrote: "We trust these words will reverberate far beyond Kabul, in Tehran, Damascus, Khartoum, and above all, in Baghdad."[30]

Initially, the hope was that Iraq's transformation from dictatorship to democracy would produce a positive domino effect by prompting spontaneous popular movements for democracy elsewhere in the Middle East. However, the United States was not going to rely on the indirect effects of an Iraqi success story and instead embarked on a policy of active promotion of democracy in the Middle East and adjacent regions, within the framework of its Greater Middle East Initiative. This initiative was introduced by President George W. Bush's speech on the occasion of the 20th anniversary of the establishment of the National Endowment for Democracy in November 2003, and it articulated a U.S. commitment to the spread of democracy in the Middle East. In short, muscular democracy promotion became the ideological underpinning of the new U.S. strategy.[31]

3. At least initially, 9/11 also brought together on the U.S. side in its war on terror not only Western allies, but also Russia and China, both of whom had their own problems with Islamic militancy.[32] It also seemed to make an international system led by the United States more palatable to other key players. An immediate result was almost unanimous international support for the U.S.-led military operations against the Taliban forces in Afghanistan, enabling the United States to establish military bases in Afghanistan and in neighboring Central Asian countries.

The U.S. decision to launch a preemptive attack on Iraq in 2003, based on allegations that it was harboring WMDs and had links to Al Qaeda operators (including the 9/11 attackers) fractured this unity. Even important U.S. allies such as France and Germany vigorously opposed U.S. plans during the United Nations Security Council (UNSC) discussions in the run-up to the U.S. attack on Iraq. Consequently, no UNSC resolution specifically sanctioning U.S. military attack on Iraq was passed, and the United States justified its action on the basis of Resolution 1141, on how to deal with Iraq's response to UN demands to inspect its nuclear sites and other suspect installations.

The U.S.-led military operations in Iraq, which began on March 18, 2003, did not result in the quick and resounding victory promised by its proponents. Nor did it lead to the breaking out of democratic revolutions in the rest of the Middle East. On the contrary, Iraq soon plunged into chaos and near civil war, and suffered tremendous human and material loss. Human and material costs of the war also steadily mounted for the United States.[33]

Meanwhile, Middle Eastern countries proved very resistant to U.S. pressures—albeit at best half-hearted—for democratization. The strength of Islamic-oriented political parties, as demonstrated by the victory of Hamas in the Palestinian elections in January 2006, brought back the specter that democracy promotion could lead to the emergence of Islamist governments in the Arab world, and it led to the abandonment of the Greater Middle East Initiative.[34] More important, a number of developments triggered a degree of reassessment of post-9/11 U.S. policies, both in the United States and among other key international players, thus presaging a potential shift away from an international system based on U.S. hegemony—characterized by its most ardent proponents as a new American Empire.[35] Paramount among these developments was the following:

+ U.S. failure to win a quick and relatively cost-free victory in either Afghanistan and Iraq or to transform the Greater Middle East.

+ Mounting economic and human costs of the wars.

+ Russia's economic recovery, in major part because of higher oil prices, leading to a more assertive foreign policy.

+ China's growing economic power, coupled with its increasing interest in the Middle East.

+ Mounting fears of the global impact of another war in the Persian Gulf, this time against Iran.

IMPLICATIONS FOR IRAN

Because of the following factors, the negative systemic consequences for Iran of the Soviet collapse were compounded by the emergence of the thesis of the clash of civilizations and the consequences of 9/11, including the growing popularity among influential circles in the United States of the theory of an existential battle between Islamic radicalism, or so-called Islamo-Fascism, potentially lasting for a hundred years:

+ The characteristics of Iran's government. Iran's entire system of government is based on Islam, and it has appointed itself as the defender of Muslim rights, most notably in Palestine.

+ The U.S. view of Iran as the main state supporter of terrorism.

+ The establishment of a U.S. military presence on Iran's borders.

+ The shift of U.S. strategic focus to Iran, following the removal of Saddam Hussein as a sizeable and, according to some the main, threat to U.S. interests. This shift was reflected in a speech by President Bush, in which he stated that Iran's quest for nuclear weapons cast the shadow of a "Nuclear Holocaust" over the Middle East and, if undeterred, could lead to "World War Three."[36] Later, during a visit to Abu Dhabi, in January 2008 he called Iran a threat to global security.[37] Other politicians and commentators compared Iran to Nazi Germany and its hard-line president, Mahmud Ahmadinejad, to Adolf Hitler.[38] The United States also justified its plan to establish a missile shield in Central Europe in terms of the Iranian threat.[39]

+ The persistence of widespread concerns about Islamic militancy leading to major players' reluctance to support Iran and risk antagonizing the United States.

The net result has been a much less congenial external environment for Iran's foreign policy.

INTERNATIONAL REACTIONS TO
U.S. HEGEMONY: PRE- AND POST-9/11

Because of the United States' economic and military weight, which enabled it to assume global leadership, along with the disequilibrium in the balance of costs and benefits in challenging America, until the mid-1990s U.S. hegemony, although resented by some other countries, was not challenged either in practice or in theory. Nevertheless, by 1995, there were growing comments on the inadvisability of a unipolar international system. The opponents of a unipolar world based on U.S. hegemony argued that such a system would mean reducing world order "to the priority of U.S. objectives," and that it would be inherently unstable. To "counterbalance [this] destabilizing factor," some commentators advised the development of counterweights to U.S. power and the United States' domination of the international system.[40]

The Russian Federation and its foreign minister, Yevgeny Primakov, first advanced the idea of a multipolar international system, which came to be known as the Primakov Doctrine. The enunciation of this doctrine heralded the end of Russian foreign policy's "Atlanticist" period and the gradual emergence of a multidimensional and less West-centered Russian foreign policy outlook. Those in Russia who favored this approach advocated the formation of a bloc by Russia, China, and India to counter U.S. hegemony. Others talked of the formation of a bloc in cooperation with China and Iran, while others included Iran in the China, Russia, and India bloc.[41]

The idea of a multipolar system also found some resonance in China and France, and at the end of President Jacques Chirac's visit to China in 1998, the two countries in their joint communiqué called for the creation of a multipolar system. Russian and Chinese leaders, too, made a similar appeal.[42] In visits to India, too, Russian officials advocated the idea of a multipolar system, as illustrated by Russian prime minister Primakov's comments in 1998 on the evolving international system. Primakov said: "A lot depends in the region on the policies of China, Russia and India. If we succeed in establishing a strategic triangle, it will be very good."[43]

The idea of creating a multipolar system was also picked up by Iranian politicians, commentators, and some intellectuals, largely because of its implicit anti-Americanism. For example, until the coming to power of the reformist president, Muhammad Khatami, who tried without much success to reintegrate Iran into the international community, key Iranian officials talked of joining with countries like India and China to form a counterweight to the United States. In 1993, in an interview with the *Hindustan Times*, Iran's President Akbar Hashemi Rafsanjani said: "One of Iran's most natural partners is India, and given our situation with the United States and some Western countries, China is another suitable partner ... if we work together we can have the last word on international affairs."[44] Iran's foreign minister, Ali Akbar Velayati, also periodically called on India and China to join Iran in counterbalancing the United States. Even reformist figures who now favor better U.S.-Iran relations, such as Behzad Nabavi, as late as 1998 supported forming alliances to counter U.S. hegemony.[45]

The proponents of a multipolar system also considered it a morally more just system. The Russian president at the time, Boris Yeltsin, said in an interview with the Italian newspaper, *Corriere della Serra*:

We don't see multipolarity as a utilitarian means to achieve some kind of aim.... A multipolar world is the wisest and most democratic system for the world.

Only in such a world will all countries, regardless of the size of their military power have a voice and can preserve their unique character. . . . Attempts by some countries to force a unique model, in other words, their exclusive leading role on the world are unrealistic and perhaps even dangerous.[46]

The following factors contributed to the emergence and popularity of the theory of multipolarity:

+ The end of ideological competition among states did not eliminate other causes of rivalry and conflict among states.

+ Despite the elimination of ideological conflict, the wholesale implementation of the Western liberal model in different cultural settings, notably Russia, proved more difficult than had been imagined, thus encouraging the reemergence of authenticist cultural and political movements.

+ The preeminence of a single power leads others to form coalitions to counter its influence.

According to Peter Rodman, efforts to counter U.S. dominance are natural and derive from the dynamics of the balance of power. He explained U.S. puzzlement at this reaction in terms of the ideological and Wilsonian bent of U.S. foreign policy. Because the United States believed that it was acting "in the name of universal moral principles," it was surprised that others saw its assertiveness as unilateralism. Yet the world was reacting to U.S. predominance in "thoroughly classical, un-Wilsonian balance of power fashion."[47]

For the following reasons, the creation of a countervailing bloc has at least so far proved impossible:

+ In the nonideological post-Soviet international system, the degree of symmetry of interests among states proved insufficient. Consequently, states had to calibrate more carefully various aspects of their international relations.

+ There were deep-rooted suspicions and ambivalences among the potential key members of such an alliance—(i.e., India/China, China/Russia).

+ All of the potential members of such an anti-American coalition, including China and India, found the potential costs of such a coalition to be higher than its benefits.

For example, given its extensive economic and trade relations with the United States and in view of the U.S. strategic importance in the Asia-Pacific region, China did not find it in its interests to burden itself with a costly policy of countering U.S. influence at the global level. India, too, found such a strategy detrimental to its interests and instead pursued a policy of increased economic and strategic cooperation with the United States. Even Russia was unwilling and unable to assume the burden of leading an anti-American coalition. Consequently, the idea of promoting a multipolar system did not go far because, as put by Vladimir Lukin, a former Russian ambassador and a member of state Duma, "there were no fools to follow us [Russia]."[48]

However, this failure did not mean that countries such as Russia and China accepted and endorsed all U.S. policy choices and actions or that they did not try to

create security and other institutions to advance their own interests in regions of particular interest to them. On the contrary, Russia became more active in reestablishing
its influence in the former Soviet republics and in reentering the Middle East. It also
established the Shanghai Cooperation Organization (SCO) with China and the participation of the Central Asian countries. Later, Mongolia, Pakistan, India, and Iran
joined the SCO as observers.

Meanwhile, China, largely driven by the need for secure energy sources and access
to other raw materials and export markets, expanded its relations with Central Asia,
the Middle East, and Africa.[49]

This systemic situation, coupled with lingering suspicions by such major international actors as Russia and China of Iran's Islamic ideology, despite the Iranian government's profession of friendship for both states, worked against Iranian interests.
Both governments throughout the 1990s and the first decade of the 2000s sacrificed
relations with Iran for the higher economic and political benefits of remaining on
good terms with the United States and other Western countries. Yet Iran continued
to pursue a foreign policy at odds with the new international realities.

IS THE ERA OF U.S. HEGEMONY/
DOMINATION OVER?

Post-9/11 events did not evolve according to expectations, and the United States',
and to some degree European, military engagements in Afghanistan and Iraq did not
yield the results that were hoped for and have taken much longer than was anticipated.
By the time President Obama assumed office the United States had been engaged in
the Afghan war for nine years. During this period, the United States and its NATO
allies had failed to eliminate the Taliban's challenge and stabilize the country. On the
contrary, by this time the Taliban had made a significant comeback. Moreover, Afghan
instability had been extended to Pakistan, and the Pakistani Taliban had become a
serious headache for both Pakistan and the United States, and had complicated operations in Afghanistan.[50] Consequently, by the end of 2009, President Obama had
decided on a policy of increasing the level of U.S. troops by 30,000 and other NATO
countries, such as Britain and France, had also announced increases in the level of
their troop contributions.[51] This was followed by the launching of major operations
against Taliban forces in Marja, followed by operations in Helmand.[52] Operations in
Marja were quite successful. However, they had not destroyed the Taliban's ability to
continue their operations even in and around Kabul as illustrated by the bombings in
Kabul on February 26, 2010.[53]

Developments in Iraq have been only marginally better. The government in Iraq
claimed that the country was capable of establishing security and order, and the United
States had decided to partially withdraw from Iraq by 2010 with full departure of U.S.
forces by the end of 2011.[54] However, deeply ethnic, sectarian, and ideological fissures
bedeviled the country and came to the fore in the months preceding the parliamentary
elections, which were held March 7, 2010. The result of the voting, however, was close
and many predicted that disputes would emerge among contending coalitions.

Financial and human costs of these wars have also exceeded what initially was expected, leading to erosion of American and European publics' support for them.[55] Furthermore, these wars had greatly contributed to the erosion of the United States' moral authority and had demonstrated the limits of its power to reshape the world according to its plans.

In recognition of these factors, the Obama administration abandoned any talk of a world order based on U.S. hegemony. Instead, it adopted a different diplomatic posture, emphasizing multilateralism and partnership with other major powers, including such emerging powers as India and Brazil, and it embarked on efforts to heal the rift with the Muslim world. Secretary of State Hillary Clinton, in a speech at the Council on Foreign Relations on July 15, 2009, described this U.S. strategy as trying to build a "multi-partner world."[56] In such a world, instead of countervailing and potentially conflicting poles of power, there would be cooperative and inclusive groups of countries. However, although not stated in her speech, the assumption is that these partners will share U.S. views and priorities, and will accept its leadership role.

The paradigm of a multipartner world is more attractive than that of a world made up of competing and antagonistic power poles. However, the notion is also naïve and ignores the fact that geographical, historical, religious, cultural, and economic factors are often at the root of many regional conflicts. They also shape countries' perception of their interests and their views on regional and global issues. The United States will find it increasingly difficult to convince countries with diverging priorities to agree to its own agenda. Nor will the United States be able to pursue successfully contradictory policies such as creating cooperative relations with Russia while supporting Ukraine's and Georgia's membership in NATO, or retaining Pakistan's cooperation on Afghanistan while forming a strategic and defense partnership with India. This phenomenon is not new. In general, global powers with vast regional relations and alliances find it difficult to reconcile their allies' diverging interests.[57] During the Cold War, anti-Communism provided certain glue for such alliances. But in the post-Soviet world, it is difficult to imagine what overarching concern could perform the same function. Yet, by spring 2010, and despite the United States's difficulties in achieving its global goals and growing talk of a U.S. decline, no single power or grouping of powers seemed ready and/or capable of replacing it on the global scene.[58]

In sum, in the near- and medium-term perspective, both the vision of a multipartner and a multipolar world appeared as equally unrealizable. Rather, international relations will remain volatile and patterns of alliances asymmetrical and limited in scope. Similarly, it is unlikely that an overarching paradigm similar to the East-West divide of the Cold War era will emerge, performing the same function.

However, even in such a world Iran will remain highly vulnerable to external pressures and threats, including from the United States, if it continues its current course and persists in a posture of defiance toward nearly all major international players. It would also certainly be excluded from all serious poles of power or partnership.

CHAPTER 2

The Domestic Context of Iran's Foreign Policy: Impact on External Behavior

‿◌◦

According to F. S. Northedge, foreign policy is a dialogue between the inside and the outside, meaning that the pattern of states' external behavior is determined by a constant interaction between its domestic needs and realities—"internal determinants"—and the characteristics of the external environment within which they operate.[1] These internal determinants greatly influence states' external behavior by providing them with certain options while excluding others.

INTERNAL REALITIES AND NEEDS

Internal determinants of state behavior can be divided into two categories, constant and changeable. The first category includes the following three factors:

1. *Geographic Location*

It is often said that "geography is destiny." This dictum may be an exaggeration. But clearly a country's geographic location greatly affects its ethnic composition, cultural makeup, and vulnerability to external attacks, thus also shaping its historical experience and influencing its worldview and self-image.[2]

Iran is among those countries whose overall evolution has been deeply affected by its geographical location. In particular, Iran's location at the crossroads of major population movements and on the route of imperial expansions has deeply affected its ethnic, religious, and linguistic composition. It has also shaped its cultural characteristics and worldview.

GEOGRAPHY AND IRAN'S CULTURAL DESTINY AND NATIONAL IDENTITY

To a great extent, Iran's geographical characteristics greatly explain its current ethnoreligious and cultural characteristics. These have led to the presence of Indo-Iranian peoples in the Iranian plateau and their cultural legacy, as well as to Iran's occupation following Greek, Arab, Turkic, and Mongol invasions, with their negative economic, political, and cultural consequences for Iran. For example, Arab and Turko-Mongol invasions, in addition to bringing tremendous physical destruction, introduced greater ethnic, linguistic, and religious diversity and hence rivalry as well as nomadism to Iran, thus undermining its national cohesion. Additionally, these periodic destructions set back for centuries Iran's economic, political, and scientific development.[3]

In the last two centuries, policies of imperial powers such as Russia and Britain have hampered Iran's economic and scientific development. According to Professor Issawi, British policy toward Iran during the 19th and early 20th centuries was to keep it "denuded of any facilities that make it easier for the Russians to advance through it to the [Indian] subcontinent."[4]

The Arab conquest of Iran in 642 c.e., leading to Iran's Islamization if not complete Arabization, in particular created deep cultural and identity-related cleavages in Iran, with significant sociopolitical consequences whose legacy is bedeviling Iran today and is deeply affecting the self-perception and worldview of important segments of its people and polity. A very important aspect of this cultural cleavage is the debate on which aspect of Iran's identity—Iranian or Islamic—should be emphasized. This debate gradually became more acute following Iran's encounter with modernity, partly because it initially was the result of military and political defeats at the hands of Russia and later Britain. These defeats raised the issue of the causes of Iran's decline, including the role that Islam as practiced in Iran may have played in it, and, as in many other Muslim societies, led some intellectuals to declare traditional Islam and the Ulema (Muslim clergy) responsible for Iran's decline. They also advocated a resurrection of Iran's pre-Islamic culture as the basis of its national identity and as part of its modernization, plus the adoption of nationalism and constitutionalism as the basis of political legitimacy instead of Islam. These developments, coupled with the process of modernization, which included the secularization of educational and judicial institutions, shifted the balance of power and influence in favor of the newly educated and mostly nationalist segments of society and against traditional classes, most notably the clerical establishment, thus inextricably linking issues of culture and identity to questions of power and legitimacy.

The Pahlavi era (1925–1979) saw the official triumph of Iranianism and, in parallel with it, a growing animosity of the clerical establishment and religiously minded groups toward Iran's pre-Islamic culture. The Left, too, for other reasons, notably the authoritarian nature of the Pahlavi regime, turned against Iranian culture. The Islamic Revolution of 1979 ushered in a period of the assertion of the Islamic pole of Iran's culture and identity, at least at the official level, and a shift of the balance of power and privilege to religious elements.[5]

However, despite the Islamic regime's systematic policy of cultural and political Islamization, pre-Islamic aspects of Iran's culture and identity have not disappeared. In the last two decades, there has been a revival of these influences, partly because of disillusionment with the performance of the Islamic regime, but essentially because of the deep-rooted nature of these influences. In fact, even the leaders of the regime have rediscovered Iran's pre-Islamic past and take pride in its achievements.[6]

This linking of issues of power and political legitimacy to culture and identity has had considerable implications for Iran's external relations and the character of its foreign policy. Generally, those who lean toward the Iranian pole favor a more nationalistic and realist foreign policy and those who privilege the Islamic pole advocate a pan-Islamist foreign policy.

GEOGRAPHY AND IRAN'S STRATEGIC PREDICAMENT

Iran's geography continues to affect its political destiny. The fact that it is located astride the Persian Gulf and the Caspian Sea, between the Arab world and the Indian subcontinent and Central Asia, and in the proximity of Russia continues to make Iran a focus of interest of major international players. This situation has advantages and disadvantages; in Iran's case it has been largely disadvantageous as it has led to greater interference and presence of key players in Iran's proximity often with the goal of limiting Iran's freedom of action in its immediate neighborhood. It has also led to a good deal of interest on the part of key players in Iran's domestic evolution and even direct or indirect interference, with the goal of determining its direction.

Moreover, the fact that Iran's immediate neighbors, notably Arabs and Turks, are some of its cultural and historic rivals has created an unfavorable strategic environment by depriving Iran of natural allies.

2. Historical Experience

Nations, like individuals, are largely the product of their life experiences, which shape their perceptions of themselves and of the outside world and their own place in it. The deeper a nation's historical roots the greater the impact of its historical experience on its behavior.

Iran's 3,000-year history of statehood is marked by dramatic ups and downs in its fortunes, with periods of splendor and expansion followed by defeat, decline, and disarray. This history has imbued the Iranians' political culture with two contradictory characteristics—namely, a sense of entitlement to an important position within the family of nations and a sense of victimhood.

The first sentiment is engendered by Iran's considerable achievements throughout its long history, and its ability to nativize its conquerors rather than losing its identity and culture. Professor Ada Bozeman's remark that although Arabs conquered Iran, Iran conquered Islam, best illustrates this Iranian ability.[7] The sense of victimhood has largely derived from Iran's experience of the last two centuries with the European powers. This experience has been one of defeat, occupation, exploitation, and manipulation.

This contradictory legacy of Iran's historical experience has had negative consequences for the management of its external relations. It has endowed Iranian foreign policy with a degree of unrealism about the country's international role and position; it has given its diplomatic style a tinge of pretentiousness not matched by its actual power and ability; and it has led it to value independence perhaps excessively and, sometimes, at great cost.

These basic characteristics not only have survived after the Islamic Revolution but have become stronger.

3. Resource Base

Countries' natural, economic, technological, and military resource base affects their external behavior by providing them with certain options while excluding others. A relatively self-sufficient country has a better chance of conducting an independent foreign policy than one that is dependent on external sources for its technological and military and—at times—economic needs. In some cases, the lack of adequate natural resources, such as water and agricultural and mineral materials, can lead to aggressive behavior on the part of countries that need such resources. Often countries that are rich in natural resources but lack adequate military and economic power become the target of more powerful states' interference because they need their resources.

Iran is a good example of a country with certain resources, namely oil and gas, that are highly desired by major international powers, while at the same time being deficient in technological, military, and financial resources. This resource deficiency has affected Iran's policy options during its modern history as well as its aspirations. For instance, early in the 19th century Iran responded positively to Napoleonic France's suggestions for an alliance in order to secure French military assistance in its war against Russia. However, after Napoleon reached an agreement with Russia at Tilsit, France abandoned Iran.[8] Reza Shah Pahlavi's befriending of Germany and his son's alliance with the West were both largely prompted by this resource deficiency.

This experience has endowed Iran's political culture with a desire for economic, technological, and military self-sufficiency as necessary for its overall independence.

The Islamic regime has been particularly influenced by this desire, which was sharpened because of its experience during the Iran-Iraq War and later because of various economic sanctions imposed by the United States and its allies. The Islamic regime has also been less willing to compromise some of its ideological stands in order to obtain resources that it has needed. Nevertheless, resource deficiency has affected its foreign policy orientation, or at least that of some elements of the regime. For instance, the Rafsanjani government's efforts to reach out to the West in the 1990s were largely determined by this factor. On other occasions, too, the regime has had to make compromises because of deficiency in its financial and technological resources.

In addition to these three principal *constant* internal determinants of state behavior, two *changeable* factors are prominent:

1. Characteristics of the Political System and Decision-Making Apparatus

The character of states' political systems and their decision-making apparatus and processes greatly influence their external behavior. In authoritarian political systems where power is centralized either in the hands of a single individual or institution, such as the army or the intelligence services, the state's behavior reflects the needs, interests, and preferences of either the autocrat or the dominant institution, and little or no attention is paid to the public's preferences in deciding the direction of foreign policy. Key foreign policy decisions are made by the leader or by the leadership of the dominant institution such as the military or the intelligence apparatus. Most Middle East countries' political systems fall within this category, as did Iran's prerevolutionary political system.

By contrast, in states with democratic systems, the legislature, civic organizations—including those representing the interests of business or ethnic groups—the press, the expert community, and ultimately the public, play significant roles in shaping external behavior. Similarly, in such systems electoral calendars and the relative role of foreign policy-related issues in electoral campaigns can influence foreign policy choices. Moreover, even in such systems individual leaders influence the character of foreign policy, at times decisively. In the case of major players, these leaders even affect global politics because

+ as put by Daniel L. Byman and Kenneth J. Pollack, these leaders' "goals, abilities and foibles . . . are crucial to the intentions, capabilities, and strategies of a state. [They] not only affect actions of their own states but also shape the reactions of other nations, which must respond to the aspirations, abilities and aggressiveness of foreign leaders";[9]

+ the ideas and beliefs of leaders affect the way they filter the information they receive from different sources. According to Hermann, Hermann, and Hagan, when leaders have a well-defined worldview, they tend to look "for cues that confirm [their] beliefs when making foreign policy. As a result [they] will be relatively insensitive to discrepant advice and data. . . . In effect the leaders[s] selectively use incoming information to support [their] predispositions";[10]

+ in many democracies, notably those of the United States, UK, France, and Germany, presidents and prime ministers enjoy extensive power and can to a great extent shape public attitudes and those of the legislature.[11]

The character of the decision-making apparatus, notably the range of institutions involved, their preferences and proclivities, the way in which decisions are made, and the character and authority of the final decision-maker are equally important.

Some theories on the making of foreign policy consider the dynamics of the process and bureaucratic politics related to it to be keys to understanding states' external behavior.[12] Moreover, these factors largely determine the means through which policies are executed.

Another influential factor is the basis of states' political legitimacy. In democratic systems, the basis of legitimacy is popular will expressed through regular elections. Authoritarian states lack popular legitimacy and their power depends on coercion and varying degrees of cooptation of elements of society. A third category is states whose governments base their legitimacy on a particular ideology. Recent examples include the

Soviet Union, China, and other Communist countries. Iran's government also legiti-
mizes itself through political and social ideology, based on Islam.

In ideological systems, the fortunes of the leadership are based on the maintenance
of the ideology, hence the need to justify all decisions in ideological terms. Therefore,
policies that risk undermining the state's ideological legitimacy are hard to adopt, and
policy changes are frequently preceded by ideological revision and often by change in
the ruling elite.

2. Ideology and Worldview

The relative impact of interest and ideology in determining states' behavior is still a
subject of debate, and different theoretical schools accord them different weight. The realists consider national interests and the desire to acquire and hold power as the main
motivations behind state behavior, and they view ideology merely as a disguise for power-
driven behavior. According to Hans Morgenthau, this cover is needed because, without it,
the state would be in an unfavorable position vis-à-vis other states in a struggle for power.
This is so because without appeal to principles other than quest for power, states cannot
gain people's support and their willingness to sacrifice, without which, Morgenthau main-
tains, "no foreign policy can pass the ultimate test of strength."[13]

Moreover, for a century now, dynastic interests, raison d'état, and the naked pursuit
of power have not been sufficient to justify state behavior, thus further enhancing the
importance of ideas and ideologies in determining that behavior.

The constructivists, meanwhile, emphasize the role of ideas, including states' ideology, in determining their external behavior.[14]

In reality, both sets of factors influence states' behavior. The role of ideas and ideology is crucial because they largely determine states' perception of what constitutes
their interests. For example, states believe that the spread of their own values and ideologies serves their interest by enhancing their security because like-minded states sel-
dom threaten each other and tend to be more cooperative on other issues. In this sense,
ideas and interests reinforce one another and jointly shape states' behavior. Ideas and
ideologies also determine states' choices of means to achieve their goals because, as put
by Zbigniew Brzezinski, ideology is essentially an "action program."[15]

However, there are limits beyond which most states cannot and do not go in pursuit of their ideological goals, if such pursuit endangers their vital interests. When
such conflicts arise, the urge to survive overrides ideological concerns and ideologically
driven goals.[16]

IRAN'S ISLAMIC POLITICAL SYSTEM:
IMPACT ON EXTERNAL BEHAVIOR

Iran's postrevolutionary political system is called the Islamic Republic, reflecting its
dual and contradictory character, which derives from an effort to combine republican-
ism with Islam. In a republic, a government's legitimacy derives from the people's will

as expressed through regular elections. But in Iran's version of Islamic government, legitimacy derives from the application of Islamic principles, and the Supreme Religious Leader (Vali-e-Faqih) is the final arbiter of both what these Islamic principles are and how they should be implemented.

For nearly two decades, the question of which aspect of Iran's political system, Islamic or republican, should be emphasized has been hotly debated and came to the fore with special force during the June 2009 presidential elections.

Some groups in Iran, including more liberal clerics, have emphasized the republican dimensions of the system and have used some of Ayatullah Khomeini's sayings to support their position. These groups base their argument on Khomeini's saying that the ultimate standard and measure of legitimacy is the people's vote (*Mizan Ray e Mardom Ast*).[17] Others, like the conservative Ayatullah Mesbah Yazdi, claim that Khomeini wanted an Islamic government in which legitimacy solely derives from Islam and, because the Leader's authority is based on religious grounds, his decisions do not require popular acceptance.[18]

Irrespective of Khomeini's real intentions, Iran's constitution, existing institutions, and their powers have a built in contradiction, but the balance is in Islam's favor. According to Article 2 of the constitution, the nature of Iran's political system is Islamic and is based on "the unity of God (*Tawhid*), His exclusive sovereignty, the right to legislate, and the necessity of submission to his commands." This clearly does not leave much room for popular will. Article 4 states that "all civil, penal, financial, economic, administrative, cultural, military, political and other laws and regulations must be based on Islamic criteria . . ." and adds that the "Fuqaha and the Guardian Council are judges in this matter." This provision, too, leaves no room for peoples' views and preferences. Finally, Article 5 establishes the guardianship of the Faqih during the time of the occultation of the 12th Imam, by stating that, until his [12th Imam] return, "the *Wilayah* and leadership of the *Ummah* devolve upon the just (*adil*) and pious (*muttaqi*) Faqih, who is fully aware of the circumstances of his age; is courageous, resourceful, and possessed of administrative ability [and who] will assume the responsibilities of this office . . ."[19]

The nonrepublican dimension of the system is enhanced by the constitution, which assigns to the parliament a consultative role based on the Koranic injunction that Muslims should consult in running their affairs. Ayatullah Khomeini also saw the parliament not as a legislative body, at least not in areas where there are clear Islamic laws, but one that develops programs (*Barnameh Gozari*) for the implementation of Islamic laws. Therefore, the people's representatives can only participate in setting programs or legislating on matters on which Islamic law is silent.[20]

Moreover, the people's role in the choice of their representatives is limited by a vetting process of candidates conducted by the Executive and Supervisory Board of Election (Shuraye Nezarat Ejraei bar Entekhabat), and the ascertaining of their suitability for office by the Guardian Council (Shuraye Negahban). Since the criteria for candidacy are vague, such as sincere commitment to the Islamic system, the Guardian Council ultimately is free to decide whom to accept. This, too, diminishes the people's role in the electoral process. Furthermore, the Guardian Council passes judgment on the acceptability of parliamentary decisions.

The powers of the president are also seriously constrained by the institution of the Velayat-e-Faqih. The president, even if he enjoys wide popular support, cannot adopt policies opposed by the leader or other influential elements of the regime. The president can even be reduced to the position of a glorified executive secretary, unless he enjoys the support of the regime's powerful elements, notably the Revolutionary Guards. The experience of Iran's highly popular President Muhammad Khatami (1997–2005) illustrates this anomalous situation.

Since the very beginning, these characteristics of the system have led to intra-regime conflict and rivalry, rendering the making of decisions on key foreign policy issues difficult, especially if this meant a fundamental departure from the established pattern of behavior. It has also made Iran's foreign policy too dependent on the ideas, worldview, and preferences of the Leader rather than on a clear calculation of national interests.

INTRA-SYSTEM IDEOLOGICAL DIFFERENCES

The existence of significant ideological differences among the system's key influential groups further complicates decision-making in foreign policy. In the last two decades, as a result of the consequences of the Iran-Iraq War, the Soviet collapse and its systemic repercussions, and post-9/11 developments, these differences have greatly sharpened. The effect has been an inconsistent and irrational foreign policy, trying to reconcile irreconcilable goals, such as pursuing an unnecessarily belligerent policy on the Arab-Israeli issue while trying to improve relations with the West.

Roots of the Ideological Divide

The ideological differences within Iran's Islamic regime are rooted in the country's sociopolitical and cultural developments, which began in the mid-19th century and accelerated in the 1940s, 50s, and 60s, and in the diverging socioeconomic and ideological backgrounds of the revolution's leaders and their lay supporters. An important division has been that between the left-leaning clergy and lay Islamists, on the one hand, and, on the other hand, those who, while supporting the revolution, were more traditional and opposed leftist ideas.[21] This division reflects the often-underestimated impact of leftist ideologies on Iran's contemporary political culture and on the mind-set of Iranian intellectuals, including those with an Islamic orientation, and on the younger and socioeconomically deprived clergy.[22] It also reflects the Iranian Left's failure to win over the religious masses, leading it to ideologize Islam and use it as an instrument of socioeconomic and political change. Ali Shariati is the major intellectual representative of this trend, and the Mujahedin-e-Khalq its institutional embodiment.[23]

The more traditional trend is represented intellectually by Ayatullah Murtaza Mutahari and politically by Ayatullahs Muhammad Beheshti and Ali Akbar Hashemi Rafsanjani. (Both were assassinated shortly after the revolution.)

Two other trends should also be mentioned—namely, the conservative and influential Islamic Coalition Party (Hizb-e-Motalefeh-e-Islami), which is inspired by the ideas of the Fedaiyan-e-Islam of Navab Safavi;[24] and the Islamo-nationalists of Iran Freedom Movement (Nehzat-e-Azadi-e-Iran).[25] During the Pahlavi regime, these groups collaborated against the Shah while each were separately planning how to shape and control the post-Pahlavi system. Immediately after the revolution, a fierce conflict emerged among these forces. The first target was the Islamo-nationalists, against which both the Left and the Islamists cooperated. Then the Mujahedin-e-Khalq (MEK) attacked the Islamist forces. They were defeated and forced into exile in Iraq, from where they have been waging a war against the Islamic regime. Some MEK members and sympathizers, along with other leftists, chose to join the system and to work from within to implement their goals. The secular left was conflict-ridden and consequently lost out to the Islamists.

During the first decade of the regime, those leftists who chose to work within the system had considerable influence over both domestic and foreign policies. In particular, they were behind the taking of the American diplomats hostage, an act whose consequences even today bedevil Iran, and in the 1990s they frustrated pragmatic elements' efforts to normalize Iran's relations with the West.[26]

Many of the leftist Islamists, including the 2009 presidential candidate, Mir Hussein Mussavi; Khatami's vice president Masumeh Ebtekar—the infamous "Mary" of the hostage operations; and the ex-Tudeh member, Behzad Nabavi; have turned reformist and proponents of either doing away with the institution of the Velayat e Faqih or greatly diluting it, and they support a pragmatic foreign policy.[27]

DIVERGING VIEWS ON FOREIGN POLICY

All of these groups had some basic traits in common in terms of their worldview and their foreign policy orientation. But they also had significant differences. The following factors, some of which had also been influential in the revolution, have shaped the Iranian revolutionaries' worldviews:

1. *Historical Experience and Anticolonialism*

To varying degrees, all groups in Iran have been influenced by its historical experience, especially its domination by the great powers and the damaging consequences that followed. One result has been a desire for independent foreign policy and non-entanglement in bloc politics. In the past, this desire was reflected in Mussadiq's policy of Positive Neutralism (Siyasat e Movazeneh e Manfi) and the Shah's National Independent Policy (Siyasat e Mustaqel e Melli).[28]

All pro-revolution groups, including liberal nationalists and Islamo-nationalists, shared this desire, but the latter groups were pragmatic and realized the importance of tempering this desire with realism, particularly in light of Iran's economic and military limitations and growing global interdependence. They also did not consider the United States as the source of all of Iran's and the world's problems, and they viewed Russia as more threatening. The Islamists' "Neither East, Nor West, Only Islam" also reflects this influence. Ayatullah Khamenei's statement to the visiting

West German foreign minister in July 1984 that Iran's Neither East Nor West policy resulted from "historic insults suffered by Iran during the last hundred and fifty years at the hands of great powers" indicates this influence.[29]

However, the views of the regime's key elements differed significantly, particularly regarding the great powers and their potential to harm Iran. The more traditionally oriented considered the USSR to be most threatening, and the leftists saw the West, especially America, as the main enemy. The reply of the one-time leftist-turned-reformist Mir Hussein Mussavi, who was prime minister between 1981 and 1989, to the question as to why Iran was less critical of the Soviet Union and Eastern bloc, indicates this difference. He said that this was because Iran "did not sustain as much damage from them [USSR and the Eastern Bloc] as we sustained from the U.S. in the last fifty years." Another leftist-turned-reformist is the Ayatullah Mussavi Khoeiniha, a mastermind of the U.S. embassy hostage crisis, who played an important role in preventing a U.S.-Iran rapprochement following the Iran-Contra debacle. He said at the time that "we [Iranians] must maintain the condition in this country in such a way that the United States will lose hope forever, and that there will not come a day when our actions or the actions of certain individuals, or those in charge, could provide the United States with a ray of hope."[30]

2. Militant Third Worldism

Iran's historical experience has also led it to embrace issues of concern to the Third World, notably the reform of the international order in all its dimensions, an order which Third World nations view as unfair, and the advancing of intra–Third World or so-called South-South cooperation. Therefore, even before the revolution, Iran championed Third World causes. However, the Islamic regime's Third Worldism is of a militant and left-leaning variety, with strong anti-Western and anti-Israel tendencies, which were popular during the 1960s and '70s and have recently made a relative comeback. This factor has greatly contributed to the regime's strong anti-imperialist tendencies, although they are articulated in Islamic terms, such as *Istikbar-e-Jahani* (global arrogance), its animosity toward Israel and conservative Arab regimes, and its anti-imperialist policy (*Siyasat e Istikbar Setizi*).

3. Islamist Influences

Early Islamist movements in Iran, such as the Fedaiyan e-Islam, were inspired by Islamist movements in the Arab World, notably the Ikhvan al Muslimin (Muslim Brotherhood), which saw the Zionist movement and later the creation of the state of Israel as major blows to the Muslim world. They also viewed the West as responsible for both phenomenon as well as for the Ottoman Empire's fall. Iranian revolutionaries shared this view. Khomeini believed that the Zionist movement and the state of Israel were part of a plan to undermine Islam and the Muslim world, a plan which began with the dismantling of the Ottoman Empire. Despite the long history of Ottoman–Iranian sectarian and power conflict, he lamented its passing.

4. *Leftist Ideas*

Leftist ideas have greatly influenced Iran's overall intellectual and sociopolitical evolution. Significant elements that participated in the revolution, including the Islamist trend, were influenced by leftist ideologies. These ideologies, too, viewed capitalism and imperialism represented by the United States as the main source of evil in the world. They also strongly opposed the so-called International Zionism and Arab Reaction. This partly explains the regime's anti-Americanism and hostility to Israel and conservative Arab regimes.

5. *Arab Radicalism*

Many Iranian revolutionaries, notably the Islamo-leftist Mujahedin-e-Khalq, but also figures like Mustapha Chamran, were trained in radical Arab countries and in the PLO (Palestine Liberation Organization) camps.[31] These Arab radicals are virulently anti-American and anti-Israel, dislike conservative Arabs, and were pro-Soviet.

6. *Khomeini's Ideas*

Khomeini's ideas, which were expressed in Islamic terms, reflected many of these influences, while also having special characteristics, notably antinationalism and pan-Islamism.

According to Khomeini, Muslims form a single community (*Ummah*), and existing borders among them are artificial and created by Islam's foreign enemies. Khomeini opposed nationalism because it fractured the Islamic world, and he believed that Islam's interest and glory should determine Muslim states policies and not narrow national interests.[32] He attributed the Muslim countries' self-interested behavior to their lack of commitment to true Islam and their adherence to what he called "American Islam." He advocated close cooperation among Muslims, saying that "no one can defeat one billion Muslims if they were united."[33] Many damaging aspects of Iran's foreign policy can be explained by the lack of adequate focus on national interests, a legacy of Khomeini's thinking.

Khomeini's worldview was polarized, and he saw all things in terms of a battle between truth and righteousness and falsehood (*Haq VA Bail*), between the arrogant powers (*Mustakberin*) and the downtrodden nations (*Mustazefin*). He also saw Iran as the standard bearer for and champion of all deprived nations and not only Muslims. This was so because, according to him, Iran's Islamic system was the only one based on true Islam.

Khomeini's simplistic and polarized worldview and his antinationalist and pan-Islamist tendencies have had disastrous consequences for Iran. By the mid-1980s, a number of developments, including the growing strength of Iranian nationalism, the Iran-Iraq War, the lack of positive Muslim response to Iran's pan-Islamist policies and the continued centrality of nation-states within the international system had led to the emergence of a more pragmatic worldview, at least on the part of some elements within Iran, and a reduction of antinationalist and pan-Islamist tendencies. These trends were strengthened during the last two decades because of the regime's domestic and external failures and systemic changes triggered by the Soviet collapse.

However, the legacy of Khomeini's worldview lingers, along with the ideological and idealistic tendencies of the early revolutionary period. Early revolutionary tendencies remain strong among influential circles, including the leadership of the Revolutionary Guards, and, after being eclipsed during the Rafsanjani and Khatami presidencies, they made a comeback during the first term of Ahmadinejad's presidency (2004–2009).

All elements within the regime were influenced by these factors, albeit to varying degrees, a difference which colored their approach to foreign policy. Broadly speaking, those whose ideas were closer to traditional interpretations of Islam and were somewhat more influenced by nationalist tendencies, favored a less revolutionary and more pragmatic foreign policy, which served Iran's national interests. They were less viscerally anti-Western and interested in normal relations with the West. Leftists, meanwhile, were anti-West and more interested in advancing Iran's revolutionary goals. In the last two decades, the leftists have gradually become reformist and advocate a more pragmatic and less revolutionary foreign policy geared to Iran's national interests.

More generally, the experiences of the Islamic regime, especially its foreign policy setbacks and its poor performance record, coupled with systemic changes triggered by the Soviet collapse, have greatly diminished the appeal of revolutionary, unrealistic, and ideological foreign policy, without ending the debate on the relative roles that realism (*Vaqe Garaei*) and idealism (*Arman Garaei*) should play in determining Iran's external behavior.

PERSONAL RIVALRIES

The Islamic Revolution changed the nature of Iran's political system but not its political culture, with its emphasis on personalities rather than institutions and the practice of either idealization or vilification of political personalities. Consequently, political personalities and their personal rivalries, animosities, and power ambitions have deeply affected Iran's foreign policy because competing personalities have used important foreign policy-related issues in their power struggles.

The system's structure, with the offices of the Supreme Leader and president, is a sure recipe for rivalry between them. This situation makes it sometimes difficult to ascertain to what extent policy differences within the leadership reflect ideological differences or personal rivalries because often ideological arguments are raised in order to hide personal issues.

Another aspect of Iran's political scene can best be characterized as the politics of revenge. Thus whenever a group which has lost in competition makes a comeback, it tries to exact revenge.[34] This aspect of Iran's political system and culture has proven harmful to Iran's foreign policy.

Because of the lack of democratic and strong political institutions in Iran, this situation is unlikely to change in the near future, with Iran's foreign policy remaining hostage to the vagaries of personal rivalries within its leadership.

IDEOLOGICAL BASIS OF REGIME LEGITIMACY

The Islamic regime's legitimacy derives from its claim to wanting to create the perfect Islamic society, to maintain Iran's independence, to combat Islam's enemies and defend Islam, and to support all downtrodden people (*Mustazafin*) against the arrogant powers (*Mustakberin*). These goals are vague and totally different policies can be justified in their name. For example, Iran can claim to be defending Islam and the oppressed while pursuing its own interests. Other states pursue their own interests while claiming to want to promote world peace, alleviate poverty, and other lofty ideas. Yet Iran has failed to adopt this strategy because ideological positions are linked to considerations of power and privilege. Moreover, early in the revolution Khomeini identified certain powers, most notably the United States and Israel, as Islam's archenemies, with whom any normal relations are impossible. This makes those who suggest any accommodation with these two countries vulnerable to charges of betraying Khomeini's and the revolution's ideals. More fundamentally, the abandonment of these positions risks undermining the basis of the Islamic elites' claim to the country's rulership.

Thus, the Islamic regime's foreign policy suffers from this ideological straightjacket, while inability to change exacerbates its dilemmas and contradictions and could lead to a violent unraveling.

THE DECISION-MAKING PROCESS

The Supreme Leader makes the final decisions on the basic direction of Iran's foreign policy and on key foreign policy issues, such as relations with the United States, Iran's position on the Arab-Israeli conflict, and the nuclear issue. Nevertheless, because of the following factors, the process of reaching decisions is quite complex: first, competing forces and views try to influence the Leader and win him over to their preferred point of view; second, changing conditions require periodic reassessment of policies even in an ideologically driven political system such as Iran's; and third, the Leader prefers to the extent possible to base his decisions on consensus.[35] This preference reflects the fact that intra-regime differences are not caused solely by ideological factors but also reflect diverging economic and other interests. Thus alienating powerful factions could undermine the entire system. Consequently, the process of decision-making on the most important foreign policy issues, which also have ideological dimensions, is long and tortuous.

Foreign policy–related issues are debated both in official forums, such as the parliament (especially its Foreign Affairs Committee), and in the press and electronic media. The press serves as a platform for various politicians, religious leaders, and intellectuals to voice their views on foreign policy challenges faced by Iran and on how to deal with them successfully. The Leader is apprised of the diverging views, and various analysis and policy options are also presented to him.

Institutionally, the organ responsible for coordinating, facilitating, and streamlining the policy-making process on security and foreign policy is the Supreme National

Security Council (SNSC). The council was created in 1989 when, following Ayatullah Khomeini's death, the constitution was revised.[36] According to Article 176, the duties of the SNSC are to

- formulate defense and national security policies within the bounds of general policies determined by the Leader;
- harmonize state programs in areas relating to politics and collect intelligence reports, as well as develop social, cultural, and economic activities in relation to general defense and security policies;
- exploit Iran's material and intellectual resources for countering threats against the country.

The president presides over the SNSC, and its membership consists of the following: the heads of the three branches of government, the chief of the Supreme Command Council of the Armed Forces, the official in charge of National Budget and Planning Affairs, two representatives from the Supreme Religious Leader, the minister of foreign affairs, the minister of interior, the minister of information, a cabinet minister as the situation may warrant, and the highest ranking officials in the armed forces and the Sepah (Islamic Revolutionary Guard Corps.)

The ministry of foreign affairs is responsible for the conduct of Iran's foreign policy and implementing decisions reached by the higher officials, especially the Leader, but it does not play a key role in formulating policies and strategies.

The internal setting of Iran's foreign policy, especially the ideological basis of the regime; the veto power of the Leader; and intra-regime divisions and rivalries have negatively impacted it's foreign policy as the following chapters will demonstrate.

PART TWO
CASE STUDIES

CHAPTER 3

Iran and the United States: Are They Destined to Eternal Enmity?

Extensive U.S.-Iranian relations date back to the early 1950s, although America became involved in Iranian affairs during the Second World War, as part of the Anglo-American and Soviet occupation of Iran in 1941. Despite being of fairly recent origin, U.S.-Iranian relations have been intense, sometimes characterized by friendship and sometimes by hostility. From 1953 to 1978, Iran and America were allies, although their alliance was at times troubled.

After the Islamic Revolution, the two countries became bitter enemies and, in the course of 30 years, have suffered from each other's actions and accumulated a long list of grievances, making reconciliation so far difficult. Moreover, in Iran, for some segment of the Islamic regime, enmity with the United States has become a cornerstone of the regime's ideology, worldview, and self-image, a foundation of its legitimacy, and as such inextricably intertwined with intra-regime ideological and power competition. Consequently, for the past 30 years, the Iranian government has not looked at relations with the United States rationally and in light of Iran's national interests.

In the United States, too, memories related to the hostage crisis of 1979–1980, the bombing of the U.S. marines in Beirut in 1982, Iran's obstruction of the Middle East peace process, along with the dynamics of American domestic politics and the influence of America's Arab and Israeli allies, have limited the United States' ability to view Iran objectively. Consequently, America has missed opportunities potentially capable of leading to some form of accommodation if not total reconciliation.

Post-Soviet systemic developments, and the effects of 9/11, despite some episodes of informal cooperation, as was the case regarding Afghanistan after the U.S. invasion, led to the hardening of the U.S. position toward Iran under presidents Bill Clinton (1993–2000) and George W. Bush (2001–2009), with the ultimate goal of changing the Iranian regime. The Bush administration even considered military action to achieve this goal.

Because of the difficulties encountered by the United States in the conduct of its wars in Afghanistan and Iraq, the administration of President Barack Obama (2009–)

initially opted for a policy of engagement with Iran, based on outreach and negotiations, and it made some positive gestures. Some positive sounds were also heard from Iranian officials, including its Supreme Leader. However, because of the continued influence of factors which, in the past, had hindered any breakthrough in the U.S.-Iranian relationship, progress toward better relations was slow. The disputed nature of Iran's June 2009 presidential elections, the repression which followed popular protests against the election results, the exposure of deep fissures within the Iranian regime, and Iranian accusations that the United States, Britain, and France were trying to foment a color/velvet revolution in Iran further undermined the prospects of better U.S.-Iranian relations.

Nevertheless, by October 1, 2009, representatives of the United States and Iran met in Geneva in the context of nuclear talks between Iran and the so-called 5+1 representatives.[1] The results of the meeting were declared to be cautiously optimistic and the group was to meet again on October 25, 2009.

However, intra-regime divisions and even petty personal rivalries such as that between Ahmadinejad and Ali Larijani, the former nuclear negotiator and the current speaker of the parliament, led Iran to delay declaring its acceptance of the draft agreement. Larijani accused the West of "chicanery" and asked why Iran should ship its uranium abroad in order to receive something—enriched uranium for the Tehran research reactor—that the West is legally bound to provide.[2] Later Iran indicated that it might not be willing to transfer the entire 75 percent of its enriched uranium at once to Russia and might instead transfer its uranium in stages as it received the more highly enriched uranium for its research reactor. Interestingly, Ahmadinejad was very positive on Iran's desire for nuclear cooperation with the West.[3] Later, Iran proposed a phased swap of fuel, but this proposal was rejected by the United States and the Europeans. By spring 2010, any prospect of improving Iranian-U.S. relations had been dashed and the U.S. shifted the focus of its policy on seeking to impose severe sanctions, while also keeping the military option on the table. Following introduction of the new U.S. nuclear strategy in April 2010 and the exclusion of Iran and North Korea from the list of states that the U.S. pledged not to attack with nuclear weapons, Iran responded with harsh criticism.

HISTORICAL BACKGROUND
OF U.S.-IRAN RELATIONS

Iran first approached the United States in 1851, when its envoy to the Ottoman court met the U.S. ambassador to Constantinople. Iran's immediate purpose was to purchase warships from the United States, in order to patrol Iran's Persian Gulf coast and protect the Iranian merchant marine and its islands and ports "from the preponderance" of an unnamed power, in other words Britain.[4] In the long term, Iran's reformist prime minister, Mirza Taqi Khan Amir-Kabir, hoped to interest America in Iranian affairs so as to mitigate the adverse effects of Russo-British competition on Iran. In 1856, Iran and the United States signed a treaty of commerce and friendship, but state-to-state relations remained limited until the outbreak of the Second World War. However, a number of Americans, notably Howard Baskerville, who died in the course of Iran's constitutional revolution; Samuel Jordan, who founded the first modern high school in Tehran; and Morgan Shuster, who tried to reform Iran's financial system; became involved in Iranian affairs, thus laying the foundation for future relations.

LACK OF INTRINSIC U.S. INTEREST IN IRAN

Iran's early efforts to interest the United States in its affairs failed, because America lacked an intrinsic interest in Iran. Like Britain, which saw Iran as useful in its competition with Russia, the United States had a derivative interest in Iran, as illustrated by its ambassador's view of it "as a serviceable potential ally against Great Britain."[5]

In the intervening decades, this basic aspect of the U.S. view of Iran as, at times, useful for the achievement of its goals, did not change or affect the U.S. approach toward Iran. Indeed, even throughout the period of their supposedly close alliance (1953–1978) the United States saw Iran essentially as a useful buffer against the USSR and as an instrument of its regional policies in the Persian Gulf, not as a country inherently valuable to it. This U.S. assessment of Iran was in contrast to its assessment of Turkey and Saudi Arabia as inherently valuable, the former because of its strategic importance and the latter for its oil reserves. America brought Turkey into NATO and in the early 1940s developed a close partnership with Saudi Arabia, but it refrained from signing a formal treaty of alliance with Iran, despite the Shah's pleadings. Moreover, the United States never engaged in sociopolitical experimentation in Turkey or Saudi Arabia, while doing so three times in Iran (1953, 1962, and 1978), with disastrous consequences for that country. Unlike its behavior toward Iran, the United States has never made much of human rights violations in either Turkey or Saudi Arabia although in the 1980s, according to Amnesty International, there were 250,000 political prisoners in Turkey, many more than in Iran under the Shah, which became a test case for the Carter administration's human rights policy, and "almost all of them [in Turkish jails] were tortured."[6] Saudi Arabia's human rights record even today is dismal.[7]

Likewise, U.S. financial aid to Iran, when they were allies and when Iran needed help, was much less than what other U.S. allies and even some pro-Soviet countries such as India received.[8]

Furthermore, at times the United States demanded that Iran perform regional tasks that were not in Iran's interest, best exemplified by the U.S. use of Iran as the instrument of its Persian Gulf policy after the British withdrawal from the east of Suez and while America was growing tired of the burdens of the Vietnam War and was in no mood to assume new responsibilities. Clearly, the Shah did not have to accept the role conferred on him by America. Yet given the fact that after the Kennedy administration's experimentation with reforms in Iran the Shah was never confident of American support, he could hardly have refused U.S. demands.

SYSTEMIC FACTORS: PERENNIAL TENSION
BETWEEN GLOBAL AND REGIONAL POWERS

Since becoming significant, U.S.-Iranian relations have been affected by the perennial tensions that exist between global powers and middle powers with regional ambitions. Because generally regional powers tend to act more independently and challenge the supremacy of great powers, the latter are often suspicious of actual and potential regional powers, even in the absence of ideological differences. They only accommodate regional players when they need them in order to confront or contain a rival global power.

Despite its economic and military shortcomings, Iran has always had the potential to become a regional power, hence British policy throughout the 19th century to keep Iran weak. The dynamics of the Cold War and later the U.S. need for Iran in the Persian Gulf prompted America to bolster Iran's military capabilities. But even before the end of the Cold War, tensions between Iran and the United States and other Western powers arose when the Shah became too ambitious and began to talk of Iran not only as a Persian Gulf power but also as an Indian Ocean power. The more serious tensions that have characterized Iran-U.S. relations in the postrevolutionary period also partly derive from this perennial tension. The Soviet collapse, by reducing America's need for Iran as a buffer against the USSR, has also enhanced this perennial tension, thus impacting major aspects of U.S. policy toward Iran in the post-Soviet era.

MORE RECENT CAUSES OF DISCORD

Over the last six decades, because of several traumatic events, Iran and the United States have accumulated negative memories, which even today hinder reconciliation, as both sides insist that all wrongs done be acknowledged and atoned for.

For Iran the following events have been most important:

1. *Romanticism gone sour.* Almost from the time it first approached the United States in the mid-19th century until the 1953 coup d'état, Iran had a romanticized vision of America. It viewed America as a country that, given its own relatively lack of a colonial experience, supported other countries struggling to free themselves from the domination of alien powers; Iranians looked to America as a counterweight to the predatory European powers. Even Dr. Musadiq, Iran's very popular and nationalist prime minister who was removed by a U.S.-sponsored coup in 1953, was hopeful that the United States would support Iran in its dispute with the British during the crisis over the nationalization of Iran's oil industry, without realizing that, as a country with extensive overseas investments, the United States could not support nationalization of foreign assets.
2. *The Anglo-American 1953 coup d'état against Dr. Muhammad Musadiq.* The coup, coupled with certain U.S. policies during the Cold War and the Vietnam War, changed Iran's and the Third World's views of the United States as

a champion of struggling countries. The coup has been seen by generations of Iranians as America's original sin against Iran.

3. *U.S. support for the Shah.* For some Iranians, who are of an age to have experienced the Shah's rule, the United States is guilty by association because it supported the Shah.

4. *U.S. support for Iraq during the Iran-Iraq War, despite the fact that Iraq was the aggressor.*

5. *The shooting down of an Iranian passenger plane by the* USS *Vincennes in 1988.*

6. *The imposition of sanctions.*

For the United States, the most traumatic event was Iran's holding of its diplomatic personnel hostage between November 1979 and January 1981, followed by the bombing of U.S. barracks in Lebanon in 1982, in which elements allegedly supported by Iran were involved, and the Khobar Towers bombings in 1996, in which Iran was again allegedly implicated. To these must be added an uninterrupted stream of hostile and derogatory discourse emanating from Tehran about the United States, best summed up by the Islamic regime's characterization of the United States as the Great Satan.

In recent years, however, Iranian perceptions of the United States have undergone considerable change and, according to a number of opinion polls, the Iranians are the most pro-American of the Middle Eastern populations. Factors responsible for this shift have been the U.S. absence from the Iranian political scene and popular disillusionment with the Islamic regime, and hence a widespread loss of Iranians' faith in its propaganda.

U.S.-IRAN RELATIONS IN THE 1980s

Since the collapse of the Shah's regime, the issue of U.S.-Iranian relations has become inextricably intertwined with Iran's domestic politics, notably ideological and power competition within its political elite. Since 1987, U.S. domestic politics have also greatly intruded in these relations.

THE FALL OF THE BAZARGAN GOVERNMENT: THE U.S. FACTOR

Conflict among the disparate forces that had coalesced against the Shah began immediately after his departure. During the first year of the revolution's victory, the leftists and the Islamists, plus self-seeking individuals such as Abol-Hassan Bani-Sadr and Sadeq Qotbzadeh, successfully undermined the interim government of Mehdi Bazargan (February 1979–November 1979), by using the question of Iran's relations with the United States.

The immediate cause of the Bazargan government's fall was the hostage crisis. But the crisis itself was the outcome of the diametrically divergent views of Bazargan on the one hand and both Khomeini and the leftists on the other, regarding the shape of

Iran's future society and government and its regional and international role. Without these fundamental differences and the determination of various competing groups to win the power game in Iran, the hostage crisis would most likely not have occurred, and, if it had, would not have lasted long.

Bazargan was a nationalist who believed that Islam should provide the ethical and moral basis of life in Iran, but he wanted the country to have a democratic, not religious form of government. In foreign policy, his priority was to secure Iran's national interests rather than to pursue ideological goals. As a realist, he recognized the fact that given Iran's military and economic shortcomings, it needed to be on good terms with all of its neighbors, including the USSR, and particularly, in order to balance the Soviet power, to have good relations with other key international players, notably the United States. Therefore, Bazargan endeavored to normalize relations with the United States, and the United States, which also wanted workable relations with Iran, responded positively.[9] President Jimmy Carter expressed a desire to maintain cooperative relations with Iran, and U.S. secretary of state Cyrus Vance met Ibrahim Yazdi, Bazargan's minister of foreign affairs, at the UN in September 1979, followed by a meeting between U.S. national security advisor Zbigniew Brzezinski and Bazargan in Algiers in November 1979.

Arguably, the Bazargan government and the U.S. administration moved too fast in trying to consolidate bilateral relations, and their mutual eagerness for good relations might have precipitated the hostage crisis. Some analysts have considered the U.S. decision to allow the Shah to enter the United States as another contributory factor.[10] However, this is unlikely, because the hostage takers' motives went beyond prevention of reasonable U.S.-Iranian relations and were linked with the struggle for power in Iran. Nevertheless, some actions by the U.S. Senate undermined efforts to maintain good relations with Iran.[11] One negative consequence of Senate actions was that the Bazargan government refused *agrément* (approval) to the U.S. appointee to be ambassador to Iran. According to some observers, the absence of an ambassador in Tehran deprived the United States of an opportunity to counter some of the more negative representations of it in Iran.[12]

THE HOSTAGE CRISIS: WHO WAS BEHIND IT AND WHY?

Even after 30 years, it is difficult to ascertain why the hostage crisis occurred and who was behind it, partly because different personalities who were involved in these operations offer diverging interpretations that may not reflect their true motivations, and partly because Iranians have obscured the role of any outside elements. Moreover, even those, such as Khomeini, Bazargan, and later Bani-Sadr, who had not ordered the hostage taking manipulated it for their own political objectives, including eliminating groups for which they had no further use. Nevertheless, it has now become clear that the left wing of the Islamist forces that today constitutes the bulk of the regime's reformist elements, including figures like Masumeh Ebtekar, Muhammad Khatami's vice president; and Hojat ul Islam Khoeiniha, nicknamed by the French *Le Mullah Rouge* (the Red Mullah); were involved in the hostage taking.

Once the crisis began, the secular left, notably the pro-Moscow Tudeh, also joined the bandwagon. The Tudeh did so because it rightly calculated that, as long as the crisis lasted, U.S.-Iranian relations would not improve and that, even after the crisis ended, its legacy would make reconciliation very difficult, as has indeed proved to be true. The Tudeh's support of the hostage operations meant that Moscow, too, was not displeased about events, as it thought that this would keep the Americans out and could hasten the coming of a true socialist revolution. Various Palestinian groups, which during the early days of the revolution had penetrated Iran, were also engaged in this operation. These groups believed that the revolution had altered the Middle East's regional balance in their favor by eliminating the Shah's regime and by reducing American influence; they wanted to make sure that American influence would not return to Iran.[13]

Ayatullah Khomeini found the crisis useful for the realization of his plans for Iran and the Muslim world. Sensing that because of the Cold War the United States would be inhibited in using military force against Iran, he manipulated the crisis to demonstrate the limits of U.S. power and to puncture the myth of its invincibility. Ironically, Cold War politics, especially the U.S. determination to deter any possible Soviet inroads in Iran as a first step toward expanding into the Persian Gulf, as best expressed in the "Carter Doctrine" and outlined in President Carter's State of the Union speech on January 23, 1980, helped Khomeini to pursue his goals.[14]

American electoral politics might have also helped prolong the crisis; allegedly, the Republicans convinced those Iranians who wanted to be rid of Bani-Sadr to delay the release of the hostages until after the 1980 U.S. presidential elections. As it happened, Jimmy Carter lost the elections and the hostages were released on the day of President Ronald Reagan's inauguration.[15]

THE IRAN-IRAQ WAR

Many in Iran and the Middle East, as well as some outside analysts, believe that Iraq invaded Iran in September 1980 with U.S. acquiescence if not encouragement. The analysts point to two factors in support of their theory: first, U.S.-Iraqi rapprochement as early as 1977; and, second, the changing views of senior members of the Carter administration, notably Zbigniew Brzezinski, who "had begun to look favorably toward Saddam Hussein as a potential counterweight to the Ayatullah Khomeini and as a force to contain Soviet expansionism in the region."[16] Some analysts have even claimed that Brzezinski had assured Saddam Hussein that the United States would not oppose the separation of Khuzestan from Iran and had met with Saddam Hussein in Amman just a few months before Iraq's invasion of Iran.[17] One journalist, Robert Parry, has written that the U.S. secretary of state, General Alexander Haig, in a 1981 memo noted that "it was also interesting to confirm that President Carter gave the Iraqis a green light to launch war against Iran through [then prince, later king] Fahd."[18]

Given the anguish and humiliation inflicted on the United States by the hostage crisis, plus the looming presidential elections, the temptation to use Iraq to punish Iran would have been strong. The idea of turning Iraq into a U.S. ally in the Middle

East would equally have been tempting. The United States might have also hoped that, faced with a foreign invasion, Iran would resolve the hostage crisis. However, the following factors argue against the United States having instigated Iraq's attack on Iran:

+ Risk of the Soviet military intrusion into Iran.
+ Risk of Iran turning to the Soviet Union.
+ Lingering anxiety about Iraq's becoming too powerful and dominating the Persian Gulf.
+ U.S. dislike of the Ba'athist ideology.

Whether the United States encouraged Saddam, once Iraq attacked Iran the United States and other Western countries did not condemn Iraq's aggression and, as Barry M. Lando has observed, "When Iraqi forces swept into Iran on September 22, 1980, there were no indignant speeches by Western leaders or calls for a U.S. embargo, as there were when Saddam Hussein invaded Kuwait ten years later."[19]

Throughout the war, the United States maintained an official policy of neutrality while, until the summer of 1982, trying to maintain a balance of power between Iran and Iraq. During this period, the Reagan administration even allowed the transfer of some military spare parts to Iran and indicated that it did not favor territorial changes in the region, as reflected in a statement of the U.S. secretary of state, Alexander Haig. He said that the United States favored a settlement to the war that would "preserve the sovereignty and territorial integrity of both Iraq and Iran."[20] The main reason behind this position was the fear of potential Soviet gains in Iran, and, according to some observers, the Soviet-centeredness of the Reagan administration in terms of its preoccupations. More cynical observers have argued that the United States and its regional allies saw the war as acceptable as long as it was confined to Iraq and Iran, because it weakened the two most powerful countries in the region. Some U.S. officials also hoped that fear of Iran would encourage the moderate Arabs to join Israel and the United States in a grand alliance of "Strategic Cooperation."[21]

By the summer of 1982, however, the following factors had changed the situation in the Middle East and hence U.S. views of the two antagonists, producing a shift in Iraq's favor:

+ Iran had managed to repulse Iraqi forces.
+ Iran's relations with the Soviet Union had become strained because of Iran's crackdown on the pro-Moscow elements, including the Tudeh party in 1983.
+ Feeling more vulnerable, Iraq had become accommodating toward the United States and the Gulf states.
+ Israel's invasion of Lebanon in 1982 had led to the establishment of an Iranian presence there, and to Iran's involvement in terrorist activities in Lebanon.

In the coming years, the United States provided Iraq with military, intelligence, economic, and other assistance, and closed its eyes to Saddam's use of chemical weapons, both against Iraqi Kurds and Iranians.[22]

However, even Iraq's invasion did not change Iran's behavior in the short term; internal bickering continued and the U.S. hostages were not released for another four months. It was only after Bani-Sadr's departure and the consolidation of Islamic forces in power that Iran began both to put up a serious defense against Iraq and to release the hostages.

American policy toward the Iran-Iraq War proved to have been a mistake. By not condemning Iraq's aggression, the United States, other Western powers, and the UN only buttressed Iran's view of their imperialist nature and the powerlessness of international organizations. When Iran drove Iraqi forces from its territory, initially this strengthened Iranians' sense that faith and resistance are more important than weapons. Finally, Western policies only emboldened Iraq, with disastrous consequences.

THE IRAN-CONTRA INTERVAL AND THE
HARDENING OF THE U.S. POSITION ON IRAN

Developments in the Middle East following the Israeli invasion of Lebanon in September 1982, including Iran's growing involvement in that country, plus changes in the top echelons of the Reagan administration, had a negative impact on U.S.-Iranian relations. Most damaging was Iran's implication in the bombing of the U.S. barracks in Beirut and hostage-taking operations in Lebanon. These acts put the Reagan administration in a serious dilemma because it had made "swift retribution" a cardinal principle of its policy toward terrorists. According to this principle, the United States should have struck Iran and Syria militarily. In any event, this did not happen. However, although Syria was most responsible for U.S. problems in Lebanon, Iran bore the brunt of U.S. regional frustrations. The start of the Tanker War by Iraq in 1983 as a means of internationalizing the conflict further strained U.S.-Iranian relations because, in order to dissuade Iraq, Iran threatened that it would close the Strait of Hormuz.[23]

The arrival of George P. Shultz as the new U.S. secretary of state, a person who was much more sensitive to Arab concerns than was Haig, contributed to a shift in the U.S. position in Iraq's favor. Disagreements between the Defense and State Departments also worked against Iran. As a former official of the National Security Council (NSC) at the time told the author, "A punitive policy on Iran was the only thing they [Schultz and Weinberger] could agree on."[24] Additionally, the proponents of arms sales to the Gulf Arab states found it useful to exaggerate the Iranian threat and thus defeat those opposing such arms transfers. Many within the U.S. political establishment were also pleased that, for key Arab states, the Iranian threat had replaced the Palestinian issue as the most significant concern in the Middle East.[25] Meanwhile, the United States' regional allies, notably Egypt, for their own reasons, plus pro-Iraq officials at the State Department and other commercial interests, worked hard to convince the United States of the advisability of a tilt in Iraq's favor.[26] One argument used was that such a policy would help compensate for the lack of progress on the Palestinian question. Moreover, while proponents of a hard-line policy on Iran were exaggerating Iran's threat, the United States was not even considering the fact that Iran's other regional policies, including its support for the Afghan mujahedin, were helping advance U.S. regional and global objectives.

The first indication of this shift was the launching of "Operation Staunch" in 1984 in order to stop arms supplies to Iran. However, although the anti-Iran view was dominant within the U.S. policy-making establishment, there were a few people, notably at the NSC, who were aware of Iran's strategic importance and its domestic complexities; they prevented Iran's complete isolation, by encouraging countries like Japan and Germany to maintain their ties to Iran.

Ironically, the hardening of the U.S. position was happening just when positive shifts were taking place in Iran's domestic and foreign policy orientation. Domestically, by 1984, an uneasy balance had emerged between the more moderate and pragmatic elements within the Iranian leadership, represented by figures such as the speaker of the parliament, Akbar Hashemi Rafsanjani, and the foreign minister, Ali Akbar Velayati, and the more hard-line personalities, such as the prime minister, Mir Hussein Mussavi, and President Ayatullah Khamenei.

In terms of foreign policy, the focus of Iranian diplomacy had shifted to state-to-state relations as opposed to the so-called people-to-people relations, and to the factoring in of national interests in determining Iran's external behavior. Consequently, Iran had begun to adopt more conventional diplomatic means in dealing with other countries. This pragmatic outlook did not extend to relations with the United States, however. Nevertheless, influential pragmatic figures, such as speaker of the parliament Rafsanjani, said that U.S.-Iranian hostility should not last until "Doomsday" (*Rouz e Qiamat*) and that Iran would be prepared for reconciliation, provided that the United States changed its ways.

It was under these circumstances that the Iran-Contra or the "Arms for Hostages" controversy occurred. A detailed discussion of this issue is beyond the scope of this book.[27] Suffice it to say that different motives, ranging from strategic to tactical, were involved in this ill-fated effort. In his television address to the nation on the so-called "Iran-gate," President Ronald Reagan put forward the strategic motive. Irrespective of the reasons behind its failure, the unfolding of the Iran-Contra affair undermined future prospects for U.S.-Iranian relations because it created a major controversy between the executive and legislative branches of the U.S. government. It also enhanced the influence of opponents of U.S.-Iranian reconciliation, including America's Gulf Arab allies. Moreover, it hardened the U.S. position toward Iran, and discredited any idea of reconciliation, until and unless Iran's regime was changed or at least its behavior was altered to such a degree that, in effect, transformed the character of the regime.

This U.S. position, with some nuances, has constituted a cardinal principle of U.S. policy toward Iran ever since. That Iran needed to change its revolutionary policies and abandon its confrontational stand toward the United States and Israel is beyond dispute. However, America's insistence that before any process of tension reduction could take place Iran must clearly declare that it was changing its policies only strengthened Iranian hard-liners and made it impossible for the moderate pragmatists to make positive, albeit incremental, moves toward the United States.

Combi in a pragmatic moment v a policy while keeping ideological intact

An immediate consequence of this shift was that the radicals, with the help of their Lebanese and Syrian allies, abducted three American nationals, thus making any U.S.-Iranian dialogue impossible. In the long term, too, this U.S. position has served the interests of Iranian hard-liners and has led America to ignore positive signals coming from Tehran.

REFLAGGING OPERATIONS AND U.S.-IRAN CONFRONTATION

Despite the tragicomic denouement of the Iran-Contra affair, Iran and the United States did not immediately close the doors to future dialogue, as illustrated by a comment by Secretary Shultz in January 1987. He recognized Iran's regional importance, the common U.S.-Iranian interest in containing the USSR, and the U.S. stake in better relations with Iran. But he added that better relations would depend on fundamental changes in Iranian policy and practice and that the United States would not pursue better ties with Iran "to the detriment of [its] many other interests and commitments in the region," meaning that the United States would not improve relations with Iran if this made its Arab allies unhappy. Earlier, during a speech at Tehran University, Iran's foreign minister, Velayati, had kept the door of dialogue with the United States open. He had also characterized those opposed to such a dialogue as "leftists with an Islamic veneer."[28]

By 1987, the U.S. opponents of an opening to Iran in the State Department and the broader policy community, who believed that Iraq was more important, had gained the upper hand. There had also been a shift in Israel's view of Iran because the Islamic regime had neither crumbled nor softened its anti-Israel stand, leading to a rethinking of Israel's peripheral strategy and the advancement of the thesis of the "Arab Option."

The premise of this strategy has been that Israel and moderate Arabs should set aside their differences and join in an anti-Iran alliance.

The combined result of these developments was a decisive shift in the U.S. position in Iraq's favor, and it led to U.S. efforts to force Iran to the bargaining table using, if need be, punitive means.

Kuwait's request that the United States protect its tankers against Iranian attacks provided a perfect opportunity to implement America's new strategy. The United States reflagged Kuwaiti tankers and offered them protection;[29] tightened the screws on Iran at the United Nations;[30] and when, on April 14, 1988, the USS *Roberts* struck a mine in Gulf waters, it attacked an Iranian oil platform with a capacity of 150,000 barrels per day. In retaliation, Iran opened fire on a U.S. Navy vessel, leading U.S. forces to destroy three Iranian warships. Finally, on July 3, 1988, the USS *Vincennes* attacked an Iranian passenger airline killing 290 people.[31] The United States persisted in saying that this was an accident, although other experts maintained that it was impossible to mistake a passenger airplane for a military aircraft.[32]

The hardening of the U.S. policy toward Iran also resulted from changing international conditions created by Mikhail Gorbachev's policy of détente with the West, and Iran's weakness. Throughout this period, Iran behaved with considerable caution, although it retained its rhetorical bravado, and it resisted the hard-liners' pressure that it launch an all-out attack on the United States, which they believed would have inflicted heavy casualties on the U.S. military. Iran also indicated that it was open to dialogue, and its deputy foreign minister told the United Nations Security General (UNSG) that Iran wanted to talk to the United States. However, the United States chose to ignore these signs.[33]

POST-SOVIET PERIOD: THE RAFSANJANI YEARS

Despite its negative effects on the long-term prospects for U.S.-Iranian reconciliation, post–Iran-Contra American policy toward the Iran-Iraq War, especially U.S. military strikes on Iranian targets, was salutary in the short term. It helped convince Iran to accept a cease-fire in August 1988, improved the moderates' position by demonstrating the risks of an adventurous foreign policy, and intensified debate on the negative consequences of past foreign policy mistakes, including those toward the West, on the country's interests. The result was a good deal of open debate about the wisdom of Iranian reconciliation with the United States in the immediate aftermath of the cease-fire agreement.

During this period, Iran was anxious for the full implementation of the provisions of UNSC Resolution 598, including the withdrawal of Iraqi troops, which still occupied parts of its territory, and recognition of the validity of the Algiers Agreement of 1975, which Iraq had denounced.

To achieve this goal, Iran was willing to be forthcoming with the United States.[34] However, for the following reasons, the United States was not open to Iranian overtures:

+ The elimination of the Soviet security threat to the Persian Gulf and hence the erosion of Iran's strategic importance.
+ The opposition of U.S. Arab allies, like Egypt, to U.S.-Iranian rapprochement.
+ A shift in Israel's assessment of Iran and the beginning of Israel's "Arab Option" strategy.
+ Continued influence of pro-Iraq elements within the U.S. policy-making community, notably the Department of State.[35]
+ Continued captivity of American and other Western hostages in Lebanon and the Iranian moderates' inability to gain their release.
+ Continued factional infighting in Iran, which undermined the moderates' ability to take bold and positive actions toward the United States in the absence of any American incentive, such as paying compensation to the victims of the *Vincennes* attack.

Consequently, this favorable opportunity to start a process of reconciliation was missed. However, in his inaugural address in January 1989, President George H. W. Bush said that "Good will begets goodwill. Good faith can be a spiral that endlessly moves on."[36] But he did not say what concrete shape this U.S. goodwill would take.

THE RUSHDIE AFFAIR, THE CONTINUING
HOSTAGE DRAMA, AND THE TRANSITION TO
THE POST-KHOMEINI ORDER

The outbreak of the Rushdie Affair caused by the publication of *The Satanic Verses*, written by the Indian-born British author Salman Rushdie, provided the Iranian radicals with a golden opportunity to shift the balance of power in their own favor and to undermine the moderates' efforts to reconcile with the West. *The Satanic Verses* generated indignation and protest throughout the Muslim world and among Muslim communities in the West; it also solicited calls for Rushdie's death from lesser known clerics, notably some in Pakistan. Iran, comparatively speaking, was slow to react, largely because the Ayatullah Khomeini at that time was ill and did not hear about this affair until September 1988. He was informed about it by the hard-liners. But when it came, Iran's reaction was extreme. In February 1989, Ayatullah Khomeini ruled that Rushdie was an apostate and hence deserving of death. Other lesser clerics offered a million dollar reward to anyone who killed Rushdie. Because of Ayatullah Khomeini's high profile, Iran came to be seen as the main culprit in the Rushdie controversy.

Meanwhile, in Western countries, notably the United States, Rushdie's case became a litmus test of the principle of freedom of speech and expression. Furthermore, the call for Rushdie's killing raised the issue of states' sovereignty and their responsibility to protect their citizens. The Rushdie controversy added another complication to Iran-U.S. relations, aggravated by Ayatullah Khomeini's death in June 1989. This made it impossible to rescind the fatwa against Rushdie, because no political or religious leader can nullify another religious leader's opinion.

The Bush administration responded to the Rushdie controversy in a relatively low-key manner, which indicated its preoccupation with the fate of its remaining hostages in Lebanon and its desire to keep open the option of reconciliation with Iran. In Iran, by contrast, the hard-liners' growing influence nearly closed the window of opportunity for better U.S.-Iranian relations that had opened after the August 1988 cease-fire. In April 1989, Iran declared that it had discovered a U.S. espionage network and accused America of having violated the terms of the 1979 Algiers Agreement.[37] The United States pleaded ignorance of Iran's charges, although later it transpired that the United States had infiltrated the Iranian military and obtained detailed information about its military planning.[38]

Ayatullah Khomeini's death in June 1989 once again raised the issue of the Islamic Republic's survival after its founder's demise, thus reducing any incentive for the United States to pursue a policy of rapprochement. However, because of the considerable warming of Soviet-Iranian relations, illustrated by Soviet foreign minister Eduard Shevardnadze's visit to Tehran in February 1989 and his meeting with the Ayatullah Khomeini, some in the United States criticized this U.S. approach and complained that the U.S. policy toward Iran was drifting. However, others countered that the United States should wait until Iran took the initiative for improved relations because it would have no choice but to do so.[39]

Developments in the Middle East also created further difficulties for U.S.-Iranian relations. The triggering event was the abduction by Israel of Sheikh Obeid, a leader of Hizbullah in Lebanon, on July 28, 1989. In response, Lebanese radicals threatened to kill Colonel William Higgins, who had been held captive since February 1988, if Obeid was not released. Israel refused to free Obeid; Colonel Higgins was killed; and his captors threatened to kill another hostage, Joseph Cicipio. However, the United States and Iran's newly elected president, Rafsanjani, behaved cautiously and avoided any confrontation. The United States, although still highlighting Iran's role, also demonstrated a greater awareness that other countries, notably Syria, were also involved in the hostage issue. Nevertheless, America warned Iran that it would hold it responsible if "any additional hostages were harmed or put to death." It also made it clear that it would, if necessary, use military force against Iran, albeit reluctantly. To make the threat convincing, America moved warships close to Iranian shores.[40] Meanwhile, the United States acknowledged signs of positive Iranian behavior and admitted that it had no reason to believe that Iran was not serious in trying to spare Joseph Cicipio.

Rafsanjani, too, tried to allay tensions, and on August 4, 1989, he said that Lebanon's and the hostages' problems had a peaceful solution. He admitted that the Bush administration's policy, compared to previous administrations, was "wiser," offered to help in the release of the hostages, expressed his regret over Higgins's killing, and condemned it.[41] Because of the opposition of the radicals, who feared that the hostages' release would lead to U.S.-Iranian reconciliation, plus Syrian obstructions, Rafsanjani could not get the release of the hostages, but no other hostages were taken or killed and a military confrontation was averted.[42] In order to establish an indirect U.S.-Iranian dialogue, Iran suggested informal talks with the United States through Pakistan.

IRANIAN ADVANCES AND AMERICAN REBUFFS

Despite obstructions from the hard-liners, encouraged by President Bush's promise of "good will begets goodwill," during 1989–1990 Rafsanjani continued his efforts for an opening to the United States through a variety of channels, including UN secretary general Perez de Cuellar's office and that of Under Secretary General Giandomenico Picco. As recounted by Picco, President Bush was eager to have an opening to Iran as early as August 1989. For this purpose, Picco was sent to Tehran to deliver a message to Rafsanjani, with whom he met on August 25, 1989. The message said that the United States would respond positively to Iranian help on the hostages, including the release of Iranian assets frozen at the time of the 1979–1981 hostage crisis. He added that because of the Iran-Contra memories and domestic political considerations, the U.S. president could not take any positive actions toward Iran before the hostages' release.[43]

According to Picco, Rafsanjani responded that, for some time, Iran had had no contacts with the hostage takers because they did not belong to the mainstream Hizbullah. He added that "when we were asked by Mr. [Robert] McFarlane [Reagan's national security advisor during the Iran-Contra affair] we did try to contact them. After the promises were not carried out, those groups became alienated." Rafsanjani noted that these groups would not respond unless Sheikh Obeid were released. He then talked about his own domestic problems, and said that [President] Bush can easily unfreeze Iran's assets. According to Picco, Velayati told him later that "the process of freeing of the hostages could begin if the U.S. released 10 per cent of the assets it had frozen after the seizure of U.S. Embassy in Tehran in 1979," and paid compensation for the victims of the Iranian Airbus shot down by the *Vincennes* in 1988.[44]

Picco recounted that when President Bush came to the UN General Assembly meeting in September 1989, he [Bush] told the UNSG that he had received Rafsanjani's message and that he would inform Perez de Cuellar of his answer before he [UNSG] met with Iran's foreign minister Velayati. However, instead, it was Secretary of State James Baker who called the UNSG. Baker told him that Washington had decided not to respond to Rafsanjani's message, because doing so "would have shown too much eagerness on the part of Washington to deal with the Iranian government."[45] According to Picco, this negative response reflected the State Department's skepticism regarding dealing with Iran. The Department, as put by Thomas Pickering, the U.S. permanent representative to the UN, believed that the United States should not reward an illegal act. According to Picco, State's objection reflected "the classic turf battle between the State Department and the White House." The State Department's opposition is not surprising because the dominant view there was that Iraq was the main prize in the Persian Gulf. Also, Secretary James Baker and the Middle East Bureau were very sensitive to Arab concerns. However, even in the White House, there were officials who were unwilling to provide Iran with incentives. It seems that only President George H. W. Bush was interested in an opening to Iran, but he was thwarted by the bureaucracy. Nevertheless, some sources have cited the Rushdie Affair and the assassinations in Europe as the main reason for the Bush administration's decision not to compensate Rafsanjani. Be that as it may, the result was Rafsanjani's weakening and the ultimate failure of his strategy of reaching out to the West.[46]

Nevertheless, Rafsanjani pursued his policy of rapprochement with the United States, and two American hostages, Robert Polhill and Frank Reed, were released in April 1990. However, the goodwill promised by George Bush never materialized.

Complications of Middle East politics limited Iran's ability to get the release of other Western hostages at the time. One such problem was the fate of the 17 members of the Lebanese Al Dawa movement (later Hizbullah) in Kuwaiti prisons. Hizbullah had always linked the release of Western hostages to the release of its members. Kuwait had consistently refused to do so, and the United States had been unwilling to pressure Kuwait, lest this appear to be making a deal with hostage takers.[47]

IRAQ ATTACKS KUWAIT

The United States believed that it had unlimited time to wait until Iran came to its senses and accepted its conditions for better relations. But Iraq's invasion of Kuwait in August 1990 unraveled the entire U.S. Persian Gulf strategy built on the expectation of U.S.-Iraq partnership.[48]

When a military confrontation with Iraq became inevitable, America was anxious that the war not appear as a conflict between the West and the Islamic world, but as the defense of a small country against a stronger aggressor. Consequently, the United States tried to form a broad-based coalition which included some Muslim states. This U.S. need for allies, or at least neutrals, changed Secretary Baker's mind regarding dealing with Iran. Even Israel's ex-defense minister and its future prime minister, Yitzhak Rabin, advised that the United States should put aside emotions as quickly as possible and make overtures to Iran.[49] However, the United States was not willing to offer Iran any incentives, unless it joined the anti-Iraq coalition, something that Iran could not do, because of continuing intra-leadership power struggles and ideological differences.

IRAN OPTS FOR NEUTRALITY

Iraq's invasion of Kuwait and the ensuing developments posed serious dilemmas for Iran. Conventional wisdom among Western and other analysts has long been that Iran was the beneficiary of the first Persian Gulf War. Certainly, Saddam's decision to attack Kuwait had a number of advantages for Iran because

+ it showed Saddam's expansionist and predatory nature;
+ it forced the Gulf States, notably Kuwait, a major Iraq supporter during the Iran-Iraq War, to apologize to Iran;
+ it forced Iraq to remove its troops from Iran's territory and recognize the validity of the Algiers Agreement;
+ it caused the Western countries, including the United States, to become somewhat more forthcoming toward Iran.

Yet Iraq's invasion of Kuwait left Iran with the unpalatable choice of either joining the anti-Iraq coalition or forming an anti-imperialist alliance with Iraq. Because of what Iran had suffered during the eight-year war with Iraq and its lack of confidence in what Saddam might do if victorious, alliance with Iraq was out of the question. Moreover, siding with Iraq would have made Iran a target of U.S. military strikes. Nevertheless, there were elements in Iran, which, for ideological reasons, favored such a strategy.[50] Joining the anti-Iraq coalition, although wiser from the perspective of Iran's national interest, was also highly problematic because of the opposition of hard-liners, including Rafsanjani's rival and Iran's Supreme Leader, Khamenei. Moreover, such a policy was against the regime's ideological principles and its self-image as the champion of true Islam.

In the long run, Iran would have lost irrespective of who won the war. Iraq's victory would have meant greater Iraqi pressure on Iran and renewed Iraqi efforts to separate Khuzestan from Iran. A U.S. victory, as has happened, would have meant a much greater U.S. military presence in the Persian Gulf and hence a much less congenial security environment for Iran. Consequently, Iran and Rafsanjani tried to strike a balance between these two extreme positions by remaining neutral, while observing the embargo against Iraq. Rafsanjani warned the radicals that "if we [Iran] help the Iraqis stay in Kuwait, they [Iraqis] will have borders with us all the way to the Strait of Hormuz . . . the Persian Gulf would become the [Arabian] Gulf." He then asked, "Is this not suicide?"[51]

Rafsanjani prevailed, and Iran remained neutral, although this neutrality was tilted in favor of the coalition. Fred Halliday has observed that Iran was not neutral in the sense that Sweden and Switzerland were in the Second World War, entitled to trade with both sides, because it did not provide military aid to Iraq and observed the UN embargo.[52] However, some food and medicine made its way to Iraq from Iran, leading James Baker to warn "sanction-busters," having Iran in mind.[53]

Iran's neutrality, and such actions as the impounding of Iraqi aircraft that had been flown to Iran for safe keeping, was of great help to the United States. Had Iran joined Iraq in an anti-U.S. coalition, it would have been much more difficult for other Muslim countries, such as Pakistan, to join the anti-Iraq coalition, and, by extending the battlefield, it would also have made the military task more complicated. By remaining neutral, Iran made it easier for Muslim countries, where popular sentiment was in Iraq's favor, to join the U.S.-led coalition. It also undercut Saddam's argument that he was fighting for Islam. Despite these facts, the United States gave no incentives to Iran. This U.S. unwillingness to reward Iran increased as Saddam's forces were defeated. The United States, contrary to its early promise of "good will begets goodwill," did not reward Iran even after the last American hostage in Lebanon was released in December 1991 as a result of Rafsanjani's personal intervention. Giandomenico Picco recounts his meeting with Rafsanjani in April 1992, after he [Picco] was told by Brent Scowcroft, the U.S. national security adviser, that the United States felt there would be no gestures toward Iran because the timing was not propitious. After relaying America's negative message to Rafsanjani, Picco says that the Iranian president told him that he should leave Tehran very quickly because "the news of what you have told me will travel fast to other quarters, and they may decide not to let you go."[54]

THE CLINTON ADMINISTRATION AND THE
DUAL CONTAINMENT

The principal reason for the first Bush administration's unwillingness to make any positive gesture toward Iran was the Soviet collapse that relieved Washington from any anxieties about Soviet advances into Iran and the Persian Gulf. It also made the United States feel vindicated that its ideas and way of life were superior to others and hence of universal applicability, and that America had the capacity to reshape the world and the new international system according to its own designs. This U.S. mind-set is best illustrated by President George H. W. Bush's comment that the new world order means that "what we [the U.S.] say goes."[55]

Under these circumstances, it is not surprising that the United States did not engage with Iran, excluded it from regional security plans, and did not invite it to the Madrid Peace Conference in October 1992, although, according to some sources, Iran would have wanted to attend. Additionally, the Bush administration made clear that it wanted to prevent Iran from gaining influence in Muslim states of Central Asia and the Caucasus.[56]

THE GOAL OF DUAL CONTAINMENT

If the Iranian government had hoped for a more positive attitude from the incoming Clinton administration, it was to be disappointed.

The foundations of the Dual Containment strategy were laid during the Bush administration, and figures that became more prominent during George W. Bush's presidency, like Paul Wolfowitz, played significant roles in it. However, it was Martin Indyk in the Clinton administration who articulated this policy. The Dual Containment strategy's ultimate purpose was to transform the Middle East's political landscape.

Indyk had criticized President Bush for not using effectively the opportunities created by the first Gulf War and the Soviet collapse to redraw the Middle East's political map.[57] Consequently, when he became a senior official in the Clinton administration with responsibility for the Middle East, he set out to do so. In a speech at the Washington Institute for Near East Policy on May 18, 1993, Indyk described the underlying principle of the new strategy as the following: in view of new geopolitical conditions, the United States no longer needs to balance Iraq against Iran. Instead, relying on its own and its regional allies' power it will "counter both the Iraqi and Iranian regimes. We [the U.S.] will not need to depend on one to counter the other."[58] Indyk made clear that the ultimate U.S. goal in Iraq was regime change, but he was less clear on Iran. However, the logical culmination of the containment policy would have been the change in regime by intensifying Iran's internal tensions and contradictions, as had happened in the case of the Soviet Union.

The Dual Containment strategy fitted well with other aspects of the Clinton administration's international strategy of promoting economic globalization and democracy, because the administration believed that their strategies would inevitably increase U.S. economic and cultural influence. To achieve its goals, the United States was willing to confront countries that resisted these trends, and which were called the "backlash states" by Clinton's national security advisor, Anthony Lake.[59] The Clinton administration, however, preferred to achieve its "transformative" goals through nonmilitary means, although it made clear that it would not shy away from the use of military force when its national interests required or the occurrence of gross human rights violations necessitated. It also favored a multilateral approach, while stressing that it would act alone if necessary.[60]

Consequently, as soon as the Clinton administration took office, it tried to convince the European countries to curtail their trade, economic, and political relations with

Iran. Martin Indyk, in his speech to the Washington Institute for Near East Policy (WINEP), said that the United States would work energetically to convince other countries that "Iran is a bad investment in both commercial and strategic terms for all responsible members of the international community."[61] The Clinton administration also developed and refined George H. W. Bush's policy of checking Iran's influence in Central Asia and the Caucasus, and excluding it from any energy export routes.[62]

Meanwhile, in Iran, Rafsanjani failed to impose his absolute control over the governmental apparatus, thus enabling the hard-liners to sabotage many of his policies by, among other things, engaging in terrorist acts inside and outside Iran. The most damaging of these acts in which Iran was allegedly implicated were two bombings in Argentina: namely, an attack on the Israeli Embassy in Buenos Aires on March 17, 1992; and an attack on the Argentine-Israeli Mutual Association (AMIA) on July 18, 1994. Initially, Arab militants were suspected of being responsible for the embassy attack. Some even pointed the finger at Syria.[63] But later Hizbullah and Iran were declared responsible for both attacks.[64]

Considering that similar attacks within the same time frame were carried out in Europe against Iranian opposition figures by Iran's intelligence ministry and its notorious head, Ali Fallahian, there is a reasonable case for suspecting Iran of complicity in these acts. Another factor which might have prompted Iranian radicals to engage in such activities, especially the 1994 Argentine bombing, was its coincidence in a particularly sensitive period in Arab-Israeli peace making.[65] In fact, Iran was blamed for the failure of Arab-Israeli peace talks by supporting Hamas and Hizbullah.[66] The bombings might have contributed to the Likud victory in 1996. But the main causes of the failure of the peace talks were Rabin's assassination by an Israeli, the backtracking of Ehud Barak's government on the implementation of the provisions of the Oslo Accords, and diverging visions of the Palestinian and Israelis on the terms and conditions of peace. In 1994, neither Hamas nor Hizbullah was strong enough to derail the peace talks. And Iran has never been, nor would it be, in a position to prevent an Arab-Israeli peace if Israel and the Palestinians were to agree to it.

However, Iran's at least rhetorical opposition to the Arab-Israeli peace, while it was pursuing better ties with the West, showed an astounding lack of understanding of both international and U.S. domestic politics. These acts made it impossible for the Clinton administration to have a positive attitude toward Iran, even if it were so inclined, which it was not. More important, it consolidated Israel's view of Iran as an implacable foe that must be contained and weakened at all costs, and led it and its U.S. supporters to ensure that America would not consider engagement with Iran.

After the attacks in Argentina, the Clinton administration's rhetoric and policy toward Iran hardened, as illustrated by the statement of Secretary of State Warren Christopher in October 1994 during a speech at Georgetown University. He said that "Iran is the world's most significant sponsor of terrorism and the most ardent opponent of the Middle East peace process . . . The evidence is overwhelming: Iran is intent on projecting terror and extremism across the Middle East and beyond . . ." He added that "the international community has been far too tolerant of Iran's outlaw behavior." He concluded that "only a concerted international effort can stop it [Iran].[67]

The Clinton administration also developed and refined the Bush administration's policy of preventing Iran from interacting with Central Asia, among other things by encouraging the emergence of the Taliban, or at least acquiescing when Pakistan helped create it.

Meanwhile, the new Republican Congress was agitating for a harder position on Iran, including the destabilization of the regime, and the American-Israel Public Affairs Committee (AIPAC) increased its lobbying to convince Congress to impose sanctions on Iran and on companies doing business with it.

IRAN SIGNS DEAL WITH CONOCO: UNITED STATES IMPOSES SANCTIONS

Since the 1979–1981 hostage crisis, the United States had imposed various types of sanctions on Iran, a trend which continued in the 1990s and culminated in the Iran-Libya Sanctions Act (ILSA). What is important to note in the sanctions trend of the 1990s is that Congress took the lead in many of them. For example, Senator John McCain introduced the Iran-Iraq Arms Non-Proliferation Act, which became law in October 1993. It extended to Iran the same export and licensing prohibitions imposed on Iraq. In January 1995, Senator Alphonse D'Amato introduced a bill to bar all trade with Iran, except humanitarian trade, and to cut off the purchase of Iranian oil, estimated at $3.5–$4 billion, by subsidiaries of U.S. companies and sold in third countries.

Yet while incapable or unwilling to make the dramatic policy changes that would have led to a breakthrough in relations with the United States, the Rafsanjani administration continued its efforts to engage with America, first through economic relations. The most dramatic sign of this Iranian desire was the granting of a $1 billion deal to a subsidiary of the U.S. oil concern Conoco in March 1995.[68] Iran intended this as a clear signal of its willingness to improve ties with the United States because, although it had been offered a similar deal by the French concern Total, it had decided to go with Conoco.

However, in view of the atmosphere created by the events described above, the United States was in no mood to respond positively to Iran. More important, Israel, which from the first had supported the Dual Containment policy, was determined that no U.S.-Iranian rapprochement should take place before a change of regime or at least a fundamental shift in Iran's Middle East policies, most notably its attitude toward the state of Israel. This is why some commentators wondered at Conoco's decision to sign a deal with Iran.[69]

The Clinton administration, including the president himself, made clear promptly that any deal with Iran "was unacceptable."[70] It followed by issuing an executive order on March 15, 1995, barring U.S. citizens and companies from financing, supervising, and managing Iran's oil development. The order did not go as far as imposing additional sanctions on Iran through specific law because changing the law required congressional acquiescence. It was the Congress, through the initiative of Senator

Alphonse D'Amato from New York, which did that. This is why some observers attributed the issuing of the executive order as a way to preempt congressional pressure for sanctions.[71]

According to many observers, Israel and its U.S. supporters played decisive roles in galvanizing congressional efforts to sanction Iran.[72] These efforts succeeded when, on December 20, 1995, the Senate approved the Foreign Oil Sanctions Act of 1995. This act required U.S. sanctions on foreign companies that invested more than $40 million in Iran's oil industry. At the last minute, Senator Edward M. Kennedy added an amendment extending sanctions to Libya, hence the law's name Iran-Libya Sanctions Act (ILSA) which, after sanctions against Libya were lifted in 2008, became known as the Iran Sanctions Act (ISA).[73] Shortly afterwards, on December 31, 1995, Congress passed a secret intelligence authorization act which included $18 million earmarked for covert action against the Tehran regime.[74] The United Arab Emirates (UAE) finally compensated Conoco with a $10 billion contract for its loss of the Iranian deal.[75]

KHOBAR TOWER BOMBING

On June 25, 1996, a bomb exploded a fuel truck adjacent to a housing complex known as Khobar Towers in Saudi Arabia, which housed a number of U.S. Air Force personnel, killing 19 Americans servicemen and one Saudi national. Those responsible were identified as members of Hizbullah Al-Hejaz.[76] Initially, Saudi officials identified the perpetrators as "Saudi Islamic militants, including many veterans of the Afghan war." Later, it emerged that Osama Bin Laden was congratulated on the success of this act. In 2007, the former secretary of defense, William Perry, said in an interview that "Al Qaeda rather than Iran was behind a truck bombing at an American military base."[77] In June 2009, Gareth Porter wrote that "blaming for the Khobar bombing was a false leak released by U.S. officials and Saudi government."[78] The purpose, according to Porter, was to save the Saudis' face and obscure the act of their complicity in Al Qaeda's attacking U.S. targets, by using charities for funding purposes, as long as Bin Laden did not target the Saudi government.[79]

However, at the time, the U.S. government believed in Iran's responsibility for the attacks. A U.S. federal court even speculated that the Ayatullah Khamenei had endorsed the attacks. Moreover, a number of arguments could be made in support of possible Iranian involvement: Iranian hard-liners might have wanted to stop any future Iranian overtures to the United States similar to the Conoco deal; to make it impossible for the United States to act positively toward Iran; and to embarrass the Saudis by demonstrating their vulnerability. Furthermore, some members of the group fled to Iran; elements in Iran and Al Qaeda might have cooperated on the attack; and the perpetrators were Shia.

Irrespective of the identity and connections of the perpetrators, the reflexive U.S. reaction was to blame Iran, and consequently Rafsanjani's presidency came to an end without any breakthrough in U.S.-Iranian relations.

KHATAMI PRESIDENCY: HOPES RAISED
AND DASHED ... AGAIN

The victory of Muhammad Khatami in Iran's 1997 presidential elections on a reformist agenda and a policy based on the principle of "reduction of tensions" (*Tashanoj Zadaei*) and Dialogue of Civilizations once more raised hopes for U.S.-Iranian reconciliation. The first indication of the willingness of Iran's new president to embark on a dialogue with the United States came in the interview that Khatami granted to CNN correspondent Christiane Amanpour in January 1998.[80] In this interview, Khatami, without exactly apologizing for the hostage crisis, said he understood that the feelings of the great American people were hurt and he regretted this fact. He also praised the values and principles which underpinned America's political, social, and moral system in such flattering terms that, according to Kenneth Pollack, even many Americans would not do.[81] Khatami also condemned terrorism, and said that it was un-Islamic because the Koran says the slaying of only one person is tantamount to the killing of all humanity. However, he added that the time for direct government-to-government talks was not ripe and suggested that a dialogue should begin at the "people-to-people level" through cultural, academic, and athletic exchanges.[82]

Perhaps more significantly, even though, due to domestic political requirements, he opposed the Arab-Israeli peace process on the grounds that it would not work, he did not attack Israel and drew a distinction between the Israeli people and their government. Later, the Khatami government stated that if Israel and the Palestinians agreed on a solution, Iran would not oppose it, thus implicitly accepting the two-state solution. Some have even argued that this statement indicated Iran's willingness indirectly to recognize Israel.[83]

The Clinton administration's response to Khatami's overtures, depending on one's perspective, was either excessively cautious or downright dismissive. The State Department responded to Khatami's statement by saying: "We listened with interest to President Khatami's interview on CNN. We welcome the fact that he wants a dialogue with the American people and welcome his appreciation of the fundamental principles that form the foundation of our nation ... Ultimately, real improvement will not depend upon what the government of Iran says but what it does."[84] This view was also shared by the NSC, where the outgoing national security advisor had warned against "Iran's seductiveness."[85] Nevertheless, the United States made some small positive gestures toward Iran, most notably by encouraging cultural and other exchanges within the framework of the so-called Track Two Diplomacy, and it lifted the import ban on some Iranian goods, such as pistachios. Additionally, Secretary of State Madeleine Albright and President Clinton acknowledged that, because of its geopolitical importance, Iran in the past "had been subject of manipulation by Western powers."[86]

However, none of these acts were sufficient for a breakthrough in relations, although the Track Two visits helped to educate a greater number of Iranians and Americans about their respective political settings, with potentially positive results for the long term. However, the benefits of this diplomacy were negligible for Iran, as many analysts who visited Iran used their knowledge better to justify their uncompromising position toward it. Indeed, some of the most hard-line opinions on Iran have come from those who benefited from these exchanges, spent time in Iran, and did research in government institutions.[87]

REFORMISTS OVERREACH: CONSERVATIVES RETALIATE

Reformist political groups that supported Khatami had diverging views on what constituted reform. Moreover, some of them harbored strong resentment toward the moderate pragmatists identified with the Rafsanjani era. The most prominent and outspoken representative of the latter group was Akbar Ganji who, in a series of articles, including one called the "Red Clocked Honorable" (*Alijanb e Sorkhpoush*), in thinly disguised terms attacked Rafsanjani. As to the others, they fell into two categories: those who wanted to pursue reforms within the limits of the Islamic system, including the acceptance of the Velayat-e-Faqih; and those who wanted eventually to eliminate the office of the Vali-e-Faqih, which in essence would have meant the end of the Islamic regime. They believed this could be done by mobilizing the people, especially the youth, whose vote had been critical in Khatami's election. They consisted mainly of the left-leaning elements of the regime that had been dominant during the first decade of the revolution and were sidelined during the Rafsanjani years. A key figure of the latter is Saeed Hajarian, widely considered to be the architect of the reform movement.

Throughout 1998, a number of reformist newspapers published articles involving veiled and sometimes not so veiled attacks on key figures of the regime, notably Ayatullah Khamenei, and on some of its foundational principles. In response, conservative newspapers such as *Keyhan* and *Abrar* published articles warning the reformists. The July 8–13, 1998, student riots, which in the reformists' and conservatives' respective mythologies have come to be known as the 18 Tir uprising and counterrevolution, were triggered by student demonstrations in front of their dormitory at Kooy e Daneshgah. They were protesting the closure of the reformist newspaper *Salam*, operated by the Militant Clergy's Organization (Sazman e Ruhaniun Mojahed), under the supervision of the leftist cleric Muhammad Mussavi Khoeiniha, and supported by President Khatami.

Local police, riot police, and some civilians, known as Ansar e Hizbullah, intervened and asked the students to return to their dormitories. Some students refused to do so. Meanwhile, the Interior Ministry intervened and, finally, the students were dispersed. However, later, another group of civilians, which in an investigative report produced by Iran's Supreme National Security Council was identified as the "Special Forces Following the Leader" (*Nirou haye Vizheh Peyrov e Velayat*) (NOPO), intervened and clashed with students. This clash left one dead and 300 wounded. Following this event, student riots broke out in other parts of the country. They were quelled, but the conflict between reformists and conservatives sharpened.[88]

The 2000 parliamentary elections provided a good opportunity for the reformists and the pragmatic moderates of the Rafsanjani era to join hands and confront the conservatives. But the actions of the more extreme reformists prevented this from happening.[89] Although the reformists won that election, the conservatives continued their obstruction and constrained Khatami's ability to pursue his conciliatory policy toward the United States. For example, in 2000, because of concern over the reaction of the Supreme Leader and other hard-line elements, Khatami missed an opportunity to shake hands with U.S. president Bill Clinton at the United Nations, something that could have had a thawing effect on relations.

In 1999, Saudi Arabia told the United States that Iran had definitely been behind the bombing of the Khobar Towers in 1996, posing a dilemma for the United States as to how to respond, especially whether to retaliate militarily. Ultimately, the United States refrained from military action, but the ability of the U.S. government to take positive measures toward Iran became even more constrained. The Clinton administration not only failed to make meaningful gestures toward Iran, which could have boosted Khatami's position and strengthened his hand vis-à-vis his domestic opponents, it took actions that weakened his position. For instance, President Clinton renewed the sanctions against Iran, thus undermining Khatami's arguments that better behavior would have positive results for the country. Frequent distinctions made by Clinton administration officials between Iran's "elected leaders," meaning Khatami, and "non-elected leaders," meaning Khamenei, made the latter more determined to frustrate Khatami's overtures. Thus the Clinton administration came to an end without any breakthrough in relations with Iran.

In short, both sides missed an opportunity to improve relations. Culprits were those elements in the U.S. foreign policy establishment determined to bring about regime change in Iran and Iranian factions that sacrificed Iran's national interests for their petty ambitions. Iran would come to regret this failure.

THE BUSH ADMINISTRATION: 9/11, WAR ON TERROR, AXIS OF EVIL, AND MOUNTING RISKS OF U.S.-IRAN MILITARY CONFRONTATION

Those personalities who ascended to key positions in George W. Bush's administration, such as Secretary of State Colin Powell and National Security Advisor Condoleezza Rice, subscribed to the realist school of international relations. This school emphasizes securing national interest through pragmatic means and considers a state's behavior to be determined principally by a desire to maximize its power and influence. Realists do not believe in the pursuit of idealistic goals, unless they help achieve other more important and power-related objectives. Traditionally, American realists have preferred to achieve America's goals through multilateral means, especially if they have involved the use of military force, although they have not been averse to unilateral military action when deemed essential for securing vital U.S. interests. There were, however, other officials in the Bush administration who by no stretch of imagination can be considered idealists in the traditional and Wilsonian sense of the word, but who believed that the United States should use its power unilaterally to change the political

[handwritten marginalia: "If the evidence isn't there, then ideas are motivated by a theory!"]

makeup of countries and regions deemed threatening to U.S. interests and those of its allies, most notably Israel. The most senior of these officials were, in order of seniority, Vice President Dick Cheney, Secretary of Defense Donald Rumsfeld, Deputy Secretary of Defense Paul Wolfowitz, Undersecretary of Defense for Policy Douglas Feith, Undersecretary of State for Arms Control John Bolton, Zalmay Khalilzad, Elliot Abrams at the NSC, and Undersecretary of State for Political Affairs Robert Zoellick.

Some of these individuals had articulated their vision as early as 1992. In 1998, a number of them, plus some academics and journalists such as Bill Kristol and Robert Kagan, sent a letter to President Clinton. In it, they complained that the administration's policy had failed to prevent Iraq's quest for nuclear weapons and demanded a change in U.S. strategy toward Iraq. Although not mentioned in their letter, these individuals also favored an activist and transformative policy toward Iran.[90]

Since the fall of the Bazargan government, the ultimate purpose of all U.S. administrations had been to bring about either the fall of the Islamic regime or to dramatically change its domestic and external behavior, through a variety of means, including sanctions, support for opposition forces, internal destabilization, and even military action, as happened during the Iran-Iraq War. However, previous U.S. administrations had not considered a full-scale preemptive military strike on Iran for the purpose of regime change. The neoconservatives favored such a strike.

[handwritten marginalia: "creates self-fulfilling prophecy"]

Nevertheless, despite their strong representation in the George W. Bush administration, the neoconservatives had not been able to implement their vision. The terrorist attacks of 9/11 provided them with the opportunity to implement their transformative agenda in the Middle East, through full-scale wars in Afghanistan and then Iraq.

It appears that the decision to change regimes in a number of countries, notably Iraq, Iran, Syria, Sudan, Libya, and Somalia was taken almost immediately after 9/11. In his book, *War and Decision*, Douglas Feith, undersecretary of defense for policy, writes that Donald Rumsfeld, in a memo to President Bush dated September 31, 2001, advised that the United States, instead of focusing on getting rid of Al Qaeda, should aim to establish new regimes in a series of states, "by aiding local peoples to rid themselves of terrorists and to free themselves of regimes that support terrorism."[91] The neocons justified their policy in terms of the war on terror, nonproliferation of WMDs, and democratization.

RAPPROCHEMENT AND BETRAYAL

The United States may have wanted regime change in Iran. Initially, however, 9/11 and the U.S. invasion of Afghanistan that immediately followed offered an opportunity to improve U.S.-Iranian relations. Iran tried to seize this opportunity when President Khatami, on behalf of himself and the Islamic Republic of Iran, condemned "the terrorist operations of hi-jacking and attacking public places in American cities" and expressed his "deep regret and condolences to the American nation."[92] There were also spontaneous public reactions of grief in Iran. As reported in the *Washington Post* on September 11, 2001, a number of Iranians held a candlelight vigil in Tehran, and on

September 19, before the start of a soccer match between Iran and Bahrain, a minute of silence was observed for the victims of 9/11. Considering the bad blood between the two countries and the ideological influence of neoconservatives in the Bush administration, the U.S. official response was quite positive. Secretary of State Colin Powell, after reiterating that because of Iran's support for terrorism the United States had serious differences with it, said that "Iran made a rather positive statement—for Iran" and added that Iran's statement was "worth exploring to see whether they now recognize that this [terrorism] is a curse on the face of the earth."[93]

Moreover, according to some sources, Khatami informed U.S. officials that a large delegation, including intelligence officials, would be accompanying him to New York when he came to attend the United Nations General Assembly (UNGA), and he suggested talks with the United States on counterterrorism.[94] However, Iran was too late again and, with the neoconservatives in charge of U.S. foreign policy, no one was interested in talks with Iran.

The European countries also tried to use this opening to bring the United States and Iran closer together. By early November 2001, there were reports that Colin Powell and Iran's foreign minister, Kamal Kharazi, might meet on the margins of the UN General Assembly. Although a formal meeting did not take place, most probably because of Iranian hard-liners' objections, they did meet informally and exchanged pleasantries. Even Donald Rumsfeld around this time admitted that U.S. and Iranian military advisors were fighting side-by-side, and he added that Iran had legitimate interests in Afghanistan.

The prospects for better U.S.-Iranian relations improved further, when Iran, by all accounts, helped the United States by brokering the deal on the future Afghan government during the Bonn Conference in 2001. According to James Dobbins, the U.S. representative at the Bonn talks on the future of Afghan government, "Iranian representatives were particularly helpful . . . It was, for instance, the Iranian delegate who first insisted that the agreement include a commitment to hold democratic elections in Afghanistan. This same Iranian persuaded the Northern Alliance to make the essential concession that allowed the meeting to conclude successfully."[95] According to Barnet R. Rubin, who attended the Bonn conference as part of the UN delegation, Iran's representative, Javad Zarif "supported efforts to frustrate Rabbani's goal of preventing the meeting from reaching agreement in the hope of consolidating his own power and formation of a broader government. Zarif's last minute intervention with the Northern Alliance delegation chair, Yunus Qanuni, convinced the latter to reduce the number of cabinet posts he demanded in the interim administration."[96] Rabbani was Afghanistan's official prime minister, whose government was removed by the Taliban but retained international recognition.

More important, Iran expressed a desire to increase cooperation with the United States regarding not only Afghanistan but other matters as well. According to Dobbins, Iranian officials offered to work under U.S. command to assist in rebuilding the Afghan army.[97] However, Iranians were told that "other issues" prevented cooperation.

The neoconservatives, within and without the U.S. administration, opposed this trend, as they had done earlier. According to Barbara Slavin, Secretary of State Colin

Powell tried to have a proactive policy toward Iran but faced "ferocious" opposition from Cheney, Rumsfeld, and Wolfowitz."[98] U.S. regional allies, notably Israel, but also Pakistan and Saudi Arabia, were not pleased with this prospect. Israel feared that rapprochement with Iran might be the beginning of a more conciliatory U.S. policy toward the Muslim world, including the Palestinians, partly because President Bush had talked about the creation of a Palestinian state. Moreover, the United States did not place Hamas and the Hizbullah on its list of more than 25 terrorist groups, an omission that, reportedly, angered Israel and increased its anxieties about the Bush administration's Middle East policies. These anxieties led Israel's prime minister, Ariel Sharon, in October 2001 to warn the United States not to repeat the Europeans' mistake in 1938 as they sacrificed Czechoslovakia in order "to reach a temporary convenient solution." He added "do not appease the Arabs at our expense."[99] Israel was also against any possible inclusion of countries like Iran and Syria in any antiterror coalition because that would doom the effort from the beginning. The reason, as put by Israel's foreign minister, Benjamin Netanyahu on September 21, 2001, during testimony before a committee of the U.S. House of Representatives, without these states' support for terrorism "the entire scaffolding of international terrorism will collapse."[100] Furthermore, he reportedly expressed Israel's specific disapproval of "any signs of U.S. cuddling up to Iran" and made clear that Israel feared any expansion of Iran's influence in Afghanistan.

Pakistan, too, was against this cooperation because it would have led to a "realignment to the detriment of Pakistan, whose military counted on monopolizing the role as the U.S.' intermediary with Afghanistan as leverage to assure U.S.-Pakistan military supply relationship."[101] Saudi Arabia, after fighting Iranian influence in Afghanistan for 40 years, did not want to see an increase in Iranian presence there either.

Eventually, those within the U.S. administration whose views were in line with the views expressed above prevailed, and the United States quickly turned against Iran in Afghanistan. It accused Iran of harboring Gulbudin Hekmatyar, who was an ally of Pakistan in the 1980s and early 1990s and who, after being abandoned by Pakistan, sought refuge in Iran. Iran expelled him. The United States also accused Iran of consolidating its influence in Herat, set out to remove its pro-Iran governor, Ismail Khan, and accused Iran of having links with al Qaeda, although the "overwhelming fact was that surviving core leadership of al Qaida all made its way to Pakistan, where their logistics and networks had been base and where they remained."[102] At this sensitive juncture in U.S-Iranian relations, as had happened so often before, the so-called *Karine-A* Affair broke.

UNANSWERED QUESTIONS

On January 4, 2002, Israel's chief of general staff, Lieutenant General Shaul Mofaz, declared that Israel had captured the ship *Karine-A*, belonging to the Palestinian Authority (PA), in the Red Sea, because it was carrying Iranian weapons. Shortly after that, Ariel Sharon said that "by his behavior Arafat [long-term leader of the PLO and head of the PA until his death in 2004] had made himself irrelevant and a bitter enemy of Israel. Arafat has taken another step by linking himself with the center of world terror—Iran."[103] Later, reports claimed that some elements in Saudi Arabia had financed the operations.[104]

Iran and the Palestinian Authority denied any involvement in this affair. Viewed purely in terms of both Iran's and the PA's interests, and given that the incident happened just when the U.S. administration was trying to pursue Arab-Israeli peacemaking and an opening to Iran, it seems strange that either of them would have done something which would adversely affect both processes.[105] This is why some analysts have suggested that Israel was behind the whole affair. Irrespective of who was behind it, this incident helped achieve a number of Israeli objectives, namely,

- undermining the idea of a Palestinian state;
- pushing Hizbullah and Syria to the top of the U.S. antiterror list;
- nipping U.S.-Iranian rapprochement in the bud.[106]

Yet it must be noted that there were elements in Iran that did not agree with Khatami's more conciliatory policy toward the United States, and therefore they might have tried to scuttle any movement in that direction through this operation. In fact, there were reports that radical elements in Iran were behind the shipping of weapons but that they intended them for the Hizbullah and not the PA.[107] At any rate, many questions regarding the affair and those responsible for it remain unanswered.[108] What is clear is that the affair put an end to the Bush administration's peacemaking efforts and opening to Iran.[109] It also consolidated the linkage between Iran and the Palestinian problem in American minds.[110]

THE AXIS OF EVIL, INVASION OF IRAQ, IRAN'S PROPOSAL FOR A GRAND BARGAIN, THE U.S. REBUFF

If one of the purposes of the *Karine-A* incident was to prevent any rapprochement between the United States and Iran, it succeeded brilliantly. Shortly after this event, when delivering his State of the Union address to the Congress on January 29, 2002, President Bush mentioned North Korea, Iraq, and Iran as forming an "Axis of Evil," who with their terrorist allies is:

arming to threaten the peace of the world. By seeking weapons of mass destruction, these regimes pose a grave and growing danger. They could provide these arms to terrorists, giving them the means to match their hatred. They could attack our allies or attempt to blackmail the United States. In any of these cases, the price of indifference would be catastrophic.[111]

Coming as it did after a period of Iranian overtures to the United States and help in Afghanistan, President Bush's speech was received with shock and disbelief in Iran. More important for the evolution of Iran's politics, this speech put the Iranian reformists on the defensive and their policy of reconciliation with the United States under serious question. Ultimately, it contributed to their defeat in the 2004 presidential elections. This United States response to Iran's cooperative gestures convinced many Iranian leaders, notably Ayatullah Khamenei, that the United States was not serious about improving ties with Iran. As he later said, Iran's problem was that it had an enemy who was always after a new excuse (*Doshman e Bahaneh Jou*).

Yet after the United States invasion of Iraq in March 2003, the Khatami government once more tried to follow the road of reconciliation. It did help the United States during the early stages of postinvasion reconstruction and did not use its Shia and Kurdish allies to complicate U.S. efforts to stabilize Iraq. This Iranian contribution is acknowledged by some U.S. analysts. But even more dramatically, Iran tried to reach a so-called grand bargain with the United States. It laid down its plans for such a deal in a letter that had been cleared by Ayatullah Khamenei and was sent to U.S. officials through the intermediary of the Swiss ambassador in Tehran in May 2003. However, it is worth noting that Iran claimed that the letter was sent in response to an American initiative.

The letter laid out what Iran was willing to do to in order to address major U.S. concerns, as well as what Iran expected from the United States in return. In the letter, Iran accepted

- to ensure full transparency regarding its nuclear program, full cooperation with the IAEA [International Atomic Energy Agency], including compliance with all non-proliferation instruments;
- to take decisive action against any terrorists in Iranian territory, especially Al Qaida members, and to cooperate fully and exchange all relevant information;
- to stop any material assistance to Palestinian groups from Iranian territory, notably Hamas and Islamic Jihad, and to pressure them to stop violent actions against civilians within the 1967 borders;
- to pressure Hizbullah to become a merely political organization;
- to accept the Arab League's 2002 Beirut declaration based on a Saudi initiative, otherwise known as the Arab League Peace Plan, which meant effectively accepting the two-state solution to the Arab-Israeli conflict;
- to use Iran's influence for stabilizing Iraq and establishing a non-religious government.

Additionally, Iran suggested specific steps and formation of working groups to address various issues, from how to proceed on Iraq to developing a long-term regional security framework. Reportedly, it also said that, if during operations in Iraq, an U.S. aircraft was shot and came down in Iran's territory and the United States sought to retrieve it, Iran would not interfere.[112]

In exchange, Iran demanded that the United States

+ accept a dialogue based on mutual respect;
+ halt its hostile actions against Iran;
+ abolish all sanctions against Iran and eliminate impediments to Iran's international trading and financial operation;
+ recognize Iran's legitimate interests in Iraq, especially its links with the holy cities of Karbala and Najaf, and support Iran's claims for reparation from Iraq;
+ recognize Iran's right to peaceful nuclear chemical and biological technology ; pursue anti-Iran terrorists, especially the MEK;
+ recognize Iran's legitimate regional security concerns which would allow for an adequate defense capability.[113]

Clearly, this letter was a major concession on Iran's part. However, as had been the case in the past, it came at a time when the United States felt that it did not need to talk to Iran or to make any concessions. A similar situation prevailed in 1991–1992 when, basking in the success of the Gulf War and the USSR's collapse, the George H. W. Bush administration felt that it did not need to compensate Rafsanjani for having secured the freedom of the last American hostage in Lebanon.

In May 2003, the United States was feeling that the Iraq operation had been a success, and there was clamor among the neoconservatives for it to pursue regime change in Iran and Syria and to reshape the Middle East through an aggressive program of democratization. The upshot of this mind-set, plus the extensive influence of the neoconservatives in the Bush administration, who, reportedly, argued that "we [the Bush administration] don't speak to evil," was that the United States did not respond to this letter.[114] Later, Condoleezza Rice said that she did not remember having seen the letter.[115] Moreover, shortly afterwards, the United States cancelled the ongoing talks between Iran's permanent representative to the United Nations, Javad Zarif, and Zalmay Khalilzad, the U.S. ambassador, which had been going on in Geneva, on the grounds of possible Iranian involvement in an al Qaeda–sponsored attack on a residential compound inhabited by U.S. and other foreign nationals in Riyadh. The United States also began providing funds to the Iranian government's opponents in Iran and abroad.

EARTHQUAKE DIPLOMACY: IRAN DROPS THE BALL

In December 2003, a strong earthquake rocked Iran's southeastern province of Kerman and devastated the historic city of Bam, with its 2,000-year-old citadel. Initially, it appeared that this tragedy might lead to some lessening of tensions between Iran and the United States. The U.S. government, including President Bush, expressed its sympathy with the Iranian people and the United States offered to send a relief team to Iran, headed by Senator Elizabeth Dole, the former head of the American Red

Cross.[116] Reportedly, Deputy Secretary of State Richard Armitage telephoned Javad Zarif, who at the time was visiting Tehran. Zarif called back within a half hour, with, according to some sources, Ayatullah Khamenei's blessing.[117] Although Iran turned down the offer of the visit, arguing that the conditions in Bam were not safe, it accepted American help, and American aid workers went to Bam.

These exchanges both raised hopes of some kind of improvement in relations and sharpened factional debate in Iran.[118] Ultimately, the Iranian government did not make the kind of gesture toward America which could have strengthened the hand of those within the U.S. administration, notably Secretary of State Colin Powell, who favored some form of engagement with Iran. This Iranian unwillingness may have been caused by: (1) fear that its overtures again might be rebuffed; (2) the fact that the Khatami administration was in its last year, and (3) increasing criticism by hard-liners of Khatami's foreign policy, which they branded as "concessionary" (*En-feali*). Be that as it may, Iran again missed an opportunity to unfreeze relations with the United States, at a time when, having failed to quickly stabilize Iraq, America might have been willing to engage with Iran.

AHMADINEJAD PRESIDENCY, IRAN'S NUCLEAR DOSSIER, AND THE GROWING RISK OF U.S.-IRANIAN MILITARY CONFRONTATION

Iran's reformists lost in the 2004 Iranian presidential elections, and the largely unknown mayor of Tehran, Mahmud Ahmadinejad, became president. Ahmadinejad declared that his administration would restore the values of the early period of the Islamic Revolution, both domestically and internationally. Internationally, this meant the adoption of a confrontational tone in relations with the West, especially the United States, the courting of socialist governments, such as those in Latin America, and resumption of a more activist approach toward the Arab-Israeli conflict, through more verbal support for groups such as Hamas and attacks on Israel.

One of the first and most damaging acts of the Ahmadinejad presidency was the holding of an international conference on the Holocaust. The conference was held under the auspices of the Institute of International Studies attached to the Ministry of Foreign Affairs. The purpose of the conference, as explained by the foreign minister, Manouchehr Muttaki, "was not to deny or confirm the Holocaust . . . Its aim [was] to create an opportunity for thinkers who cannot express their views freely in Europe about the Holocaust." Nevertheless, given the kind of people who participated in the conference, including the American white supremacist and a former leader of the Ku Klux Klan, David Duke, the goal was clearly to cast doubt on it.[119] Iran later organized a competition for cartoons on the subject, perhaps partially in response to cartoons published in Denmark insulting the Prophet of Islam.[120] Earlier, Ahmadinejad, at a conference entitled World without Zionism, had repeated Khomeini's saying that Israel must disappear from the face of the earth (*Az Sahneh e Rouzegar Mahv Shavad*).[121] This statement was translated as "Israel must be wiped out of the face of the earth," which is not accurate. But the damage was done, and these statements and actions, in addition to being morally wrong, seriously harmed Iran's national interests. Domestically, a large number of Iranians were embarrassed and outraged by them, and Iran's Jewish minority felt seriously hurt. Internationally, they intensified Israel's and Western powers' fears about the ultimate intentions of the Iranian government and hardened their position on Iran's nuclear program, thus making any engagement with Iran more difficult.

IRAN'S NUCLEAR PROGRAM, SANCTIONS, AND THE THREAT OF WAR

The history of Iran's quest for nuclear technology goes back to the mid-1950s. In 1957, Iran signed an agreement with the United States "for cooperation in research on the peaceful uses of nuclear energy." Shortly afterwards, Iran established a Nuclear Research Center at Tehran University and purchased a small research reactor. Iran was among the first countries to sign and ratify the Nuclear Nonproliferation Treaty (NPT).[122]

However, it was only in the early 1970s that Iran began to talk of the need to develop nuclear power plants to produce electricity and to save its oil and gas reserves for industrial goals and export. At the time, Iran looked to the United States and Europe for required reactors, know-how, and fuel. Because, at the time, Iran was a close Western ally, the Shah's nuclear ambitions did not generate strong anxiety, although there was some suspicion that he might eventually want to acquire nuclear weapons. Later, according to the first director of Iran's atomic energy organization, Dr. Akbar Etemad, the Carter administration had developed some concerns over Iran's plans, leading the Shah to send him to Washington in 1977 to dispel them.[123]

Work was begun on Iran's first nuclear plant began in 1978 by a German concern, Kraftwerk Union. Iran also joined EURODIF.[124] All these ambitions were abandoned after the revolution and the Iran-Iraq War that followed. The Bushehr power plant, which at the time of the Iraqi attack was 80 percent complete, suffered serious damage.

After the war, Iran asked the Germans to complete the power plant, but the German government opposed it. Finally in 1995, Russia, in the context of its 1992 agreement with Iran on comprehensive nuclear cooperation, took over the building of the plant.[125]

IRAN AND NUCLEAR WEAPONS

The Shah was suspected of seeking nuclear weapons, but the United States and other Western powers, according to most observers, did not look with alarm at this prospect, although, as noted earlier, this view is disputed by the first director of Iran's atomic energy organization. Anxiety over Iran's nuclear weapon ambitions began as early as the 1980s, when reports about Iran's intentions begun to circulate. After the Soviet collapse, there were erroneous reports that Iran had obtained nuclear warheads mounted on missiles from Kazakhstan. Other reports claimed that China, India, Brazil, and Pakistan were helping Iran's nuclear program, and that by 2002 Iran would have nuclear weapons, or, according to some observers, by 2000. Many of these reports were attributed to the MEK.

Consequently, preventing Iran from acquiring a nuclear-weapon capability became a cornerstone of the Clinton administration's Iran policy. However, Iran's nuclear program did not become a major issue in its relations with the United States and other Western countries until 2002. On August 14, 2002, the MEK declared that it had discovered that Iran was constructing one nuclear enrichment facility in Natanz and a heavy water reactor in Arak. The construction of these facilities, strictly speaking, did not amount to a violation of the NPT. Moreover, it seems that the IAEA and perhaps the intelligence services of Western countries, including the United States, knew about Iran's activities. Nevertheless, the fact that Iran had not formally informed the IAEA of these activities made them appear suspect. According to some reports, the director of the IAEA told reporters that "it would have been better if we had been informed earlier about the decision to build these facilities."[126]

This revelation led to a lengthy process of negotiation between Iran on the one hand and the IAEA and three European countries (the UK, Britain, and Germany—the Troika, plus the European Union's High Representative for the Common Foreign and Security Policy, Javier Solana) on the other.[127] Iran-U.S. interaction in this connection was essentially in the context of the IAEA. The United States lobbied for stringent measures against Iran, which finally led to the referral of Iran's dossier to the UNSC and the imposition of economic sanctions. The United States, according to many sources, also prevented the reaching of a settlement between Iran and Europe on this issue, which could have closed Iran's nuclear dossier.

In August 2009, Iran agreed to the inspection of its heavy water nuclear plant in Arak by the IAEA inspectors.[128] In its August 2009 report, the director general of the IAEA recognized this and other signs of Iranian cooperation with the agency. It noted that "Iran has cooperated in improving safeguard measures at FEP [Fuel enrichment Plant] in Natanz." It also noted that the agency was able to continue to "verify the non-diversion of declared nuclear material in Iran." However, the report also said that Iran had not implemented the Additional Protocol or the UNSC resolutions.[129]

CORRESPONDENCE AMID TENSIONS

Despite their criticism of Khatami's foreign policy, conservatives who won the presidency in 2005 were anxious to talk to the United States, not least because they feared a possible military attack. Moreover, since the mid-1980s, the question in U.S.-Iranian relations had not been merely whether Iran should talk to the United States but also who within the Iranian leadership should do the talking and hence reap the benefits of an improved relationship. Therefore, it is no surprise that even in Ahmadinejad's first presidency Iran indicated that it was ready to engage with the United States. According to Barbara Slavin, by 2005–2006 a consensus seemed to have emerged within the Iranian political establishment, from left to right, that the time was ripe for talks with America. She relates that an Iranian reformist figure and former official of the Khatami administration, Saeed Leylaz, informed her that a taxi driver told him that U.S. ambassador to Iraq, Zalmay Khalilzad, had been seen in Tehran. He added that he believed that the government of Ahmadinejad was ready for talks with the United States.[130]

This Iranian willingness to open a dialogue with the United States was indicated in a quite clumsy and roundabout fashion by Ahmadinejad's letter to President George W. Bush, dated May 9, 2006. Instead of making concrete suggestions as to how to proceed to resolve outstanding differences between the two countries, the letter listed the world's ills, the unjust international system, the plight of the Palestinians, and the U.S. role in them. This was followed by a call for the United States to change its behavior and to adopt policies in line with the teachings of the prophets.[131]

President Bush did not answer the letter. Many believe that he missed a good opportunity to explain the U.S. position on various issues mentioned in Ahmadinejad's letter and to offer constructive ways of approaching them.[132] Such a response, they argued, could have started a process that might have led to an improvement in bilateral relations.

In Iran, many criticized Ahmadinejad, not for writing the letter, but for its content. However, if Ahmadinejad was offended by not receiving an answer he did not show it. He merely commented that President Bush's decision not to answer his letter was in itself an answer. This comment indicates that he interpreted the lack of answer to his letter as a sign of the Bush administration's lack of interest in a dialogue with Iran.

In addition, the United States hardened its rhetoric against Iran. A White House global strategy document issued in 2006 put Iran at the top of U.S. security concerns and stated that, if a military confrontation were to be avoided, diplomacy to halt Iran's nuclear program must succeed, but it did not say what would happen if diplomacy failed.[133] Then the administration proceeded to allocate $66 million for democracy promotion in Iran. Later, the United States allocated another $420 million for operations to destabilize Iran and to bring about regime change, including support for activities of separatist groups, like Kurdish Pejak and the Baluchi Jund Ullah. Consequently, when in 2008 reports emerged that the United States intended to send its diplomats to Tehran to serve in its Interests Section at the Swiss embassy, they were greeted with anxiety by those in the United States opposed to improvement in U.S.-Iranian relations. To quell these suspicions, the Bush administration argued that the U.S. diplomatic presence in Iran would enable it to have a better picture of what was going on there and to establish contact with individual Iranians.[134] The Iranian government, therefore, viewed this act as part of U.S. efforts to bring about what they characterized as "soft regime change" (Barandazi e Narm). The current speaker of the Iranian Parliament, Ali Larijani, reflected this mind-set when he said that "I would not take the issue seriously as there might be a mischievous reason behind it." He added, "What we need in the region is to change the strategies not the tactics."[135] Oddly enough, reportedly, the Ahmadinejad government, including Larijani, who had become the secretary of the Iranian National Security Council, had suggested the stationing of U.S. diplomats at the Swiss embassy in Tehran provided the United States agreed to direct flights between Tehran and New York by Iran Air.[136]

By the late spring of 2007, the United States had agreed to participate in the nuclear talks between Iran and the three European countries, plus China and Russia, but mostly as a silent partner.

Trapped in its regime-change rhetoric and excessively concerned that in dealings with Iran it should not appear as "caving in," the United States approached contacts with Iran in a fashion akin to "holding its nose while it stretched a pinky toward Tehran."[137] This U.S. attitude, coupled with the Iranian leaders' lack of appreciation of the fact that they could not pursue dialogue with the United States while denying the Holocaust, meant that nothing came of all this letter writing.

THE UNITED STATES AND IRAN IN IRAQ: ANOTHER MISSED OPPORTUNITY FOR RECONCILIATION

The U.S. invasion of Iraq in March 2003 created opportunities for engaging with Iran after America's expectation of early stabilization of Iraq and spontaneous revolutions in the rest of the Middle East did not materialize. However, the United States did not seize the opportunity during either the Khatami or Ahmadinejad presidencies.

President Khatami signaled Iran's readiness to reach a modus vivendi with the United States in Iraq by sending the 2003 letter and by indicating that Iran had no interest in the establishment of an Islamic government in Iraq. What Iran hoped for in exchange was a more cooperative U.S. posture on the MEK, which at the time was still on the U.S. terrorist list. The organization had also been criticized by Human Rights Watch for running prison camps in Iraq, and by others for being run as a cult under the dictatorial leadership of Mas'ud and Mariam Rajavi.[138] However, the United States argued that the MEK had been a good source of intelligence on Iran, especially on its nuclear program, and could in the future help it fight Iranian influence in Iraq; thus the United States declared the MEK "protected people" under the Geneva Convention.

As the situation in Iraq deteriorated, the United States increased charges that Iran was responsible for its Iraq frustration, ignoring the following important facts:

+ The Iraqi insurgents were Sunni and anti-Iran and were helped by Arab countries, including such U.S. allies as Saudi Arabia, Jordan, and Egypt, and Arab volunteers came to Iraq through Syria.
+ The overwhelming majority of those killed were Shias.
+ More Americans were killed by Sunnis rather than by Shias.
+ Shia militant groups, such as Moqtada Al Sadr's Mahdi Army, were not Iran's main Shia allies in Iraq, who were under the leadership of Ayatullah Hakim.

Nevertheless, by 2005 American ambassador in Iraq Zalmay Khalilzad had begun to cultivate the Sunnis, including the insurgents.[139] These contacts did not reduce the insurgents' attacks on U.S. targets but led to the most devastating attack on the Shia holy places, notably the Al Asker Mosque in Samara on February 22, 2006.[140] That mosque holds a special significance for the Shias: it is where the 10th Shia Imam, who was exiled to Samara, died; it is where the 11th Shia Imam died; and the cave where the 12th Imam became occluded is close to the mosque.

Shia religious leaders, notably the Grand Ayatullah Sistani, tried hard to limit anti-Sunni violence, but Iraq's prime minister criticized Sunni religious leaders for failing to issue fatwas, declaring them acts against religion. Some Iranian authorities, notably Ali Larijani, blamed Khalilzad's courting of the insurgents as responsible for the attack. However, the Ahmadinejad government and the Ayatullah Khamenei backed talks with the United States on Iraq, and some talks did take place between U.S. ambassador Ryan Crocker and Iran's ambassador, Kazemi Qomi.[141] Iran's foreign minister, Manouchehr Muttaki, also indicated in June 2007 that Iran would be willing to consider talks at a higher level if the United States requested, demonstrating Iran's desire to broaden the scope of the talks beyond the Iraqi situation.[142] Muttaki's suggestion is also interesting because it happened after Iranian diplomats in Iraq were seized by U.S. forces.

As usual, Iran was late, and by 2007 the U.S. position had hardened even more, as indicated by a number of events, notably the kidnapping of five Iranian diplomats, one by the name of Jalal Sharifi, who was the second secretary at the Iranian embassy in Baghdad and the fourth secretary in Iran's Liaison Office in Erbil, which was to be upgraded to consulate status.[143] The United States accused the latter of being in reality members of the Islamic Revolutionary Guards Corp's (IRGC) Qud's force, Ramadan Section. The Iranian government denied this allegation, and the authorities of the Kurdish regional government also said that the Iranians were operating in Erbil with official sanction.[144]

Shortly afterwards, the United States allocated $420 million to encourage change in Iran and stepped up support for Iran's Kurdish and Baluchi separatists.[145]

These U.S. policies did not bear fruit because they failed to dissuade the Sunni insurgents from their acts and did not help to stabilize Iraq. They only exacerbated sectarian tensions in Iraq and problems with Iran. By focusing on Iran as the main factor responsible for Iraq's instability and ignoring help given by its Arab allies such as Saudi Arabia, Jordan, and Egypt, among others, to Sunni insurgents, the United States allowed its Arab allies to continue sabotaging its efforts in Iraq with impunity. Had the United States approached talks with Iran on Iraq seriously, it might have helped resolve other problems, too. Meanwhile, Iran could have been less timid in expressing a desire for talks with the United States, not just on Iraq but on broader issues. But having been burnt in Afghanistan, Iran's reticence was understandable.

By the end of 2009, as the political competition in Iraq heated up prior to the parliamentary election, the United States, including the commander of American Forces in Iraq, General Ray Odierno, again accused Iran of being responsible for these difficulties.[146] Yet the main problem was the United States and the Arab countries' efforts to bring back some of the ex-Ba'athists to power, something that angered the Maliki government and the majority Shias.[147]

OBAMA PRESIDENCY: ENGAGEMENT
OR MORE OF THE SAME

During the 2008 presidential campaign, Barack Obama had criticized the Bush administration's unwillingness to engage diplomatically with Iran and promised a different policy, creating the expectation in Iran that Obama's election would fundamentally alter its relationship with the United States. However, a close scrutiny of Obama's statements on Iran, most important his 2008 speech to the AIPAC annual conference, indicates that there was no essential difference in his attitude on Iran from that of the Bush administration during its last year in office. In that speech, Obama accused Iran of the same wrongdoings as previous administrations had done. He called Iran "the greatest strategic challenge to the U.S. and Israel," thus establishing a commonality of interest between the United States and Israel on Iran.[148] He justified his desire to engage in "robust diplomacy" toward Iran on the basis of the argument that, if Iran did not accept U.S. and Western conditions, it would be easier to enlist China's and Russia's cooperation in imposing harsher sanctions on Iran.[149] Obama also kept the military option on the table and insisted that Iran stop enrichment activities, a condition that Iran, in the past, had refused to accept.[150]

Nevertheless, Obama's election did create hopes in Iran that he might be more forthcoming, prompting Ahmadinejad to send a congratulatory letter to Obama on the occasion of his presidential victory. In it, he expressed the hope that the new president would make meaningful changes in U.S. foreign policy, and Ahmadinejad advised him to keep American government interventions "within its own country's borders."[151]

At the time, it was reported that President Obama was considering a reply to this letter, and that several drafts had been prepared. However, Ahmadinejad's letter went unanswered. Later, President Obama reportedly sent a letter to Supreme Leader Khamenei. Further, on the occasion of the Persian New Year (Norouz) on March 20, 2009, President Obama sent greetings to the Iranian people and said that the United States extended a hand to Iran, provided that the Iranians "unclenched their fist." The rest of the message consisted of a list of Iran's sins and U.S. conditions for better relations, including the phrase that, in exchange for an extended hand, Iran must accept some "real responsibilities." The most important aspect of President Obama's message was that it was addressed to the people and leaders of the Islamic Republic of Iran, which was meant to indicate that he did not seek regime change in Iran and was only seeking a change in Iran's behavior.[152]

Iran's response to this message was mixed and cautious, but it also contained positive elements. Its most positive aspect was that Ayatullah Khamenei said that if the United States changed its behavior toward Iran, Iran would also change its behavior toward America. Moreover, this time he was more specific on what aspects of American policy he wanted to see changed and referred to the alleged U.S. interference in Baluchistan and Kurdistan by supporting separatist elements.[153] Later, however, other Iranian officials, including the speaker of the Iranian parliament, Ali Larijani, said that Iran could not be swayed by mere words and that the United States must prove that it is serious about change through concrete actions.[154]

However, internal developments in Iran, strong opposition by U.S. Arab allies and Israel to any meaningful opening to Iran, and the opposition of key Obama administration officials, notably Secretary of State Hillary Clinton and Dennis Ross, special envoy for Iran and the Persian Gulf, reduced the U.S. diplomatic option to an exercise in futility and served as a prelude to harsher sanctions.

During the 2008 presidential campaign, Hillary Clinton had adopted a very tough line on Iran, stating that the United States "will obliterate Iran if it attacked Israel."[155] Shortly before President Obama's greeting to the Iranians, during a trip to the Middle East, she made hawkish remarks on Iran. She called Iran a threat not only to the Middle East but also to Russia and Europe, and she mentioned engaging Iran only in regard to the specific cases of Afghanistan and Iraq, areas where the United States felt a need for Iran's cooperation.[156] Later, in meetings with UAE officials, during the Sharm Al Sheikh donor countries meeting on Iraq in March 2009, she said that she did not think that Iran would respond positively to U.S. overtures.

Secretary Clinton is also reported to believe that negotiations are useful only to show their futility in convincing Iran to stop its enrichment program, thus paving the way for "crippling sanctions." Moreover, she and other U.S. officials made clear that improving ties with Iran cannot and will not come at the expense of U.S. relations with its Arab allies, which had expressed anxiety over possible U.S.-Iran reconciliation. To prove this point, Secretary of Defense Robert Gates toured the Persian Gulf Arab states, and President Obama visited Saudi Arabia in April 2009.[157] The same pattern continued in the coming months, with key U.S. officials trying to reassure Israel and Arabs on Iran.

Israel expressed even more anxiety over a potential softening of the U.S. attitude toward Iran. To forestall such a move, Israeli leaders, from Benjamin Netanyahu to Shimon Peres, warned that in such a case Israel might attack Iran unilaterally.[158] The United States seems to have taken this threat seriously enough that, according to some reports, it sent the director of the Central Intelligence Agency to Tel Aviv to dissuade Israel from doing so.[159] The United States succeeded in this effort because Israeli officials, including the extreme right-wing foreign minister, Evigdor Lieberman, stopped talking about attacking Iran.[160] However, when Benjamin Netanyahu visited President Obama in Washington, he convinced him that any negotiations with Iran must have a time limit and not drag on indefinitely. Netanyahu suggested the end of September 2009, but this was later extended to end of December.

By the middle of May 2009, the Obama administration's policy toward Iran was confused enough to lead two ex-U.S. officials, who had been critical of the U.S. refusal to answer positively to Iran's 2003 offer of a grand bargain, to write in the *New York Times* that President Obama had made "several personnel and policy decisions that [had] undermined the promise of his encouraging rhetoric on Iran."[161] Meanwhile, partly because of Israel's and its U.S. supporters' pressure, the House and the Senate in July 2009 passed a resolution to impose sanctions on companies selling gasoline to Iran.[162] Later, they suspended action on this resolution until the end of September, but they finalized it in October.

THE ROXANA SABERI INCIDENT

In Iran, too, opponents of rapprochement with the United States were active and resorted to an old trick, namely the jailing of U.S. citizens with an Iranian heritage. This time the victim was Roxana Saberi, an American citizen of mixed Iranian-Japanese parentage who was arrested on January 31, 2009, only one week into the Obama administration. Saberi also had Iranian citizenship and had entered Iran on her Iranian passport. She had been living in Iran for six years, working as a freelance journalist for the BBC, NPR, and FOX News. Reportedly, her permission to work in Iran had expired, and she worked without a legal permit. Initially, it was reported that she had been arrested for buying a bottle of wine. Later, however, the charges were changed to espionage. The latter charge was based on evidence that she had obtained a top secret report prepared by the research institute of the Expediency Council, through what Iranian media characterized as an "admirer." She was condemned to an eight-year prison term. However, in an interesting move, which can be interpreted as sending a positive signal to the United States, Iran's president interfered and her case was examined in an appeals court. According to her new lawyer, there were some suspicious aspects to her case, including a trip she took to Israel and to the restive province of Zahedan, plus her connections to some U.S. officials. However, she managed to convince the judges that she had no intention of spying, and her sentence was reduced to two years in prison and suspended without any restrictions on her movement. She left Iran in May 2009.[163]

The Saberi case was an unnecessary complication for the fragile and timid U.S.-Iranian engagement. It showed the continuing disarray within the Iranian leadership. But Ahmadinejad's intervention to reduce her sentence and free her could be read as an indication of Iran's desire to explore engagement with the United States, especially given that both President Obama and Secretary of State Hillary Clinton had called for her release.

A COUNTERREVOLUTION IN THE MAKING? IRAN'S CONTESTED PRESIDENTIAL ELECTION

From the very beginning of the Obama presidency, the fact that Iran was also to have its presidential elections in June 2009 posed some difficulty in regard to possible U.S.-Iranian talks. Understandably, the U.S. government preferred dealing with Iran's new president, be it Ahmadinejad or, preferably, someone with less negative baggage. U.S. hopes regarding the possibility of having a more congenial interlocutor in Tehran were raised when Iranian reformists showed determination in challenging Ahmadinejad at the polls. Meanwhile, the United States took some modestly positive steps and declared that it would join the 5+1 talks with Iran. It also instructed U.S. embassies abroad to invite Iranian diplomats to the Fourth of July celebrations.[164] Furthermore, in May, the Guardian Council revealed that President Obama had sent a letter to Ayatullah Khamenei.

Postelection developments, however, derailed this positive trend. After voting was over, both leading candidates, the reformist Mir Hussein Mussavi and Ahmadinejad, declared victory. However, election officials said that Ahmadinejad had gained a resounding victory by capturing more than 62 percent of the votes. This declaration led to massive protests by Mussavi's supporters, which lasted for more than a week and led to many injured and between 7 and 15 people dead. Mussavi's supporters charged the government with electoral fraud and demanded the annulment of the elections and the holding of another election. Initially, the authorities reacted with caution and several supporters of Ahmadinejad, such as the former speaker of the parliament, Had Adel, called on Mussavi and his supporters to accept the election results and pursue any complaints through legal channels.

As the protests continued and became violent, Supreme Leader Ali Khamenei intervened and, in a bold and blunt speech, said that the government would not tolerate lawlessness and would not succumb to pressure. Moreover, he stated that Ahmadinejad's views were closer to his own than those of the reformists, including former president Rafsanjani. Meanwhile, the Guardian Council, which was charged with investigating alleged electoral irregularities, declared that although there had been some irregularities they had not been of a magnitude to affect the results.[165]

As the protests continued and became violent, the Iranian government began to accuse the foreign media and governments of fomenting violence, with the goal of instigating a velvet/color revolution in Iran. In his speech, Khamenei particularly targeted the BBC and the Voice of America.[166] The Islamic regime seized upon European governments' expressions of concern over the Iranian government's crackdown on demonstrators by accusing them of interfering in Iran's domestic affairs.

Initially, President Obama adopted a cautions and neutral attitude toward Iran's electoral dispute, for which he was criticized by Republican lawmakers. However, as the protests continued and became violent, he voiced his concern for the way the crisis was handled and for those who were subjected to harsh treatment and imprisonment. In another sign of its displeasure, the United States withdrew its invitation to Iranian diplomats for Fourth of July celebrations because, it said, under Iran's current conditions the presence of representatives of the Iranian government in an event that celebrates American values would be incongruous.[167]

In response to the hardening of the U.S. position, in a speech on June 25, 2009, on the occasion of the inauguration of a petrochemical factory, Ahmadinejad said that "regarding the governments of England and of one or two European countries, whose past and whose actions are known to all, and who have no shame vis-à-vis the world—we do not expect anything from them. But the question is why Mr. Obama fell into this trap. Why did he commit this mistake?"[168] He then added, "I sincerely advise him to correct himself before committing Bush's mistakes."[169]

The postelection disarray in Iran also meant that Iran did not give its response to the offer of 5+1 on its nuclear dossier, despite saying that it was preparing a comprehensive package that would include suggestions on how Iran could cooperate with the United States and Europe to solve global problems.

IRAN-U.S. TALKS IN GENEVA: POSSIBLE
BREAKTHROUGH OR ANOTHER FALSE HOPE?

Iran finally presented its packages of proposals to the representatives of 5+1 in September, and it was agreed that 5+1 and Iran would begin talks in Geneva on October 1, 2009. These proposals did not address Iran's nuclear problem per se but rather mentioned a number of areas regarding global matters, including the issue of nuclear weapons in general, where Iran and other countries could cooperate. This Iranian tactic was most likely followed because of Iran's previous insistence that its nuclear program was not negotiable. The United States, by contrast, insisted that its main objective in the talks was to raise the issue of Iran's nuclear program and that it was not interested in talks for the sake of talks.

The contrasting approaches of the United States and Iran to the talks raised the fear that the talks would go nowhere, especially because the United States continued to speak of severe sanctions on Iran and the U.S. Department of Treasury began to discuss with a number of countries, including Saudi Arabia and the UAE, a list of crippling sanctions on Iran. In short, the Obama administration adopted what they called a "two track" approach toward Iran, namely talks and preparing for sanctions simultaneously.

European countries, notably France and Britain, continued their tough talk on Iran. In particular, during an interview with the BBC, the UK foreign minister, David Miliband, refused to rule out the military option against Iran.[170]

Iran's declaration just a few days before the talks that it had been building another enrichment plant in the village of Fardo near Qum further clouded the prospects of success in the talks, especially since more or less at the same time Iran had tested new missiles.[171] This led to speculation that Iran might already have learned how to make nuclear warheads.[172] Iran argued that, according to the NPT, it was required only to inform the IAEA 180 days before injecting nuclear material into the plant, whereas it had done so 18 months in advance. Nevertheless, Western experts and some officials used this as evidence of Iran's continued duplicity in regard to its nuclear activities.[173]

Yet the talks were fairly successful, especially since Iran's principal representative, Saeid Jalili, and the U.S. undersecretary of state for political affairs, William Burns, had a fairly good meeting and among other things discussed the fate of three American hikers, who, by mistake, had crossed into Iran from Iraqi Kurdistan in August 2009.[174] As a good will gesture, Iran earlier had allowed the Swiss ambassador to see the detainees.[175] Before that, Ahmadinejad had said that although the final decision on this matter is with the judiciary, he would request leniency toward U.S. citizens. Also, while in New York for the UNGA meeting, Ahmadinejad had expressed the desire to buy nuclear fuel from the United States for the research reactor in Tehran, which produces medical isotopes.

The Geneva talks were a relative success because

+ both sides agreed to meet again on October 25;
+ Iran agreed to allow IAEA inspectors to visit the Fardo facility;

+ Iran agreed to consider the proposal to send most of its low-enriched uranium to Russia and then to France for further enrichment and transformation into fuel. Reportedly, this proposal was worked out through the IAEA and between Russia and the United States. According to the *Washington Post*, during President Obama's July 2009 trip to Moscow, U.S. official Gary Samore had raised the issue with Sergei Kirienko, head of Russia's Atomic Energy Agency.[176]

Initially, the Iranian government, in general, appeared anxious to strike a deal that would forestall military attack and stringent sanctions. The fact that the leadership after the 2009 presidential election was ideologically more cohesive gave further hope that this time Iran would be able to reach an agreement and implement it. Ahmadinejad had already made the same proposal a few days earlier in a speech.

However, in the coming months the following factors led to the dashing of hopes raised by the Geneva talks:

1. Conflicting U.S.-Iran objectives: The United States's main purpose of these talks was to eventually stop Iran's nuclear program altogether, and the U.S. authorities clearly said that the nuclear issue was the main focus of Geneva talks. By contrast, Iran was interested in broadening the talks to include other issues of concern to Iran as well as regional and global questions. This Iranian desire was largely because the Ahmadinejad government did not want to appear to be negotiating about Iran's nuclear program, which it had criticized the Khatami administration of having done in the past.

2. Iran's mistrust of both Russia and France as reliable suppliers of enriched uranium it would need for the Tehran research reactor: In light of Russia's long history of defaulting on its promises to Iran, be it regarding the Bushehr Power Plant or the delivery of S300 missiles, Iran's mistrust of Russia understandable. In fact, because of these Russian defaults Russo-Iranian relations had begun to cool considerably by late 2009. France's history with Iran was not much more confidence-inspiring than that of Russia. In fact, Iran's representative to the IAEA, in a letter to the agency, cited the following instances as the West's default on their promises to Iran: (a) the U.S. government's decision to stop the supply of fuels to the Tehran reactor in 1980 by the American firm AMF, and the latter's refusal to refund the $2 million paid in advance for the fuel, (b) Germany's refusal to provide fuel for the Bushehr plant and (c) France's refusal to provide enriched uranium to Iran despite Iran being a shareholder in Eurodif. France, and particularly, Sarkozy's very hard-line stance on Iran also made France appear an unreliable partner in this venture.[177] Because of ideological reasons, Iran felt some hesitance in handing over its uranium to Russia and France. To overcome this trust barrier, countries like Turkey and Japan expressed their willingness to be the place where the swap of material would take place. Reportedly, Japan offered to enrich Iran's uranium.[178]

3. Iran's domestic politics and intra-regime rivalries: The opponents of the Ahmadinejad government and some of its rivals, notably the Speaker of the Iranian

parliament and one-time nuclear negotiator Ali Larijani, also raised doubts about the wisdom of fuel exchange. Even Hassan Rowhani, Iran's nuclear negotiator under Khatami, said that Iran should pay money for the highly enriched uranium for the Tehran reactor and not low enriched uranium.[179] In fact, it seemed as if Ahmadinejad was the one most eager for some sort of a deal.

Iran continued to express its willingness to work out a deal. One Iranian proposal was that the swap of low enriched uranium for high enriched should take place simultaneously and in stages; Iran would deliver low enriched uranium and at the same time would receive high enriched uranium. Moreover, Iran said that the swap should take place in Iranian territory. Iran further elaborated on this proposal and in January 2010, at a conference in Bahrain organized by the UK-based International Institute of Strategic Studies, Iran's foreign minister Manouchehr Muttaki declared that Iran was ready to swap 400 kilograms of uranium in the Kish Island.[180] Ahmadinejad later made the same proposal in a speech in February.[181]

The United states rejected both ideas and called the Muttaki proposal unacceptable. It did, however, offer to sell Iran medical isotopes.

The United States's refusal to consider Iran's proposals led Iran, in early 2010, to declare that it will begin to enrich its own uranium to the level of 20 percent for the Tehran reactor under IAEA supervision, but it still insisted that it was willing for the fuel exchange.[182]

The United States, the European countries, and Russia reacted negatively to this Iranian decision and interpreted it as a sign of Iran's more sinister designs. This Iranian declaration further intensified efforts on the part of the United States and the European countries to move in the direction of tougher sanctions on Iran.

Even at the time of the Geneva talks, the United States indicating that the Geneva agreement, if implemented, would be a step forward, it sought a more comprehensive solution to Iran's nuclear program. It also continued its efforts to gain support for stringent sanctions on Iran should negotiations fail. Conservative politicians and experts argued that instead of talks the United States should encourage regime change by supporting the opposition.[183] Israel, too, expressed unhappiness with the prospect of Russia's further enriching Iranian uranium. However, later Netanyahu endorsed the Geneva agreement perhaps sensing that it had not much chance of being finalized.[184] The U.S. Congress, meanwhile, went ahead with the gasoline sanction plan, although the Obama administration requested that Congress delay the implementation until the result of talks became clear.[185]

Even within the administration, key figures, notably Secretary of State Hillary Clinton, were in favor of more pressure on Iran. Secretary Clinton undertook a campaign of gathering support for sanctions on Iran among Arab states of the Persian Gulf, as well as trying to convince countries such as China and Brazil to support more sanctions on Iran in the United Nations Security Council.[186] Even President Obama said that Iran was pursuing a nuclear weapons program and added that the world was moving fast on Iran sanctions.[187] Other U.S. officials such as Deputy Secretary of State Jim Steinberg and Undersecretary of State for Political Affairs William Burns, visited Turkey, Azerbaijan, and Syria for the same purpose.[188]

A new argument in favor of sanctions was that it will help bring the regime down by intensifying popular disenchantment, which was demonstrated during the June 2009 elections.[189]

The report of the IAEA, under its new director, the Japanese Yukiya Amano, which came out in March 2010, but was leaked in February, was harsher than the previous report. While not offering any new evidence indicating that Iran was after nuclear weapons, and admitting that there had been no diversion of nuclear material, it said that there were "concerns about the *possible existence in Iran of past or current undisclosed activities of a nuclear payload for a missile*" [Emphasis added].[190] This is in contrast with El Baradei's report that said "there remain a number of outstanding issues *which need to be clarified to exclude the existence of possible military dimensions to Iran's nuclear programme*" [Emphasis added].[191]

The United States was happy with the report while Iran reacted sharply to it, as did the group of the Non-Aligned (NAM) countries.[192] The report also seemed to strengthen the position of those in the United States and in other countries advocating for very harsh sanctions. Israel again was in the forefront and its Prime Minister Netanyahu said that Iran should be prevented from the sale of its oil. Israel's foreign minister Avigdor Lieberman, called for a Cuba-style embargo on Iran.[193]

By spring 2010, whatever hopes the Geneva talks had generated were evaporated. It appeared that the proponents of a harder diplomacy on Iran rather than engagement had gained ascendance within the U.S. administration.[194] The United States, however, seemed wary of a military encounter with Iran. In particular, the U.S. military appeared not to favor a military option, while also saying that it might become inevitable.[195]

ASSESSING IRAN'S POLICY TOWARD THE UNITED STATES

More than any other aspect of its foreign policy, Iran's handling of relations with the United States demonstrates the negative impact of its leaders' lack of understanding of the domestic political dynamics of U.S. foreign policy; the dimensions of post-Soviet systemic changes, including the United States' reappraisal of Iran's importance, and the accentuation of competitive dimensions of great power/regional power relations; plus the ideological nature of the Islamic regime; the role of anti-imperialism in its self-image and as a basis of regime legitimacy; and intra-regime ideological differences and personal rivalries. For example, Iran's leaders have even now not fully realized that, without the Soviet ideological and military threat, Iran does not have the same strategic significance, or that a too-strong and belligerent Iran is unlikely to be tolerated by other great powers.

Also, despite bemoaning the influence of the so-called Zionist lobby in the United States and the frequent intimations of Israel that for Tehran "the road to Washington goes through Tel Aviv," Iran's leaders have tried to improve relations with the United States without changing their policy toward Israel. This has meant that, several times, Iran has been helpful to the United States (e.g., the Gulf War in 1990–1991, Bosnia in 1995, Afghanistan in 2001–2002, and even Iraq) only to be punished by the United States afterward.

Moreover, Iran has missed opportunities to resolve its disputes with the United States at those times when the United States was in need of Iranian cooperation, while approaching the United States when its help was no longer needed. Iran's inability to define its role in the post-Soviet world in a more positive manner, such as becoming the representative of a more democratic and progressive Islam, has kept it trapped in the outdated Cold War mold of international relations and reduced its ability to deal effectively with the United States.

The Khatami administration, with its idea of a Dialogue of Civilizations, tried to change the paradigm of Iran's foreign policy and replace past confrontation and anti-imperialist struggle with cooperation to reform the inequities of the international system. Khatami also tried to present his version of a rationalist, democratic, and civil Islam as an antidote to the Islam of the Taliban. But he failed in his efforts because of the hard-liners' and Khamenei's opposition, who saw their privileged position likely to suffer as a result of this paradigm shift.

No doubt, U.S. unwillingness to respond to Iran's overtures has also played important roles in Iran and America's continued estrangement. But Iran should look after its own interests and not hope that others will keep its interests in mind. In the future, too, Iran will not be able to reach a modus vivendi with the United States unless it fully understands U.S. domestic realities and the importance of the Israel factor in its relations with America.

CHAPTER 4

Iran and Europe: Not So Constructive Engagement

Iran's interaction with Europe goes back to ancient times. Some of the images created in European minds of Iran and Iranians resulting from these early relations are still influential. They affect the contemporary Europeans' perceptions of today's Iran and Iranians and their tendencies and aspirations, thus partly shaping European attitudes and policies toward Iran.

Most European accounts of these early interactions with Iran emphasize their negative dimensions by focusing on wars and conflicts. In European narratives, Iran stands for stereotypical Eastern despotism and barbarism while ancient Athens and Rome are seen as beacons of civilization and democracy.[1] Iran's misdeeds in Greece are still the subjects of movies in the West, while Alexander's gratuitous burning of Persepolis and his destruction of Persian cultural heritage is passed over lightly.[2] Much is said about Xerxes' military adventures and the excessive luxury of the Achaemenid court, but Cyrus's policies of religious and cultural tolerance, plus his culturally pluralistic mode of governance, are ignored, and the impact of ancient Iranian civilization is minimized. For example, in European—and other Western—history books dealing with the ancient world, the Iranian world is treated as a subsection of the so-called Mesopotamian empires, although Iranian civilization is different from those of Assyria and Babylon. By contrast, Egypt, China, and India are treated separately, yet no fair-minded person can compare the political and cultural reach of the Achaemenid and Sassanid empires, especially in terms of their impact on Europe, with those of Babylon, Assyria, India and China.[3]

In short, the European view of ancient Iran is that of a "hostile other" lacking in any redeeming characteristics. Yet Iran's interaction with centers of ancient European civilizations was not solely conflictual. On the contrary, there were significant flows of ideas and artistic and philosophical influences between them. For example, Plato was familiar with and admired Iranian wisdom (wisdom of the magi).[4] During the Sassanid Empire, many Christian scientists and medical experts worked at the famous university of Jundi Shapur, in present-day Ahwaz, while they were persecuted in

Rome.[5] Iranian religious ideas from Zoroastrianism to Manicheanism and Mithraism exerted significant influence in the development of European religious traditions.[6]

Moreover, for centuries, Iran protected Europe from the incursion of Turkic and Mongol nomadic peoples and served as a bridge between Europe and China. The original Silk Road linked China to Byzantium through the Sassanid Empire. Yet there is no recognition of these realities and Europeans have had very little intrinsic interest in Iran and its civilization. This European attitude is succinctly summed up in the following observation by J. H. Iliffe:

> Hebrew, Greek, and Roman civilization is absorbed more or less by the Western man with his mother's milk; the vast Iranian panorama in which our ancestors arose and flourished seems as remote to the majority as the moon. For us [the Europeans] its early history is restricted to those occasions when it formed part of Israel or of Greece. Our sympathies are enlisted on behalf of the Jewish exiles, the drama of Marathon and Thermopylae, the March of the ten thousand or Alexander's meteoric career; incidental to our minds to these events are the extent of the realm of Ahasuerus, the background to the decree of Cyrus, King of Persia, the initiative shown by Darius on his accession to the throne.[7]

European treatment of Islamic Iran has not been much better. For example, while recognizing the contributions of Islamic civilization to Europe's cultural renaissance, most Europeans identify Islamic civilization solely with Arabs. Yet as noted by the great British Iranologist, Edward Brown, "Take of what is wrongly known as Arabian sciences . . . what has been contributed by the Persians and the best is gone."[8] A recent example of this attitude is the BBC's calling the great Iranian philosopher and scientist Abu Ali Sina (Avicenna), who was born in Bukhara and died in Hamadan and who wrote in Persian as well as Arabic, an "Arab."[9]

In modern times, too, European interest in Iran has derived from other more fundamental concerns, such as coping with the Ottoman Empire, preventing Russian influence in India and its access to the Persian Gulf, and using Iran as a buffer against Soviet expansionism.

This lack of intrinsic interest in Iran is reflected in the fact that no major European country, notably Britain, arguably the most influential power in Iran, was interested in Iran as a colony. According to a former British ambassador in Iran, Sir Dennis Wright, Britain "never considered Iran a place worth colonizing."[10] Rather, as put by Charles Issawi, Britain saw Iran as "a glacier to be kept denuded of any facilities which might make it easier for the Russians to advance through it to the [Indian] subcontinent." In other words, Britain pursued a policy of hampering Iran's advancement.[11]

This aspect of British policy toward Iran, as well as of European policy in general, also stemmed from their recognition of Iran's past achievements and its potential for regeneration, despite its long period of decline in modern times, as reflected in the comment of the British envoy in Iran, Scheel, about the potential impact of a railroad on Iran and why Britain should prevent its construction. Scheel wrote to the British foreign secretary, Lord Palmerston, that "of course the building of a railroad would awaken Iran's talents which, because of need and poverty have remained dormant."[12] This factor also explains certain European policies toward Iran both under the Shah and during the Islamic regime, such as disregarding Iran's neutrality during both world wars, applying different standards of human rights performance to Iran and Arab states and Turkey, and opposing its development of nuclear energy.

IRANIAN-EUROPEAN RELATIONS DURING THE 1980s

By the mid-1970s, tensions had appeared in Iran's relations with Europe, triggered by what the Europeans saw as the Shah's megalomania, hawkish policies on oil prices, regional ambitions, hectoring language, and Iran's independent foreign policy, especially in regard to the Arab-Israeli conflict—in short, the Shah's insistence on being treated like an ally rather than a client. At heart, however, European powers, like the United States, were concerned about Iran's competitive potential economically and politically, reflecting the perennial conflicts and tensions between great powers and regional powers, including those that only aspire to that status.

Thus, when Iran's political crisis began in 1977 and accelerated in 1978, European states, notably Britain and France, adopted what at best could be called a complacent attitude toward Iranian events and at worst, as some Iranians believe, a policy in support of replacing the Shah. Indeed, some Iranians have maintained that because of factors noted above, already by 1977 a decision to oust the Shah had been reached in the West.[13]

This European complacency toward the challenge to the Shah's rule was exemplified in France's admittance of Ayatullah Khomeini and the provision of exceptional media access to him and his cohorts. It appears that a group of semisecular opposition figures, notably Ibrahim Yazdi, had convinced the Europeans that after the Shah's ouster, Khomeini would return to his religious studies, and a more democratic and less ambitious government would come to power.

Events in Iran, however, did not progress as the Europeans had hoped, and an Islamic government with clear anti-Western orientation and revolutionary aspirations replaced the Pahlavi regime. This turn of events ushered in a long and still ongoing period of tense Iranian-European relations. Therefore, when the Iran-Iraq War began in September 1980, most European countries, especially France, supported Iraq, justifying their policy as defending civilization against barbarism.

DETERMINANTS OF IRANIAN-EUROPEAN RELATIONS IN THE 1980s

During the first decade of the Islamic regime, a number of contradictory factors, most notably the new government's ideological leanings and aspirations on the one hand and its economic needs on the other, determined the character of Iran's relations with European countries.

Ideologically speaking, the new regime's determination to stay aloof from both the East and the West extended to Europe, because most European countries at the time belonged to either the Western or the pro-Soviet Eastern bloc. However, because in practice the Islamic regime's hostility was much stronger toward the West, partly because it feared the attractiveness to the Iranian people of Western culture, the regime's relations with Western Europe suffered more, and one consequence was the closure of European cultural centers in Iran.

However, since most European countries have not had a long history of domination in Iran, the new government was not averse to normal economic and political relations with them. Iran's economic realties and needs, notably its need for export markets for its oil and for imports of industrial and agricultural products, especially during its eight-year war with Iraq, further mitigated the negative impact of the ideological factors. Consequently, during the 1980s, Iran maintained a reasonable level of economic and political relations with most European countries.

Moreover, there were more pragmatic elements within the leadership of the Islamic regime that disliked and feared the Soviet Union more than they did Europe. These factors, coupled with the Europeans' fear of potential Soviet inroads in Iran, made them more willing to deal with the Islamic regime, which meant that

1. the attitude of individual European governments toward the Iran-Iraq War;
2. the spillover of U.S.-Iran tensions;
3. Iran's engagement in terrorist acts in Europe and in the Middle East;
4. European countries' domestic politics.

THE PATTERN OF IRANIAN-EUROPEAN RELATIONS

Broadly speaking, during the first decade of the Islamic regime, Iran's relations with East European countries, which under the Shah had been relatively cool, improved. The existence of leftist and pro-Soviet sympathies within the regime's leadership, notably the long-serving prime minister, Mir Hussein Mussavi, plus Iran's need for new economic partners and sources of weaponry, were responsible for this improvement.[14]

Relations with the smaller and less powerful European countries, such as Finland, Denmark, Spain, Ireland, and Sweden, also expanded, particularly in the economic field, although the total value of economic exchanges remained limited.[15] Iran's relations with Italy also expanded, largely because Italy adopted a more balanced position on the Iran-Iraq War. It waited longer than others before sending ships to the Persian Gulf in 1987 in support of the U.S. reflagging operations, expressed the belief that resolving the conflict required the recognition of Iran's legitimate grievances, and called for the condemnation of Iraq's use of chemical weapons.[16] Iran's relations with Germany, too, were essentially good, and by 1987 Germany's share of the Iranian market was 20 percent. Principal reasons for this satisfactory situation were the lack of any bad historical memories, Germany's basically neutral stance in the Iran-Iraq War, and Iran's need for economic partners.[17]

Meanwhile, with its support for Iraq in its war with Iran, France squandered the goodwill it had garnered with Iran's revolutionaries by admitting Ayatullah Khomeini to France, and Franco-Iranian relations seriously deteriorated. For a period, even diplomatic relations were interrupted. Other contributory factors to tense Franco-Iranian relations were Iran's involvement in terrorist incidents in France, plus a number of disputes dating form Shah-era agreements.[18]

Largely for similar reasons, plus British support for U.S. policies regarding Iran and the Persian Gulf, Iran's relations with Britain were also tense. The activities of some Iranian opposition groups in the UK, including the seizure of the Iranian embassy in London in May 1980 by a group calling itself the Democratic Revolutionary Movement for the Liberation of [Arabistan], also contributed to the worsening of Anglo-Iranian relations. The Iranians' bitter memories of past British policies toward Iran further created a background of mistrust, which amplified even mundane differences.[19]

The outbreak of the Rushdie Affair in September 1988, notably the Ayatullah Khomeini's fatwa against him, created new tensions in Iran's relations with all European countries, including those with whom Iran had had reasonable relations. However, because Rushdie was a British citizen and resident of that country, the negative impact of the Rushdie Affair was strongest on Iranian-British ties. Initially, both countries tried to limit the damage done to relations by this affair. The UK foreign secretary, Sir Geoffrey Howe, said that he understood that Rushdie's book had been found deeply offensive by people of the Muslim faith. Rafsanjani, too, tried to calm the aroused passions.[20] However, for many in Europe, the Rushdie question became a litmus test for freedom of speech and expression and the safeguarding of Europe's liberal democratic values, even at diplomatic and commercial cost. Consequently, the Rushdie controversy became a serious hindrance to the improvement in Iranian-European relations well into the 1990s, with Britain maintaining the most uncompromising position.[21]

The Rushdie dispute was only resolved in 1998, after the coming to power of President Khatami.

POST-SOVIET PERIOD: THE RAFSANJANI YEARS

As noted earlier, even before the fall of the USSR, Iran had been trying to repair its damaged external relations. Relations with Europe were a priority partly because Iran needed European cooperation in rescheduling its $32 billion debt to European banks.[22] Initially, most European countries were open to better ties with Iran, which would have ensured their return to the Iranian market where, because of postwar reconstruction, there were considerable business opportunities. However, a number of outstanding issues, such as the continued captivity of some European—that is, British—hostages and the fall out of the Rushdie Affair, slowed the pace of improvement of Iranian-European relations. Later, the end of the Cold War and the Soviet Union's inexorable unraveling led some European countries to feel that there was no urgent need for better ties with Iran.

Notwithstanding the above, however, the greatest barrier to better European-Iranian ties was the Iranian hard-liners' determination to undermine Rafsanjani's policies of economic liberalism at home and improved relations abroad, especially with the West.

A major change took place following Iraq's invasion of Kuwait in August 1990. This invalidated the dominant view in the West, including Europe, that Iraq could be the West's new partner in the Persian Gulf, replacing post-Shah Iran. This factor, plus the need to secure, at least, Iran's neutrality in the war between the U.S.-led coalition and Iraq, inclined the European countries to pursue better relations with Iran. By 1991, the atmosphere of Iranian-European relations—with few exceptions—had improved so much that Iran's vice president in July 1991 declared that several European heads of state were to visit Iran.[23] The French president, Francois Mitterrand, was one of these world leaders. He was supposed to visit Iran in autumn 1991.[24] German chancellor Helmut Kohl was also expected to come to Iran.

However, because of the assassination of the Shah's last prime minister, Shapur Bakhtiar, in Paris in August 1991, in which high Iranian officials were implicated by one of the perpetrators, neither of these visits took place. It appears that the assassination was the work of either radical or rogue elements within the Iranian intelligence community, or of the Mujahedin-e-Khalq, which did not welcome improvement in Iranian-European relations.[25]

Progress in relations with Germany was also halted by the assassination of the leader of the Kurdish Democratic Party of Iran, Sadeq Sharifkandi, and two of his associates, in September 1992, in a restaurant called Mykonos in a suburb of Berlin.[26] Allegedly, the assassination was carried out on the orders of the chief of Iran's intelligence apparatus, Ali Fallahian, with the full knowledge and support of President Rafsanjani and Foreign Minister Ali Akbar Velayati.[27] The reverberations of this incident, especially the verdict of the German court directly implicating Iran's leaders, up to and including the Supreme Leader, went beyond German-Iranian relations and cast a very dark shadow over the entire spectrum of Iran's relations with Europe. Questions relating to those responsible for this incident, and the extent of top Iranian leaders' involvement in it, are still shrouded in mystery.

In Iran, different factions within the regime have accused each other of this act, while others have pointed at rogue elements within the intelligence services, acting as Israeli spies, as the culprits.[28] The Iranian government has questioned the reliability of witnesses, including former president Abol-Hassan Bani-Sadr—upon whose testimony the German verdict was issued—as have done some European commentators.[29]

A full analysis of the arguments and counterarguments is beyond the scope of the present work. What is clear is that the Islamic government has assassinated its opponents in Europe as well as within Iran. In the specific case of the Mykonos assassinations, the key question to be asked is why, following the disastrous impact of the Bakhtiar assassination on Rafsanjani's plans for improving Iran's ties with Europe, he would almost immediately proceed with another assassination, this time in Germany, when the target did not even pose a serious threat to the regime.[30] Therefore, the more plausible arguments are that either his opponents within the system were responsible for this act or that the president could not control the intelligence apparatus.

Even before the verdict of the German court on the Mykonos Affair, Iran took a number of retaliatory measures against Germany, including mass anti-German demonstration and the imprisonment of German nationals. These acts exacerbated tensions not only with Germany but with Europe in general.

Germany's domestic politics, notably the opposition of the Social Democrats to the more accommodating policy of the German foreign minister, Klaus Kinkel, toward Iran, coupled with pressures from the United States and Israel on the German government to sharply reduce its dealings with Iran, further contributed to the worsening of Iranian-German relations.

Other contributory factors to deteriorating Iranian-European relations were Iran's human rights record and the activities of Iranian opposition groups in Europe.

Meanwhile, the elimination of the Warsaw Pact and the transformation of the nature of East European governments into pro-Western and democratic—to varying degrees—states made them subject to the same influences that determined Iran's relations with West European countries. By the end of 1993, because of the hardening of the U.S. policy toward Iran in the context of the Dual Containment strategy, the creation of the European Union (EU), and the development of its Common Security and Foreign Policy (CFSP) in the context of the Maastricht Treaty (November 1993), Iran's relations with Europe had become even more complicated and fraught.

CRITICAL DIALOGUE: MORE CRITICISM THAN DIALOGUE

The upshot of the European Community's (EC) transformation into the EU and the Europeans' efforts to develop the CSFP was that relations of individual European countries with Iran became constrained by broader EU policies. Thus, even countries that wanted to have better ties with Iran could not easily do so because of the influence or objections of more influential EU members, such as Germany, France, and the UK.[31] In effect, since 1994, Iranian-European relations have been mostly conducted within the EU framework and in the context of, first, the Critical Dialogue and, later, the Comprehensive Dialogue. Nevertheless, the character and extent of Iran's relations with individual European countries has to some degree varied as different European countries have calibrated and fine-tuned their bilateral relations with Iran within the limitations of the broader EU strategy.

CFSP, HUMAN RIGHTS, AND THE CRITICAL DIALOGUE

According to Article J of the Maastricht Treaty, the CFSP's core aims are: "to preserve peace and security," to promote "international cooperation," and "to develop and consolidate democracy and the rule of law, and respect for human rights and fundamental freedoms."[32] In the conduct of its foreign policy, however, the EU has not applied these principles with equal rigor in the case of all countries. On the contrary, countries with special strategic and economic importance for Europe, such as Saudi Arabia and other Persian Gulf Arab states, Egypt, Morocco, and Jordan, have been exempt from this principle. By contrast, in Iran's case, the emphasis on human rights has served as an excuse to implement a policy based essentially on the premise that pressure would be more successful than incentives in generating change in Iran's behavior in the first place and in its regime in the long run. In fact, the double standard applied by the Europeans toward Iran, as compared to conservative Arab states, has been a major Iranian complaint.[33]

The emphasis on pressure in bringing about change in Iran predates the formation of the EU and the beginning of the Critical Dialogue. The logic of this strategy, as a British diplomat told the author in the late 1980s, is to show that extremism does not pay, and thus to strengthen the moderates' position within the Iranian leadership and political and security structures.

However, at the end of the Rafsanjani administration, despite some early hopes and some progress, the Critical Dialogue had failed to achieve either Europe's or Iran's goals. On the contrary, Iranian-European relations had reached a point of crisis following the 1997 guilty verdict pronounced in the Mykonos trial and the recalling of the EU ambassadors from Tehran.

CAUSES OF THE CRITICAL DIALOGUE'S FAILURE

According to Seyyed Hossein Mousavian, Iran's ambassador to Germany during the Rafsanjani years, the Critical Dialogue initially succeeded in eliciting a more open Iranian attitude on issues of concern to the EU, notably the highly charged question of human rights.[34] For example, in 1995 Iran set up the Islamic Human Rights Commission, and the foreign ministry established a Department of Human Rights, which reflected Iran's awareness of the importance of human rights issues for the country's external relations. Furthermore, in 1996, Iran allowed Professor Maurice Copthorne, the United Nations' special human rights representative (UNSR), to visit Iran. No further visits followed because Iran complained that the UNSR's report was abused by certain countries in order to reinforce "their prejudgments and predrawn conclusions against Iran."[35]

According to Mousavian, the Critical Dialogue also contributed to a change in Iran's position on the Palestinian issue, another major European concern. This change was signaled when Iran issued a formal statement declaring that it would not hinder negotiations between Israel and the Palestinians.[36] Ultimately, the Critical Dialogue did not succeed because it was based on the principle that pressures and not incentives would produce change in Iran's behavior and eventually in its regime. Other contributing factors were:

1. the reduced importance of Iran following the USSR's dismantlement, the near destruction of Iraq's military power in 1991, and the opening up of new opportunities for Europe in the former USSR;

2. factionalism in Iran and the sabotage of Rafsanjani's policies by the hardliners;

3. occasional damage-causing statements by Iranian leaders on the Palestinian issue, such as Rafsanjani's statement that Rabin's assassination was divine punishment;[37]

4. the impact of domestic politics of European countries, including pressure by leftist parties for a harsher EU approach to Iran;

5. the activities of Iranian opposition groups in Europe, especially the Mujahedin-e-Khalq, aimed at compromising the Iranian government. For example, there is some evidence, or at least reasonable suspicion, that the MEK was involved in planting a consignment of mortar shells in an Iranian vessel, the *Iran Kolahdooz*, destined for Antwerp. The vessel was impounded in March 1996;[38]

6. the European countries' use of talks with these groups as a means of pressure on Iran.

However, the negative impact of these factors could have been mitigated had it not been for the strong opposition of Israel to the Critical Dialogue, which predated Rafsanjani's unfortunate statement on Itzhak Rabin. U.S. pressures, strengthened by Israeli lobbying, also helped doom the Critical Dialogue.

The evolution of U.S. policy toward Iran was discussed in chapter 3. To recapitulate briefly, after the introduction of the Dual Containment policy with the ultimate goal of changing the nature of Iran's government, the United States imposed sanctions on Iran.[39] It also pressured the Europeans into doing the same. In June 1993, U.S. secretary of state Warren Christopher urged the Europeans to impose a joint economic embargo on Iran or, failing that, to reduce the export of dual-use technology to that country. At the time, the United States did not get EU agreement on a trade embargo. Therefore, it shifted its attention to convincing those EU members, like Germany, with extensive economic and other relations with Iran, to reduce the level of their ties.

COMPREHENSIVE DIALOGUE AND CONSTRUCTIVE ENGAGEMENT: THE KHATAMI PRESIDENCY

The election of Muhammad Khatami to Iran's presidency in 1997 ushered in a new stage in Iran's international relations. His emphasis on dialogue as the underlying principle of his diplomacy, for domestic reform and a conciliatory Iranian foreign policy, facilitated the Europeans' adoption of a more positive attitude toward Iran. This new attitude was first reflected in the European countries' agreement to resolve the Rushdie problem through what was essentially the same formula that had been offered by the Rafsanjani government. According to this formula, the Iranian government would not seek or encourage Rushdie's killing, while not officially rescinding the fatwa. A second important development was the return of the EU ambassadors to Iran by November 1997, followed by the EU decision in 1998 to engage in a Comprehensive Dialogue and Constructive Engagement with Iran.

The following contributed to this shift in the EU's position:

1. Disappointment of the Europeans' early expectations of a close Russia-West co-operation, and growing Russian assertiveness
2. Reduced expectations for Caspian Basin energy and hence a revival of interest in Iran's energy resources
3. A more forthcoming U.S. policy toward Khatami
4. The failure of past policy to bring about change in Iran

The changes in Iran and in the Europeans' attitude toward Iran resulted in a flurry of high-level official visits between Iran and EU member states. First, Italy's minister of foreign affairs, Lombarto Dini, visited Iran in March 1998, less than a year after Khatami's assumption of the presidency.[40] Then in September 1999, Austria's president Thomas Klestil visited Tehran,[41] followed, in October 2000, by Spain's prime minister Jose Maria Aznar.[42]

Following the resolution of the Rushdie Affair, which had been a particularly thorny question in its relation with Britain, Iran's foreign minister Kamal Kharazi met with the British foreign secretary, Robin Cook, following which the two sides restored full diplomatic relations. The terrorist attacks of 9/11, the impending U.S. invasion of Afghanistan, and the West's need for Iran's help in Afghanistan helped improve Anglo-Iranian relations further and led to the visit of the UK foreign secretary, Jack Straw, to Tehran in September 2001.[43] But relations again deteriorated when Iran denied *agrément* to UK designate ambassador to Tehran, accusing him of being a spy.

The U.S. invasion of Iraq in 2003, British support for the United States, plus the presence of British military forces in Iran's proximity created other sources of tensions, especially as the United States and the UK began to accuse Iran of destabilizing Iraq and even of supporting the Taliban in Afghanistan. Other irritants in British-Iranian relations included the August 2003 arrest in London of an Iranian diplomat wanted by the Argentine government on terror charges and the holding of eight British sailors by the Iranian authorities in June 2004, after their vessel, according to Iran, had "strayed" into Iranian waters; Britain insisted that they were in international waters. The sailors were released after three days.[44]

Meanwhile, Iran's relations with other European countries entered a more promising era, with landmark visits by Khatami to France, Italy, Germany, Greece, Austria, and Spain. Khatami's principal goals in these visits, in addition to improving the atmosphere of Iranian-European relations, were to encourage European investment in Iran, especially in the energy sector; to continue with the rescheduling of Iran's debts; and to gain new lines of credit. This aspect of Iran's new diplomacy was noted by the French daily, *Le Figaro*, which wrote:

Rome and Paris were not chosen randomly to be the first capitals of Europe where President Khatami comes in an attempt to show that Iran has changed. Elf and ENI recently signed joint, important oil contracts with Tehran.

Khatami's visit to France also procured credit lines from major French banks that were reportedly worth $2 billion. In July 2000, Khatami visited Germany with high expectations of German economic involvement in Iran's third Five Year Economic Development Plan. As an initial step, Germany increased cover for business with Iran to DM 1 billion, and the two countries' joint economic commission was reactivated.[45]

However, despite these auspicious beginnings, at the end of the Khatami presidency, Iranian-European relations had entered another period of crisis, this time over Iran's nuclear program. At the most fundamental level, the same factors that had led to the failure of Rafsanjani's policy of opening also marred the prospects of solid and lasting reconciliation under Khatami. Paramount among these factors were

1. continued, and even worsened, intra-regime frictions and tensions. This was caused by the position of the left wing of Khatami's reform movement, which in effect demanded the elimination of the institution of the Velayat-e-Faqih, thus openly challenging Ayatullah Khamenei's position. This made the Khatami government vulnerable to charges that its reforms, including openings to the West, were ultimately aimed at radical transformation of the system. The upshot of this situation was that Khatami's adversaries created situations which at times caused problems for him in his foreign travels. For example, when Salman Rushdie showed up in Paris for a book event, the conservative *Jomhuri-e-Islami* wrote that: "inviting the apostate Salman Rushdie to Paris on the eve of the Iranian president's visit is tantamount to an act of spite by the French government toward the Islamic Republic."[46] Later, Khatami's visit to Spain in 2002 was nearly torpedoed when the Iranians insisted that wine should not be served at the official banquet and that women should cover their head when being introduced to him.[47] More serious was Iran's accusing of 13 Iranian Jews of spying for Israel and jailing them. The *Independent* rightly wrote that they were pawns "caught up in the tense power struggle for Iran's destiny between the popular reformers of President Mohamed Khatami, and the hard-line mullahs who do not want to let go of a country they have ruled for two decades."[48] Here it must be noted that the Europeans' ignoring of Khamenei's pivotal role in Iranian politics and their pinning their hopes on Khatami alone did not help the latter. Rather, it intensified suspicions of his ultimate goals and increased his opponents' obstructive activities;

2. opposition within Europe to improved ties with Iran. Certain groups in Europe, either for domestic political purposes or for principled reasons, opposed improvement of ties with the Islamic regime. Thus, they created conditions that put both Khatami and his European counterparts in difficult positions. For example, while Rushdie has a right to go to Paris whenever he wants to, the scheduling of his visit to coincidence with Khatami's trip to Europe could be construed as an attempt to mar it;

3. activities of Iranian opposition groups, notably the MEK, and the support of some European governments, such as Germany and Britain both for MEK and for Iran's separatist groups, like the Kurdish group PJAK, and the Jundullah;

4. continued overemphasis on human rights, beyond what European countries demand from their Arab partners. This European attitude gave the Iranian hardliners a unique opportunity to arrest someone or accuse someone of wrongdoing, knowing full well how Europeans will react;

5. Iran's negative role in the Arab-Israeli peace process, although, from the time of Yitzhak Rabin's assassination until the Clinton administration's effort in 2000, there had been no peace process to speak of;

6. lack of progress in U.S.-Iranian relations.

However, the main culprit for lack of improvement in Iranian-European relations again was intra-regime divisions, which made it impossible for Khatami to change those aspects of Iran's foreign policy most objectionable to Europe.

Nevertheless, Iranian-European relations might have improved more during Khatami's presidency had it not been for 9/11, which led to the U.S. policy of a Global War on Terror and promotion of regime change in Iraq, Iran, and a few other countries, by military means if necessary, partly reflected in President Bush's 2002 Axis of Evil speech.

Then, on February 3, 2003, the MEK representative, Ali Reza Jafarzadeh, revealed that Iran was building sophisticated facilities in Natanz and several other cities, which could eventually produce enriched uranium. Later, Iran officially admitted that it was enriching uranium in Natanz as a pilot project.

These revelations created yet another crisis in Iran's relations with Europe and destroyed any remaining chances of progress in Iranian–European relations. In fact, since 2003 Iran's relations with Europe have been dominated by the dynamics and twists and turns of the nuclear issue.

IRAN'S NUCLEAR DOSSIER AND
IRANIAN-EUROPEAN RELATIONS

The background of Iran's nuclear activities and the causes of the outbreak of the nuclear crisis in 2003 were discussed in chapter 3. Here, the unfolding of this crisis and its impact on Iran's relations with Europe will be discussed.

EU, IRAN, AND THE NUCLEAR PROBLEM

As noted earlier, when the nuclear crisis first erupted, the IAEA and its director, Muhammad El Baradei, took the initiative to deal with it according to the NPT's requirements. However, the United States and the EU also became vocal on the matter and made demands on Iran.

As a first step, on August 6, 2003, France, Germany, and the UK sent a joint letter to the Iranian foreign minister. In it, they demanded that Iran ratify and implement the 93+2 additional protocols and freeze its enrichment activities. Then, on June 16, the General Affairs and External Relations of the European Council concluded that "the nature of some aspects of Iran's [nuclear] program raises serious concerns, in par-ticular as regards the closing of the nuclear fuel cycle, especially the uranium centrifuge announced by President Khatami." And it called on the Iranian government to cooper-ate fully with the IAEA and to answer all the outstanding questions adequately and in a timely fashion.[49] The EU's high representative for CFSP, Javier Solana, also called on Tehran to make rapid progress in its negotiations with the IAEA so as to avoid "unwelcome effects on the EU's relations with Iran."[50]

During the last remaining two years of the Khatami administration, Iran's main goals regarding the nuclear issue were to prevent the sending of its nuclear dossier from IAEA to the UN Security Council; and to prevent the United States from ob-taining a global consensus on how to deal with this issue. As part of this strategy, Iran approached the EU for talks on its nuclear program.

TEHRAN AND SAADABAD STATEMENTS
AND THE BRUSSELS AGREEMENT

The first round of Iranian-European talks was held in Tehran in October 2003 and led to the issuing of the Tehran Statement.[51] At the outset of the talks, European representatives insisted that Iran unilaterally stop its enrichment program without ex-pecting any quid pro quo on Europe's part. However, they finally settled for suspension of enrichment, and later, agreed to a formula based on "mutual commitments" by Eu-rope and Iran.

The Tehran Statement was followed by the so-called Saadabad Statement, agreed upon on October 21, 2003, according to which Iran suspended its enrichment activi-ties as defined by IAEA director El Baradei to mean avoidance of "introducing gas into centrifuges."[52] Shortly afterward, however, the atmosphere of Iranian-European nu-clear talks was darkened and Europeans' suspicions of Iran's real intentions heightened. The cause was the discovery by the IAEA inspectors of some discrepancies in Iran's previous statements on the type of centrifuges, polonium, contamination, and gas test.

Yet negotiations continued and, after long and arduous efforts, on February 23, 2004, Iran and three European countries—the UK, France, and Germany—along with the support of the EU high representative, settled on the so-called Brussels Agreement, according to which Iran accepted to suspend the manufacture of parts and assembly of centrifuges. Iran's hope was that, with the coming into effect of this agreement, the E3/EU would close Iran's nuclear case at the June 2004 meeting of the IAEA Board of Governors' meeting.

The introduction of the Brussels Agreement deals with the "setting out of the principles on which a long-term relationship between the E3/EU and Iran would be based." It then enumerates the elements upon which this long-term relationship should be based:

A. Developing relations of trust and cooperation between the E3/EU and Iran;

B. Defining the relationship between the E3/EU process and the EU-Iranian negotiations on a Political Dialogue and a Trade & Cooperation Agreement as complementary and mutually reinforcing;

C. Committing themselves to establishing a long-term relationship in the security and political fields, based upon shared principles and conditional on both sides' adherence to all the principles and commitments set out in the overall agreement;

D. Welcoming Iran's commitment that, in accordance with Article II of the Treaty on the Non Proliferation of Nuclear Weapons, it does not and will not seek to acquire nuclear weapons or other weapons of mass destruction;

E. Recalling that Article IV of the NPT stipulates that "nothing in the Treaty shall be interpreted as affecting the inalienable rights of all the parties to the Treaty to develop research, production and use of nuclear energy for peaceful purposes without discrimination and in conformity with Articles I and II of this Treaty;"

F. Affirming that a final agreement on long-term arrangements providing objective guarantees that Iran's nuclear programme is exclusively for peaceful purposes would lead immediately to a higher state of relations based on a process of collaboration in different areas; and

G. Underlining their determination to strengthen their long-term relationship through an enhanced programme of economic and technological cooperation, particularly through the early completion of negotiations between Iran and the European Union on Trade & Cooperation Agreement, and the Associated Political Dialogue Agreement.[53]

The second part of the agreement deals with Political and Security Cooperation between Iran and the EU. It consists of sections dealing with:

A. General Principles. The most important component of this section is the commitment given to Iran by France and Britain That: 1) ". . . they will not use nuclear weapons against a non-nuclear weapon state party to the Treaty on the Non-Proliferation of Nuclear Weapons, except in the case of an invasion or any attack on them, their dependent territories, their armed forces or other troops, their allies or on a State towards which they have a security commitment, carried out or sustained by such a non-nuclear weapon state in association or alliance with a nuclear weapon State"; 2) they "Would recall and reaffirm their intention, as Permanent Members of the Security Council, to seek immediate action to provide assistance, in accordance with the Charter, to any non-nuclear weapon state, party to the Treaty on the Non-Proliferation of Nuclear Weapons that is a victim of aggression in which nuclear weapons are used."

B. Areas of Cooperation of Special Interest. This section includes: 1) issues of non-proliferation, including the objective of creating a verifiable Middle zone free of "weapons of mass destruction, nuclear, biological and chemical, and their means of delivery . . ."; 2) regional security. In this section the EU recognizes Iran's contributions to the reconstruction of Afghanistan and Iraq; 3) Terrorism; 4) combating drug trafficking.

C. Implementation Mechanism. In this section, the E3/EU proposes " the creation of a high-level committee on political and security issues, which would be made up of representatives from respective Foreign Affairs and Defence authorities. This Committee which would meet periodically, would review progress on this part of the agreement and provide a forum for discussing issues of regional, international and mutual interest. The Committee would report regularly to the appropriate EU bodies and to the Government of Iran."

D. Long-Term Support For Iran's Civil Nuclear Programme. In this section, the E3/EU recognize Iran's right to peaceful nuclear energy and declare their willingness to help Iran develop a safe and proliferation proof civil nuclear power generation and research programme that conforms with its energy needs. This assistance, however, would be contingent on the following:

1. Iran's full implementation of its relevant international obligations and commitments, including the long-term arrangements agreed between the E3/EU and Iran, resolution by the IAEA of all questions raised under Iran's Safeguards Agreement and Additional Protocol, and continued cooperation with the IAEA;

2. Implementation by Iran and the E3/EU of export controls in a non-discriminatory manner, bearing in mind the new context that would be created by the confidence building measures and commitments undertaken by Iran under an overall agreement.

E. Iranian Access to The International Nuclear Fuel Market And Cooperation In Nuclear Energy. An important part of this section is the assurances given by E3/EU on fuel for Iran's nuclear facilities and the start of negotiations for an agreement between EURATOM and Iran.

F. Confidence Building. As part of this effort Iran must not pursue fuel cycle activities other than the construction and operation of light water power and research reactors and undertake to:

1. Not withdraw from the NPT and to keep all [its] nuclear facilities under IAEA safeguards under all circumstances;

2. Ratify its [IAEA] Additional protocol, in accordance with its existing commitment, by the end of 2005;

3. In the meantime fully implement the Additional protocol pending its ratification and to cooperate proactively and in a transparent manner with the IAEA to solve all outstanding problems, including by allowing IAEA inspectors to visit any site or interview any person they deem relevant to their monitoring of nuclear activity in Iran; and

4. In line with IAEA Board Resolutions to stop construction of the heavy water research reactor in Arak. In exchange, the E3/EU offer to send an expert mission to Iran to help identify research requirements and the most suitable type of equipment to meet those requirements.

The rest of the agreement deals with EU-Iranian economic and technological cooperation and provides information on areas where the EU would be willing to cooperate with Iran.

Had it been implemented, this agreement not only would have resolved Iran's nuclear controversy, but it would have led to a breakthrough in Iranian-European relations. However, the agreement was never to be implemented and, as early as the March 2004 meeting of the IAEA Board, the three European countries would present Iran with new demands that would be difficult to meet in view of changing domestic political conditions.

CAUSES OF THE COLLAPSE OF THE BRUSSELS AGREEMENT

A number of factors contributed to the failure of the agreement, including:

1. discrepancies in Iran's reporting and the IAEA's findings;
2. the impact of Libya's unilateral abandonment of its nuclear ambitions;
3. Iran's domestic politics, especially the entanglement of nuclear diplomacy with presidential election politics;
4. strong U.S. opposition.

Of all the above-noted causes, U.S. opposition was the most important. At the time, America was bent on regime change in Iran, including, if need be, by military means. Iran's nuclear program was an important element—together with Iran's sponsorship of terrorism and its human rights abuses—that would serve as justification for such a policy. If the Iranian-European agreement became operational, it would have deprived the United States of its main argument for military action, as well as for referring Iran's dossier to the UN Security Council and thus setting the stage for military strike, at least against Iran's nuclear facilities. The UK's half-hearted endorsement of the agreement also contributed to its unraveling.

According to Ali Larijani, who later became Iran's negotiator on nuclear issues, the British prime minister, Tony Blair, believed that Iran's agreement to suspend its enrichment activities was the result of the Iraq War, reflected in his comments while reviewing British troops in Basra. He told them: "We [the British] reaped the fruit of Iraq's invasion in Iran."[54] In other words, the British continued to believe that pressure and not incentives work with Iran.

Meanwhile, inside Iran opposition groups were claiming that the Khatami government was submitting to Western pressures and was making real concessions in exchange for mere promises. This attitude is best captured by Larijani's famous comment that, in nuclear negotiations, Iran gave up pearls in exchange for a box of chocolates.

At the same time, the United States intensified its anti-Iranian lobbying at the IAEA. Initially, the Europeans resisted these efforts. However, when the IAEA indicated in its June 2, 2004, report that Iran had presented "contradictory information," the European countries refrained from normalizing Iran's nuclear dossier accord-ing to the Brussels Agreement, leading Iran to cancel its obligations under the agreement.[55]

PARIS AND ROWHANI-CHIRAC AGREEMENTS

Following the collapse of the Brussels Agreement and the end of Iran's voluntary suspension of its enrichment program, the Khatami administration came under heavy, albeit contradictory, pressures from international and domestic sources. Internation-ally, the greatest pressure came from the United States, which wanted to send Iran's dossier to the United Nations Security Council, as a prelude to the imposition of sanc-tions. The European countries, meanwhile, insisted that Iran return to the pre-June 2004 IAEA Board meeting situation—namely, suspension of enrichment activities.

Domestically, opponents of the Khatami government stepped up their opposition to his conciliatory policy; some even called for Iran's withdrawal from the NPT and the expulsion of the IAEA inspectors.

To diffuse the crisis and prevent the referral of its dossier to the UNSC Iran sub-mitted a proposal on July 24, 2004, to the Troika (France, Germany, and the UK) entitled "Framework for Mutual Guarantees." In this proposal, Iran developed what it considered to be "a large-scale strategy for crisis management," with the goal of turning threats into opportunities." In it, Iran assured the Troika that

1. it had not deviated from peaceful activities and that it will not leave the NPT;
2. it will control its advanced technology and will cooperate with the IAEA inspec-tors, according to the Additional Protocol;
3. it will assume full responsibility for the use of advanced technology.

In return, Iran demanded that European countries

1. recognize Iran's basic rights according to the NPT to develop the fuel cycle;
2. elevate their ties with Iran to the level of strategic relations;
3. transfer technology, including dual use technology;
4. expand economic relations, initiate defense cooperation, and grant Iran security assurances.

By this time, however, an international consensus was forming around the position that Iran must suspend enrichment activities indefinitely. Therefore, when the Euro-pean countries made a proposal to Iran entitled "the way forward," in it they included the following demands and threats:

1. Europe would support reporting Iran to the UNSC if it did not suspend its enrichment activities.
2. The period of suspension must be unlimited.

3. Nonproliferation policies were defined in a way which would pave the way for pressuring Iran on its missile program.
4. Iran must immediately ratify the Additional Protocol and the Complete Test Ban Treaty (CTBT).
5. Transparence was defined in a way that could have exceeded the requirements of the Additional Protocol.
6. "Objective guarantees" were demanded from Iran according to a definition which amounted to ending its nuclear program.

However, as pressures were gathering to refer Iran's dossier to the UNSC during the November 2004 meeting of the IAEA Board of Governors, Iran and the European countries tried to avert this. After exchanging various proposals, finally they reached what is known as the Paris Agreement that satisfied the basic requirements of both sides.

The Paris Agreement called for temporary suspension of Iran's enrichment program, and the EU's support for the resumption of enrichment activity, after a negotiated solution was reached on the entire program, plus other EU incentives for Iran. The Europeans' emphasis was on Iran providing them with "objective guarantees."

The Paris Agreement bought Iran some time. The IAEA Board of Governors' resolution of November 29, 2004, was less severe than the previous one, and Iran's case was not referred to the UNSC. However, a major problem remained—namely, what constituted "objective guarantees." Iran argued that the NPT, the Additional Protocol, and cooperation with the IAEA constituted objective guarantees demanded by the EU, because they would ensure that there would be no diversion of nuclear activities to nonpeaceful purposes. However, the Europeans insisted that these were not sufficient because they did not eliminate the risks of concealment of illegal activities.

Iran proceeded to supplement the Paris Agreement with other accords. In March 2004, Iran's nuclear negotiator, Hojat ul Islam Dr. Hassan Rowhani, met with French President Jacques Chirac. The goal of their meeting was to ask the IAEA to help solve the questions of "objective guarantees" by identifying mechanisms through which such guarantees could be defined. However, according to a member of Iran's negotiating team, the French government seemed to be divided on this issue, and the foreign minister opposed this measure, thus leading the German and British foreign ministries to follow his suit.[56] However, according to a senior EU official, had the EU made any concrete gestures to Iran after the signing of the Paris Agreement, Iran's nuclear controversy would have ended. As an example of such a concrete gesture, he mentioned the signing of a memorandum of understanding, according to which European countries would help build a nuclear plant in Iran. *He added that U.S. opposition made such a gesture impossible.*[57]

According to the Iranian source noted above, the Europeans had also agreed to a limited enrichment program for Iran, but a final solution was made impossible because of Iran's presidential politics and the coming to power of the Ahmadinejad administration in August 2005.[58]

AHMADINEJAD PERIOD: RESUMPTION OF IRAN'S NUCLEAR ACTIVITIES AND GROWING TENSIONS WITH EUROPE

One of the main issues in the 2005 presidential elections was the Khatami government's so-called concessionary foreign policy. According to his opponents, this policy had helped Western countries, without their making any concession to Iran and indeed with their hardening their positions. These opponents also argued that Khatami's policies had been contrary to the revolution's principles. Thus Ahmadinejad's priority was to restore the revolutionary and idealistic/ideological (*Armangera*) dimensions of Iran's foreign policy.

As discussed earlier, a hallmark of Iran's revolutionary ideology has been striving for independence and self-sufficiency, notably in scientific and technological areas, because such self-sufficiency is necessary for political independence. Given this outlook, during Ahmadinejad's presidency Iran's nuclear program was declared to be essential for its overall scientific and technological development. Recalling past occasions, when great powers had prevented Iran from acquiring technology and even building railways and steel mills, Ahmadinejad characterized Western opposition to Iran's nuclear program as "technological apartheid."[59] The nuclear issue also became a matter of Iran's sovereignty and its undeniable right to acquire technology for peaceful and nonmilitary uses according to the NPT's Article 4. Consequently, Ahmadinejad embarked on a nationwide propaganda campaign to make the nuclear issue a litmus test of Iran's sovereignty and independence similar to the case of oil nationalization in 1951.

NUCLEAR DIPLOMACY UNDER AHMADINEJAD

The decision to leave the Paris Agreement and resume work on the Isfahan Uranium Conversion Facility was reached by the outgoing Khatami government in July 2004. This decision was prompted by the hardening of the Europeans' position; they were now demanding total cessation of enrichment activities by Iran for a period of 10 years.

However, the Ahmadinejad government gave a new push to enrichment activities, while trying to fend off the sending of its dossier to the Security Council. Consequently, during the first sixth months of Ahmadinejad's government, Iran tried to gain the support of Russia, China, and other non-European countries, in order to prevent the referral of its case to the UNSC, and it did not pursue negotiations with Europe vigorously. But Iran's new diplomatic strategy failed, and, on January 3, 2006, its case was referred to the UNSC by the IAEA Board of Governors. The UNSC passed Resolution 1696 on July 31, 2006, placing Iran's dossier in the context of chapter 7 of the UN Charter, which deals with security matters ("threats to the peace"), thus paving the way for the passing of Resolution 1737 and the imposition of sanctions on Iran.

Following these developments, Iran resumed negotiations with the European countries, albeit under conditions far more detrimental to its interests, not least because now its nuclear dossier would be discussed in the context of the so-called 5+1 (five permanent members of the UNSC plus Germany), instead of the European Troika. However, the EU and its chief foreign policy official, Javier Solana, also remained involved.

The first round of negotiations took place in 2006 between Ali Larijani, Iran's chief negotiator, and Javier Solana, who had the lead role for Europe. During the early part of the renewed talks, hopes were raised that a possible compromise could be reached. However, these hopes were soon dashed, partly because of the negative attitude of some European countries, especially the UK. For example, when in spring 2007 it was reported that Larijani and Solana were close to an agreement, a British diplomat supposedly insisted that for negotiations to move ahead Iran must end enrichment activities as demanded by the UNSC, adding that "Solana won't be making any fresh offers."[60]

The election of Nicholas Sarkozy to the French presidency in May 2007 also hardened France's position, partly because of Sarkozy's strong pro-Israeli sentiments. Thus, in one of his first speeches as president, Sarkozy called Iran's nuclear ambitions "without doubt the most serious crisis that weighs today on the international scene."[61] Then, the French foreign minister, Bernard Kouchner, said that the world must prepare itself for war with Iran.[62] Moreover, under Sarkozy Franco-American relations became much warmer than they had been for decades.

Political changes in Germany, notably the victory in August 2005 of the Christian Democrat Union (CDU)—which historically has shown greater receptivity to U.S. concerns—over the Social Democrats, and the assumption of the office of German Chancellor by Angela Merkel hardened German attitudes. Meanwhile, Britain's hardline position under Tony Blair continued when Gordon Brown became UK prime minister in June 2008.

In short, Europe's political landscape had changed in a direction which made European concessions to Iran less likely. Meanwhile, the United States was intensifying its anti-Iranian rhetoric and was insisting on complete suspension of its enrichment program.

In view of these changes, some Iranian officials and foreign observers have maintained that key European countries were not serious in reaching a negotiated solution. Rather, they wanted the talks to fail in order to justify the imposition of more severe sanctions and even perhaps the use of force. The above noted statements by the French officials give some credence to this claim. Larijani has criticized the negotiating tactics of the French foreign minister, Philippe Douste-Blazy, who apparently asked Larajani to answer yes or no to the offer made to Iran. Larijani also has claimed that following the failure of the 2007 negotiations, Solana telephoned him and told him that "the saboteurs did their work."[63]

In Iran, too, disagreement on the basis upon which a compromise could be reached was emerging. These disagreements plus personal rivalry between Larijani and Ahmadinejad led to Larijani's replacement by Saeid Jalili as Iran's chief negotiator.

However, although Iran adopted a more defiant attitude on its nuclear plans and periodically declared that it had commissioned new centrifuges, no fundamental shift occurred in its negotiating position. It declared that the question of suspension had been moot because it had already mastered the nuclear fuel cycle, but it also signaled its readiness to take measures in order to allay international fears about the weaponization of its program. Such measures included creating a consortium or a fuel bank for the production of nuclear fuel. However, Iran insisted that in any bilateral agreement between itself and one or several other countries on fuel production that production must be carried out in Iran. This Iranian insistence was the reason why the Russian proposal that Iran and Russia jointly produce fuel on Russian territory did not go very far. Iran's insistence, in turn, derived from its fear that fuel produced abroad would not be delivered. This fear was not totally unreasonable, especially given the history of the Bushehr power plant built with Russian help.

Other aspects of Ahmadinejad's diplomacy, notably its more militant position on the Palestine question and his remarks regarding the Holocaust, increased regional and international fears and made it difficult for the Europeans to reach a compromise on Iran's nuclear program.

Interestingly, when in 2009 the new Obama administration indicated a willingness to engage with Iran, the UK and France grew uneasy. The British foreign secretary, David Miliband, in a speech in the UAE singled out a nuclear-armed Iran as "the most immediate" threat to Middle East stability and called on the Arabs to put pressure on Iran to abandon its nuclear program.[64] Then the British prime minister, Gordon Brown, in a speech at Chatham House, accused Iran, despite evidence to the contrary, of not cooperating with the IAEA and flouting UN resolutions.[65] And Sarkozy called on President Obama to be firm in any talks with Iran.

OTHER ASPECTS OF
IRANIAN-EUROPEAN RELATIONS

Iranian-European tensions were intensified in this period not just by the continued dispute over the nuclear issue, but also by other incidents, notably the capture of British sailors who had entered what Iran considers its territorial waters and what the British claimed to be disputed waters;[66] Iran's allegations that the British were involved in a bombing incident in Ahwaz; and Iranian accusations of British support for the Jundullah in Baluchistan.[67] However, even during Ahmadinejad's presidency, Iran maintained economic and other relations with Europe and endeavored to convince the Europeans to see it as a reliable source of energy supply and a promising place for investment. For example, during a visit to Germany in May 2009, Iran's oil minister tried to convince German investors to become involved in Iran's gas industry and said that Iran could be a reliable source of energy for Europe.[68]

Yet while Iran's major European trading partners have continued their commercial relations with the Islamic Republic (see table 4.1), they have not changed their positions on issues like opposing the inclusion of Iran in pipeline projects such as the

Table 4.1   Iranian–EU Trade in Billion Euros in 2008

EU Exports to Iran	EU Imports from Iran
14.1	11.3 (90% energy)

Source: Eurostat.

Nabucco, which is to transfer Central Asian gas to Europe via Turkey. Nor has there been any major European investment in Iran. On the contrary, companies like France's Total, which reportedly was intending to invest $5 billion in a gas project in Iran, have cut back their presence there. The Total decision largely reflected response to pressure by the Sarkozy administration and economic sanctions.[69] In October 2009, Norway's Statoil Hydro declared that it would not make any new investments in Iran.[70] Even Europe's problems with Russia over gas supplies in 2008–2009 did not change the Europeans' position on investment in Iran.[71] Angela Merkel's government also tried to persuade German companies to reduce the level of their trade with Iran, including by cutting credit guarantees.[72]

Some smaller European countries, such as Austria and Switzerland, have shown some degree of willingness to engage economically with Iran. For example, both countries signed agreements for the development of Iranian gas and its export to their countries.[73] However, a number of problems have to be overcome before these projects can become operational. One problem is opposition from the United States and Israel. Both countries severely criticized Austria and Switzerland for dealing with Iran. The other is the transport issue. For example, according to some sources, the export of gas to Switzerland depends on the construction of the Trans-Adriatic Pipeline.

Iran's relations with East European countries continued to stagnate under Ahmadinejad as they had under the Rafsanjani and Khatami presidencies, reflecting the dramatically changed political nature of these countries and their foreign policy orientation. The only country of the former Eastern Bloc with which Iran has maintained considerable economic and political ties is Belarus, which has not undergone a democratic transformation and has strained relations with the West. Iran has established a car factory in that country and cooperates with it in energy and other fields.[74] There has also been a series of high level—including presidential—visits between Iran and Belarus, including the 2007 visit of Ahmadinejad to Belarus. In February 2010 the foreign minister of Belarus, Sergei Martinov visited Tehran.[75] In 2008, Iran also seemed to be improving relations with Poland. Following a visit by Iran's minister of mines and industry to Warsaw in January 2008, the two sides agreed to revive their joint economic cooperation committee and the Polish media reported that "Poland will activate its stagnant relations with Iran."[76]

As can be seen, Iran's trade with non-EU European countries is negligible, especially in terms of Iran's exports (see table 4.2).

Table 4.2 Iranian Trade with Non-EU European Countries in 2008

Country	Exports	Imports
Belarus	6.3	62.6
Norway	5.8	22.8
Switzerland	24.9	565.8

Source: Eurostat.

THE 2009 PRESIDENTIAL ELECTIONS AND POSTELECTION TURMOIL: IMPACT ON EU-IRAN RELATIONS

The contested nature of Iran's 2009 presidential election had a negative impact on the course of Iranian-European relations. With the wave of demonstrations and arrests continuing throughout June, European countries were forced to protest to the Iranian government and to voice their criticism of its handling of the crisis.[77] In the communiqué following their meeting of June 26, 2009 in Trieste, the G8 foreign ministers voiced their concern over events in Iran. They expressed their solidarity "with those who have suffered repression while peacefully demonstrating, . . . and [urged] Iran to respect fundamental human rights, . . . and [urged]the Iranian government to guarantee that the will of the Iranian people is reflected in the electoral process."[78] In response, the Iranian government called in a number of European ambassadors to the foreign ministry and protested against such criticisms.[79]

Relations with Europe further deteriorated when Iran accused Britain and France of interfering in its internal affairs and fomenting revolution. On June 22, 2009, Iran expelled two British diplomats and, in retaliation, Britain expelled two Iranian diplomats.[80] Iran later imprisoned nine members of the British Embassy's local staff, as well as a French researcher, Clotilde Reiss, and a local French embassy staff member, Nazak Afshar.[81] As could be expected, both governments denied any involvement in Iran's election and protested against the arrests. Britain also demanded that if its embassy staff were not released, the EU's ambassadors should be recalled from Tehran. In the course of the following weeks, Iran released the British embassy staff. And in August, French citizen Reiss was released on bail. Charges brought against these prisoners included reporting on Iran's political scene, encouraging protesters, and giving them shelter in the embassy.

As a result of these problems, for a time, France refused to recognize the Ahmadinejad government, but by August 2009 it had relented. However, with the shadow cast over the fairness of his election and hence the legitimacy of his government, Ahmadinejad was placed in a much weaker position in dealing with Europe than before.

After Iran submitted its package of proposals in September 2009 and the 5+1 talks resumed in Geneva on October 1, 2009, France and the UK maintained a hard line. Reportedly, even President Obama had some difficulty with Sarkozy in this regard at the UN meeting.[82]

With the failure of the Geneva talks and the gradual shift in the Obama administration's policy toward Iran from one of engagement to one of more sanctions and pressure, coupled with active Israeli lobbying of the European countries, the European countries policy toward Iran hardened.

Iran's relations with the UK became particularly tense by late 2009, and there were demands in the Iranian parliament to downgrade diplomatic and economic ties with the UK. This prompted the British ambassador in Tehran to write a letter to Chairman of the Foreign Affairs Committee of the Iranian Parliament Alaeddin Boroujerdi advising against such move.[83]

Relations with Italy and Germany also deteriorated in early 2010. In Italy's case the triggering event was the arrest of an Iranian journalist on charges of arms smuggling to Iran.[84] In Germany's case the culprit was the decision of Germany not to hand the leader of the Kurdish separatist movement in Iran, PJAK (Partyia Jyana Azad Kurdistane), who had been apprehended in Germany, to either Belgium where he faced charges of terrorism, or Iran, which demanded his extradition. Rather, it released Abdul Rahman Hadji Ahmadi, who is a German citizen. Iran complained that Germany was supporting terrorism. Iran pointed out that it had provided Interpol a 1,000-page report on Hajiahmadi's activities, which had led to the killing of civilians.[85]

An upshot of these developments was that a number of European companies, including Germany's Siemens, decided not to undertake any new projects in Iran and curtail or stop delivery of certain materials, notably gasoline. Earlier in November 2009 Italy had pulled out of Iran's satellite project.

In short, by early 2010, Iran-Europe relations had further worsened with no potential improvement in sight in the near future, barring an expected and positive turn in Iran's nuclear dossier.[86]

ASSESSING IRAN'S EUROPEAN DIPLOMACY

Iran's diplomacy toward Europe has suffered from the same flaws that have also hampered the success of other aspects of its foreign policy, namely the following:

1. The inadequate appreciation of the extent of systemic changes in the post-Soviet era.
2. The nonrealization of the extent of commonality of interests and views between the United States and Europe on major global issues, including the Arab-Israeli question.
3. Failure to realize that, any time faced with a choice between the United States and Iran, European countries would chose America, and that Iran's bemoaning Europe's lack of independence is useless.

Consequently, for two decades, Iran has tried to improve relations with Europe, expand economic ties, and attract European investment, while ignoring these factors. For instance, Iran has pursued better ties with Europe while continuing to pursue a hard-line position on the Arab-Israeli issue. The naïveté of Iran's policy becomes clear when one reads the statement of Total's chairman, who said that if Iran wants the company to invest there, it must improve relations with Israel.[87]

Iran's European diplomacy, like other aspects of its foreign policy, has suffered badly from the divided nature of its leadership, the ideological nature of the regime, and the saliency of some issues, such as that of Palestine, both for the regime's self-image and for its legitimacy. The adverse effect of intra-regime differences and rivalries was reflected in terrorist activities and assassinations carried out in Europe and in the country itself at sensitive junctures of evolving relations with Europe. These scuttled Rafsanjani's efforts to improve ties with Europe. The same factors, albeit to a somewhat lesser extent, also sabotaged Khatami's European policy.

In the future, the state of Iran's relations with the EU, as well as with individual European countries, will be determined by the following factors: the fate of its nuclear dossier; change in aspects of its external behavior that is opposed by the European countries; the state of U.S.-Iranian ties; and, most important, the evolution of its internal political conditions. Positive developments in these regards would lead to the expansion of Iranian-European economic and other relations, whereas a worsening of Iran's nuclear crisis and other negative developments would augur badly for Iranian-European relations.

However, it should be added that Europe, too, missed several opportunities in trying to influence Iran's internal developments and its foreign policy in more positive directions. Lack of response to Iran's positive moves, insistence that Iran a priori meet all of Europe's preconditions, including on human rights beyond anything that Europe demanded from other Middle Eastern countries, only served to validate the position of those in Iran who believed that Europe's problem with the Iranian government was not its behavior but its very character as an Islamic Republic bent on pursuing an independent foreign policy.

Its ideological nature conflicts with its desire for trade, etc.

CHAPTER 5

Iran and Russia: Strategic Partnership or a Fool's Bargain?

Iran and Russia have had a long and turbulent history. From Iran's perspective, the legacy of this history has been largely negative. Russia's southern expansion was achieved at Iran's expense, as best exemplified by the Russo-Iranian wars of 1804–1813 and 1824–1828. As a result of these wars, Iran lost its Transcaucasian provinces and came under the regime of capitulation. Throughout the 19th and early 20th centuries, Russo-British rivalry undermined Iran's independence and hindered its economic and political development. At times, such as 1907, Britain and Russia tried to divide Iran between them.[1]

The Bolshevik Revolution of 1917 initially had a positive effect on Iran, since it ended the Russo-British entente. The revolutionary government removed Russian troops from Iran and denounced the Anglo-Russian agreements and the regime of capitulation. It also helped obtain the removal of British troops. Iran's sense of relief at this Russian change of heart is reflected in the following statement by a renowned Iranian literary and political figure, Muhammad Taqi Bahar (Malek e Sho'ara): "Two enemies, each pulling one side of a rope, were trying to strangle a man. Suddenly, one of them let the rope go and said, 'Poor man I am your brother, and the unfortunate man was released. The man who let the rope go from our throat was Lenin.'"[2]

However, the Bolshevik regime soon reverted to the czarist pattern of behavior toward Iran and tried to dominate it, this time by spreading Communism and revolutionary ideas. Between 1918 and 1921, Russia tried to manipulate the Jangali movement and set up a socialist republic in Iran's Gilan province.[3] However, after the signing of the Soviet-Iranian friendship treaty of 1921, the USSR withdrew its support from the movement.[4]

A generation later, however, in an act reminiscent of the 1907 agreement, the Soviet Union signed a pact with Nazi Germany (Molotov-Ribbentrop Pact), which recognized "the Asiatic area to the south of the Soviet Union as Russia's sphere of influence." In the 1940s, the USSR took advantage of the allied invasion of Iran to establish pro-Soviet socialist republics in Iran's Kurdistan and Azerbaijan provinces, and throughout the Pahlavis' rule it supported Iran's leftist groups.

However, in a pattern that it also applied to other Third World countries, during the 1960s and 1970s, the USSR pursued a dual policy toward Iran, characterized by reasonable state-to-state relations and support of left-leaning opposition groups.[5] During this period, Soviet-Iranian relations were also affected by the dynamics of the Cold War, the state of East-West relations, and Iran's desire for an independent foreign policy.

THE ISLAMIC REVOLUTION
AND SOVIET-IRANIAN RELATIONS

The Soviet Union's initial reaction to the Islamic Revolution of 1979 was ambivalent. It welcomed the fall of the pro-American Pahlavi regime and the changes introduced in Iran's foreign policy by Mehdi Bazargan's government. But it remained uncertain about the long-term effects of the revolution and concerned about potential turmoil in Iran, which could elicit U.S. intervention.

The Soviet Union was also suspicious of the true character of the new regime, partly because it found hard to believe that the United States had allowed the Shah to fall without ensuring that the successor regime would be friendly toward America. The USSR was aware of U.S. dissatisfaction with aspects of the Shah's policy and, therefore, suspected U.S. complicity in Iran's political changeover. Moscow's suspicions were strengthened by the Bazargan government's efforts to normalize relations with the United States and by the fact that characters like Abol-Hassan Bani-Sadr and Sadeq Qotbzadeh were more anti-Soviet than anti-American.[6]

Meanwhile, Moscow was aware of the role played by the Left in the revolution and placed no faith in religion as a revolutionary ideology. It hoped and even expected that the Islamic revolution would be followed by a socialist revolution. Consequently, it criticized the Bazargan and Bani-Sadr governments and supported Khomeini. According to Noureddin Kianouri, leader of the pro-Soviet Soviet Tudeh party, the period following the revolution's victory was characterized by a duality of power, symbolized by the revolutionary center headed by the Ayatullah Khomeini and the liberal "opportunistic bourgeoisie."[7] In this view, the hostage crisis was partly organized to undermine the Bazargan government and was also used to oust the more accommodationist Bani-Sadr government. In view of the leftist and pro-Soviet tendencies of those involved in the crisis, some sort of Soviet involvement could not be ruled out.

During the first decade of the revolution, depending on the fortunes of various factions within the leadership, Soviet-Iranian relations fluctuated between rapprochement and hostility. Another important factor was variation in the prospects for improved U.S.-Iranian relations.[8] By early 1989, however, Soviet-Iranian relations had stabilized and the two sides had decided to improve and expand their bilateral ties. This new Russo-Iranian understanding was reflected in the visit of the Soviet foreign minister Eduard Shevardnadze to Tehran in June 1989, and his meeting with Ayatullah Khomeini.[9] This meeting was of great importance because it showed Khomeini's approval of expanded Soviet-Iranian relations.

RUSSIAN-IRANIAN RELATIONS IN
THE POST-SOVIET ERA

The Soviet collapse in 1991 was not welcome news for Iran because at the time it happened good relations with the USSR were very important for Iran. Stable relations with the Soviet Union had meant that for the first time in two centuries Iran did not face a serious security threat on its northern borders. Furthermore, given the West's tepid response to Iran's overtures immediately after the 1988 cease-fire in the Iraq-Iran War, plus domestic opposition to better ties with the West, the Soviet Union was the most attractive economic and military partner for Iran during its postwar reconstruction era.

The Soviet demise changed all this. It left Iran with three unstable immediate neighbors—Azerbaijan, Armenia, and Turkmenistan—and several more distant and equally unstable neighbors in the South Caucasus and Central Asia. Two of these neighbors—Armenia and Azerbaijan—were engaged in armed conflict over the disputed region of Nagorno-Karabakh. This conflict faced Iran with unpalatable policy choices and made it vulnerable to negative consequences, such as the inflow of Azerbaijani refugees.[10]

Moreover, because some of Iran's ethnic minorities overlap with the populations of these post-Soviet republics, notably with those of Azerbaijan and Turkmenistan, and because of Azerbaijan's and potentially Turkmenistan's territorial irredentism toward Iranian territories, Iran faced new security threats.

Faced with these new threats, plus a hardened Western policy toward Iran, Tehran found it imperative to have good relations with Russia, and throughout the post-Soviet era it has tried to maintain good relations with Moscow, despite Moscow's frequent lack of enthusiasm for such ties. Consequently, during the last two decades, it has been Russian priorities and Moscow's evolving foreign policy outlook that have determined the state of Russian-Iranian relations, while Iran has responded eagerly whenever Russia has expressed a desire for better ties.

Therefore, Russo-Iranian relations should be analyzed in light of Russia's changing foreign policy priorities and Iran's place within them. Of course, beyond the more mutable dynamics, Russian-Iranian relations have also been influenced by a set of converging and conflicting interests.

FACTORS OF COMPETITION AND
COOPERATION IN RUSSIAN-IRANIAN
RELATIONS

The following are the most significant areas of common interest between Iran and Russia:

+ Commitment to the territorial status-quo in the southern rim of the post-Soviet space.[11] Russia and Iran both have ethnic minorities, some with separatist tendencies.

Common concern over the potential domination of the region by the West. These concerns were exacerbated following the setting up of American military bases in Central Asia, close military relations between the United States on the one hand and Azerbaijan and Georgia on the other, and talk of Georgia's and Ukraine's membership in NATO.[12]

Common concern over Turkish ambitions in the region and the potential emergence of a Turkic bloc. However, these fears have subsided in the last 10 years, especially as far as Russia is concerned since Turkey has not been able to replace Russia in Central Asia.

At the same time, Russian and Iranian interests and ambitions collide in the following areas:

- *Energy.* Russia and Iran are competitors in energy, especially natural gas. Russia wants to become the most important purveyor of gas to Europe which, by making European countries dependent on Russian energy, enhances its influence in the Continent.

- *Pipelines.* Russia wants to remain the main export route for the energy resources of Central Asia and sees Iran as a potential rival.

- *Iran's regional influence.* Russia wants to be the principal player in its southern neighborhood. Therefore, it is opposed to the significant presence of any other regional country with ethnic and cultural affinity with the peoples of this region.

- *Lingering concern over Iran's Islamic ideology.* Russia is still suspicious of Iran's revolutionary Islamic ideology and fears its impact on its Muslim-inhabited neighbors.

- *Ambitions in the Arab World.* Russia wants to increase its economic presence in the Arab World, especially the oil-rich countries of the Persian Gulf where it hopes to find clients for its arms. Therefore, it shies away from a too-close partnership with Iran.

- *Diverging positions regarding relations with the West.* Russia would like to regain its great power status and be treated as equal with the EU and the United States. However, Russia neither wants, nor can afford, another Cold War with the West. Hence, as long as Iran's relations remain unsettled with the West, the Russians will not go beyond a certain point in nurturing ties with Iran, if this were to cause significant problems in relations with the West.

- *The perennial tension between great powers and regional powers.* Like Western powers, Russia would not like Iran to acquire significant economic, military, and political power sufficient to make it a serious competitor in regions of Russia's interest.

- *The U.S. factor.* The U.S. policy of isolating Iran, coupled with Russia's desire not to jeopardize relations with America and, at times, with Europe, has limited the scope of Russian-Iranian relations.

RUSSIA'S FOREIGN POLICY DEBATE AND ITS IMPACT ON RUSSO-IRANIAN RELATIONS

Changes in Russia's foreign policy thinking predate the USSR's collapse. They began, when, as part of its overall reform program, Mikhail Gorbachev introduced his "New Thinking."[13] The principal underpinnings of the New Thinking were

1. the importance of economic vitality and power for national security and international status and social well-being. Soviet policy makers seem to have concluded that because "economic strength was proving more decisive than military strength in resolving many global issues . . . only by reversing its precipitous economic slide and establishing linkages to the international economy could the USSR qualify as a true superpower'";

2. the de-ideologization of Soviet foreign policy and the emphasis on national interests. Soviet leaders had concluded that classic tenets of Marxism and Leninism, including the belief that international relations are a zero-sum game, were no longer sufficient guides for a successful foreign policy. The USSR's economic problems, which made it impossible for it to bankroll ineffective Third World countries simply because they espoused Marxism, also contributed to the shift in its perspective.

The main problem with the New Thinking was that it did not provide clear guidance for action. Nor did it define what constituted Soviet national interests and the nature of threats to these interests. Moreover, although progressive for its time, this theory was the outcome of Cold War and bloc politics and could not be a sufficient guide for a post-Soviet foreign policy. Consequently, after the Soviet demise, Russia was faced with a theoretical vacuum, leading to the emergence of diverging views on the best guidelines for a successful foreign policy.

EURO-ATLANTICISM AND EURASIANISM

During the period immediately following the USSR's collapse, two broad concepts, closely related to debates about Russia's identity, emerged as basic frameworks for Russia's foreign policy orientation.[14] These were: Euro-Atlanticism, which was dominant from 1992 to the middle of 1993 and was identified with Russia's first foreign minister, Andrei Kozyrev; and Eurasianism.

The following are the underlying concepts of Euro-Atlanticism and reflect Russia's priorities during the early post-Soviet years:

- Opposition to Islamic extremism in the South. This aspect reflected the impact of separatist movements in the Muslim-inhabited North Caucasus and the belief that because Russia was adopting Western values, it would become the target of Islamist animosity.[15]

+ Promoting an external environment conducive to Russia's internal reforms.

+ Restoring Russia's status as a great power.

+ Integrating Russia into the Western-dominated global order or, as Andrey Kozyrev put it, making Russia a member of the "civilized club."[16]

+ Preserving Russia's role as a civilizing agent and a preeminent power in Central Asia and the South Caucasus.

However, between 1991 and 1994, the Euro-Atlanticists' main objective was Russia's integration in the global order and the forging of a strategic alliance with the West, as reflected in Boris Yeltsin's suggestion that Russia and the United States form a "joint U.S.-Russian defense system (directed against potential aggressors in the south)."[17]

The Euro-Atlanticists also shared Western views of key Muslim regions and countries, such as Iran.

Given the perspectives of the Euro-Atlanticists, during the period of their ascendancy Russian-Iranian relations cooled. However, for a number of reasons, Russo-Iranian relations did not deteriorate beyond a certain point. These reasons were Iran's patience, its cautious policy toward the Muslim-inhabited republics of the former Soviet Union, its strategic importance, and Russia's need for export markets for some of its failing industries.

EURASIANISM AND THE SEARCH FOR MULTIPOLARITY

The Euro-Atlanticists were criticized by a variety of groups, including various shades of Russian nationalists, for their naïveté, idealism, concessionary attitude, neglect of the East, and lack of a sense of mission for Russia.[18] Their critics argued that Russia should not again become a "messianic" country but should have a higher purpose in its foreign policy.[19]

The most coherent alternative to the Euro-Atlanticist perspective was offered by the Eurasianists. The principal underpinnings of their perspective are the following:

1. The link between foreign policy and Russian statehood. The Eurasianists considered the reassertion of Russian statehood, which had been undermined by domestic and external challenges, a precondition for the success of domestic reforms.

2. The primacy of interests over ideals. According to the Eurasianists, even in the post-Soviet era, interstate relations are determined by the pursuit of interests. Ruslan Khasbulatov, speaker of the Russian Duma in 1993, admonished: "We [the Russians] must always bear in mind that the struggle for political and economic influence is continuing in the world. There remains a complex hierarchy of relations conditioned by the real power of this or that country, even if the struggle may have taken a more civilized as well as a more complex form than before."[20]

3. Russia's cultural superiority over the West or, at least, its equality with the West, especially, according to them, because of the spiritual dimensions of the Russian culture as opposed to the West's material culture.[21]

The more reasonable Eurasianists recognized the importance of good relations with the West. Nevertheless, they favored a less West-centered policy that included good relations with China and other Pacific Rim countries, the former Soviet Republics, and the Muslim countries of the Middle East and South Asia.

Various Eurasianist schools held diverging views on Islam, which have evolved over time. Broadly-speaking, Eurasianists, like the Euro-Atlanticists, have been concerned about the potential emergence of a Turko-Muslim front against Russia and the potential threat posed by Islamic extremism. However, they have maintained that Russia must deal with the Islamic world in a constructive way and should not allow Russia's centuries-old investment in the Islamic world to "melt" away.[22]

Meanwhile, some Eurasianists, like Alexander Dugin, identified different types of Islam and argued for much closer relations with the so-called "Eurasit Islam."[23] According to him, the "Eurasit Islam," especially Shiism, is a potential ally of Russia.[24] However, this division of Islam reflects more the attitude of various Muslim countries toward Russia and the West rather than Islam's reality.

Dugin considered Iran, with its anti-Western policy and Shia majority, as representing the Eurasit Islam. Therefore, he advocated the formation of a Moscow, Beijing, Delhi, Tehran axis, while other Eurasianists did not include Iran in such a potential grouping.

Euasianist ideas influenced aspects of Russian foreign policy even during the Kozyrev period. However, their influence did not extend to Iran. Even after Kozyrev's departure and gradual changes in Russia's foreign policy orientation, because of the continued importance of relations with the West it would be some time before Russia would reach out to Iran.

THE PRIMAKOV DOCTRINE AND MULTIPOLARISM

The more nuanced expression of Eurasianism is Yevgeny Primakov's theory of multipolarity. It sought to balance U.S. domination of the international political system by forging countervailing alliances between Russia and Europe and between Russia and such Asian countries as China and India.[25] After 2000, the term "multipolarity" has been used less frequently by Russia, and instead terms such as "multivector diplomacy" have been adopted, although recently the term has made a comeback.

For a brief period after 9/11, the Western countries, Russia, and China appeared to be united in a common struggle against Islamic extremism. This unity, however, was undermined by the U.S. attack on Iraq in 2003, problems in Kosovo, further NATO expansion, U.S. plans to station an antimissile shield in Poland and the Czech Republic, and American support for Georgia in its war with Russia in 2008. Meanwhile, the gradual improvement in Russia's security conditions, following the end of full-scale war in Chechnya, along with improvements in its economy, thanks to rising oil revenues, led Russia to pursue a more assertive foreign policy, even if it displeased the West. Shortly afterward, however, Russia was adversely affected by falling oil prices in 2008 and the global financial crisis. Moreover, the end of Vladimir Putin's second term and the election of Dmitri Medvedev to the Russian presidency, while Putin became prime minister, introduced greater ambiguity to Russian foreign policy, including its attitude toward Iran.

RUSSIAN–IRANIAN RELATIONS: RAFSANJANI YEARS

Developments in the Soviet Union, triggered by Gorbachev's reforms , especially in the USSR's Muslim republics, strained nascent Soviet-Iranian cooperation, heralded by Soviet foreign minister Eduard Shevardnadze's visit to Tehran in February 1989, the return visit by Akbar Hashemi Rafsanjani to Moscow in June 1989, and the signing of agreements, including one on military cooperation.[26]

Meanwhile, Gorbachev's policy of political opening (*Glasnost*) led to an outpouring of ethnic and religious grievances and the emergence of separatist movements, including in Muslim majority republics, notably Azerbaijan. These developments presented Iran with a difficult dilemma, namely, whether to ignore the demands of Soviet Muslims and lose its Islamic credibility or to react sympathetically to them and jeopardize its relations with the USSR. Iran chose a pragmatic approach and tired hard not to antagonize the Soviet Union, albeit with mixed success. For instance, when nationalist and anti-Moscow stirrings began in the USSR's Muslim republics, Tehran said that these related to the USSR's "internal affairs." Nevertheless, Moscow accused Iran of fomenting Islamic fundamentalism in its Muslim republics. This attitude was partly designed to prevent Western criticism of Soviet policies toward these republics, especially Azerbaijan, where Soviet troops entered in October 1990.

During the Euro-Atlanticists' ascendancy, Russia viewed Iran more as a potential threat than an attractive partner.[27] However, because certain powerful economic and military interests in Russia, such as the energy industry giants Lukoil and Gasprom, and the Defense and Atomic Energy Ministry, favored good relations with Iran, Russia did not go beyond a certain point in antagonizing Iran.[28] The Eurasianists also favored good relations with Iran.[29]

By early 1994, because of the nonrealization of Russia's expectations of partnership with the West, the Euro-Atlanticists' perspective had lost most of its influence. This Russian disillusionment was due to different Western and Russian understanding of what their partnership entailed. Put simply, by "partnership," the West meant Russia's acquiescence in all of its policy choices, even in regions of historical concern to Russia such as Central Asia, the Middle East, and the Balkans, and its total openness to Western capital and political and cultural influence. The West was willing to make symbolic concessions to Russia, such as admitting it to the Group of Seven industrial states, but it viewed any reassertion of Russian influence in the post-Soviet space as the revival of Russian imperialism.

Russia, by contrast, had in mind an equal partnership with Europe and the United States in managing the world along the lines of a new version of the old Concert of Europe. In particular, Russia—including even Kozyrev—had expected that, in the southern rim of the former Soviet space, Russia would be the main actor within a broad partnership with the West and it would act as the only bridge between these regions and the West.[30]

Other Western policies, such as expanding NATO, favoring Turkey in Central Asia, including former Soviet republics in NATO's Partnership for Peace (PFP), coupled with Russia's suspicions that some of the West's Muslim allies were helping the Chechen rebels, and what Russia saw as the West's uneven approach to Islamic militancy and terrorism, intensified Russia's disillusionment in the coming years.[31]

Russia's shift away from an excessively West-centered strategy revived its interest in better relations in Iran, and by 1995 the two sides were talking about a strategic partnership. The first signs of improved Russo-Iranian relations were the agreement for Russia to build the Bushehr nuclear power plant and the visit of Iran's foreign minister, Ali Akbar Velayati, to Moscow in 1996.

In the coming years, Iran's good behavior in Central Asia and the Caucasus, especially in regard to Chechnya, along with regional developments, such as the rise of the Taliban in Afghanistan, further contributed to Moscow-Tehran rapprochement. Iran was instrumental in ending the Tajik civil war, although Russia did not acknowledge its contribution until much later.[32] Iran also kept Chechnya out of the 1997 Organization of the Islamic Conference (OIC) Summit agenda, an inclusion that Turkey had wanted. Iran's help was acknowledged by Russia's minister of interior Anatolii Kulikov, when he thanked Iran for its "circumspect position on the Chechen issue."[33] Iran also created a special committee on Chechnya within the OIC for consultation with Russia. Iran and Russia also supported the Northern Alliance of Ahmad Shah Masud in Afghanistan. However, it was not until 1999 that Russia began to think of Iran as a potential strategic partner. Until that time, Russia, limited by the Gore-Chernomyrdin agreement, did not sell Iran any sophisticated weapons. Reportedly, the U.S. vice president, Al Gore, had told then-Russian prime minister Victor Chernomyrdin that the United States might be forced to impose sanctions on Russia if it sold arms to Iran.[34] Nor did Russia work seriously on the Bushehr power plant. Even the submarines that Russia sold Iran were defective. However, Western sources maintain that Russia helped Iran acquire missile technology, and also that Iranian students have received training in Russia on nuclear-related skills.[35]

THE KHATAMI PRESIDENCY AND RUSSIAN-IRANIAN RELATIONS

The Khatami presidency in Iran coincided with Vladimir Putin's rise to power in Russia. Putin's priority was to restore Russia's statehood by ending the Chechen rebellion, even if this meant first resuming full-scale war. The resumption of the Chechen war in December 1998 again presented Iran with a difficult dilemma—namely, whether to criticize Russia and risk antagonizing it or to keep quiet and be accused of betraying the Muslims. Once more, Iran chose the latter option, and Khatami declared that Chechnya was Russia's internal affair.

Iran's continued "good behavior" in the post-Soviet south, Russia's anxiety over possible U.S.-Iran rapprochement under Khatami, and Putin's determination to show Russia's independence from America created a better atmosphere for improved Russian-Iranian relations.

Russia's new foreign policy direction was reflected in its withdrawal from the Gore-Chernomyrdin agreement. This development eliminated a major barrier to expanded Russia-Iran military and economic cooperation. Then, the 2000 Foreign Policy Concept of the Russian Federation declared that "it is important to develop further relations with Iran."[36]

Earlier, in the fall of 1999, two Muslim members of the Duma had traveled to Iran. After meeting with President Khatami, one delegate, Abdul Vahid Niazov, stated that "the development of Russian-Iranian relations can no longer be contingent on the view of a third party [the United States], a view that was imposed on us."[37]

The next big event was the visit of President Khatami to Moscow in March 2001. The trip was high on hype—Primakov called it the biggest event in the history of Moscow-Tehran relations—but quite meager in results. Putin declared that Russia would resume arms sales to Iran, but this declaration did not lead to the kind of military cooperation and strategic partnership that Iran had hoped for. A document entitled "The Treaty on Foundations of Relations and Principles of Cooperation" was signed. However, it fell short of being a strategic agreement because it only said that if one side were the subject of aggression, the other side would not help the aggressor. This point was emphasized by Alexander Luskov, Russia's deputy defense minister, when he stated that "the planned treaty will not make Russia and Iran strategic partners."[38] Robert Freedman, too, noted that "given the background of deteriorating U.S.-Russian relations, one might have expected more to come out of the Putin-Khatami meeting than actually happened."[39]

However, given substantial conflict of interest between Iran and Russia in many areas, this outcome was not surprising. One area of disagreement related to the sharing of Caspian resources. Russian-Iranian rapprochement, even before Khatami's visit, was marred by the change in Russia's position. Initially, Russia, like Iran, had favored the "condominium" approach to the sharing of Caspian resources, but in a reversal of policy and, largely because of pressure by its energy lobby, it signed bilateral agreements with Azerbaijan, Turkmenistan, and Kazakhstan on the exploitation of Caspian energy resources.[40] Iran bitterly resented this Russian betrayal. It reminded Moscow that in 1998 its deputy foreign minister had signed an agreement promising Iran that Russia would take Iran's insistence on a 20 percent share into account.[41] Yet Russia's behavior on this matter was in line with its overall pattern of behavior toward Iran, characterized by its frequent default on its agreements.[42]

Iran was also concerned about Russia's military activities in the Caspian Sea. After Russian military exercises there in 2001, the Iranian news agency said that "Iran believes that that there is no threat in the Caspian Sea to justify the war games and military presence, and that such measures will harm the confidence building efforts of the littoral states."[43] However, this reflected another area of conflict of interest between Iran and Russia: Russia has wanted to remain the dominant player in the Caspian region and military exercises derived from this overriding objective.

Another source of tension in Tehran-Moscow ties was the ill-fated Bushehr nuclear power plant. The agreement to build the plant was made in 1995 and construction was expected to be completed by 1999. However, given the volatile relations between Russia and Iran, the completion of the plant was first delayed to 2004, then to 2005 and 2007. As of spring 2010, the Russians had promised that the Bushehr plan would become operational by September 2010. Pretexts used by Russia for the delays have included technical difficulties, Iranian nonpayment, and the question of spent fuel. To resolve the last-named issue, Iran agreed to send the fuel back to Russia, but Moscow's delaying tactics continued.

Russia's defaults on its promises have seriously undermined Iran's confidence in Russia, but Iran "still favors nuclear cooperation with Russia because European countries decline to help Iran in the nuclear field."[44] This rule applies to other areas of Russo-Iranian cooperation.

The events of 9/11 and the ensuing Russian-U.S. rapprochement led America both to pressure Russia and offer it incentives so that it would stop the construction of the Bushehr plant. America, in an effort to convince Moscow "to dump Tehran, agreed to allocate a $20 billion aid package to Russia to scrap its weapons of mass destruction."[45] Russia did not succumb to these pressures, and in August 2002 the representative of Atomeneroproject, the company building the plant, said that it would be completed on schedule in 2004. However, this date was changed to 2005 then 2007, and 2009. In October 2009, however, Iranian authorities indicated that it was 96 percent complete. At times, Iranian officials have said that Iran will finish the plant itself.

Despite the Russian show of unreliability, Iran continued its efforts for expanded relations with Moscow. Russia, meanwhile, stopped just short of totally abandoning Iran and instead used the Iran card to get concessions from the West.

However, although Iran had been eager since the Yeltsin years to receive a high-level Russian visitor to Teheran—that is, at the president or prime minister level—and despite rumors of an impending Putin visit to Iran in 2003, no such visit took place until 2007.

AHMADINEJAD PRESIDENCY, IRAN'S NUCLEAR PROGRAM, AND RUSSIAN-IRANIAN RELATIONS

The U.S. attack on Iraq in 2003 undermined the post-9/11 Russian-American entente. In the following years, the steep rise in oil prices, which enriched Russia's treasury, elicited a more assertive Russian behavior, and, as noted above, the U.S. decision to station antimissile sites in Poland and the Czech Republic exacerbated relations. However, these developments did not change the basic dynamics of Russo-Iranian relations. What affected those relations, and in a mostly negative fashion, was Iran's resumption of nuclear activities and its unresponsiveness to Russian proposals regarding how to resolve the dispute over Iran's nuclear program.

Until February 2006, when the IAEA, with Russia's approval, finally referred Iran's nuclear dossier to the United Nations Security Council, Russia had been supportive of Iran's right to peaceful nuclear energy and had opposed imposing sanctions on Iran and the use of force against it. Additionally, Russia had offered Iran certain inducements, such as helping it launch a remote-sensing satellite in October 2005 and agreeing to sell it an air-defense system—the S 300—worth $1 billion.[46] Moreover, in order to resolve Iran's nuclear problem, Russia offered to enrich uranium for Iran in Russia to the level required to make fuel for power plants. Iran did not respond positively and said that uranium enrichment, even in cooperation with other countries, must be done in Iran. Russia, in a concession to Iran, then suggested that Iran and Russia jointly enrich uranium.[47] Initially, Iran rejected this proposal, too. Instead, when it looked very likely that the IAEA would refer its dossier to the UNSC, it tried to persuade Russia from voting for it and indicated that it would seriously consider Russia's proposal.[48] But Russia was not convinced and, irritated by Iran's lack of responsiveness to its proposals, voted in favor of Iran's referral to the UNSC.

Despite Russia's positive vote, and later its agreement to the imposition of UN economic sanctions on Iran, Tehran continued its policy of courting Moscow. Russia, too, despite its irritation with Iran, tried to prevent excessive deterioration of relations. An important Russian motive was to retain the Iran card in its relations with the West.

This Russian desire to maintain good relations with Iran was demonstrated by Vladimir Putin's visit to Tehran in October 2007. That visit was almost cancelled because of rumors of a plan to assassinate Putin and, when the visit did take place, it lasted only 24 hours. It was not strictly speaking a state visit; it took place on the occasion of the summit meeting of the heads of states of the Caspian region.[49] Nevertheless, Iran finally got to welcome a Russian president. .

Putin's visit did not change the basic dynamics of Russian-Iranian relations, as shown by Russia's foot dragging on the Bushehr power plant, its refusal to deliver the promised air-defense system—largely because of U.S. and Israeli pressures[50]—and its use of the Bushehr plant as a tool to pressure Iran on its nuclear program.[51] Moreover, Russia successfully used the Iran card to obtain concessions from the United States. It was no accident that after President Obama declared the change in U.S. policy on antimissile sites in Central Europe, Russian President Dmitry Medvedev indicated that Russia would be willing to consider harsher sanctions on Iran.[52] By the beginning of October 2009, during talks with the 5+1 countries, Iran appeared to have agreed in principle to something akin to the Russian proposal on its uranium enrichment, although, as noted in chapter 3, it changed its position.

The disputed nature of Iran's June 2009 presidential elections created anti-Russian sentiments among Iran's reformist movement opposed to Ahmadinejad and led to some questioning on the part of the Russian press of the advisability of Russia's continuing a business-as-usual approach to the second Ahmadinejad administration.[53] The presence of Ahmadinejad in Moscow on June 17, 2009, on the occasion of the Shanghai Cooperation Organization (SCO) summit meeting was partly responsible for this criticism.[54] But as Western criticism of the Iranian elections finally subsided and the European countries recognized the Ahmadinejad government, the Russian position did not appear out of the ordinary.

Table 5.1   Iran-Russia Trade in 2008 (million EUROS)

Iran's Exports	Iran's Imports
283.3	2,659.3

Source: European Commission.

As can be seen in table 5.1, the balance of trade is heavily weighted in Russia's favor. Also the volume of Russo-Iranian trade is much lower than that with the EU, and China, and in 2008, Russia was Iran's eight most important trade partner.

However, despite economic advantages that relation with Iran entails for Russia, Russo-Iranian relations continued to deteriorate during the rest of 2009 and early 2010. Some Iranian publications referred to the "Cold winter of Russo-Iranian relations."

From the Iranian side, Russia's default on its promises, especially its unwillingness to deliver the promised S300 missiles to Tehran and the continued delay on the completion of the Bushehr power plant, as well as Russia's unwillingness to side with Iran on its nuclear dossier were the main culprits.

On the Russian side, two factors played the most significant roles: First Medvedev is more West-oriented than Putin was and consequently was unwilling to jeopardize Russia's relations with the West because of Iran. It is worth noting that Medvedev's statements on Russia's willingness to impose sanctions on Iran were far more forthcoming than those of Putin or Foreign Minister Sergei Lavorov.[55] Second, Russia' economic problems made the continuation of a very assertive policy toward the West unrealistic. Additionally, Russia, which wanted to score a diplomatic coup by brokering a nuclear deal between Iran and the West, was exacerbated by Iran's negative response to the proposal made to it during the Geneva talks.[56]

Last but not least, Israel's relentless lobbying also greatly contributed to change in Russia's approach to Iran.

In addition, Western countries accommodated Russia on such questions as the missile defense shield to be stationed in Poland, and France agreed to sell warships to Russia.

As a sign of how much Russo-Iranian relations had deteriorated in March 2010, Iran declared that it had given Russian pilots working in Iran's civilian air transport industry two months to leave the country.[57]

ASSESSMENT OF IRAN'S RUSSIA POLICY

Iran's approach to relations with Russia, has reflected the impact of several factors. These include the anti-Americanism of the Iranian regime, in particular some elements within it; the leftist tendencies within the regime's leadership, which carried over their pro-Soviet leanings into relations with Russia; the lack of appreciation of the magnitude of systemic changes; and basic divergence of economic and strategic interests as between Russia and Iran. Largely because of these factors, the Iranians did not realize that a Cold War-era type Russian-Iranian alliance would be impossible in the postideological world. For example, while Russia had its disagreements and conflicts of interest with the United States and wanted more say for itself internationally, it was not prepared to engage in a global competition with America. But this is precisely what Iran expected, a full-blown anti-American alliance.

Iran failed to realize that Russia, as a great power bent on retaining its influence on its southern frontiers, would not want to see Iran, a regional power, become too strong. It also failed to recognize the fact that as in the post–Cold War era, Russia and the West would be willing to make deals at Iran's expense. More seriously, Iran did not realize that remaining at odds with the West weakened its hand in dealing with Russia. Consequently, Iran's efforts to befriend Russia did not yield the results it had hoped for.

On the contrary, because of its overall policy mistakes, Iran's relations with Russia, instead of leading to strategic alliance, became a fool's bargain.

CHAPTER 6

Looking East: Iran's Relations with India, China, and Other Asian Countries

Iran's policy of expanding economic and other relations with key Asian countries, such as China and India, has been generally interpreted as an effort to circumvent the Western countries' mounting economic and political pressures. Clearly, Iran's economic needs and its desire to escape international isolation have partly motivated this strategy. However, two other factors have also been important:

1. Iran's unwillingness to accept the emerging post-Soviet international system, based on U.S./Western hegemony, and hence its efforts to help create a multipolar world by the formation of a grouping of countries to serve as a viable counterweight to the Western powers.
2. The desire to find a home for itself in Asia, since historically it has been rejected by the largely Arab Middle East because of its Persian and Shia character, and because in the post-Soviet era it has faced the challenge of pan-Turkist movements in Central Asia. Consequently, Iran has hoped that the development of a pan-Asian identity and movement toward intra-Asian cooperation and even eventually an Asian Union would mitigate its ethnic and cultural isolation.[1] In fact, the roots of Iran's quest to become integrated in Asia can be traced to the early 1970s.

Consequently, even before the Islamic Revolution and before China and, increasingly, India had become global economic powers, they loomed large in Iran's foreign policy. In China's case, its permanent membership on the UN Security Council, possession of nuclear weapons, and efforts to spread its own brand of Communism abroad—including to Iran and its neighborhood—made China an important factor in Iran's foreign policy calculations.[2]

Iran's cultural and other ties with India date to pre-Islamic times.[3] From the 1950s to the 1970s, the following factors enhanced India's importance in Iran's foreign policy:

+ The Indo-Pakistani conflict.

+ India's leadership of the Non-Aligned Movement (NAM).

+ India's close military and economic ties to the Soviet Union and to such Soviet allies in the Middle East as Iraq.

The oil revolution of 1973 added an economic dimension to Iran's interest in India and China, which until then had been largely based on security concerns and led the Shah to pursue his own eastern strategy. The reasons, as illustrated by the following quote, were similar to those behind the Islamic government's eastward strategy: "Bound by the USSR to the north and blocked by the Arab-Israeli conflict to the West, Iran is looking East in search of new friends and areas for economic and political activity."[4]

However, Cold War dynamics dominated Iran's relations with India and China for the rest of the Shah's regime. Consequently, when China joined the West in containing the Soviet Union, Iran's relations with China improved and led to the signing on August 17, 1971, of a bilateral agreement on mutual recognition and the establishment of diplomatic relations. However, there was no major expansion in Sino-Iranian economic and political relations, although the trend was in that direction.[5] This lack of progress, in addition to lingering ideological suspicions, reflected the state of China's economy, which was not capable of satisfying Iran's desire for high technology.

India's closeness to the USSR and its economic and technological limitations also limited the scope of Indo-Iranian cooperation. In fact, during the 1970s, Japan, a Western ally and the most developed Asian country, was Iran's main economic partner in Asia.

SINO-IRANIAN RELATIONS AFTER THE ISLAMIC REVOLUTION: THE 1980s

The following factors made China an attractive economic and political partner for the Islamic government:

+ China had had a genuine socioeconomic and political revolution.

+ It had successfully defied both the United States and the USSR and had achieved a degree of economic and military advancement.

+ It had championed the aspirations of Third World countries.

+ It had the potential to become an alternative source of civilian and military goods and technology for Iran, even if of a comparatively inferior quality.

China, meanwhile, had established a good working relationship with Iran in the 1970s and was concerned about political instability in Iran, the impact of the war with

Iraq, and potential Soviet inroads in Iran and hence in the Persian Gulf. These Chinese fears were exacerbated by the Soviet invasion of Afghanistan in November 1979. Therefore, when in 1984 the Islamic government began to think of its external relations in more traditional and state-centered fashion and started to normalize its diplomatic relations, China responded positively.

The first important step in renewed Sino-Iranian relations was the visit of the speaker of the Iranian parliament, Ali Akbar Hashemi Rafsanjani, to Beijing in July 1985, followed in May 1989 by the visit of Iran's president and the current Supreme Leader, Ali Khamenei.[6] A number of agreements were signed during these trips, including one between the atomic energy organizations of the two countries.[7]

Iran's reaching out to China paid off. Beijing helped Iran during its war with Iraq and provided it with military supplies and technical assistance, including Silkworm missiles.[8] Therefore, when the Chinese deputy foreign minister visited Tehran in August 1988, Rafsanjani said that "China is a true friend of Iran."[9]

However, the pace of progress in Sino-Iranian relations, which if continued could have led to a deeper partnership, slowed down as China's domestic policies and priorities, and hence its international orientation, shifted. China's market-oriented economic reforms, its desire to become integrated in the global economic system, and its need for investment and market access, especially in the United States, necessitated changes in its foreign policy, notably a greater sensitivity to American political concerns, including those regarding Iran. Table 6.1 indicates the extent of China's economic relations with the United States.

Strained Arab-Iranian relations, coupled with China's reliance on imports from the Gulf Arab countries, further limited the expansion of Sino-Iranian ties, as China tried to prevent its relationship with Iran from harming its relations with the Arab oil exporters. As China's energy needs have grown and are expected to grow more in the future, China will be forced to continue this balancing act between Iran and the Gulf Arabs.

Meanwhile, by the time Iran was finally coming out of its debilitating war with Iraq and concentrating on rebuilding its war-torn economy and reintegrating into the international community, new developments were changing the global geopolitical conditions to Iran's detriment. The main factor behind these changes was Gorbachev's reforms, including the change in the premises of Soviet foreign policy in the context of

Table 6.1   The Volume of U.S.-China Trade in 2008 in Billion Dollars

Chinese Exports to the United States	Chinese Imports from the United States
338.8	9.5

Source: U.S.-China Business Council.

his so-called New Thinking. This new Soviet outlook vastly diminished international tensions, including those between the USSR and China, thus undermining China's interest in Iran as a bulwark against Soviet expansionism. The changing international conditions and the Soviet withdrawal from Afghanistan in 1989 eased Sino-Indian relations and thus further undermined the strategic rationale for China's interest in Iran.

INDO-IRANIAN RELATIONS IN THE 1980s

Unlike its relations with China, Iran's relations with India had never been overly hostile. There were, however, tensions in Indo-Iranian relations deriving primarily from the dynamics of the Cold War and the Indo-Pakistan conflict. India, although professing nonalignment, had close relations with the USSR, including a friendship treaty signed in 1971, which Iran viewed with alarm and as part of the Soviet strategy of encircling it. India and Iran also had widely diverging regional relationships. Iran was an ally of Pakistan, India's major foe, while India supported radical Arab states such as Nasser's Egypt and Saddam's Iraq, which were actively working against the Shah's regime.

Nevertheless, throughout the turbulent postwar years, both sides managed to maintain reasonable relations. Iran, conscious of India's regional and international weight, tried to reassure it that its Western ties were not directed against India. Thus, when in 1954 Iran joined the Baghdad Pact (renamed the Central Treaty Organization following the 1958 revolution in Iraq) in order to reassure India, the Shah visited New Delhi in 1956. In September 1959, Indian prime minister Jawaharlal Nehru visited Tehran, and in January 1960 the Shah paid a return visit to India.

The relative détente in East-West relations, following the end the Cuban missile crisis, also led to an improvement in Soviet-Iranian ties, which in turn positively impacted Iran's relations with India. Iran's support to India during its war with China in 1962 further improved their ties. This positive trend stopped after the 1965 Indo-Pakistani war, during which Iran fully supported Pakistan, and only resumed in the early 1970s.

The following factors contributed to the new and more positive phase of Indo-Iranian relations, which continued throughout the 1970s:

+ The Shah's more independent foreign policy.
+ Changes in the relationship between the oil producers and major oil companies even before the oil revolution of 1973, which enhanced Iran's economic attraction as a potential partner and allowed it to play a more active regional role.
+ Iran's and India's disillusionment with their respective regional allies. India was saddened by the lack of support from its Arab allies during its 1965 war with Pakistan, while the Iranian-Pakistani alliance had begun to unravel because of growing friendship between Pakistan and the Gulf Arab countries, especially Saudi Arabia; the growing influence of Islam in Pakistani society and politics;

and Pakistani-Arab competition with Iran for influence in Afghanistan. The result was the growing importance of India and Iran for each other.

However, even during this period, Indo-Iranian relations were not free of misgivings, especially on India's part. The main cause of India's misgivings was Iran's ambitions to play a leading role in the Persian Gulf and the Indian Ocean at a time when India was building up its navy and saw itself as a Persian Gulf power.[10] In particular, Prime Minister Indira Gandhi did not like the Shah's pretensions to a leadership role in the Indian Ocean.[11] Nevertheless, during the 1970s, Indo-Iranian economic and military cooperation increased, and Prime Minister Gandhi visited Tehran in 1974. Economic and military cooperation included Iranian investment in a coal mine in India, provision of economic help to ease the burden of oil-price increases, and the training by India of Iran's naval personnel.[12] The two countries also agreed to cooperate in the field of nuclear energy.

The Islamic Revolution in many ways adversely affected Indo-Iranian relations, while also removing some causes of their discord. The most serious damage was done by the regime's Islam-based ideology. Before the revolution, the Shah had used the two countries' Aryan heritage and their deep-rooted cultural bonds to cement relations.[13] Also, pursuing a nationalist foreign policy, the Shah did not particularly concern himself with the fate of other Muslims, including those of India. By contrast, the Islamic regime considered itself the champion of all Muslims and hence sensitive to issues related to Hindu-Muslim relations. Thus, during periods of Hindu-Muslim tensions, some members of the Iranian parliament made comments that alarmed Indian officials, and India was in general apprehensive about the impact of the Iranian Revolution on its own Muslim population.

These negative factors were partially mitigated by the end of Iran's alliance with the United States and the new government's view of India as a Third World country that had achieved a considerable degree of economic and military self-sufficiency.[14] However, the Soviet invasion of Afghanistan in November 1979 and the Iran-Iraq War (September 1980–August 1988) complicated Indo-Iranian relations because India had close ties to Iraq and supported the Soviet presence in Afghanistan.

SINO-IRANIAN RELATIONS IN THE POST-SOVIET ERA

The Soviet Union's collapse eroded the security rationale for close Sino-Iranian relations. However, other systemic consequences of the USSR's dismantling, most notably the United States' international ascendancy as the sole superpower, acted as impetus to better Sino-Iranian relations.

Despite its growing trade and economic ties to the United States, China, as an aspiring great power, could not have been overjoyed by U.S. global hegemony, which, if consolidated and perpetuated, would have inevitably limited China's freedom of action. Moreover, tensions remained in U.S.-China relations, deriving partly from human rights-related issues. Consequently, when Russia began to promote the idea of multipolarity, China responded positively because this concept corresponded to China's desire to maintain its presence in key strategic regions and countries and further expand this presence into new regions, such as Africa.

IRAN'S ATTRACTIONS TO CHINA

Iran's attraction to China derives from the following factors:

+ Iran's vast oil and gas reserves.

+ Substantial markets.

+ Iran's nonideological approach to China and regions of interest to it, such as Central Asia. For instance, Iran has not emphasized the Islamic factor in its relations with China and has refrained from supporting Chinese Muslims' grievances against Beijing. This attitude was best illustrated by Iran's near silence in the face of the harsh Chinese crackdown on its Muslim Uighur minority during riots that broke out in Urumqi in July 2009. This official attitude generated comments in the Iranian media, especially among those opposed to the government's ideological approach to other foreign policy issues, such as the Arab-Israeli dispute, at the expense of Iran's national interests.[15] This Iranian attitude is in sharp contrast to that of some elements in the West who are supportive of such groups. Some in the West would not even mind China's territorial disintegration.[16]

+ Mutual commitment to the territorial *status quo* and opposition to secessionist movements.

+ Absence of any Iranian preconditions for better ties.

In its relations with China, Iran has not imposed any prior political conditions, as it has done in the case of the United States. Thus, while Iran has cited close U.S.-Israeli ties as one reason for not having relations with America, it has ignored Sino-Israeli relations, which include large Israeli arms sales to China.[17]

CHINA'S ATTRACTIONS FOR IRAN

China is attractive to Iran for the following reasons:

+ It is a source of goods, services, technology and investment. This factor became more important after the failure of Iran's diplomacy of outreach to Europe and partially to the United States.

+ It is a potential strategic and political counterweight to the United States.

+ The lack of Chinese preconditions for better ties, such as improved human rights performance or support for the Arab-Israeli peace.

+ It is a model of socioeconomic and political development.

+ There is a lack of any disagreements within the Iranian regime's key elements on having good relations with China.

Because of these factors, throughout the 1990s and 2000s Sino-Iranian economic and political relations expanded, although the pace and scope of this expansion would have been more significant had it not been for the effects of other aspects of Iran's foreign policy, particularly its conflict with the United States. Even so, between September 1992 and June 2006, there were more than 15 high-level visits by Iranian and Chinese leaders to each other's countries, including by three Iranian presidents to China.[18] In addition, over the last two decades, the two countries have signed and implemented a number of important agreements in various fields.

In February 1993, during the visit of the Chinese foreign minister to Tehran, the two sides signed an agreement for the construction of two 300-megawatt nuclear power plants. This agreement angered the United States, which, in response, impounded a Chinese cargo ship, accusing it of carrying chemical weapons to Iran.

Sino-Iranian economic and technological cooperation became more difficult after the United States imposed economic sanctions on Iran. Initially, China opposed these sanctions and resisted American pressures to cancel its nuclear agreement with Iran. However, under U.S. pressure, in 1996 China declared that it would not construct the two nuclear power plants.

During the last decade, Sino-Iranian economic relations have been focused mainly on the energy sector, because of Iran's acute need for investments that are not forthcoming from Western sources. Meanwhile, China is keen to have a diversified and secure source of energy supplies. Consequently, in the last six years, China has become an important investor in Iran's energy sector. Some of the more important examples of Chinese-Iranian energy relations are the following:

+ The agreement with the state-owned Zhuhai Zhenong Corporation in March 2004 for the purchase over 25 years of 110 million tons of Iranian LNG (Liquefied Natural Gas) at an estimated cost of $20 billion.

+ The October 2004 agreement between the Iranian National Oil Company (NIOC) and China Petroleum and Chemical Corporation (SINOPEC), according to which China will participate in the development of the Yadavaran oil field, and Iran will sell 150,000 bpd (barrels per day) of this oil to China.

+ The June 2005 agreement with the China National Petroleum Corporation (CNPC) to develop the Khoudasht oil field in southwestern Iran.[19]

+ The June 2009 agreement with CNPC to replace Total in the development of Phase 11 of the South Pars gas field. Total withdrew under pressure from the Sarkozy government. The value of this contract is $4.7 billion.

+ The Memorandum of Understanding between CNCP and NIOC to develop the North Azadegan oil field.

Table 6.2   China's Top Export Destinations in 2008 in Billion Dollars

Rank	Country/Region	Volume
1	The United States	252.3
2	Hong Kong	190.7
3	Japan	116.0
4	South Korea	74.0
5	Germany	59.2
6	Netherlands	46.0
7	UK	36.1
8	Russia	33.0
9	Singapore	32.3
10	India	31.5

Source: U.S.-China Business Council.

In addition, the China National Offshore Oil Corporation has held talks with Iran to finalize a $16 billion deal to develop the North Pars gas field and build an LNG plant. Meanwhile, CNCP has held talks to develop energy reserves in Iran's Caspian region.[20] Iranian sources claim that China intends to invest $40 billion in Iran's energy industry.

Chinese companies are also involved in drilling activities, the building of oil and gas pipelines, and downstream operations. Iran is seeking China's help in expanding its refining capacity, by helping construct the Hormuz refinery and renovate the Abadan refinery.[21] Other areas of China's participation have been shipbuilding, the construction of the Tehran metro, dam-building, and other activities. According to some sources, there are close to 250 Chinese companies of various sizes that are active in various sectors of the Iranian economy.[22]

During a conference in Tehran in May 2009 to discuss the global financial crisis and bilateral Sino-Iranian relations, it was said that the two countries intended to increase the volume of their trade to $50 billion. Noting the tremendous boost in bilateral trade over the past 15 years, Iran's foreign minister, Manouchehr Muttaki, said that the volume of trade had increase from $448 million in 1994 to $29 billion in 2008.[23] Even so, Iran is not yet among China's top trading partners. It is even behind Saudi Arabia as a major source of imports for China. This means that China imports more oil from Saudi Arabia than it does from Iran. The discrepancy between the volume of China's oil imports from Saudi Arabia and those from Iran will widen in the future, if the declining trend in China's oil purchases from Iran in 2009 by fifty per cent continues. This decline was reportedly prompted by growing talk of sanctions against Iran and increased risk of a military strike by the U.S., Israel, or both. Moreover, the trade volume of China with all Gulf Cooperation Council (GCC) states is even larger and in 2005 stood at $46 billion, $21.4 billion of which consisted of China's exports (see tables 6.2, 6.3, and 6.4).[24]

ARMS SALES TO IRAN: NOT VERY SIGNIFICANT

Much as been written by Western experts and observers about China's contribution to Iran's arms industry and Chinese arms sales to Iran, including antiship missiles, notably the HY-2 (Silkworm) and C-801 missiles.

However, in the post-Soviet era, China's sales of sophisticated arms to Iran has not been considerable.[25] Other areas of China's military assistance to Iran, including nuclear and missile technology, are mostly in the realm of speculation. The main reason for this situation has been U.S. pressure, which at times has led China to cancel deals with Iran. For example, in 1997, during President Bill Clinton's visit to China, that country agreed to stop the sale of missiles to Iran and to stop its help in developing Iran's civilian nuclear energy sector.[26] In January 1998, the Chinese president, Jiang Zemin, assured the U.S. secretary of defense that China had halted "all transfers of anti-ship missiles to Iran, and that Beijing would not assist Iran in upgrading its [current] cruise missile inventory." In 2002, China also published a comprehensive list of export controls, largely corresponding to the Missile Technology Control Regime (MTCR). Even so, since the publication of this list, Chinese firms have been sanctioned for missile-related exports to Iran. However, it appears that these were dual-use items not covered by MTCR.[27]

Consequently, although according to the Swedish Peace Research Institute (SIPRI), Iran is the second largest importer of Chinese arms in terms of volume, as table 6.5 demonstrates, the amount is negligible.

IMPEDIMENTS TO AN IRANIAN-CHINESE STRATEGIC ALLIANCE

Iran has been eager to forge close economic, military, and political ties with China in an effort to prevent the perpetuation of a unipolar world. However, the following factors have frustrated Iran's ambitions in this direction:

+ *The U.S. factor.* U.S. international weight and influence, plus the extensive and complicated economic, trade, and financial relations between America and China, have played important roles in China's decision to curtail its military ties to Iran. The United States's opposition has also limited the scope of China's economic relations with Iran. With the increase in U.S. pressures on China to join in anti-Iran sanctions, Sino-Iranian relations will come to a crossroads. If China joins in sanctioning Iran or even if it merely abstains in the UNSC voting on Iran, its relations with Iran will no doubt suffer. But going against U.S. wishes will add another source of tension to Sino-American relations, which have been growing tense since the latter part of 2009. However, other factors have also been important in determining China's approach.

+ *Saudi competition.* As Sino-Iranian relations expanded in the early 2000s, especially in the energy field, Saudi Arabia took measures to wean China away from

Table 6.3 China's Top Import Suppliers in 2008 in Billion Dollars

Rank	Country/Region	Volume
1	Japan	150.7
2	South Korea	190.7
3	Taiwan	103.3
4	The United States	81.4
5	Germany	55.8
6	Australia	37.4
7	Malaysia	32.3
8	Saudi Arabia	31.0
9	Brazil	29.7
10	Thailand	25.6

Source: U.S.-China Business Council.

Table 6.4 Volume of Iran-China Trade in 2008 in Million Euros

Iran's Exports	Iran's Imports
13,611.0	6,348.5

Source: European Commission.

further involvement in Iran. This Saudi activism was signaled by the visit of King Abdullah to China on January 22, 2006,[28] and by the visit of China's president Hu Jianto to Riyadh in February 2006.[29] Since 2009, Saudi Arabia, partly on U.S. urging, has been actively lobbying China to reduce its ties to Iran. Reportedly, the Saudis have argued that Iran's nuclear program threatens the Middle East's stability and also reportedly, the Saudis have offered China to make up for Iranian oil, perhaps even at a lower price. Meanwhile, some Chinese commentators, notably Yin Gang, have argued that China should not undertake "to please Iran and at the same time hurt the feelings of the Arabs and other countries."[30]

+ *The Israel factor.* Since the latter part of 2009 Israel's lobbying of China to join in sanctioning Iran has become an added barrier to closer Sino-Iranian relations. At the end of February 2010, Israel sent a high level group of officials to China. China has good relations with Israel, which has in the past been an important supplier of military hardware to China.[31] In view of close U.S.-Israeli ties, the souring of relations with Israel over Iran would also negatively impact Sino-American relations.

+ *The systemic tension between global and regional powers.* China is aspiring to become a great power with a global role. As a rule, great powers with a global reach are wary of middle powers, especially if they are located in a strategically sensitive region. Iran, clearly, is such a country. Consequently, China would want good relations with Iran and might even go some distance to prevent the United States or any other rival power to dominate it and the region. But it would not want to see a very strong Iran capable of exerting significant influence in a region as sensitive as the Persian Gulf, and potentially in Central Asia, which is also emerging as an area of great importance to China.

+ *The impact of Iran's domestic politics.* Positive changes in Iran's domestic politics in the direction of greater internal openness and moderation in external behavior have led to an expansion of bilateral relations. By contrast, a hardening of Iran's domestic and external policies, as has happened since 2005, has negatively affected bilateral relations. For instance, it is important to note that while visiting the Persian Gulf region in 2006, China's president did not visit Iran.

+ *Diverging expectations.* Iran and China have had diverging expectations of their relations. China has viewed Iran in a classic great-power perspective as a source of energy supplies and export markets, and as an instrument to balance the influence of other key international players. Iran, by contrast, has viewed China principally as a potential counterweight to the United States that would be willing to join it in an anti-U.S. alliance and defend it against U.S. pressures.

Although uneasy about a global system dominated by the United States, China has had no intention of resuming an all-out rivalry with America. Moreover, barring the intensification of Sino-American tensions and potential rivalry for global influence, as China joins the ranks of great powers it would develop a stake in the current international system and would not welcome the emergence of other major regional and international players, such as a militarily and economically stronger Iran, potentially capable of challenging its influence in places such as the Persian Gulf and possibly Central Asia.

This discrepancy between Iran's and China's expectations of their relationship became evident during the drawn-out crisis over Iran's nuclear program. Despite Iran's hopes, China refused to veto UN-imposed economic sanctions on Iran. True, China has opposed military attacks on Iran if it does not stop its uranium enrichment program, and it has resisted the imposition of so-called crippling sanctions on Iran. But if the United States decides to attack Iran, with or without UN authorization, China will not risk its ties to the United States and other Western countries for Iran's sake.

China has also been unwilling to help Iran achieve lesser goals, such as gaining full membership of the Shanghai Cooperation Organization.

In short, as far as China is concerned, the results of Iran's efforts to mitigate Western pressures by pursuing an eastward strategy have been mixed.

Table 6.5   China's Arms Exports to Iran

Year	Amount in $ Millions
2000	59
2001	83
2002	111
2003	84
2004	86
2005	59
2006	73
2007	73
2008	73
Total	701

Source: SIPRI at: http://www.sipri.org/contents/armstrad/
output_types_TIV.html

POST-SOVIET DEVELOPMENTS: INDIA

During the 1990s and the 2000s, the worsening of Iranian-Pakistani relations, the disappointing results of Iran's policy of opening to the West, and India's economic progress enhanced Iran's interest in India as a potential regional partner. Meanwhile, the systemic consequences of the USSR's demise created new challenges and opportunities for India, as did India's economic transformation.

The USSR's collapse eliminated an important pillar of Indian foreign policy, namely close relations with the Soviet Union, especially in terms of arms supplies, and it undermined the rationale behind India's Soviet-leaning nonaligned posture.

Meanwhile, India's economic progress and its ambitions to become a global player necessitated a new direction for its foreign policy and set off a debate on how best to proceed. One issue was whether India should join a potential alliance, which would include China and Russia and possibly Iran, to challenge U.S. global hegemony, as the proponents of a multipolar order wished to do.

Some analysts believed that India should continue its close ties with Russia and join those wanting to create a multipolar order. Others, such as Satish Kumar, argued that India's new economic realities and aspirations, plus growing convergence of interests between the United States and India in Central, South, and Southeast Asia, required India to forge closer ties and even a strategic alliance with the United States.[32]

As in the case with China, because of economic factors, especially the desire to become integrated into the globalized world, India chose to pursue its national interests rather than become entangled in any global competition with the United States. This policy resulted in increasingly close U.S.-Indian relations, including in the military and nuclear areas, culminating in the strategic agreement signed by India and the United

States during Secretary of State Hillary Clinton's visit to India in July 2009, according to which the United States will provide India with sophisticated weapons.[33]

Meanwhile, India has maintained its good relations with Russia, including in terms of arms supply. India has joined Russia and Iran in the project of building a North-South transportation and trade corridor. The agreement, which was signed in St. Petersburg in 2001, aims to link the Indian Ocean to the Caspian region via Iran and from there through Russia to other North European countries.[34]

Other factors, notably India's growing energy requirements, its need for access to Central Asia, and developments in Afghanistan, especially Pakistan's support for the Taliban while Iran and India supported the Northern Alliance, have brought India and Iran closer together. Iran's nonideological approach toward India and its downplaying of the Islamic factor have further contributed to their rapprochement. Iran has kept out of Hindu-Muslim disputes and, as told to the author by an Indian diplomat, has even occasionally been helpful to India in Muslim-related issues. Furthermore, Iran has not imposed any prior conditions on improved relations with India and has ignored India's close relations with Israel. Finally, establishing good relations with India has had the support of all factions of the regime.

These factors have resulted in a gradual but steady improvement and expansion in Indo-Iranian relations in the post-Soviet era. The first manifestations of this positive trend were the visit of Indian prime minister Narasimha Rao to Tehran in September 1992 and the return visit of Iranian president Hashemi Rafsanjani to India in April 1995.

The coming to power of the reformist Muhammad Khatami created a better atmosphere for Indo-Iranian cooperation. This new era of expanding relations was heralded by the visit of the Indian prime minister Atal Behari Vajpayee to Tehran in April 2001, during which the two sides signed the Tehran Declaration, setting out the framework for future expansion of Indo-Iranian relations. In the declaration, the two countries announced their determination to "launch a new phase" in constructive and mutually beneficial cooperation, covering, in particular, the areas of energy, transport, industry, agriculture, and services. They reaffirmed their commitment to strengthen transport and transit cooperation, the active promotion of scientific and technological cooperation, including among other things, joint research projects, short and long training courses, and the exchange of related information on a regular basis. Furthermore, the declaration stressed the importance of developing a comprehensive convention against international terrorism at the United Nations, a plan that India had proposed.

This declaration was followed by the New Delhi Declaration, signed during the visit of Muhammad Khatami to India in January 2002. As a sign of the growing importance of Indo-Iranian relations, Khatami was invited as a guest at the Independence Day celebrations of India, an honor bestowed on few visitors.

The New Delhi Declaration went one step further than the Tehran Declaration toward a strategic partnership. The details of this partnership were laid out in the Road Map to Strategic Cooperation. Among various other agreements signed during this trip was one on cooperation in defense, including the training of Iranian military personnel by India and the exchange of visits between the two countries' militaries.

However, since then various factors have caused Indo—Iranian relations to stagnate. Meanwhile India has tried to consolidate its energy and other relations with the Persian Gulf Arab states, as demonstrated by prime minister Manmohan Singh's visit on November 10, 2008, to Oman and Qatar.[35] Earlier, in April 2008, India's minister for external affairs, Pranab Mukherjee, had visited Saudi Arabia. The visit to Qatar was particularly significant because of Qatar's large gas deposits. Iran's omission from Singh's Persian Gulf itinerary was viewed by the Iranian government as a snub and resented.

This is why, according to a report of a roundtable discussion on "Engaging Iran: Opportunities and Challenges for India" organized by India's Institute for Defence Studies and Analysis, the Iranian participants characterized Indo-Iranian elations only as good and not "excellent," complained that many of the agreements, especially in defense cooperation, have not been implemented, and said that India should clarify its stand on Iran. They also expressed unhappiness that the Indian prime minister had ignored Iran during his visit to the Persian Gulf.[36]

According to statistics available from international sources the volume of Iran-India trade still is not very high. However, Iranian sources put the volume quite high. According to the official Iranian news agency, bilateral trade between the two countries had reached $13 billion in 2008, from $6.1 billion in 2005–2006. However, if trade through third parties—mainly the UAE—is taken into account the volume of trade is $30 billion. Iran wants that trade to be conducted without intermediaries, and Indian officials and businessmen have expressed interest in creating an India trade hub in Iran.[37] Thus far there has been no substantial Indian investment in Iran. However, reportedly India's Oil and Natural Gas Corporation (ONGC), the Indian Oil Company (IOC), and the Oil India Trade Limited are negotiating a $3.5 billion deal to develop the Fars block oil field. ONGC is also in talks for a role in the Azadegan oil field and to develop Caspian oil.[38] In addition, Iran and India signed an agreement according to which India will build a 6,000-megawatt gas-fueled power plant in Iran plus a 1,500-kilometer transmission line to export the electricity to India (see table 6.6).[39]

THE TORTURED STORY OF THE PEACE PIPELINE

A major reason for India's interest in Iran has been its growing energy needs. One project, in particular, has held special interest for India—namely, to build a pipeline to bring Iranian LNG to India. The idea of such a project dates from 1989. Reportedly, it was developed by Dr. Rajandra K. Pachauri and Ali Shams Ardakani, a former deputy foreign minister of Iran, and was proposed to the Iranian and Indian governments. Initially, the Australian energy company BHP was interested in building a pipeline and different options, including an undersea pipeline, were envisaged. U.S. opposition scared off BHP and tense Indo-Pakistan ties made an overland pipeline a risky proposition.[40] However, by the late 1990s, Pakistan's own rising energy needs had made such a project attractive to it, and Pakistan indicated that it would be interested in such a project even if India decided not to join.

The warming Indo-Iranian ties revived the pipeline project. However, two factors—namely, dispute over the price of Iranian gas and, more important, U.S. opposition—have so far prevented its construction. In the last two years, growing instability in regions bordering Iran and Pakistan has increased the risks of such a project.

U.S. opposition to the pipeline has been in line with its overall policy of squeezing Iran economically and preventing the building of pipelines either *through* Iran or *from* Iran. In order to prevent India from going through with this project, the United States proposed the sale of nuclear reactors to India to meet its energy needs, despite anxieties expressed by some members of the U.S. Congress regarding the negative impact of such a deal on the nuclear nonproliferation regime.[41]

Following the brief visit of Ahmadinejad to India in 2008, it seemed that the agreement might be finalized and the pipeline become a reality. However, by spring 2010 it seemed that India would not join the pipeline. It has always been quite unlikely that the pipeline would become a reality without U.S. acquiescence. Indeed, some Indian commentators have maintained that knowing Washington's near obsession with Iran, it was unrealistic of India to think that it could develop a strategic relationship with the United States while cozying up to Tehran.[42]

In addition to the United States, Israel, which has close ties to India, has been opposed to closer Indo-Iranian relations, including the pipeline project. It is even conceivable that Israel has influenced the U.S. approach to the pipeline.[43]

IRAN'S NUCLEAR PROGRAM:
IMPACT ON INDO-IRANIAN TIES

Iran's determination to pursue its uranium enrichment program, despite strong U.S. and European opposition and serious misgivings on the part of many other countries, including Iran's neighbors, has acted as another obstacle to the realization of the ambitious goals set in the Tehran and New Delhi Declarations.

India did not sign the NPT and developed nuclear weapons. But it now opposes other countries, Iran included, acquiring nuclear technology even for peaceful purposes. This is quite natural on India's part. India wants to limit the membership of the exclusive nuclear club. Moreover, regarding Iran's specific case, India, as an aspiring global power and an actual Indian Ocean power, does not want Iran to emerge as a strong regional power.[44]

India has had to admit that, according to Article 4 of the NPT, Iran has the right to develop nuclear energy for civilian purposes, and it has supported Iran's right to do so. However, because of the above-noted considerations, but mostly because of U.S. opposition, during a crucial meeting of the IAEA in September 2006 India voted in favor of sending Iran's nuclear dossier to the UN Security Council. Iran felt betrayed by India's decision, leading its nuclear negotiator, Ali Larijani, to express surprise at India's behavior, saying "India is Iran's friend." India's opposition parties also claimed that India had succumbed to U.S. "coercion."[45]

However, because of its weak hand, Iran could do nothing but express hurt at India's behavior, while India played its Iran card to convince the Bush administration to get congressional agreement for the U.S.-India nuclear deal before Bush left office in 2009. The deal went through after the members of the nuclear suppliers group in September 2008 agreed to allow it.

In short, in terms of relations with India, too, Iran's hostile relations with the West and the latter's determination to contain what it sees as Iran's destabilizing and destructive behavior have prevented Iran from leveraging its assets, such as energy resources, considerable markets, and strategic position as the gateway to Central Asia, in its relations with India. Meanwhile, India has used its Iran card to get preferential treatment from the United States and alluring offers from the Gulf Arab states.

RELATIONS WITH OTHER ASIAN COUNTRIES

Notwithstanding its desire to expand its relations with Asian countries, some of Iran's traditional ties in Asia, notably those with Japan, have suffered in the post-Soviet period, thus dealing another blow to Iran's eastward strategy.

JAPAN

The cooling and stagnation of Iranian-Japanese ties have directly resulted from Iran's hostile relations with the United States and the U.S. policy of isolating Iran.[46] U.S. efforts to limit Japan's economic and other engagement with Iran predates the end of the Cold War and the Clinton administration's dual containment policy and sanctions, followed by the Bush administration's policy of regime change in Iran. In the 1980s, U.S. pressure led Japan to stop helping in the building of a major dam on Iran's Karun River, reduced its development assistance, and led it to refrain from making substantial investments in Iran. Even Iranian-Japanese trade has suffered because of U.S. pressures. For instance, the United States has pressured Japan to stop importing pistachios from Iran and instead import California nuts, which are of lower quality.[47]

The case of the Azadeghan oil field best illustrates the essentially political reasons behind the lack of significant Japanese investment in Iran, especially in energy, despite Japan's quest for secure sources of energy.

THE SAGA OF AZADEGHAN OIL FIELD: AN EXAMPLE OF CONFLICTED IRANIAN-JAPANESE RELATIONS

While being responsive to U.S. concerns, throughout the 1990s and the early years of the 2000s, Japan tried to maintain reasonable relations with Iran. For the following reasons, in a pattern similar to those of the European countries' attitudes toward Iran, Japan maintained diplomatic and trade ties with it:

+ Japan's considerable interest in Iran as a key strategic country in the Middle East and a major source of energy.

+ The belief that the Iranian leadership had many moderate or at least pragmatic members who could, in time, bring about a fundamental change in Iran's behavior.

The coming to power of Muhammad Khatami in 1997 and his efforts to mend Iran's international ties, including with the United States, seemed to vindicate Japan's view. As the U.S. stance on Iran somewhat eased during the first years of Khatami's presidency, Iranian-Japanese relations also improved, as reflected in President Khatami's visit to Japan in 2000.[48] During this trip, Khatami and Japan's prime minister, Yoshiro Mori, agreed on plans for the expansion of economic relations. In the context of this agreement, Iran gave Japan preferential rights regarding the development of the Azadeghan oil field, estimated to hold 26 billion barrels of crude oil.

The Japanese Ministry of Trade and Industry (MITI), headed at the time by Takeo Hiranuma, supported the involvement of the Japanese government, and a company was formed (Inpex Holdings) by merging the Inpex Corporation and the Teikoku Oil Company. However, because of a number of problems, including a change in the leadership of MITI, negotiations took a long time. Iran twice extended the deadline for Japan to make a decision on the subject. Finally, with the preferential treatment close to expiring, Japan signed the agreement in 2004 and took a controlling 75 percent interest in the $2 billion project. According to the agreement, by 2006, 300,000 barrels per day, amounting to 6 percent of Japan's oil needs, would have been exported from the field.[49] However, because of U.S. opposition, from the beginning the agreement was ill-fated. Japan did not start work on the project and, finally, it nearly withdrew from it when it reduced its stake from 75 percent to 10 percent.[50]

Despite this disappointment, Iranian authorities have continued to stress their interest in expanded economic ties with Japan. In July 2008, Iran's ambassador to Tokyo, Abbas Araqchi, after noting that "the US administration has created several hindrances in the expansion of economic cooperation between Japan and Iran," said that "the potential for further cooperation between Iran and Japan exists and we hope that our Japanese partners further develop their presence in the Iranian markets."[51]

This statement shows Iran's weak hand in its relations with Japan, and it came after Japan agreed in February 2007 to new UN sanctions on Iran and took measures, including the freezing of the assets of 10 Iranian entities and 12 individuals believed to be involved in Iran's nuclear program. In justifying the measure, Japan's chief cabinet secretary, Yasuhisa Shiozaki, said that "resolute action is needed over the Iran nuclear issue from the viewpoint of maintaining nuclear non-proliferation and in view of the impact on the North Korean nuclear issue and peace in the Middle East."[52]

Table 6.6   Iran-India Trade in 2008 in Million Euros

Iran's Exports	Iran's Imports
760.2	1,798.1

Source: European Commission.

Nevertheless, by early 2010 Iran had embarked on a policy rapprochement with Japan, and Japan seemed willing to explore possibilities for better ties. Several factors contributed to this trend:

1. The new government of Prime Minister Yukio Hatoyama in Japan had indicated that in the future Japan will pursue more independent foreign policy. This meant that Japan may no longer follow the U.S. position on all foreign policy issues. Some commentators have attributed this change in Japanese outlook to both Japan's economic problems and the rise of China, thus creating a feeling among some Japanese commentators and politicians that the 21rst century will be "the age of Asia";[53]
2. The assumption of the directorship of the IAEA by a Japanese national Yukio Amano. Iran might have felt that Japan might exercise a moderating influence on the new director vis-à-vis Iran;
3. The intensification of U.S. efforts to gain consensus on harsher sanctions on Iran.

These factors led to a new activism in Japan-Iran relations. In 2009 the countries celebrated 89 years of diplomatic relations with the participation of the foreign ministers of the two countries in the celebration in Tokyo and in Tehran. Japan's foreign minister visited Iran, the first visit of a Japanese foreign minister to Iran in five years, and the Iranian foreign minister returned the visit.[54] But the most important Iranian visitor to Japan was the speaker of its parliament Ali Larijani. He went to Japan in late February 2010 and spent five days there.[55] While there he met with Japanese politicians, lawmakers, journalists, and academics. He visited Nagasaki, and there both recalled the use nuclear weapons by the U.S. against Japan and spoke against such weapons.[56]

Meanwhile the Japanese prime minister praised Iran's contributions to Japan's economic development and said that Japan was ready to help solve the nuclear problem between Iran and the West.[57]

Iran is clearly of importance to Japan, especially as a source of energy, although reportedly Japan's import of Iranian oil declined in 2009.[58] (See table 6.7.) Japan has not been happy about that its one dominant position in Iran has eroded while that of China has grown strong. Yet as long as tensions between Iran and the West, especially the US continues even an independent minded Japanese government can go very far in relations with Iran. Moreover, the potential return of a more pro-American government in Japan as it has generally been the case again would put improvement

Table 6.7 Iranian-Japanese Trade in 2008 in Million Euros

Iran's Exports	Iran's Imports
11,277.6	1,428.0

Source: European Commission.

of Iran-Japan relations on ice. Therefore, in the future, too, progress in Iran's relations with Japan will depend largely on the state of U.S.-Iran relations, especially whether Iran's nuclear problem is resolved by diplomatic means.

MALAYSIA AND INDONESIA

As two Muslim countries with substantial economic potential Indonesia and Malaysia have been important in Iran's diplomacy, especially in the context of its eastward strategy. However, relations with these two countries, too, have not always been smooth. Certainly, Iran has not received the kind of diplomatic support that it would have wished from fellow Muslim states on its nuclear program. Although both Indonesia and Malaysia have supported Iran's right to the peaceful use of nuclear energy, they have not voted against measures designed to scuttle Iran's program, as illustrated by Indonesia's abstention, instead of opposition, during the 2007 voting in the UN on sanctions on Iran.

Several reasons, some related to the U.S. opposition, and others to Iran's religious character and its particular brand of Islamic ideology, have been responsible for the limited level of economic and political cooperation between Iran and Malaysia and Indonesia. In the last decade or so, the desire not to antagonize the United States for Iran's sake has played a role. For instance, Indonesia's decision to abstain in the UN vote on sanctions on Iran was because of concern over the United States'—and other Western countries'—reactions. Even Malaysia under Muhammad Mahathir, who has been critical of the West, has been careful not to antagonize the West over Iran. This tendency has strengthened under the premiership of Abdullah Ahmad Badawi and his successor. Iran's Shia character, lingering anxiety about Iran's more revolutionary Islamic ideology, and the excessively confrontational tone of its diplomacy have been other culprits.

In Indonesia, the anti-Shia and anti-Iran Wahhabi groups, which have gained considerable influence in the last two decades, accuse the Islamic Republic of spreading Shiism in Southeast Asia. Opposition to Shia infiltration has been even stronger in Malaysia, as has been suspicion of Iran's revolutionary ideology and concern over its possible spread to Malaysia. This was particularly the case during the 1980s, when Malaysia distanced itself from Iran and, according to some sources, "considered banning visits to Iran by Malaysian citizens."[59] In 1996, Malaysia cracked down on the country's indigenous Shia population.

Despite these impediments, Iran has pursued a policy of fostering ties with both countries and has not reacted strongly to some of their policies, such as Malaysia's mistreatment of the Shias or Indonesia's lack of support in the UN.[60] On the contrary, during a visit to Indonesia in 2007, Iran's president, Mahmoud Ahmadinejad, thanked Indonesia for not supporting the UN resolution.[61]

EVOLUTION OF RELATIONS

Iranian efforts to nurture relations with Malaysia and Indonesia started in the early 1990s during the Rafsanjani presidency. The first results of Iran's new policy were the visit of the Malaysian prime minister Muhammad Mahathir to Tehran in April 1994 and Rafsanjani's visit to Malaysia in October 1994. These visits laid the foundation for a new era in the two countries' relations and ushered in a period of expanded economic and other relations. During Rafsanjani's trip, the two sides signed a number of agreements covering areas ranging from trade and technology sharing to housing and agriculture, which led to an increase in the volume of bilateral trade and some Malaysian investment in the development of Iranian oil. Petronas, the Malaysian oil company, acquired a 30 percent stake in Iran's Sirri A and E offshore oil fields, and it was awarded a contract for the 40,000-barrel-per-day Balal field.

The expansion of economic relations was helped by certain affinities in the political philosophy of Iran's more moderate president, Ali Akbar Hashemi Rafsanjani, and Prime Minister Mahathir, who had been a defender of the rights of Muslim and Third World countries. Thus when, in 1996, the U.S. Congress passed the Iran-Libya Sanctions Act (ILSA), Mahathir criticized this U.S. action.

The coming to power of the reformist president, Muhammad Khatami, in 1997, created even more auspicious conditions for the expansion of Iranian-Malaysian relations, by eliminating some of Malaysia's earlier ambivalences regarding more expanded ties with Iran. President Khatami's visit to Malaysia in July 2002 gave a further boost to Iranian-Malaysian.[62] During this visit, the two sides signed several agreements, including one in the field of multimedia creative technology application.[63]

In 2005, Malaysia's new prime minister, Abdullah Ahmad Badawi, visited Iran. During his visit, he addressed the trade exhibition of Malaysia in Isfahan. In his address to the Malaysia-Iran Business Forum, which also met in Isfahan, he expressed satisfaction that the volume of Iranian-Malaysian trade had reached the level of U.S. $604.4 million in 2004, a 41.1 percent increase over the previous year. But he regretted that this still presented a very small fraction of Malaysia's foreign trade.[64]

In March 2006, Iran's new president, Mahmud Ahmadinejad, paid an official visit to Malaysia. As a result of these contacts, Malaysian firms became involved in various activities in Iran. The main Malaysian companies involved in Iran are Petronas, which is engaged in the exploration of oil and gas; the Amona Group in housing; TM International in developing mobile telecommunication in Isfahan; and Malaysian Mining Corporation in oil refineries.[65] Amona Group also signed an agreement with Iran in June 2008, worth U.S. $1.5 billion, to develop the Resalat oil field. In addition, the Malaysian automaker Proton has a partnership with Iran's Zagros Khodro and is engaged in making cars in a factory in the Iranian city of Borujerd.[66] Petronas's most important deal, agreed to in 2004 was a 20 percent stake in the development of the Pars LNG complex, together with the French energy company, Total, worth U.S. $2 billion. However, the agreement became a casualty of U.S. pressures, and Petronas withdrew from the project in October 2008 after Total did so earlier.[67] One reason cited by the Petronas officials was that "given the present geopolitical situation, there will be constraints in the sourcing of equipment that will be required for the project."[68] This, of course, refers to sanctions imposed on Iran by the United States and other Western countries.

However, most of these deals were paid for by Iran and did not involve substantial investment by Malaysia. Iran's most important deal with Malaysia, which involved large-scale investment in the country, was the agreement between NIOC (National Iranian Oil Company) and the SKS group, linked to business magnate Mokhtar Al Bukhary. The deal is to develop the Golshan and Firdows gas fields and to build plants to produce liquefied gas, valued at U.S. $16 billion and signed in December 2006.[69] The deal raised U.S. concerns. However, so far Malaysia has stood firm and has gone as far as saying that it would end negotiation for a free trade agreement with the United States if the latter insisted on Malaysia's cancelling its agreement with Iran.[70]

Iran's relations with Indonesia, too, have suffered from the same factors that have handicapped Iran in its other ties, although relations today are fairly good, albeit rather limited, in both economic and political fields. Generally speaking, despite the fact that most of Indonesia's population is Muslim, forging close relations with other Muslim states has not traditionally been a priority of Indonesia's foreign policy. Rather, its focus has been on the immediate neighborhood. Despite its membership in the OIC, until the early 1990s Indonesia's involvement in the Muslim world had been mostly through the Non-Aligned Movement.[71]

However, by the early 1980s, growing contacts between Indonesia's Muslims and Arab countries, notably Saudi Arabia, had led to the spread of more Orthodox and strict forms of Islam and the rise of political Islam in the country, although Islam's politicization had other roots, too, notably the lower economic conditions of Indonesia's Muslims compared to certain minorities, especially the Chinese.[72]

The Indonesian government under Suharto viewed these developments with alarm. Consequently, the Indonesian authorities had serious misgivings about Iran's new revolutionary regime and the possible impact of its ideology in Indonesia. Therefore, throughout the 1980s, Iran's relations with Indonesia remained limited, and Iran was mainly preoccupied with countering accusations of spreading revolution in Indonesia.[73]

The situation began to change in the early 1990s, as a result of both changes in Iran's diplomacy under the more pragmatic President Rafsanjani and the systemic changes generated by the Soviet collapse. The moderation of Iran's policy under Rafsanjani eliminated some of Indonesia's anxieties about the possible impact of Iran's revolutionary ideology on its own Muslims. Meanwhile, the end of the Soviet Union required that Indonesia in its relations with non-Western countries look for a different paradigm than that of nonalignment, although this concept remained important for Indonesia.

Furthermore, Indonesia's considerable industrial development in the preceding decades also necessitated a search for new export markets, including in the newly independent Muslim republics of the former Soviet Union, thus increasing its interest in more expanded relations with other Muslim states. In this new context, Iran as a large export market and as a gateway to the Middle East and Central Asia became important for Indonesia. As a sign of this newfound interest, President Suharto visited Iran in 1993, the first visit by an Indonesian president to Tehran since the 1979 revolution. His visit was reciprocated by Rafsanjani in 1994. During this visit, a joint commission on economic and trade cooperation was established, which has met regularly since then. Also, Indonesia agreed to sell Iran Super Puma helicopters. These high-level visits were followed by other visits at the ministerial level.[74]

The creation in 1997 of the organization of eight developing countries (D-8) at the initiative of the Turkish prime minister, Necmettin Erbakan, and Indonesia's membership in it both demonstrated Indonesia's continued interest in Muslim countries and provided another venue for cooperation with Iran.

The turmoil that gripped Indonesia in 1998 and led to the fall of the Suharto regime put the implementation of many economic agreements on ice. But Iran tried to remain on friendly terms with Indonesia, despite fundamental differences of outlook on relations with the West and Israel, which became more serious after the coming to power of President Abdurrahman Wahid. Wahid in 1999 stated that Indonesia could establish trade relations with Israel and, indeed, in 2006, the two countries signed their first trade agreement.[75]

Yet during a visit to Jakarta in 2004, Iran's foreign minister, Kamal Kharazi, made clear that Iran had no intention of allowing this difference to affect Iranian-Indonesian bilateral relations. To prove its sincerity, Iran supported Indonesia on the issue of Irian Jaya, or Papua New Guinea, a remnant of the Dutch colonial era.[76]

In February 2003, Indonesian president Megawati Sukarnoputi visited Iran in the context of the summit meeting of the D-8 countries and met with president Khatami and Supreme Leader Khamenei. However, there were no major breakthroughs in the countries' relations or the level of their economic cooperation.[77]

A major boost to relations occurred in May 2006, with the visit of Iran's president Mahmud Ahmadinejad to Jakarta and the return visit of the Indonesian president, Susilo Bambung Yudhoyono, to Iran in March 2008.[78] A major goal of Ahmadinejad's visit was to gain Indonesia's support for its nuclear program. Indonesia expressed support for Iran's right to develop peaceful nuclear energy and offered to mediate between Iran and the Western countries on this matter.[79]

Indonesia, meanwhile, was interested in obtaining Iranian investment in its oil and gas sector, and also investing in Iran's energy programs. This was partly because Indonesia has, since 2005, become a major oil importer.[80] A concrete result of this mutual desire was agreement between the countries for the building of an oil refinery in Indonesia's Banten province, with the participation of the Iranian Oil Refining and Distribution Company (NIORDC), the Indonesian State Oil Company (PERTAMINA), and Petrofield Refining of Malaysia.[81] However, the building of the refinery has reportedly been delayed until 2016. Other areas of cooperation that had been discussed during previous visits were agriculture, education, and nuclear energy for peaceful purposes.[82]

SOUTH KOREA AND THAILAND

Despite ideological differences and different patterns of alliances, Iran has managed to retain reasonable relation with non-Muslim Asian countries, notably Thailand and South Korea. Iran's relations with Thailand have a nearly four-century history, and there is a small Iranian community in Thailand.[83] Throughout the 1980s, Iran remained a major importer of Thai rice. However, with Iran's efforts to become self-sufficient in rice production, limits have been imposed on the import of Thai jasmine rice. Nevertheless, Thailand enjoys a trade surplus with Iran. Thailand is interested in having Iran invest in energy-related projects, notably in the Strategic Energy Land Bridge in its southern region.[84]

There are no major problems between Iran and Thailand, and Iran has taken a cautious approach to the question of Thailand's Muslim population and its grievances. However, the future of relations between the two countries will depend on the restoration of political stability in Thailand and on Iran's financial outlook.

Iran also maintained reasonable relations with South Korea throughout the 1980s, despite ideological differences and Iran's close relations with North Korea. In 1987, there were approximately 2,000 South Korean nationals working in various projects in Iran. Following the end of the war with Iraq and the start of the period of reconstruction, Iran hoped to enlist South Korea in its rebuilding activities. However, for most of the 1990s, Iran's economic relations with South Korea were limited to trade. From 2000 onwards, South Korea began investing in Iran, mostly in the energy sector. A major event in the evolution of Iran–South Korea relations was the visit of the South Korean minister of foreign affairs, Hang Seung Soo, to Tehran in August 2001. During this trip, he met with President Khatami, who said that this trip marked a new chapter in the two countries' relations, and he called for greater South Korean investment in Iran.[85]

Relations, however, hit a snag in 2003 when South Korea supported an IAEA decision to reprimand Iran for not meeting the UN's demands. This prompted Iran's foreign minister, Kamal Kharazi, to say that "the Islamic Republic of Iran will pay attention to balancing economic cooperation with political ties in its relations with other countries."[86] Again, in 2005 relations hit a low point when South Korea voted in the IAEA to refer Iran's nuclear dossier to the United Nations Security Council, leading Iranian authorities to indicate that they might ban the import of South Korean goods.[87] However, efforts by South Korea, along with Iran's economic and investment needs, prevented a rupture in relations.

In February 2005, the head of South Korea's Chamber of Commerce visited Iran to discuss ways to improve trade and investment conditions for Korean businessmen in Iran.[88] In 2007, the two countries signed an agreement, according to which South Korea will invest U.S. $500 million in an LNG project, with gas from the South

Pars (Phase 12),[89] and in 2008 they established a joint investment committee.[90] In October 2009, Iran's Mehr News Agency reported that Iran and South Korea's GS (an energy company) had signed a new agreement for the development of Iran's Pars gas field, worth 1.2 billion euros.[91]

In short, Iran managed to retain its commercial relations with South Korea, but the level of these relations would have been much higher in the absence of political irritants.

Interestingly, Iran's relations with North Korea, which were close in the 1980s, have remained stagnant in the post-Soviet era. This situation reflects Iran's new needs and North Korea's economic shortcomings (see table 6.8).

OTHER ASPECTS OF IRAN'S EASTWARD STRATEGY

In the last decade and especially during the first term of Ahmadinejad's presidency (2005–2009), Iran has tried both to find a presence in existing Asian groupings and to promote various types of intra-Asian cooperation. Consequently, Iran has acquired observer status in SAARC (South Asian Association for Regional Cooperation)[92] and is trying to get the same position in ASEAN (Association of Southeast Asian Nations).[93] Iran has also tried to encourage cooperation among various Asian groupings. In the political area, Iran has been engaged in the Asian Cooperation Dialogue (ACD) established in 2002 by the initiative of the Thai prime minister. The next meeting of the foreign ministers of member countries of ACD will be held in Tehran in 2010. Iran was also instrumental in setting up the Asian Parliamentary Assembly (APA) in 2006. Because of Iran's role, the headquarters of the APA is in Tehran. Reportedly, Iran will further emphasize the Asian dimension of its foreign policy during Ahmadinejad's second term.[94]

ASSESSMENT

Iran's eastward strategy has been only marginally successful in achieving its economic and political goals. Economically, Asian investment in Iran has not been sufficient to compensate for the near stoppage of Western investment, especially in

Table 6.8   Iran's Trade with Other Asian Countries in 2008 in Million Euros

Country	Iran's Exports	Iran's Imports
Indonesia	171,180	521,600
Malaysia	367,400	586,400
South Korea	5,006,500	2,887,400
Thailand	436,300	148,500

Source: European Commission.

the vital oil and gas sectors. Moreover, Iran's political problems with the West have scuttled a number of important investment projects by Asian countries, as illustrated by Japan's withdrawal from the development of the Azadegan field, after the withdrawal of Total and Royal Dutch Shell.

There has been even less success in the political area. None of Iran's principal Asian partners have been willing to support it in its disputes with the West, notably over its controversial nuclear program. On the contrary, some of them, like India, have used the prospect of support for Iran to gain concessions from the West on matters of importance to themselves. Similarly, Iran's regional rivals, notably Saudi Arabia, use Iran's problems with the West and hence hesitations on the part of Asian states vis-à-vis Iran to lure them with better energy and other offers.

The reasons for the failure of the eastward strategy have been a glaring lack of understanding of the dynamics of the international political system and the factors that drive state behavior in a postideological world; an overestimation of Iran's attractions; and the underestimation of the potential of its rivals, notably the Persian Gulf Arab States.

Despite Iran's declared intention to pursue its Asian strategy with greater determination, without changes in other aspects of its foreign policy, the chances of success will remain limited at best.

CHAPTER 7

Iran and Its Neighbors: Pakistan, Afghanistan, and Turkey

The Soviet Union's collapse adversely affected Iran's relations with its neighbors. The reason was that the character of Iran's relations with Turkey and Afghanistan since the 1920s and with Pakistan since its creation in 1947 had been largely determined by the Soviet factor. Broadly speaking, until the USSR's disintegration, common fear of the Soviet Union and the potential consequences of Soviet inroads in any of the three countries had moderated the competitive aspects of their relations and had served as impetus to cooperation.[1] During the 1950s and 1960s, the Soviet threat was the main reason why Iran, Pakistan, and Turkey joined U.S.-sponsored regional security arrangements, notably the Baghdad Pact, later named the Central Treaty Organization.

After the Islamic Revolution and despite ideological and policy differences because of concern over Soviet inroads in Iran, Turkey and Pakistan approached the Islamic regime with caution. Meanwhile, for the first two decades of the Islamic Republic's life relations with Afghanistan were dominated at first by the Soviet-Afghan War and later by the Afghan Civil War.

The Soviet Union's demise removed the fear of its potential inroads among the regional states and produced the following changes in the dynamics of regional relations:

+ It reduced the incentive for Turkey and Pakistan to placate Iran.
+ It intensified the competitive aspects of their relations and added new elements of rivalry, such as competition for influence in the newly independent republics of Central Asia and the Caucasus and competition to become the main export route for these regions' energy exports.
+ It generated anxiety in Pakistan and Turkey about their diminishing value to their Western allies and thus led them to use the West's fear of Iran and their own role as counterweights to Iran to demonstrate their continued value to their allies.[2]

This point is illustrated by a statement made by Pakistani general Naseerullah Baber, who in late 1993 assumed responsibility for Pakistan's Afghan policy and who is believed to have played a pivotal role in the emergence of the Taliban. He said: "I will see to it that Iran is neutralized in Afghanistan." He also indicated that Pakistan would check Iran's influence in Central Asia.[3] Turkey, meanwhile, portrayed its own model of secular government and more progressive Islam as the best barrier to the spread of Iran's Islamic ideology.

Even Afghanistan became embroiled in the energy game, despite the fact that the withdrawal of Soviet troops in 1989 was followed by a fierce civil war. Developments there, especially after the emergence of the Taliban in 1994, created significant security threats for Iran and adversely impacted its relations with Pakistan.

Soviet demise also enabled the Western powers, notably the United States, to pursue a harsher policy toward Iran, which, in turn, emboldened Iran's neighbors, especially Pakistan, to pursue policies detrimental to Iran's interests and security.

RELATIONS WITH PAKISTAN: OUTWARD FRIENDSHIP, SECRET ENMITY?

By the mid-1970s, once-close Pakistani-Iranian relations, because of Pakistan's courting of Arab countries, including such radical states as Gadhafi's Libya, and Iran's friendly overtures to India, had grown cool and tense. This trend continued and intensified after the Islamic Revolution in Iran in 1979 and General Zia ul Haq's takeover of power in Pakistan in 1978 and his policy of Pakistan's Islamization.[4]

Throughout the 1980s and 1990s, the following developments contributed to the shift in Iranian-Pakistani relations from close friendship to thinly disguised hostility:

+ Political and cultural changes in Iran and Pakistan, especially the spread of a more strict, Saudi-inspired version of Sunni Islam in Pakistan.

+ Increasing Arab influence in Pakistan, especially that of Saudi Arabia and the UAE.

+ Growing sectarian tensions in Pakistan between the more strict Sunnis and the Shias.

+ Developments in Afghanistan, notably the Soviet-Afghan and Afghan civil wars, the rise of the anti-Shia and anti-Iran Taliban with Pakistan's help.

+ The intensification of competitive aspects of regional politics following the Soviet collapse.

INTERNAL CHANGES IN IRAN AND PAKISTAN

Iran's and Pakistan's diametrically opposed processes of Islamization and the cultural and political consequences have been a major source of discord in their relations.

Pakistan was created as a home for the Indian subcontinent's Muslims. Yet the vision of Pakistan held by its founder, Muhammad Ali Jinnah, was that of a secular state. Others, however, notably members of the Jama'at-i-Islami, saw Pakistan as an Islamic state ruled by the Sharia.[5]

For the first 25 years of Pakistan's existence, Jinnah's vision largely prevailed, although Islam remained the most important identity and cultural marker in the country. By the late 1960s, Islam became an increasingly important factor in Pakistan's domestic politics and in its foreign policy. Zulfighar Ali Bhutto was the first Pakistani politician consciously to use Islam as an instrument of its domestic and foreign policies.

Domestically, in forming his Pakistan Peoples Party (PPP), he combined Islam and socialism.[6] Bhutto also used the Islamic factor in order to pressure Pakistan's regional foes, like Afghanistan, to expand security and other relations with oil-rich Arab states, notably Saudi Arabia and Libya. In the 1970s, many Pakistani military, including General Zia ul Haq, served as military advisers in the Gulf Arab states, and, in the early 1980s, Pakistani troops were stationed in Saudi Arabia.[7] Saudi Arabia also began encouraging the spread of its version of Islam in Pakistan, especially after the outbreak of the Soviet-Afghan War.[8] Competition with Iran for influence in South Asia, even before the Islamic Revolution, was a major impetus behind Saudi activities in Pakistan.

Pakistan's Islamization under President Zia ul Haq triggered sectarian tensions in the country as Pakistani Shias, in response to Zia's policies, which they saw as discriminatory, organized politically.[9] Iran's Islamic Revolution further contributed to Shia activism in Pakistan. Since then, Pakistan's sectarian tensions have been a major irritant in Iranian-Pakistani relations.

Meanwhile, because Iran's Islamic Revolution was influenced by Shia Islam and radical Third Worldism, Iran's Islamization led the two countries to draw further apart. The shift in Iran's foreign policy away from a pro-Western direction, while Pakistan remained a Western ally, plus growing Saudi-Pakistani relations, also contributed to Iranian-Pakistani estrangement. However, geographical proximity, the lack of any major territorial or ethnic disputes, Pakistan's energy needs, and the existence of pockets of pro-Iran sentiments in Pakistan, coupled with Iran's weak hand in its diplomatic relations across the board, have enabled the two states to avoid outright conflict and to pursue some cooperative policies, thus retaining a facade of friendship.

REGIONALIZATION OF PAKISTAN'S SECTARIAN TENSIONS: IMPACT ON IRANIAN-PAKISTANI RELATIONS

In addition to exacerbating Pakistan's sectarian tensions by emboldening its Shia population, Iran's Islamic Revolution also led to Shia disturbances in the Persian Gulf Arab States and a general deterioration in Iran-Arab relations, resulting in a conscious manipulation of sectarian divisions in Arab-Iranian rivalry. Consequently, Iran courted Arab Shias while Saudi Arabia supported Sunni groups, including some extremists, in their competition for regional influence, including in Pakistan, thus exacerbating sectarian tensions and violence.[10]

Since the 1980s, rising sectarian tensions in Pakistan, growing attacks on the Shias by militant Sunni groups, and the Pakistani government's desultory way of dealing with the perpetrators of anti-Shia violence have posed a serious dilemma for Iran. As the only Shia government, Iran has been expected to speak up in their defense. However, doing so would have made it vulnerable to charges of interference in Pakistan's internal affairs and possibly to retaliatory measures by Pakistan. Iran's other problems—the war with Iraq in the 1980s and problems with the West in the post-Soviet era—further limited its ability to challenge Pakistan on this issue.

Iran's dilemma became more acute when anti-Shia sentiments of Pakistan's Sunni militants became conflated with anti-Iranian sentiments, leading to attacks on Iranian diplomatic and cultural centers and personnel. In 1990, Sadiq Ganji, head of Iran's cultural center in Lahore, was gunned down by members of the Sipah-e-Sahaba. His killers, among them Zakiuddin Zaki, escaped from a prison in Dera Ghazi Khan, allegedly with the connivance of security officials. In January 1996, Agha Rahimi, the head of Iran's cultural center in Multan, and six others were attacked and killed, and in May 1996 the Pakistani police officer who apprehended the killers of Agha Rahimi was killed in Gujranwalla. In September 1996, six Iranian air force cadets were killed in Rawalpindi. In 1997, Iran's cultural centers in Lahore and Multan were burned down.[11] In November 2008, Iran's commercial attaché in Peshawar was abducted.

Over the years, Pakistani authorities have not dealt seriously with the perpetrators of these attacks, thus eliciting Iran's complaints.[12] Pakistan has claimed ignorance of the links and hiding places of those responsible.[13] However, this claim is not credible because, when it has been important, Pakistan has identified and apprehended the perpetrators of other terrorist attacks, such as those in Mumbai in 2008. Pakistani authorities captured one of the masterminds of the attacks.[14]

Nevertheless, Iran has not allowed this Pakistani behavior to cause serious deterioration in bilateral relations and has continued to placate Pakistan. The Iranian media, however, have been critical of Pakistan.

AFGHANISTAN: A SOURCE OF DISCORD IN IRANIAN-PAKISTANI RELATIONS

Since the late 1960s, albeit for different reasons, Afghanistan has loomed large in Iranian-Pakistani relations. Before the revolution, Iran's concern with Afghanistan derived from its preoccupation with the Soviet threat. Iran feared that Afghanistan could turn from being an essentially neutral, though somewhat pro-Soviet, country into a Soviet satellite. Flanked by the USSR in the north and by the pro-Soviet Iraqi Ba'athist government in the west and south, Iran worried that a change in Afghanistan's position vis-à-vis the USSR would complete its encirclement by Russia.

Iran's fears were exacerbated after the 1972 coup in Kabul that ousted King Zahir Shah and created a republic under the leadership of General Daoud Khan, the king's cousin. Throughout the 1970s, Iran attempted to prevent the new regime from falling under Soviet sway by trying to involve Afghanistan in regional cooperative arrangements, such as RCD (Regional Cooperation for Development),[15] offering it financial and other aid, and resolving the dispute over the sharing of the waters of the Hirmand River.[16]

Pakistan's preoccupation with Afghanistan stemmed from the existence of large Pashtun populations in its territory and Afghanistan's irredentist claim to Pakistan's Pashtu-inhabited regions. Pakistan was also concerned about increased Soviet and Indian influence in Afghanistan. To guard against these potential threats, Pakistan has always wanted a government in Afghanistan under Islamabad's influence, and, since the early 1970s it has tried to achieve this goal.

During the pre-Revolution era, Iran and Pakistan shared certain common goals in Afghanistan. But they used totally different cultural paradigms to achieve their goals. The Shah, who also wanted to wean India away from the USSR, used the idea of generating an Aryan renaissance,[17] while Pakistan resorted to Islam in its approach toward Afghanistan.[18] In this policy, Pakistan was supported by Saudi Arabia, which was bent on checking Iran's regional influence. In short, the causes of future Iranian-Pakistani rivalry and indirect conflict in Afghanistan should be traced to the Shah's era.

SOVIET-AFGHAN WAR (1979–1989): IRANIAN PASSIVITY, PAKISTANI ACTIVISM

The Soviet-Afghan War (1979–1989) occurred almost simultaneously with the Iran-Iraq War (1980–1988) and lasted nearly as long. The coincidence of these two conflicts greatly influenced both Iran's and Pakistan's positions in Afghanistan and the character of their bilateral relations in the following two decades.

The Soviet-Afghan War, coming shortly after the Iranian Revolution, which had effectively taken Iran out of the regional equation, enhanced Pakistan's strategic importance to the West as the latter's main regional instrument in countering Soviet aggression and led to growing military, intelligence, and political cooperation between Pakistan and the United States. Saudi Arabia, as the financial backer of the anti-Soviet forces, also acquired a larger profile.

Limited by its ideology and trapped by the war with Iraq, Iran remained largely on the sidelines of the Afghan conflict, while bearing the burden of Afghan refugees. Fear of antagonizing the Soviet Union, which could have led Russia to support Iraq more actively, contributed to Iran's passivity. Iran provided some help to the Shia groups fighting the Soviets, which generated resentment among the Afghan and Pakistani Sunnis, resulting in Iran's losing ground in Afghanistan on the political, religious, and cultural fronts.

SOVIET WITHDRAWAL AND THE AFGHAN CIVIL WAR

In 1988, within the framework of the Geneva Accords, Afghanistan, Pakistan, the USSR, and the United States agreed on the modalities of Soviet withdrawal from

Afghanistan, to be completed by February 15, 1989.[19] The Geneva Accords did not address questions related to the future of the Communist regime headed by Najibullah and his party the Hizb-e-Watan, or on the form of a post-Communist Afghan government. This omission led to infighting among competing Afghan groups with diverging ethnic, sectarian, and ideological affiliations and also to competition among regional actors over Afghanistan's future government and its external orientation—developments which ended in civil war.

The United States, meanwhile, adopted a policy of neglect toward Afghanistan, thus leaving its fate largely in the hands of Pakistan and Saudi Arabia, with devastating consequences for Afghanistan and, as it turned out, for Pakistan and the United States.[20] This outcome was inevitable because Pakistan and Saudi Arabia were interested in advancing their own interests and not those of Afghanistan. As put by one author, "Saudi Arabia was not interested in self-determination for the people of Afghanistan. Riyadh, like Islamabad, believed that a military defeat of the Communist regime in Kabul would facilitate the realization of its objectives in Afghanistan. *Thus from mid-1988 to 1991, Saudi Arabia, like Pakistan, insisted on the military solution to the conflict*" [emphasis added].[21]

Unlike the period of the Soviet-Afghan War, Iran, relieved from the burden of the war with Iraq, became more involved in Afghanistan. Iran's main goal in this period was to prevent the establishment of an anti-Iran government there. Iran's new activism in Afghanistan strained its relations with Pakistan because they backed different Afghan groups.

The Collapse of the USSR, the U.S. Dual Containment Strategy, Competition in Central Asia and the Rise of the Taliban

Post-Soviet developments added new sources of tension to Iranian-Pakistani relations and exacerbated their existing differences. A major new area of rivalry has arisen in Central Asia.

Pakistan lacks significant ethnic, linguistic, and cultural ties to Central Asia and is geographically handicapped in terms of access to the region; hence, as compared to Iran, Pakistan is not a viable export route for Central Asian energy resources. It thus needed to control and pacify Afghanistan and, to achieve this goal, needed to keep Iran out of Afghanistan. Implementation of this Pakistani policy was facilitated by Iran's estrangement from the West, U.S. determination to block Iran's influence in Central Asia (as early as January 1992), and later the Clinton administration's policy of dual containment.[22] Pakistan's main instrument in Afghanistan was the Taliban, in whose creation, training, and expansion it played a central role, with support from Saudi Arabia and the UAE, and with at least U.S. acquiescence.

The rise of the Taliban, with their anti-Shia and anti-Iran tendencies, posed a clear security threat to Iran. Yet until 1996, Iran did not do much to stem the rise of the Taliban or to hold Pakistan responsible for their anti-Iran and anti-Shia actions. It was only after 1996 and the fall of Kabul to the Taliban that Iran finally decided to support more forcefully the anti-Taliban groups in Afghanistan. In this it had the support of India and Russia.

Iran's lack of firm action in face of Pakistan's policies in Afghanistan stemmed from its other security preoccupations, which were largely the by-product of its hostile relations with the West. Iran's inability to counter the activities of the Afghan Taliban and their Pakistani (and Saudi and UAE) sponsors was embarrassingly demonstrated in September 1998 when the Taliban killed Iranian diplomats in Mazar Sharif, despite Pakistan's assurances that it would protect Iran's diplomats.[23] Following these killings, there were calls in Iran for military retaliation against the Taliban. Iran's Supreme Leader put the Iranian military on alert and called on Pakistan to stop supporting the Taliban. However, the government of President Muhammad Khatami, aware of Iran's disadvantageous position, chose to exercise restraint.

In short, developments in Afghanistan and the determination of Pakistan and its allies to dominate Afghanistan further strained already tense Iranian-Pakistani relations.[24]

9/11, War on Terror, Regime Change in Iran, and the Development of New Sources of Tension in Iranian-Pakistani Relations

The Taliban were created as part of a strategy of isolating and containing Iran. They were supposed to be pro-Pakistan, pro-Saudi Arabia and other Gulf Arabs, and pro-United States. These expectations were disappointed when the Taliban associated themselves with the anti-American terrorist organization, Al Qaeda, which in 1998 attacked the American embassies in Kenya and Tanzania and led the United States to change its attitude toward the group. However, it was only after the tragic events of 9/11 that the United States decided to be rid of the Taliban by invading its strongholds in Afghanistan in October 2001.

Because Afghanistan, especially the Taliban, was a major source of tension in Iranian-Pakistani relations, after the Taliban's removal from power Iranian-Pakistani ties should have improved. Indeed, immediately after 9/11, relations seemed to be improving, especially since the Iranian government adopted a constructive and cooperative approach to the establishment of a post-Taliban Afghan government, a role acknowledged even by the United States.[25] In November 2001, Iran's foreign minister, Kamal Kharazi, visited Islamabad and, in a joint press conference with Pakistan's foreign minister, Abdul Sattar, declared that the two countries had decided to collaborate in Afghanistan's stabilization.[26]

However, after putting in place the new Afghan government, the United States adopted a more hostile policy toward Iran, aimed at changing its political system and reducing its influence in Afghanistan, by among other things forcing out pro-Iran Afghan elements from leadership positions.[27] As a result, hopes of better Iranian-Pakistani relations evaporated. Meanwhile, as early as 2002 Pakistan began to pursue its own interests in Afghanistan, again through support for the Taliban which, fairly soon after the U.S. invasion, began gradually to regain their influence. Pakistan's interests in Afghanistan widely diverged from those of the United States and the Afghan government, leading to complaints from Afghan president Hamid Karzai.[28]

When Saddam Hussein's fall did not lead to spontaneous regime change in Iran and U.S. difficulties in Iraq and Afghanistan made the military option against Iran less attractive, America opted for regime change through destabilization and began, among other things, encouraging Iran's ethnic and religious minorities, especially in Kurdistan, Sistan, and Baluchistan, to rebel against Tehran. In this effort, the United States was supported by Saudi Arabia and Pakistan.

Pakistan, through its Inter-Services Intelligence (ISI), and Saudi Arabia, through funding, have been helping the Baluch separatist movement in Iran and its leader, Abdulmalek Rigi. Rigi and his group have committed terrorist acts in Iran and have abducted Iranian military and law-enforcement personnel.[29] A particularly flagrant Rigi-sponsored operation took place on October 18, 2009, in which a number of high-level Revolutionary Guard commanders and ordinary people were killed.[30] Rigi, who directs the Sunni militant group the Jundullah (the Army of God), claims that he is campaigning for the rights of Iran's Sunni population not only in Baluchistan but throughout Iran.[31] Iranian authorities have complained to Pakistan about the lack of adequate cooperation of its security forces but to no avail. However, Iran's response to the October 2009 Jund Ullah attacks and Pakistan's involvement in them was sharper than before. Iranian authorities this time openly accused ISI of being involved in these attacks, and Iran's minister of interior in Pakistan produced evidence of their involvement and demanded that Pakistan hand over the Rigi group, which Iranian officials claim move easily between Iran and Pakistan.[32]

To make Iran's case more strongly, Iran's minister of interior traveled to Islamabad. During this trip, the Pakistani minister of interior promised cooperation with Iran in apprehending the terrorists.[33] The two sides also declared that they would sign a comprehensive security agreement to deal with issues of drug trafficking, terrorism, border security, and exchange of intelligence.[34] Iran's minister of interior also met with Pakistan's president Asif Ali Zardari, and Ahmadinejad phoned Zardari. However, soon after the visit of Iran's minister of interior, Pakistani border officials captured 11 Iranian security personnel whom they claimed to be Revolutionary Guards. Iran denied that they were and said they were border security in pursuit of drug traffickers. Pakistan apologized for their capture and freed them, but the incident demonstrated tensions in relations.[35]

Barring fundamental changes in Iran's relations with the West, it is unlikely that Pakistan will respond positively to Iranian demands, although in his meeting with the Iranian minister of the interior his Pakistani counterpart promised cooperation with Iran in apprehending those responsible for terrorist attacks.[36] Iranian news media also reported that the Rigi group could be transported to other parts of Pakistan or even to Saudi Arabia or the UAE. It is equally unlikely that Iran will be able to take any harsh measures against Pakistan. This prognosis is based on the fact that Pakistan could not have carried out its actions against Iranian personnel if the policy were not backed by the West. The fact that reportedly Pakistan once threatened the United States that it would deliver to Iran the members of the Rigi group, which would have revealed their U.S. links, also indicates such connection. In May 2008, ABC News reported current and former U.S. intelligence officers as saying that "they [U.S. intelligence] frequently meet and advise Jund Ullah leaders . . ."[37]

The late 2009 terrorist attacks risked setting back Iranian-Pakistani relations, which had experienced some improvement at the beginning of 2009 with the visit of the new Pakistani president, Asaf Ali Zardari, to Tehran in March, on the occasion of the meeting of the Economic Cooperation Organization (ECO) heads of states.[38] In May 2009, Iran hosted a trilateral summit with the participation of Zardari and the Afghan president, Hamid Karzai, and Iran and Pakistan also signed a number of agreements, including one providing for the construction of a pipeline to carry Iranian gas to Pakistan.[39]

However, Pakistan took the initiative in trying to stop further deterioration of relations, and in early February 2010 Speaker of Pakistan's National Assembly Fahmida Mirza, who hails from a Shia family in Sind, visited Iran for a five-day visit. During this visit she met with the family of the kidnapped Iranian diplomat.[40]

Then on February 22, 2010, by forcing the airplane carrying him from Dubai to Kyrgyzstan to land in Iranian territory, Iran captured Abdulmalek Rigi, the notorious head of Jundullah responsible for killing at least 140 Iranian nationals, including revolutionary guards, in Sistan and Baluchistan.[41]

Iranian authorities claimed that they had succeeded in his arrest without any help from the intelligence services of other countries, including Pakistan. However, Pakistani press wrote that Pakistan handed both Rigi brothers to Tehran.[42] It seems difficult to believe that Iran could have managed to apprehend Rigi without some help from the Pakistanis. Pakistan might have decided that the risks of overly antagonizing Iran were too high. In fact, Ahmadinejad, during his visit to Kabul on March 10, 2010, admitted that in apprehending Rigi Iran had had help from Afghan and Pakistani intelligence.[43] However, Rigi's arrest does not mean the end of Jundullah. Even if Pakistan ends its support for the movement they can always operate from Afghanistan. In fact, according to Iranian sources, Rigi easily traveled to Afghanistan, including to U.S. military bases there. In spring 2010, Iran announced that its intelligence officers had freed the captured Iranian diplomat, thus indicating the continued trend of intelligence cooperation between Iran and Pakistan.

Yet, despite relative improvement in Iran-Pak relations by early 2010, fundamental causes of strain in their relations persist. Some of these are a by-product of tensions in Iran's relations with the West and the Gulf Arab states, the consequences of U.S. post-9/11 regional policies, and other divergences of interest and rivalries (see table 7.1).

Table 7.1 Iranian-Pakistani Trade in 2008

Iran's Exports	Iran's Imports
269.5	447.2

Source: European Commission.

Conclusions

By the beginning of the 1980s, internal changes in Iran and Pakistan, stemming from the Islamic Revolution and Zia ul Haq's Islamization policies, growing Saudi-Iranian rivalry in parallel with an increasingly close Saudi-Pakistani alliance, the drastic shift in Iran's relations with the West, and the Soviet-Afghan War, had fundamentally changed the dynamics of Iranian-Pakistani relations. The USSR's collapse added new sources of competition to their relations, thus pulling them further apart.

Yet against all odds, Iran has tried to retain the fiction of good neighborly relations and Islamic solidarity with Pakistan and has not retaliated against Pakistan's hostile policies. As with all aspects of its foreign policy, the Iranian attitude toward Pakistan has been a direct result of its hostile relations with the West, which have put it in a disadvantaged situation vis-à-vis all of its neighbors, including Pakistan.

Some Pakistani politicians and intellectuals believe that its policy toward Iran has not been wise. However, as compared to other groups and personalities with close ties to Saudi Arabia and the Gulf Arab states, their influence is limited. Moreover, the Arab countries can help Pakistan more than can Iran. More important, Pakistan needs U.S. military and financial assistance, which has made the state of Iranian-Pakistani relations dependent on the state of U.S.-Iranian relations.

It is unlikely that Iranian-Pakistani relations can again return to the state of close friendship that prevailed in the 1950s and 1960s. However, an improvement in Iran's relations with the West and Iran's international rehabilitation would eliminate some sources of friction in their relations and would encourage Pakistan to change some of its negative policies toward Iran, such as its periodic support for its separatist movements, as it had done in Jundullah's case.

RELATIONS WITH AFGHANISTAN:
A MODEL OF MISMANAGEMENT

Iran has the closest ethnic, linguistic, and cultural links with Afghanistan, and the two countries' ancient and modern histories have been intertwined.[44] However, during the last three decades, the spread of Wahhabism in Afghanistan and, with it, a degree of cultural Arabization, especially among the Pashtuns, have diminished Iranian-Afghan cultural similarities. Yet cultural and historical links, instead of bringing Iran and Afghanistan together, have distanced them by generating resentment on the part of the Afghans and feelings of betrayal on Iran's part. This has been true partly because when Afghanistan emerged as an independent state in the 1920s, in the pattern of many new states it appropriated Iran's history and culture as its own in the construction of its national, historical, and cultural narrative, without acknowledging that both belong to the same Iranian civilization.[45]

The Iranians have resented this Afghan behavior and have protested against it, leading the Afghans to accuse them of cultural arrogance. Such disputes have not determined the state of Iranian-Afghan relations. But they have created among Afghans an underlying sense of mistrust of Iran and the fear of being culturally absorbed by Iran. This mistrust exacerbates other problems between them and impedes cooperation.

Since the 1930s and the signing of the Saadabad agreement, until the rise of the Taliban, Iranian-Afghan relations had been essentially peaceful, although never warm. Before the revolution, the major bone of contention in Iranian-Afghan relations was the sharing of the waters of the Hirmand River and Iran's fears of possible Soviet inroads in Afghanistan. The latter factor was the main reason for the Shah of Iran's efforts to wean Afghanistan away from the USSR during the 1970s.

Throughout the 1980s and during most of the 1990s, Iran's policy toward Afghanistan was passive. In the 1980s, the war with Iraq, plus the constraints imposed by Iran's Islamic ideology, were responsible for this passive policy. The result was that Iran's Afghan policy neither benefited its security interests nor endeared it to the Afghans and other Muslims. For instance, Iran could have sided with the Soviets in exchange for military and other aid in its war with Iraq, or it could have joined the anti-Soviet coalition. By doing neither, it angered the Afghans and other Muslims, lost influence in Afghanistan, and did not get any Soviet support, while bearing the brunt of Afghan refugees, without any outside financial help.

After the Soviet withdrawal and no longer burdened by the Iraq War, Iran tried to remedy past mistakes, gain some say over Afghanistan's future, and thus prevent it from posing a security threat. However, by that time it was too late, and countries like Pakistan and Saudi Arabia would not allow Iran to recoup its losses.

COLLAPSE OF THE USSR, COMPETITION OVER
ENERGY ROUTES, AND THE RISE OF THE TALIBAN

The consequences of the USSR's dismantlement and the U.S. policy of isolating Iran also enhanced the competitive dimensions of Iranian-Afghan relations.

Initially, the Taliban's rise, which challenged the Afghan government's authority, helped improve Iran's relations with the Rabbani administration (1992–1996). However, even the Rabbani government, anxious to gain the West's support, kept its distance from Iran until Kabul's fall to the Taliban in 1996.[46] After the Taliban's capture of Kabul and creation of the Islamic Emirate of Afghanistan, which was promptly recognized by Pakistan, Saudi Arabia and the UAE, Iranian-Afghan relations entered a period of intense hostility, bringing the two countries to the brink of war in 1998, after the Taliban killed Iranian diplomats in Mazar Sharif. War was avoided because Iran was weak, isolated, and wary of Pakistan's nuclear power.

The Taliban's creation was also linked to competition among outside powers and major energy companies over the energy resources of Central Asia and export routes. The Rabbani government had signed an agreement with the Argentinean energy company Bridas for the export of Turkmen gas through Afghanistan. Meanwhile, the U.S. energy company UNOCAL was interested in Turkmen gas and its export through Afghanistan. Consequently, UNOCAL supported the Taliban and played an important role in gaining the U.S. government's support for them.[47] The Taliban were also supposed "to provide security for roads and, potentially, oil and gas pipelines that would link the states of Central Asia to the international markets through Pakistan rather than Iran."[48] To counter the Taliban's influence, Iran joined India and Russia in support of the Northern Alliance and Ahmad Shah Masud, the Tajik commander.

In the 1990s, Iran's Afghan diplomacy suffered from the same lack of understanding of international realities that had stymied other aspects of its foreign policy. Most important, Iran did not understand that regional countries, even if they wanted to, could not deal with Iran against the wishes of Western powers and other key regional states, because Iran could not meet their economic and other needs.

IRAN AND THE POST-TALIBAN AFGHANISTAN

The U.S. invasion of Afghanistan in October 2001, while eliminating the Taliban threat, did not result in a more auspicious security environment for Iran. On the contrary, the introduction of American and NATO military forces into the country posed new security threats to Iran. Meanwhile, the growing profile of Turkey in Afghanistan created new rivals for Iran. Overall, postinvasion developments limited Iran's ability to improve relations with Kabul. Most of these negative consequences could have been avoided if Iran's postinvasion Afghan diplomacy had been more skillful.

IRAN AND THE CREATION OF THE NEW AFGHAN GOVERNMENT: A FOOL'S BARGAIN

By all accounts, Iran was instrumental in the success of the Bonn Conference, which set up the post-Taliban Afghan government. However, in terms of securing Iran's interests in Afghanistan, Iran's postinvasion Afghan policy was an utter failure, as it was unable to get adequate representation for its former Northern Alliance allies in the new government. Iran also failed to obtain any concessions from the United States, such as an end to economic sanctions, in exchange for its cooperation on the Afghan issue.

On the contrary, shortly after the formation of the new government, America hardened its policy toward Iran in Afghanistan and elsewhere. It tried to block Iran's influence in Herat, the Afghan region historically closest to Iran; forced out its pro-Iran governor Ismail Khan; began building military bases near Herat, which potentially could be used for military strikes on Iran; discouraged close Afghan-Iranian economic cooperation, despite the obvious benefits that this would have for Afghanistan; and accused Iran of helping the Taliban and destabilizing Afghanistan.[49]

However, for security and economic reasons, the government of Hamid Karzai wanted to maintain workable relations with Iran. From a security perspective, a hostile Iran could have complicated Afghanistan's efforts to pacify the country, especially since Pakistan and Saudi Arabia supported the Taliban, which, after a period of retreat, resumed their armed challenge to the central government. Economically, Iran could be a valuable partner for Afghanistan, especially by providing it with rail and road access to the sea.

In fact, in the last eight years, Iran has contributed to Afghanistan's rebuilding, especially in regions close to Iran. During the January 2002 Tokyo conference on Afghan reconstruction, Iran pledged $560 million, which, according to the Iranian representative to the United Nations, on a per capita basis was the highest of any donor nation. By November 29, 2005, $180 million of this pledge had been disbursed.[50] In October 2009, Iran's ambassador in Kabul declared that Iran's disbursed aid had reached $350 million.

These funds were spent on road building, including a rail project to link Herat to the Iranian rail network, provision of electricity to Herat, paving of roads in Kabul, and other industrial projects.[51] A major 120 kilometer road linking Dogharun in Iran to Herat, built by Iran at a cost of $60 million, was opened in January 2005. The road is expected to carry half of Afghan import/export trade. President Hamid Karzai, in his first visit to Iran since being elected to the presidency, participated in the opening ceremonies of the road and a power plant.[52] Iran has also offered scholarships for Afghan students in its universities.

Iran's assistance was essentially motivated by its own security interests. Herat, for instance, is only 65 miles from Mashhad, the capital of Iran's Khorasan Province. Consequently, an unstable Herat would pose a serious security threat for Iran. The upgrading of Afghanistan's road system and linking it to Iran's also serves Iran's interest of becoming a major transportation hub linking China and Central Asia to Europe. Self-interested or not, Iran's Afghan policy has been constructive and has been viewed as such by the government of President Hamid Karzai. After George W. Bush blamed Iran for Afghanistan's instability, Hamid Karzai, in an interview with CNN during his visit to Washington in August 2007, characterized Iran as a "helper and a solution."[53]

Given their significant interests in good neighborly relations, Iranian and Afghan leaders have made official visits to each other's capitals. In November 2001, Hamid Karzai, who at the time was head of the Afghan interim government, visited Iran, and in August 2002, Iran's Muhammad Khatami visited Kabul. During this trip, Khatami denied any Iranian intention to interfere in Afghanistan's affairs because, he said, the Afghans would not tolerate interference.[54] This was followed by the visit of Iran's next president, the controversial Mahmud Ahmadinejad, to Afghanistan in August 2007.[55] In addition, the two countries' foreign ministers and other high officials have kept in regular contact. By early 2010, with mounting casualties, some Western countries—notably Britain—put increased pressure on the Afghan government to negotiate with the Taliban.[56] Meanwhile the United States, notably Secretary of Defense Robert Gates, again accused Iran of helping the Taliban and playing a "double game" in Afghanistan.[57] Ahmadinejad responded by accusing the United States of fighting the terrorists that it had helped create, referring to the alleged U.S. role in the creation of the Taliban.[58]

These developments, especially the prospect of a return of the Taliban to power in Afghanistan—if not through military victory then through negotiations—alarmed Iran and led to Ahmadinejad's trip to Kabul on March 10, 2010, during which he met officials in the executive, legislative, and judiciary branches.[59]

Reportedly, the trip was initially scheduled for March 8, but because of overlap with Secretary Gates's trip, it was delayed. There was even speculation that the trip might be cancelled, however, the Afghan government did not want to overly antagonize Iran. Moreover, Karzai, whose relations with the U.S. had become tense, used relations with Iran and China as levers in ties with America.

AFGHAN REFUGEES: A SOURCE OF TENSION AND RESENTMENT

A major source of tension in Iranian-Afghan relations has been Iran's efforts to expel the illegal Afghan refugees from Iran and to encourage the repatriation of those residing legally in the country. This policy was necessitated by Iran's own problems of unemployment and security concerns and the financial burden of the refugees. In the wake of Iran's decision in 2007 to expel Afghan refugees, its minister of the interior said that the "world community must be sensitive to this issue [Afghan refugees]. Many abnormalities have been imposed on us: production of narcotics has increased three to four times; insecurity, terror and trouble making are among the things imposed on us."[60] Moreover, according to Iranian officials, Iran does not feel responsible for new refugees who entered Iran following the U.S. invasion of Afghanistan, as illustrated by the following statement by its minister of interior: "During the internal war in Afghanistan a large group of Afghans stayed in Iran for a long period. But there is no reason why we should tolerate a large number of refugees who have entered Iran in the past 2 or 3 years . . . *Why should a group of people (the U.S. and NATO) come from the other side of the world to Afghanistan and Iranians pay the price?"* [emphasis added].[61]

Therefore, Iran's desire to encourage the return of the refugees to Afghanistan is quite understandable. Nevertheless, Iran's decision to expel unregistered illegal Afghan refugees in 2007 created serious tensions in its relations with the Afghan government. It also led to official and popular protests against its decision.[62]

Meanwhile, Western analysts interpreted Iran's action as retaliation against Western accusations of Iranian assistance to the Taliban and as a demonstration of the potential problems that Iran can create for Afghanistan if pressured too much.[63]

Clearly, Iran has legitimate motives to want the return of Afghan refugees to their lands. But it also uses the periodic expulsion of refugees to show Afghanistan that it cannot take Iran's friendship for granted. However, this strategy risks generating ill will toward Iran among the Afghans, thus undoing its efforts to portray itself as a good partner for Afghanistan.

However, Iran did not aggressively implement this policy, and more than two million Afghan refugees are still in Iran and, according to some sources, the value of their annual remittances to family members still in Afghanistan is around $2.5 billion or the equivalent of Afghanistan's entire annual budget.[64]

There are no official figures for Iranian-Afghanistan trade. But Iran's ambassador in Kabul in October 2009 stated that commercial exchanges between the two countries in 2009 had amounted to $600 million.

Conclusion

The Islamic Republic's handling of relations with Afghanistan in the last three decades, and especially in the post-Soviet era, has been very inept. Even under the best conditions, because of cultural rivalries and sectarian differences, Iran's relations with Afghanistan would not be very easy. Developments in the last three decades, especially the cultural changes produced in Afghanistan by the spread of Wahhabism, have created new difficulties. However, Iran could have minimized the negative effects of these factors if its overall foreign policy was more realistic and determined by its national interests.

In Afghanistan's case, too, most damaging has been Iran's estrangement from the United States and American opposition to the Iranian presence in Afghanistan. Moreover, at times, Iran's policy toward Afghanistan has been careless as when, during Taliban rule, it trusted Pakistan to protect its interests, including the safety of its diplomats in Afghanistan. The same was true of Iran's diplomacy in the immediate postinvasion period.

In the future, the shape of Iran's relations with Afghanistan will depend first and foremost on the unfolding of Afghanistan's internal situation. A resurgence of the Taliban, leading possibly to some form of compromise between the international forces in Afghanistan and the Taliban and hence a government wherein the Taliban hold a significant place, would damage relations with Iran. The failure of the international forces to defeat the Taliban, coupled with popular disenchantment with the Karzai government, and the disputed nature of the 2009 Afghan presidential elections, and the growing desire of some of America's European partners, notably the Netherlands and Britain, to end military operations in Afghanistan, makes this scenario quite plausible. Even if this were not to happen, so long as Iran's relations with the West are strained, even under the most favorable of circumstances its efforts to woo Afghanistan will be at best only partially successful.

RELATIONS WITH TURKEY: BETWEEN COMPETITION AND COOPERATION

Since the creation of modern Turkey and after the resolution of border disputes between the two countries in 1932, Turkish-Iranian relations have been essentially peaceful, without ever being warm. This was true even when both countries faced the threat of Soviet expansionism and were members of Western-sponsored regional security pacts.

A number of ethnic, religious, and cultural factors, some rooted in history, have been responsible for this lack of true warmth in Turkish-Iranian relations. Recurring Turko-Mongol invasions of Iran beginning in the ninth century c.e. were economically and culturally devastating to Iran and have left bitter memory with many Iranians. Turkic invasions also changed Iran's ethnic balance and its linguistic equilibrium, further eroding its national identity and cohesion, which had already been undermined by the Arab invasion. These invasions also created ethnic and linguistic cleavages in Iran, with significant political and security ramifications.[65] Since the late 19th century, because of the rise of ethnic nationalism and transnationalism, such as Pan-Arabism and Pan-Turkism, security threats to Iran deriving from ethnolinguistic cleavages have increased. At times, Iran's neighbors have manipulated its ethnolinguistic divisions either to undermine its territorial integrity or to pressure it.

This phenomenon has affected Iran's relations with Turkey since the Ottoman era.[66] After the Soviet collapse, this factor again became important, as a number of Turkish intellectuals and politicians searching for a new paradigm for Turkish foreign policy resurrected pan-Turkist ideas and used them to advance Turkey's goals in Central Asia and the Caucasus. The influence of pan-Turkist ideas in Turkey's policy toward Iran has historically been reflected in its wooing of Iran's Turkic-speaking populations and personalities, albeit with varying degrees of intensity.[67]

In the past, religious differences have also affected Iran's relations with Turkey, but in modern times their influence has vastly diminished, although they still constitute a source of misgiving on Turkey's part toward Iran.

However, ethnic and sectarian differences have never been insurmountable barriers to good Turkish-Iranian relations when other factors, such as a common security threat, have favored cooperation, as was the case during the Cold War; or a common outlook, as was the case during the Atatürk's rule in Turkey and Reza Shah Pahlavi's rule in Iran. Even during the first decade of the Islamic Revolution and, despite their ideological differences, the threat of Soviet inroads in Iran prompted Turkey to maintain reasonable ties with Iran, as illustrated by the following remark by a Turkish scholar that Turkey's efforts to maintain a workable relationship with the Islamic Republic was "a deliberate attempt to prevent Tehran from falling into the Soviet sphere of influence."[68] This policy was sanctioned by the United States for the same reason.[69]

Despite its occasional support for Iranian separatists, Turkey's policy during the 1980s was also motivated by its fear of Iran's fragmentation along ethnic lines, which could potentially have endangered Turkey's own territorial integrity. Turkey has been particularly concerned about its Kurdish population's separatist tendencies, hence its concern that "the failure of the revolution and the subsequent fragmentation of Iran would lead to the creation of a Kurdish state."[70] Meanwhile, during the 1980s Iran's approach toward Turkey was determined largely by its need for economic and trade partners, leading it to be pragmatic in its relations with Turkey.

TURKISH POLITICAL GROUPS AND TURKISH-IRANIAN RELATIONS

From the early 1930s until the Islamic Revolution, Iran and Turkey both shared a secular outlook and a similar worldview, which accounted for their basically friendly relations. The Islamic Revolution changed this situation and, since then, Turkish-Iranian relations have been affected by the character of the Turkish leadership, because different Turkish political groups have had diverging views on Iran, including its potential ideological threat to Turkey.

For different reasons, two groups in Turkey have a hostile view of Iran: (1) the military establishment and the ultra-Kemalist elite; and (2) the ultranationalists with pan-Turkist aspirations, exemplified by groups such as the Grey Wolves (Bozkurt). By contrast, the more moderate Kemalist and the Islamically oriented groups have a more nuanced view of Iran, including a less alarmist perception of its ideological threat, and they favor a balanced and realistic approach to relations with Iran.

For most of the 1980s, Turgut Özal, a pragmatic politician with Islamic leanings, was Turkey's prime minister. This factor greatly contributed to the maintenance of reasonable relations between Turkey and Iran, largely because, unlike the generals, Özal did not see Iran's Islamic ideology as an immediate threat to Turkey.[71] Turkish pragmatists were helped in their efforts to maintain workable relations with Iran by the fact that Iran, too, played down the ideological factor in its relations with Turkey. This Iranian policy was essentially a function of its war with Iraq, plus the fact that, in terms of the export of Islamic ideology, Turkey was never Iran's main target.[72] Iranian-Turkish ideological competition was essentially limited to articles written in the two countries' newspaper critical, respectively, of Atatürk, whom the Islamic regime viewed as anti-Islamic, and Ayatullah Khomeini.

In the post-Soviet era, too, the evolution of Turkey's political scene and the shifting fortunes of its different political groups have affected Turkish-Iranian relations. Particularly important has been the rise of a new economic and political Islamic elite, which has challenged the exclusive hold of the Kemalist elite on power, thus leading to growing secular-Islamist tensions in Turkey during the 1990s, including the assassination of some prominent secular figures, notably the author Ugur Mumcu.

Rising secular-Islamist tensions in Turkey adversely affected Turkish-Iranian relations, as Turkish secularists blamed Iran for this development and acts that grew from it, such as Mumcu's killing. Turks demonstrated against his killing and chanted slogans like: "Turkey will not be Iran" and "Mullahs out."[73] However, the Turkish government was careful not to point fingers at Iran, and the Turkish president Suleiman Demirel said that "we must be careful and have very accurate information before attributing any blame to Iran as a state."[74] The Iranian government denied involvement, and there was no evidence to prove otherwise. However, this was a time when other assassinations, in which elements of the Iranian government were implicated, had taken place in Europe, and thus accusations by MEK members in Turkey that Iran had been behind Mumcu's assassination were given some credit.

Other Islam-related issues that caused tensions in Iran's relations with Turkey were the following:

A. The crisis over the Sincan Affair of 1997. The crisis emerged when the town of Sincan, on the weekend of January 31–February 2, staged a "Jerusalem Memorial Night," similar to the Quds Day activities that were initiated by Iran. The organizers invited Iran's ambassador to Turkey and the Palestinian representative to the event. Reportedly, Iran's ambassador told the crowds not to be afraid of being called radicals. The secular leaders and the Turkish military considered the event to be a direct attack on Turkey's secular foundations and sent 50 tanks to the town. Some opposition leaders like Mesut Yilmaz called Iran's ambassador a terrorist, and eventually the ambassador and the head of Iran's consulate in Istanbul were expelled from Turkey.[75]

At the time of the Sincan affair, Necmettin Erbakan, the leader of the Islamic party Refah (Welfare), was prime minister and had, since coming to power in 1995, tried to expand Turkey's relations with Muslim countries, including Iran. The Sincan affair eventually caused his removal from power.

  B.   Merve Kavakci Affair. The crisis occurred in May 1998 when Merve Kavakci, a woman who was elected to parliament, insisted on wearing the Islamic headdress. Eventually she was barred from parliament and was stripped of her Turkish citizenship because she was born in the United States and had dual citizenship. The Turkish prime minister, Bülent Ecevit, accused Iran of spreading Islamism in Turkey, and Iran defended Kavakci's right to wear the headscarf.[76]
  C.   Accusations against Iran for training Islamist militants and being behind assassinations. The Turkish government in January 2000 accused Iran, especially the Quds Brigade of the Revolutionary Guards, of having trained the Hizbullah, an Islamist group in the Kurdish regions of Turkey. The Hizbullah was originally created by the Turkish security and intelligence organizations and, according to some Turkish politicians and journalists, the Turkish Armed Forces, in order to undermine the PKK (the Kurdistan Workers Party). However, when the Turkish police in 1999 began a crack down on Hizbullah hideouts, Turkish politicians accused Iran of having created the Hizbullah and claimed that the Hizbullah members were spies for Iran.[77]

It is conceivable that Iran might have used the Hizbullah once it was created, especially after the Turkish-Israeli strategic agreement. However, it is generally agreed that the Hizbullah's emergence was an outgrowth of Turkey's war with the PKK and that the Turkish military and the Kemalist establishment, embarrassed by charges of having created the group, found Iran an easy scapegoat.

Turkey also accused Iran of having been behind the assassination of the journalist and professor Ahmet Taner Kislali, training Imams for Turkey's Shias, and paying their salaries. Most of these accusations were made by ex-officials, the interior ministry, and the media, while the Turkish Foreign Ministry remained circumspect. Nevertheless, Bülent Ecevit, the prime minister, and Ahmet Necdet Sezer, the president, criticized Iran for having always helped the PKK and exported its revolution to Turkey. However, Ecevit distinguished between the Khatami administration and Iran's military and intelligence agencies. Iran responded by denying these charges, stressing the point that Turkey should not blame the rise of Islamist tendencies in Turkey on Iran, and asserting that such accusations were made on the instigation of Israel and Zionist groups.[78]

Turkey's secular-Islamist divide, coupled with Iran's Islamic revolutionary ideology, has generally had adverse consequences for their bilateral relations. However, during times when Islamically oriented parties have been in power, relations with Iran have tended to improve. This was the case during the brief premiership of Necmettin Erbakan (1995–1997), and relations with the Justice and Development Party (AKP) government, although not always warm, have been better than under previous governments. However, sectarian differences, nationalist tendencies of Turkey's Islamists, and the desire of the mainstream Turkish Islamists, such as those of the AKP, to distance themselves from Iranian-style Islamism have prevented close cooperation between Iran and the Islamically oriented governments of Turkey.[79]

OTHER AREAS OF FRICTION

The following issues have been other sources of tension in Iranian-Turkish relations, albeit to varying degrees at different times:

Presence of Iranian diaspora and opposition in Turkey. During the 1980s, there were at least one million Iranian exiles in Turkey, including some armed opposition groups that counted among their number MEK members and some royalist groups. Even today, there are close to 500,000 Iranians residing in Turkey. This large Iranian diaspora has caused problems in Iranian-Turkish relations. This was particularly the case in the 1980s. After the royalist opposition petered out by the early 1980s and the MEK moved to Iraq, some of these problems disappeared.[80] Furthermore, to deal with these issues, in 1984 the two countries signed a security agreement requiring "each country to prohibit any activity on its territory aimed against the other's security."[81] Iran's concern was its opposition groups, while Turkey was worried about possible Iranian aid to the PKK.

However, the continued presence of Iranian opposition figures in Turkey and Iran's activities to stop them from acting against the Islamic regime, including through assassinations, continued to cause strains in their bilateral relations in the 1990s and beyond. In the last several years, however, this issue has figured less prominently.

Consequences of the Iran-Iraq War. The Iran-Iraq War posed a number of dilemmas for Turkey. On the one hand, Turkey did not want Iran's disintegration, because this would have opened it up to Soviet penetration and could possibly have unleashed Turkey's own centrifugal forces. On the other hand, Turkey did not want an Iranian victory, because that would have changed the balance of power against Turkey. To prevent such an outcome, in case of an Iranian victory Turkey seems to have had plans to occupy Mosul and Kirkuk, with their considerable oil resources. Iran viewed such a possibility with alarm and insisted on maintaining Iraq's territorial integrity.

The Kurdish connection. During the Iran-Iraq War, Iran maintained good relations with Iraq's Kurdish population and their armed groups, while Turkey viewed the activities of Iraqi Kurds with alarm. Consequently, these groups' activities became a problem in Turkish-Iranian relations. For instance, after a group of Iraqi Kurds ambushed some Turkish soldiers in August 1986, the Turkish Air Force bombed Kurdish sites, killing close to 200 people. Iran saw this as a warning to itself that Turkey would not allow Iran to win by pressuring Iraq on its northern flank through the manipulation of Iraq's Kurdish population.

The first Gulf War, Turkey's participation on the side of the anti-Saddam alliance, and the creation of the safe haven for the Kurds in northern Iraq caused new difficulties for Iranian-Turkish relations, especially as they each supported different Kurdish groups: Iran the Patriotic Union of Kurdistan (PUK) under the leadership of Jalal Talebani, and Turkey the Democratic Party of Kurdistan (DPK), under Masud Barzani.

In the 1990s and early 2000s, when hostilities between the PKK and the Turkish military escalated, the Kurdish issue intruded even more in Iranian-Turkish relations, with Turkey accusing Iran of giving sanctuary to PKK fighters and even training them. In July 1999, the Turkish Air Force bombed Iranian territory on the grounds that there were PKK camps there. Iran called this raid an "invasion." Turkey replied that it "reserves the right to retaliate," supposedly for Iran's giving shelter to the PKK, and Ecevit rejected Iran's claims of invasion by saying that "if we wanted to invade Iran we would not do it with two soldiers." Iran saw a more sinister pattern behind this Turkish action, largely because the attack occurred two days after Turkish president Suleiman Demirel's visit to Israel.

Throughout the 1990s, Iran and Turkey signed a number of security agreements to deal with problems, arising from the Kurdish issue. But because of other problems in their bilateral relations these agreements were never fully implemented.

The capture of the PKK leader, Abdullah Öcalan, and the de-escalation of the anti-PKK conflict, followed by the U.S. invasion of Iraq in 2003, dramatically changed the dynamics of the Kurdish issue and the approach of regional countries toward it and hence the impact of the Kurdish factor on Iranian-Turkish ties.

COLLAPSE OF THE USSR: IMPACT ON TURKISH-IRANIAN RELATIONS

As was the case with Iran's relations with Pakistan, the Soviet collapse intensified the competitive dimensions of Turkish-Iranian relations. The end of the Cold War eroded Turkey's strategic value to the West, leading some Western, notably American, politicians to argue that, with the Soviet threat eliminated, the United States should no longer provide economic and military assistance to countries such as Turkey, forcing Turkey, too, to find new ways of making itself valuable to key international players. One way was to portray Turkey as a barrier to the spread of Islamic militancy, political Islam, and Iranian influence, and thus to ask for special treatment by Western powers, including membership in the EU.[82] Like Iran's other neighbors, Turkey largely succeeded in this goal because of Iran's inability to end its estrangement from the West, especially the United States.

The emergence of independent republics in Central Asia and the Caucasus added another zone of competition to Turkish-Iranian relations.

Iran and Turkey as Opposing Models of Development for Central Asia

Even before the Soviet collapse, Mikhail Gorbachev's reforms had led to the emergence of various nationalist and Islamic groups in the Muslim republics of the former Soviet Union.[83] These reforms had also brought down the "Islamic Iron Curtain," leading to increased contacts between Soviet Muslims and their neighbors and other Muslims.[84] The result of these developments was a growing competition among Muslim states, especially Iran and Turkey, for influence in the Soviet Muslim Republics.

Turkey used Turkic solidarity and its position as the only secular democratic Muslim state to become the main actor in the post-Soviet Muslim states. Between 1988 and 1993, the ideas of Pan-Turkism became popular in Turkey as a framework for Turkish policy toward the Muslim Republics of Central Asia, Azerbaijan, and Muslim-inhabited parts of the Russian Federation, as illustrated by the following statements by the Turkish academic, Aydin Yalçin, and Bilal Samir, a member of the Turkish Ministry of Foreign Affairs. According to Professor Yalçin, Pan-Turkism was an ideology whose time had finally come. The collapse of the Soviet Union and the discrediting of Communism had "finally given a public expression and support to pan-Turkism."[85] Bilal Samir, however, did not use the term "Pan-Turkism." Instead, he employed terms such as "Turkic community" or "Turkic commonwealth." According to him, Turkey's efforts to develop ties with the new republics could lead to the emergence of "something similar to the Nordic Council, the Arab League, or the Organization of American States." He added, "What is more natural than Turkey taking the lead in creating such a grouping? . . . This is not pan-Turkism in the wrong meaning, it is not expansionism . . . The Nordics, the Arabs, the Latins and others have such groups. Why should not the Turkish people?"[86] Considering the fact that Iran has a considerable Turkic-speaking population, some of whom have pan-Turkist tendencies, the reemergence of such talk in Turkey did not help bilateral relations with Iran. In fact, as early as 1990 the Republic of Azerbaijan, with a majority Shia population and close links to Iran, became an area of Turkish-Iranian rivalry. Turkey, both directly and through ultranationalist groups such as the Grey Wolves, supported pan-Turkist elements, initially led by Abülfaz Elçibey, who had strong anti-Iran feelings during the 1992 presidential elections. It also undermined Iran's efforts to mediate between Armenia and Azerbaijan in the Nagorno–Karabagh dispute.[87] Turkey also supported separatist elements in the Iranian province of Azerbaijan, further straining relations.[88]

Ultimately, neither Turkey nor Iran could exert a determining influence either on Central Asian countries' domestic developments or on their external behavior. In the meantime, however, this competition adversely affected their bilateral relations.

COMPETITION OVER PIPELINE ROUTES

Iran and Turkey also became competitors as the conduit for the export of Central Asia's energy resources, with Turkey wanting to make its Mediterranean port of Jeyhan a main export hub. From an economic and geographic perspective, Iran, which has common borders with these countries and large export terminals in the Persian Gulf, offered the most logical and economical export route. However, pipeline routes were not merely a question of economics and geography, but of geopolitics. For two reasons, Iran was excluded as a viable export route: first, pipelines through Iran would increase dependence on the volatile Persian Gulf region; second, running the pipelines through Iran would enhance its strategic importance and benefit it economically at a time when the West was trying to isolate it in the hope of generating political change there.

Despite Iran's efforts and the early preference of the oil companies and the Central Asian states for an Iranian route, ultimately the Turkish alternative was chosen, and Iran, because of its lack of realization of the dimensions of systemic changes and its inability to adjust to them, lost out to Turkey.

TURKEY AS A MIDDLE EAST PLAYER, THE TURKISH-ISRAELI ALLIANCE: IMPACT ON TURKO-IRANIAN RELATIONS

For most of its history, modern Turkey had remained aloof from Middle East politics. However, in the post-Soviet era, as it looked for new justifications for its continued strategic importance, Turkey has sought to market itself as a pillar of security in the Middle East and in the Persian Gulf. Turkey was interested in being included in the various security schemes in the Persian Gulf offered after the first Gulf War.

Iran, which was excluded from all these schemes, did not look favorably at yet another competitor in a region of vital security and economic interest to itself. However, it was Turkey's strategic alliance with Israel that most adversely affected Turkish-Iranian relations. Turkey was the first Muslim state to recognize Israel and always had good relations with the Jewish state. However, it was after the international and regional shifts in the balance of power caused by the Soviet collapse that Turkey felt it to be both necessary and safe to upgrade its relations with Israel to the level of a strategic alliance.

One reason behind Turkey's new policy was to gain the support of the American Israeli lobby, as illustrated by the following article by a former Turkish Ambassador to the United States, Sükrü Elekdag, in the nationalist secularist daily *Miliyat*: "The Israeli lobby in the United States is far superior to all other ethnic lobbies put together. Whenever this lobby has worked for us, Turkey's interests have been perfectly protected against the fools in the United States. The development of relations between Turkey and Israel and the formalization of their *de facto* alliance will place this lobby permanently on our side."[89] This expectation was correct: the pro-Israel groups and personalities promoted Turkey as the West's preferred partner in the post-Soviet space, and Israel and Turkey cooperated in this space, especially in Azerbaijan. Alliance with Israel had other advantages for Turkey, including assistance in the development of its military industries.[90]

Iran was concerned that Israel could spy on it from Turkey and try to penetrate its disgruntled minorities, especially the Kurds. This concern played a role in the cancellation in 2004, under pressure from the Revolutionary Guard and the conservative-dominated parliament, of a contract given to a Turkish-Austrian company, Tepe Afken-Vie (TVA), to manage the newly opened Imam Khomeini Airport, and to Turk Cell to build and distribute mobile phones in Iran. The excuse used for cancelling the Turk Cell agreement was that it also had investments in Israel, and, therefore, their presence could pose security risks to Iran.

Because of this cancellation, President Khatami had to postpone a planned trip to Turkey. This incident also eroded the confidence of Turkish business and government circles in the reliability of deals made with Iran, at a time that Iran needed all the investment it could get.[91] Later in 2008, the Israeli government tried hard to prevent an official visit by Ahmadinejad to Turkey. The trip was not cancelled. But the incident demonstrated the limiting impact of Turkish-Israeli ties on the expansion and improvement of relations with Iran.[92]

Following the U.S. invasions of Iraq and Afghanistan and the worsening of U.S.-Iranian relations, Turkey has expanded its regional role to include South Asia. It has even ventured to mediate between Syria and Israel.[93] By being part of the NATO-led International Security Assistance Force (ISAF) and encouraged by the United States, Turkey has become a player in Afghanistan. For instance, in 2008 Turkey hosted a meeting between the presidents of Pakistan and Afghanistan, while Iran, which has common borders with these countries, closer cultural and linguistic ties, and hosts close to two million Afghan refugees, was excluded from the meeting.[94]

Turkey's newly found activism in the Middle East and South Asia has been attributed both to Turkey's growing despair of full EU membership and the Islamic tendencies of the AKP government.[95] Turkey has called its new foreign policy "all inclusive," based on the principle that Turkey wants to be friends with everyone and have no enemies.[96] Others, including Iranian commentators, have seen a more expansionist design, influenced by the neo-Ottomanist outlook behind Turkey's new foreign policy. The appointment of Ahmet Davutoğlu, who is known for his neo-Ottomanist views, as Turkey's foreign minister has been noted in support of this thesis.[97]

The long-term effects of this shift in Turkish outlook on Iran and Turko-Iranian relations, provided that it continues, cannot be predicted. So far, however, this development has benefited Turkish-Iranian relations. Growing tensions between Turkey and Israel following the Gaza events in 2008–2009 have also benefited relations with Iran.[98]

Nevertheless, unless Iran changes some fundamental aspects of its foreign policy, Turkey's eastward policy will further undermine Iran's regional position, as it has already done to some degree. Turkey cannot be blamed for this situation, since Iran has forfeited its role as an important regional player by refusing to accept new systemic realities.

THE U.S. FACTOR IN IRANIAN-TURKISH RELATIONS

Given close Turkish-American relations over time (despite the downturn that came with the U.S.-led invasion of Iraq in 2003), the U.S. attitude toward Iran has influenced the character of Iranian-Turkish relations. In the 1980s, the United States did not object to reasonable relations between Iran and Turkey because it believed that such relations would prevent Iran from falling under Soviet influence. In the 1990s and the first decade of the 2000s, however, U.S. policy of containing Iran limited the scope of Turkish-Iranian cooperation, including in economic areas, and this emboldened Turkish groups hostile to Iran. Moreover, U.S. support gave Turkey a strong competitive edge against Iran in the Middle East, Central Asia, and Afghanistan.[99]

FACTORS RESPONSIBLE FOR TURKO-IRANIAN ACCOMMODATION

Historically, certain common security and economic interests and geographical realities have mitigated the competitive and conflictual aspects of the Turkish-Iranian relationship and thus have prevented the excessive deterioration of their relations. Prior to the Soviet collapse, the threat of gains by the USSR in Iran moderated Turkey's behavior toward the latter. Since the Soviet collapse, both countries have shared an interest in checking the spread of Kurdish nationalism and preventing the emergence of an independent Kurdish state, although both, at different times, have manipulated each other's Kurdish problem.[100] Iran and Turkey have also had a common interest in maintaining Iraq's territorial integrity, although, in other respects, especially regarding the Shias' role in the Iraqi political structure and power equilibrium, their interests there have diverged.[101]

Economically, since the revolution, and particularly since the imposition of U.S. sanctions in 1994 and 1996, Iran has increasingly needed Turkey as an economic partner. Meanwhile, Turkey's increasing energy needs and its desire to diversify its sources of supply, plus Iran's large market, have made Iran a potentially attractive partner for Turkey. Iran's economic importance for Turkey was enhanced after its early euphoria regarding its prospects in Central Asia was dissipated. Iran's geographical position as gateway to Central and South Asia and even farther east has also made it important to Turkey, which is not territorially linked to these regions.

Consequently, amid tensions, the two states have tried to maintain a workable relationship. In the post-Soviet era, the first breakthrough in Turkish-Iranian relations occurred with the July 1994 visit of Suleiman Demirel, then Turkish prime minister, to Iran and his meeting with his Iranian counterpart, Ali Akbar Hashemi Rafsanjani. During this visit, Rafsanjani assured Demirel that Iran was not supporting the PKK and said that the creation of a Kurdish state was impossible. However, this statement, like other agreements, did not end the two states' use and abuse of the Kurdish problem.

Iranian-Turkish relations experienced a period of relative warmth during Erbakan's presidency. Erbakan had always been a supporter of cooperation among Muslim states, and, during his premiership, he helped create the so-called D-8 countries, with Turkey, Iran, Pakistan, Malaysia, Egypt, Nigeria, Indonesia, and Bangladesh. Erbakan visited Iran in August 1996, despite U.S. opposition, and the two countries signed a $20 billion gas deal.[102] Rafsanjani returned Erbakan's visit in December 1996.[103] However,

Erbakan was soon removed, and Turkish-Iranian relations became tense again. The implementation of the gas deal, which depended on Turkey building its portion of the pipeline, languished, and Turkey looked to energy deals with other countries, including Russia, through the so-called Blue Stream.

The next important visit indicating a certain thaw in Iranian-Turkish relations was the visit of Turkey's ultrasecularist president, Necdet Sezer, to Iran in June 2002. This visit was partly prompted by developments unleashed by 9/11, the U.S. invasion of Afghanistan, and increased talk of a U.S. attack on Iraq.

Regional developments and the coming to power of an Islamically oriented, albeit pragmatic, government in Turkey in 2003, intent on improving Turkey's relations with its neighbors and pursing a more active regional policy, led to an improvement in Iranian-Turkish ties, despite pressures from the United States. Trying to calm anxieties about closer Iranian-Turkish ties during his visit to Tehran in 2004, Prime Minister Recep Tayyip Erdogan said that: "we haven't made any discrimination among Iran, Iraq, Syria, Bulgaria, Greece and Jordan ... Turkey is determined to further improve its relations with neighboring countries and make joint investments with them."[104]

Consequently, there were several high-level visits between officials of the two countries—Erdogan to Tehran in 2004, Khatami to Turkey in 2004, Ahmadinejad to Turkey in 2007, and Turkish foreign minister Ahmet Davutoğlu in 2009—and the two states talked of increasing the level of bilateral trade to $20 billion. However, throughout, Iran has shown more eagerness for better ties, and Turkey retained the initiative in determining the state of Turkish-Iranian relations.

NEW CHALLENGES: IRAN'S NUCLEAR PROGRAM AND RISK OF IRAN-WEST MILITARY CONFRONTATION

Since 2002, Iran's nuclear program, increasing Iran-West tension over this program, and the possibility of a military exchange between Iran and Western states and possibly Israel has become another problem in Turkish-Iranian relations. In particular, it has presented Turkey with a serious dilemma—namely, how far it should go along with the Western policy of pressuring Iran. Clearly, Turkey would not want to see a nuclear Iran because this would undermine Turkey's position in its relations with that country. However, because of geographical proximity, Turkey would be adversely affected by increasing confrontation between Iran and the West, which could lead to armed conflict.

It is difficult to judge what the Turkish position would have been under a staunchly secularist government. However, the attitude of the AK government on this matter has been in line with that of other Third World countries. The Turkish government has supported Iran's right to peaceful nuclear energy, while working for overall nuclear disarmament, especially in the Middle East. Turkey's prime minister, Recep Tayyip Erdogan, has called the West's approach toward Iran's nuclear issue "unfair" and has emphasized that Israel's nuclear weapons never get any mention.[105]

During a landmark visit to Tehran on October 26–28, 2009, Erdogan again emphasized these points. This visit was important on other fronts, as well. Iran hailed it as the beginning of a new Turkish-Iranian partnership.[106] Before Erdogan's trip, Iran's Mohsen Rezaei, secretary of the Expediency Council, had said that Iran and Turkey could perform in the Middle East a role similar to that of Germany and France in Europe. Erdogan seemed to favor Turkish-Iranian cooperation, which could extend to Syria and possibly Iraq. But clearly, Turkey would want to be the senior partner and Iran is in no position to challenge Turkey.

Toward the end of 2009, it appeared that Iran and Turkey had concluded that better political and more extensive economic relations were in their interest. The two sides again signed another agreement on energy cooperation, including a $3.5 billion Turkish investment in Iran's Pars gas field, and the building of a 6,000-megawatt power plant. However, only time will tell whether these agreements are implemented or languish like earlier agreements. The future of Iranian-Turkish relations remains dependent on the continuation of the AK government in power in Turkey. The return of a military-controlled government would inevitably increase tensions in Turkish–Iranian relations. Such a possibility cannot be ruled out, as the discovery of secret coup plans against the AK government illustrates.[107] Equally important would be the degree of U.S. pressure on Turkey to join in anti-Iran sanctions.[108]

CONCLUSION

Compared to Iran's relations with its other neighbors, Turkish-Iranian relations, although at times very tense, have never deteriorated beyond a certain level and have been improving since 2004. This relatively positive score has been partly due to Iran's mostly, although not always, pragmatic approach toward Turkey and its patience in the face of certain Turkish policies, such as support for separatist groups in Iranian Azerbaijan. However, unlike the case of Pakistan and Saudi Arabia, Turkey's support has never included actual arming and inciting to terrorism. In other respects, too, Turkey has shown considerable patience in the face of some Iranian actions and statements, including the denigration of Atatürk, the refusal of Iranian visitors to perform ceremonies at his mausoleum, and Iran's making inflammatory statements regarding aspects of Turkish politics.

If Turkish-Iranian relations have not been more fruitful and if Turkey has taken advantage of Iran in certain respects, such as energy deals, it has largely been because of overall ineptness and naïveté of Iranian diplomacy. These aspects of Iran's foreign policy have also meant that Turkey has held the initiative in deciding the direction of bilateral relations (see table 7.2).

The bulk of Iran's exports are oil and gas.

ASSESSMENT OF IRAN'S POLICY TOWARD ITS NEIGHBORS

Iran's handling of relations with its neighbors has been one of the weakest aspects of its astonishingly inept foreign policy. Iran has pursued a concessionary policy toward

Table 7.2   Turkey-Iran Trade in 2008 in Million Euros

Iran's Exports	Iran's Imports
568.1	1517.4

Source: European Commission.

its neighbors and has closed its eyes to many of their transgressions against it. This has been especially true of Pakistan.

In Afghanistan, Iran's policy has left the field open to its regional competitors and, despite considerable help provided to Afghan refugees and, since 2001, to the Afghan government, it has gained no goodwill and is blamed by many Afghans for interference there. Iran's policy in Afghanistan during the immediate period after the U.S. invasion was remarkably naïve.

Iran's handling of Turkey has been somewhat better, but the positive state of Turkish-Iranian relation as of this writing has had more to do with the foresight of such Turkish politicians as Turgut Özal during the 1980s and Turkey's political shifts and changing foreign policy orientation under the AK party than with any skillful Iranian diplomacy. Here, too, the main culprits have been the ideological basis of Iran's foreign policy and its determination to ignore changing systemic dynamics and insist on self-defeating policies.

CHAPTER 8

Iran, Central Asia, and the Caucasus: Unfulfilled Expectations

The USSR's collapse worsened Iran's strategic predicament and posed a number of new and serious security challenges to it. These new challenges resulted from the creation of six new republics in Iran's proximity, all of which faced serious challenges of nation-and state-building. Moreover, some of them, such as Armenia and Azerbaijan, were involved in territorial conflicts, the consequences of which could affect Iran's security.[1] The following factors further exacerbated Iran's security dilemmas:

+ The overlap between Iran's Turkic-speaking minorities with the populations of two of its new neighbors, Azerbaijan and Turkmenistan, and their potential manipulation by these republics against Iran.
+ Azerbaijan's irredentism toward Iran's northern provinces.
+ The intensification of the competitive dimensions of Iran's relations with Turkey and Pakistan, especially in Central Asia and the Caucasus.

However, the creation of these new republics made it possible for Iran to reconnect with regions with which it has had close ethnic, linguistic, and cultural ties for three millennia, and offered it opportunities for economic cooperation.

IRAN'S ASSETS AND LIABILITIES IN RELATIONS WITH CENTRAL ASIA AND THE CAUCASUS

In its efforts to develop effective, productive, and eventually lucrative relations with Central Asian countries, Iran benefited from certain assets and suffered from some liabilities. Some of Iran's liabilities had ethnic, sectarian, and historic roots, while others derived from the dynamics and characteristics of the international and regional systems, aspects of Iran's overall external behavior, and the character of its political system and ideology.

Iran's Assets

Iran's most significant assets in its relations with the nations of Central Asia and the Caucasus have been

+ its geographical location astride the Persian Gulf/Sea of Oman and the Caspian Sea. This position has made Iran the most efficient bridge between the land-locked Central Asian and South Caucasian states of Armenia and Azerbaijan and the open seas. (The Caspian Sea is a closed sea or, in fact, a very large lake.) Iran is also the best road and rail link between Central Asia and Turkey and from there to Europe;[2]

+ cultural and linguistic ties. Iran has considerable cultural links with Central Asia and the Caucasus, including with its Turkic peoples. Culturally speaking, until the Russian conquest in the 19th century, these people were largely Persianized. The title of an article by Daniel Pipes, "Turkic Peoples and Persian Cultures," accurately reflected this reality.[3] Iran's civilizational influence is strongest in Uzbekistan and in Persian-speaking and ethnically Iranian Tajikistan. However, Iran's cultural influence is present, albeit to a lesser degree, in other republics, as illustrated by the statement of the Kyrgyz president, Askar Akayev, to Iran's foreign minister, Ali Akbar Velayati, that he was proud to have been brought up in a family that was familiar with the works of Firdowsi and Saedi. With Azerbaijan, in addition to strong cultural links, Iran shares the Shia faith;

+ its large market;

+ its potential as a source of energy for energy-poor republics;

+ Iran's ability, albeit limited, to assist in these countries' economic development.

Iran's Liabilities

The following are Iran's most significant liabilities:

A. *Ethnic and Linguistic Differences and the Historic Turko-Persian Rivalry*

Many Turkic-speaking populations of these countries and their leaders, especially those with pan-Turkist leanings, resent their debt to Iranian civilization. They also feel culturally competitive with Iran. These feelings are strongest in Uzbekistan and with its leader, Islam Karimov. This situation is mainly due to the fact that a considerable number of Uzbeks are in fact Turkified Tajiks; the existence of a Tajik minority in such cities as Bukhara and Samarqand; and the existence of latent separatist tendencies among them. During the period of Perestroika and Glasnost, some members of Uzbekistan's Tajik population demanded greater cultural rights, while simultaneously in neighboring Tajikistan there were calls for the joining of Samarqand and Bukhara to Tajikistan.[4] Consequently, the Uzbek government does not want a significant Iranian presence there. Moreover, it has pursued a policy of cultural repression against its Tajik minority, approaching cultural genocide. Another reason is that Uzbeks—and especially Karimov—view themselves as the main power in the region and the inheritor of Teimour's (Tamerlane) empire and hence as the symbol of Turkic unity and splendor. Naturally, such ambitions are not compatible with a resurgence of Tajik-Iranian cultural and political presence in the region.

A similar factor affects Iran's relations with Azerbaijan, where the population is ethnically closer to the Iranians, but the language is Turkic. Moreover, nearly all of Azerbaijan's literary luminaries, such as Nizami, Khaghani, and others, have written their work in Persian on Persian historic and romantic themes. Yet Azerbaijan has a culturally pan-Turkist tendency, illustrated by the banning of the works of the above-mentioned poets in their original Persian. A substantial Iranian presence, therefore, would run counter to this Turko-centric cultural identity-building.

B. *Sectarian Differences*

Most Central Asian Muslims are Sunni, while Iran is a majority Shia country. This religious difference is a liability for Iran and, in some cases, nullifies the positive effects of linguistic and cultural affinities. This sectarian barrier has grown stronger in the last several decades because of the growing influence of Wahhabi and Salafi groups. These groups, unlike the traditionally dominant Hanafi School, which does not have an overly hostile attitude toward the Shias, have viscerally anti-Shia tendencies. Iran as a Shia state is particularly disliked by them.

Logically, the common bond of Shia Islam should bring Iran and the Republic of Azerbaijan closer. Yet in practice, this has been a source of estrangement between them because the secular government of Azerbaijan has been wary of Iran's influence among its Shia population.

C. *Limited Economic, Financial, and Technological Capabilities*

Since their independence, the Central Asian and South Caucasian countries have needed economic, financial, and technological assistance. Consequently, a central goal of their foreign policies has been to gain access to these resources, which has led them to gravitate toward those states that could satisfy their economic and financial needs.

Iran, because of its economic, financial, and technological limitations, coupled with its own developmental needs, has been a less attractive partner for these republics, compared to the Western states, China, Russia, or even Turkey and the Gulf Arab states. Iran's ability to help these countries was further limited because of its own reconstruction needs in the aftermath of its war with Iraq. It is difficult to determine whether the availability of economic assets would have enabled Iran to overcome the impact of its other liabilities, although certainly it would have lessened their negative impact.

D. *Iran's Revolutionary Ideology and Governmental System*

By the time of the Central Asian countries' independence, the most intense period of Iran's revolutionary foreign policy had ended, and under presidents Rafsanjani and Khatami, Iran pursued a less ideologically driven foreign policy, especially in regard to Central Asia and the Caucasus. However, Iranian politics remained ideological and its political leadership and its bureaucracy highly divided because of ideological and other differences. These factors, especially, influenced the rhetoric of Iranian diplomacy, even if not its substance. This contradiction between Iran's rhetoric and policy caused Central Asian states to mistrust Iran and to remain hesitant about establishing closer ties with it. Some of them, especially majority-Shia Azerbaijan, have periodically accused Iran of trying to influence their population.

Systemic Factors

As discussed in chapter 1, the systemic changes triggered by the USSR's collapse adversely affected Iran, largely because they enhanced the position of the Western countries, with which Iran had hostile relations. Because of the hostile nature of Iranian-West relations, the Western countries pursued a policy of preventing Iranian influence in Central Asia and excluding it from any regional economic and political arrangements. They also discouraged regional states from cooperating with Iran. Consequently, even those regional states otherwise well-disposed to cooperation with Iran refrained from doing so beyond a certain level. Some of them even used the so-called Iran card to enhance their own regional position and their value to the West.

Because of these systemic conditions, plus peculiarities of Iran's foreign policy, even its most important asset—namely, its extremely favorable geographic position, worked against it. This was so because these systemic conditions and Iranian failures allowed countries like Russia and Turkey to market themselves as outlets for the Central Asian and Caucasian countries and to limit Iran's presence and influence.[5] Additionally, they made the character and range of Iran's relation with Central Asian and Caucasian countries dependent on the latter's and not Iran's priorities and objectives.

Partly, this situation has been natural because

- the character of interstate relations is the outcome of the interaction among objectives and priorities of different states;
- early expectations of most commentators that Central Asian and Caucasian states would gravitate either toward Iran or Turkey have proven incorrect;
- Central Asian and Caucasian states have acted according to a model common to all small, postcolonial states. This has meant that, instead of allowing a particular country unduly to influence their foreign policy, they have tried to use relations with a wide range of states to maximize their own interests.[6]

Nevertheless, given the disparities in Iran's and these countries' size and resources, Iran should have been able to set the priorities and character of their mutual relations to a greater extent, had it not been for the adverse consequences of aspects of its foreign policy, notably the West's determination to contain its influence in the region and exclude it from major regional schemes.

PRINCIPAL GOALS AND CHARACTERISTICS OF IRAN'S POLICY TOWARD CENTRAL ASIA AND THE CAUCASUS

Even before the USSR's collapse, Iran's policy toward Central Asia and the Caucasus was centered on the following objectives:

+ To guard against negative effects of regional developments on its security.

+ To expand economic ties with these countries as part of its of post-Iraq War economic reconstruction and revitalization. Following the imposition of economic sanction by the United States and its policy of Iran's isolation, relations with these regions acquired more importance.

+ To avoid antagonizing Russia, even when Russia's policy toward Iran was not friendly.

In fact, Iran's policy toward these regions has suffered from excessive Russo-centrism.

PRAGMATISM, REGIONALISM, AND MEDIATION

Iran's policy toward Central Asia and the Caucasus has been nonideological and pragmatic. Even in Tajikistan, when between 1992 and 1997 an Islamic opposition was engaged in a civil war with the secular government, Iran did not provide substantial support to the Islamists. Instead, it tried, with some success, to mediate between them, in order to end the civil war.[7] Iran's mediation efforts in Tajikistan succeeded largely because Russia, too, wanted to end the conflict. Because of the rise of the Taliban, even Uzbekistan, which had contributed to the instigation of the civil war, favored ending it.

However, Iran's efforts in 1992 to mediate in the Karabagh dispute were thwarted because of the manipulation of the conflict by competing political forces in Azerbaijan; and by Turkish and Western obstructionists who did not want Iran to succeed.[8]

The following have been the main reasons for this aspect of Iran's Central Asia policy:

+ The primacy of security and economic goals.

+ Concern about Russian sensitivities.

• The lack of ideological connection with Central Asia's Islamist movements.

 • The lack of Central Asia's symbolic and ideological importance, contrary to the Palestinian issue.

 • Central Asia's lack of importance for the regime's legitimacy and self-image as opposed to the Palestinian issue.

 • The fact that Central Asia's Islamist movements have been more influenced by Arab, Afghan, and Pakistani Islamists.

Iran has also emphasized regional cooperation in its relations with Central Asian countries, both in the context of the Regional Cooperation Organization (ECO) and the Shanghai Cooperation Organization (SCO).[9] Iran has supported the inclusion of the six Muslim majority republics of Central Asia and the Caucasus in ECO. Iran has shown great interest in SCO and has obtained observer status in it, but so far has failed to gain full membership.[10] Iran's interest in SCO partly derives from its desire to encourage the evolution of the international system in a multipolar direction.

FACTORS AFFECTING THE EVOLUTION OF IRANIAN-CENTRAL ASIAN RELATIONS

Iran began to establish cultural and other links with the Central Asian and Caucasian countries, especially Tajikistan and Azerbaijan, during the period of Gorbachev's reforms.[11] Once these republics became independent, Iran swiftly established diplomatic ties, initiated visits to these countries by Iranian officials, and invited Central Asian leaders to visit Iran.

In December 1991, before the official dismantling of the USSR, Iran's foreign minister, Ali Akbar Velayati, visited Central Asia and was well received.[12] In November 1992, Uzbek president Islam Karimov visited Tehran, and in October 1993 President Hashemi Rafsanjani toured the Central Asian countries, except Tajikistan, because of the ongoing civil war, plus Azerbaijan. During Rafsanjani's visit, Iran signed 60 different agreements with these countries. In the following years, regular visits at different levels have continued to take place between Iranian officials and those of Central Asia and the Caucasus. Iran also moved to stabilize its borders with these countries. In Central Asia, Iran has land borders with Turkmenistan and shares the Caspian Sea with Kazakhstan. In the Caucasus, Iran has a long land border with Azerbaijan and a shorter border with Armenia, and it shares the Caspian Sea with Azerbaijan.

Iran's approach toward the issue of regional borders is that of a status quo power. Iran wants to maintain current borders. In the Caspian Sea, Iran favors keeping Soviet-era borders, which are more beneficial to it than what some countries such as Azerbaijan would like to see happen. However, Azerbaijan has an irredentist claim toward Iran's northwestern provinces, where most of the population is Turkic-speaking. Baku republic refers to these provinces as "Southern Azerbaijan," a term popularized by the USSR and its Iranian supporters following the Soviet occupation of Iranian Azerbaijan.[13]

Unlike Azerbaijan, Turkmenistan has, so far, made no territorial claims against Iran. Nor has it made any reference to the existence of ethnic Turkmens in Iran who are concentrated in the Gorgan province, especially in Turkmen Sahra. This attitude is accounted for by the desire of Turkmenistan's authorities, especially its first president, Saparmurat Niyazov, for good relations with Iran. According to the Moscow-based Turkmen political analyst Artem Ulunyan, when there was some talk about Iran's Turkmen minority in Turkmenistan, Niyazov said, "Don't even think about that, don't ask any questions that could be considered as antagonistic in Tehran." He also warned that he would punish those who did so.[14] However, after his death in 2006, and despite the new president's pledge that he would continue his predecessor's policy of neutrality, both internationally and regionally, Turkmenistan has become more Western-oriented. This change in the orientation of Turkmenistan's foreign policy has made relations with Iran more volatile, although the new president, Kurban Kuli Berdimohammadov, has said that he is committed to good relations with Iran. So far, Turkmenistan's new leadership has not made any public references to Iran's treatment of its Turkmen minorities. Nevertheless, some Western sources have speculated that they may do so in the future, especially if other irritants develop in their relations.[15] As a sign of potential ethnic tensions, in June 2009 Iranian media reported that Turkmenistan's ambassador to Iran was summoned to the foreign ministry. The reason was the mistreatment of Iranian citizens by Turkmen customs officers, the confiscation of their property, and even their beating.[16]

Iran also disagrees with Azerbaijan and Kazakhstan over the sharing of Caspian resources. Initially, Russia was in agreement with the Iranian position. However, later it adopted a position close to that of Azerbaijan and Kazakhstan, and signed agreements with them establishing bilateral borders. Only Turkmenistan partly shares Iran's position, although that too might be changing. Broadly speaking, Iran favors either the equal sharing of the Caspian Sea resources or their joint exploitation by all littoral states based on a system of "condominium."[17] Iran has maintained that until a new legal regime is established for the Caspian Sea, Russo/Soviet-Iranian treaties are still valid.

This Iranian position has a solid foundation in international law dealing with the question of succession of states, as embodied in the Vienna Convention on the Succession of States. Moreover, when they became independent, Soviet successor states declared that they would be bound by the Soviet-era treaties.[18] Iran's position would give everyone a 20 percent share of the Caspian. Other littoral states, meanwhile, argue that the Caspian is a sea, and, therefore, the rules of the 1982 Law of the Sea Treaty apply to it. On the basis of this position, Iran would get only a 13 percent share of the Caspian or even less.

Diverging views on the sharing of the Caspian have been a source of tension between Iran on the one hand and Kazakhstan and, more seriously, Azerbaijan on the other. In July 2001, this disagreement resulted in a skirmish between the Iranian navy and an Azerbaijani vessel exploring for oil in a disputed zone.[19]

Officially speaking, Iran does not have any outstanding border problems with the Republic of Azerbaijan, and the Soviet-era borders remain intact. Iran's territorial problems with Azerbaijan derive from the irredentist claims of the Republic of Azerbaijan toward a number of Iranian provinces. In pursuit of these claims, Baku has published maps, which include Iranian provinces as part of the Azerbaijan Republic; campaigns for the rights of the inhabitants of Iranian Azerbaijan; and supports separatist groups, notably the Front for the Liberation of Southern Azerbaijan, also known as the Front for the Awakening of Southern Azerbaijan, led by Mahmud Ali Chehreganli.[20] These activities of the Republic of Azerbaijan have constituted a major irritant in Iranian-Azerbaijani relations.

Iran does not have common borders with other Central Asian countries, nor does it have Uzbek, Kyrgyz, or Kazakh minorities. Therefore, border and minority issues do not constitute a major irritant in their relations.

Even today, however, Iran has a relatively large Armenian minority, estimated around 200,000. However, they are fairly evenly distributed in certain parts of the country, notably Tehran and Isfahan, and are not identified with a particular territory. Therefore, there is no question of an Armenian separatist movement in Iran. Moreover, Armenians, historically, have been better treated in Iran than, say, Turkey. Also, in the post-Soviet era, Iran and Armenia have shared a number of security concerns, including the threat of a potential Turkic coalition. Consequently, both sides have used Iran's Armenian minority to cement bilateral relations, instead of Armenia's using them as a lever of pressure against Iran.

Developing the Transportation Infrastructure and Expanding Trade and Investment

In the last two decades, Iran has tried to develop its transportation networks—both road and rail—and to expand and improve its ports, in order to enhance its attractiveness to Central Asian and Caucasian countries as the best bridge between them and the outside world.

A first step in this direction was the inauguration in May 1996 of the railroad linking Mashhad in northeastern Iran to Sarakhs at the Iran-Turkmenistan border. The ceremony was attended by heads of states and governments of Central Asian and other neighboring countries, including Turkish president Suleiman Demirel. He hailed the event as the coming to life of "a historic legend" referring to the Silk Road.[21] This was followed by the completion of the Bafgh-Mashhad railroad, which effectively links Central Asia to the port of Bandar Abbas in the Persian Gulf. In November 2007, during the summit meeting of the Caspian littoral states, the Turkmen president declared his country's agreement to build 700 kilometers of the 900-kilometer-long railroad, which eventually will link Iran to Kazakhstan via Turkmenistan.[22] The construction of the system was started in 2007 and reportedly some Iranian experts will help in its building.[23] In 2008, Uzbekistan also expressed its readiness to join this project.

Additionally, with India's cooperation, Iran is building a railroad to link its Chahbahar port in the Sea of Oman to Zaranj on the Afghan border. This railroad will enable transit trade between India and Afghanistan through Iran and will offer another outlet to the sea for Afghanistan.[24] Iran has also been upgrading its rail system and building new connections, notably a rail link from Kerman Province to Zahedan, which is linked by rail to Quetta in Pakistan, and a railroad linking Mashhad to Herat in Afghanistan. These networks will eventually link Iran to India, and will also run through Afghanistan to Tajikistan.

Iran has also promoted transportation links within the ECO. In August 2009, the so-called ECO Train linking Islamabad in Pakistan with Istanbul in Turkey via Iran arrived in Tehran. This is a container train and covers a 6,500-kilometer journey.[25] Iran has also been working to connect its rail system to that of Turkey, and in September 2007 they agreed in principle to build a railroad linking Turkey to Iran, most probably from the northern banks of Lake Van.[26]

In the Caucasus, Iran already has a rail link with Azerbaijan, and, as part of the North-South Corridor project, in cooperation with Azerbaijan and Russia, it will build new railroads linking the Iranian cities of Rasht and Qazvin to Astara at the Azerbaijani border. Once completed, this link will connect Iran to the Russian railroad system.[27]

Also in 2008, the Armenian government declared that it had decided to build a rail link to Iran. Iran, meanwhile, agreed to build the section which will connect its northwestern city of Tabriz to the border with Armenia.[28] Russia expressed its support for the project, which, given Moscow's influence in Yerevan, improves the prospects of the successful completion of the project.[29] Meanwhile, Armenia is building a second highway linking itself to Iran.[30]

Assistance to Develop Central Asia's Road, Electricity, and Energy Networks

Iran has been helping some Central Asian countries to develop and/or repair their road networks. Iranian companies have been active in repairing and building a number of roads in Kyrgyzstan, including two phases of the Jalalabad-Azgen road. In Tajikistan, Iran is helping in the construction of the Aznab Hydro Tunnel, as well as the road linking Dushanbe to China. In Turkmenistan, Iran took the responsibility to build the road linking Bajgiran in Iran to Ashgabat in Turkmenistan, plus the Turkmenbashi-Ashgabat road, which is 500 kilometers long.[31]

In Tajikistan, Iran is involved in the building and financing of a number of dams and hydraulic power plants, including the Sangtoudeh and Raqoun power plants. In 2004, during his visit to Tajikistan, Iran's president, Muhammad Khatami, committed Iran to covering half of the $500 million cost of the hydroelectric plant on the Vakhsh River. Additionally, Iranian engineers and companies are engaged in the technical planning and development of the Eini electric power station in Tajikistan and a factory to build low consumption lamps.[32] Iran's private sector has been involved in upgrading the republic's medical infrastructure. It was reported that Iranian doctors have built Central

Asia's best-equipped cardiology hospital in Dushanbe, the Tajik capital. The hospital is staffed with Iranian doctors and nurses.[33]

Iran has been eager to establish energy links with Central Asian and Caucasian countries, as both a reliable energy source and export market, and as the best export route. Iran's aspirations to become a major export route have so far been thwarted largely because of Western opposition. However, Russia, too, has not been eager to see Iran emerge as a rival to itself for the export of Central Asian energy.[34] Nevertheless, Iran has built a pipeline providing gas to Armenia, which became operational in October 2008.[35] It also has swap arrangements with Kazakhstan and Azerbaijan and imports 14 billion cubic meters of natural gas from Turkmenistan through the Korbeje (Turkmenistan) and Kordkuy (Iran) pipeline.

In January 2009, during the official visit of Turkmenistan president Kurban Kuli Berdimohammdov to Iran, it was announced that Iran will invest in the expansion of Turkmenistan's gas fields.[36]

INVESTMENT, AID, AND TRADE

One of Iran's most serious liabilities in dealing with Central Asia and the Caucasus has been its limited financial resources, which have made it very difficult for Iran to provide substantial aid and investment to these countries. Iran has not only lagged behind industrialized countries in this respect, but also Turkey.

In Central Asia, because of ethnic and linguistic affinities, Tajikistan has received the bulk of Iranian aid. This aid, according to Utker Omarev, the World Bank's economic affairs expert in Tajikistan, has helped to stabilize Tajikistan to some degree, especially given that, prior to the U.S. invasion of Afghanistan, Tajikistan was of little interest to the United States and Europe and received little aid.[37]

The volume of trade between Iran and these countries, with the exception of energy with Turkmenistan, which consists mostly of Iran's import of Turkmen gas, has not been substantial (see table 8.1).

ASSESSING THE RESULTS OF IRAN'S POLICY

Despite its basically nonideological, accommodating, and constructive policy toward the countries of Central Asia and the Caucasus, Iran has failed to capitalize on its tremendous geographical and other advantages. More seriously, because of the effects of its broader foreign policy, Iran has made itself vulnerable to manipulation by some of these countries, and in, some cases, to insulting behavior on their part. Furthermore, as noted before, regional countries and not Iran have shaped the nature of bilateral relations.

Thus, the course of Iran's relations with Azerbaijan has been determined by the evolution of that country's domestic and foreign policies. Until the coming to power of the ultranationalist, pan-Turkist and anti-Iranian Abülfaz Elçibey to the presidency in

Table 8.1   Iran's Trade with Central Asia and the Caucasus in 2008 in Million Euros

Country	Exports	Imports
Armenia	124.5	18.8
Azerbaijan	85.2	425.7
Georgia	—	—
Kazakhstan	19.7	1,307.0 (energy and wheat)
Tajikistan	49.5	71.3
Turkmenistan	162.9	1,073.0 (natural gas)
Uzbekistan	—	144.7

Source: European Commission.

Azerbaijan in June 1992, Iran had reasonably good relations with Azerbaijan. However, Elçibey pursued a pro-Turkish, pro-West, pro-Israel, and anti-Iran policy. Azerbaijan also used Iran's problems with the West to enhance its own value to Western countries. Had Iran appreciated the extent of systemic changes triggered by the USSR's collapse and adjusted its foreign policy accordingly, Azerbaijan could not have acquired such a strategic value for the West.

Another important aspect of Azerbaijan's strategy has been the establishment of close formal and informal ties with Israel. Azerbaijan is important for Israel as a source of energy—reportedly Israel gets 30 percent of its oil from Azerbaijan through the Baku-Jeyhan line—and as a listening post on Iran. Meanwhile, Israel uses its influence in the United States in Azerbaijan's favor.[38]

Following the fall of Elçibey in 1993 and the coming to power of Haidar Aliev in 1994, there was an improvement in Iranian-Azerbaijani relations because, initially, Aliev tried to pursue what he called a balanced foreign policy combining good relations with the West and Turkey with good relations with Iran and Russia. Later, however, Aliev largely abandoned his efforts to improve ties with Iran, despite Iran's eagerness for better relations and its help to the Azerbaijani enclave of Nakhjivan, which is separated from the rest of the republic by Iranian territory.[39] Many aspects of Baku's policies toward Iran under Aliev, father and son, notably its support of separatist movements in Iranian Azerbaijan, have been similar to those of the Elçibey government. Azerbaijan's anti-Iranian cultural policies have also continued unabated.

Baku has also used Iran's estrangement from the West to obtain concessions from it. Meanwhile, through occasional rapprochement with Iran, it has forced the United

States to treat Azerbaijan with greater indulgence, notably in regard to its human rights record. Thus when the United States was unhappy with the process of elections that led to Haidar Aliev's son Ilham to become president, Azerbaijan cozied up to Iran, and Aliev visited Tehran on January 24–25, 2005. During this trip, Iran gave in to the Republic of Azerbaijan's demands to open a consulate in Tabriz, which would better enable Baku to stir up anti-Tehran sentiments in the region, and made concessions on the Caspian Sea. More seriously, Iran risked damaging its close relations with Armenia by publicly supporting Baku in its conflict with Armenia and in favor of the territorial integrity of Azerbaijan. This Iranian posture certainly contributed to Armenia's move in the last few years to improve its relations with Ankara and Israel.[40] In exchange, Azerbaijan promised not to allow its territory to become a launching pad for an attack on Iran. Iran was forced to make these concessions because, in previous years in a bid to join NATO, the Republic of Azerbaijan had reportedly allowed the United States to station troops on its territory near the Iranian border, to establish radar stations, and to modernize its Caspian fleet.

However, alarmed by Iranian-Azerbaijani rapprochement, the United States changed its position toward Baku, invited Aliev to visit the United States, and once again opened the option of attacking Iran from Azerbaijan.[41] Iran had to warn Azerbaijan that if it allowed its territory to be used to attack Iran, it would take retaliatory measures.

In short, if so far Azerbaijan has retained some level of relations with Iran, it has been because of its economic, geographic, and military limitations. The Russian factor has also had some impact. In dealing with Iran, especially in the last five years, Azerbaijan, which is dependent on the remittances of its nationals working in Moscow, had to consider Russian sensitivities. Also, despite the government's anti-Iran policy, Iran has a degree of cultural influence in the Azerbaijani Republic and is popular with the more religious Shias. For example, according to an Azerbaijani author, in 2006, when there was increased talk of a possible U.S. attack on Iran and allegedly the United States was urging Azerbaijan to allow it to station troops there and to participate in an attack on Iran, a poll conducted by Azerbaijan's Center for Economic and Political Studies (FAR Centre) in cooperation with the U.S. National Endowment for Democracy showed that 34 percent of Azerbaijanis supported Iran in its dispute with the United States over Iran's nuclear program and only 20 percent the United States and the West; and only 9 percent of the Azerbaijanis were of the opinion that a U.S. attack on Iran would benefit the republic.[42]

The same pattern is observable in Iran's relations with Turkmenistan. The good Iranian-Turkmen relations were the result of the policies of Niyazov, and since his death these relations have changed. Thus immediately after Niyazov's death in 2006, Turkmenistan halted its export of gas to Iran until a new treaty was signed. Then in the winter of 2007–2008, Turkmenistan, ostensibly because of a dispute over the price of Turkmen gas sold to Iran, cut gas supplies to the latter, causing hardship for the people and embarrassment for the government. Some have speculated that the United States may have encouraged Turkmenistan in this act.[43] Later, Iran was forced to agree to a much higher price, according to a treaty that, because of its unfavorable nature from the Iranian perspective, has been likened by the Iranian press and commentators to the shameful treaty of Turkmenchai, which established the regime of capitulation in Iran following Iran's defeat in the 1824–1828 Russo-Iranian wars. This Turkmen action was, as put by John Daly of the Jamestown Foundation, a particularly "bitter recompense" for Iran, because it had helped Turkmenistan to break Russia's stranglehold on its gas exports, thus making it possible for foreign investments to pour into Turkmenistan, while Iran's energy fields are deteriorating because U.S. sanctions have starved them of capital.[44] Similarly, under its new president and ignoring Iran's sensitivities, Turkmenistan has established diplomatic relations with Israel.[45] Yet Iran not only did not retaliate but Ahmadinejad received the Turkmen president in Tehran in April 2009 to discuss more Iranian investment in Turkmenistan's oil and gas.[46]

By the beginning of 2010, it seemed that Iran-Turkmenistan had weathered tensions that developed in their relations when Turkmenistan, for a period, cut its gas supplies to Iran in winter 2007–2008. As a sign of improving relations, Ahmadinejad visited Turkmenistan in January 2010. During this visit, together with the Turkmen president, inaugurated the second pipeline carrying Turkmen gas to Iran built with Iran's assistance. The two sides also launched the construction of the Gorgan-Atrak-Barakat railway, which is part of the larger network linking Iran, Turkmenistan, and Kazakhstan through Iran to the Persian Gulf and Europe. Iran will lend $300 million to Turkmenistan for the project, but Iranian firms will do the construction work.[47]

Uzbekistan, too, has calibrated its relations with Iran based on its own orientation, whether in a more pro-Western or Russian direction, and on its assessment of the costs and benefits of ties with Iran. Thus early on, despite certain reservations regarding an Iranian presence in the region, Uzbekistan welcomed relations with Iran, and President Islam Karimov visited Tehran in 1992. By 1994, however, Uzbekistan had changed its foreign policy orientation in a Western direction and was marketing itself as a regional counterweight to both Russia and Iran. By 1995, during the visit to Uzbekistan by the U.S. secretary of defense William Perry, the two countries signed an agreement which included the possible training of Uzbek military personnel by the United States.[48] This Iranian willingness was the result of Iran's need for Turkmen gas, which is the result of the lack of available financing for the development of Iran's own vast natural gas resources because of its anti-United States foreign policy.

This shift in Uzbek policy was a direct result of gradually deteriorating Russo-American relations, following the fall of Andrei Kozyrev, and the U.S. policy of Dual Containment. Following this shift, Uzbekistan adopted a hostile policy toward Iran and was the only non-Western country to openly support the imposition of U.S. sanctions on Iran in 1994.[49] However, the Uzbek foreign minister, during a later visit to Tehran, denied that his government had done so.[50]

U.S.-Uzbek relations grew closer when Uzbekistan allowed the United States to use its air bases in Karshi-Khanabad in the southern part of the country for military operations in Afghanistan. Meanwhile, Uzbekistan adopted an increasingly friendly approach toward Israel, as illustrated by the visit of Israeli foreign minister Simon

Peres to Tashkent in 1994, during which he warned Central Asian states of Iran and its intentions.[51] This trip was followed by other visits by Israeli officials, including Prime Minister Benjamin Netanyahu in 1998, and return visits by Uzbek officials, including President Karimov. Because of these Uzbek policies, Uzbek-Iranian relations have remained at best cool for nearly a decade. Yet Iran has chosen to ignore Uzbekistan's less-than-friendly attitude.

In May 2005, large protests by Islamist groups broke out in Andijan. They were harshly dealt with, led to criticism by the U.S. government, and strained U.S.-Uzbek relations. In retaliation, Uzbekistan asked the United States to remove its personnel from Uzbek air bases.[52] Meanwhile, Iran remained silent on the Andijan events. All these developments led to a degree of improvement in Uzbek-Iranian relations. The important point is that, in the last two decades, it has been the Uzbek government that has determined the state of Uzbek-Iranian relations, while Iran has always been in a state of eagerness for expanded relations, when and how it suited Uzbekistan.

Factors such as cultural competitiveness and fear of Iranian cultural influence have not seriously impacted Iran's relations with Kazakhstan. There are no Tajik-speaking minorities in Kazakhstan, nor any territorial dispute or cultural rivalry between Kazakhstan and Tajikistan. Kazakhstan is also distant from Iran, and there are no Kazakh minorities of any significance in Iran. Also, because of its ethnic and religious composition, notably a large Russian population, pan-Turkist ideas were never embraced by Kazakhstan. Consequently, Kazakhstan was initially interested in cooperation with Iran and favored a southern export route for its energy. The following remark by the Kazakh ambassador in Iran illustrates this early interest: "Unfortunately, to this day we have a perception of this very important strategic partner that is not always objective and is limited by the so-called Islamic fundamentalism. This is a very simplified approach and it would be a mistake to follow it. Iran's geopolitical situation and status have ensured for it a key position not only in the region but in the entire world."[53]

However, while Iranian-Kazakh relations have developed in a number of areas, U.S. opposition has limited their scope, especially in the energy field, which held the most potential for greater cooperation. On some occasions, the United States has even opposed high-level visits by Iranian officials to Kazakhstan. For example, it was reported that the United States in 2002 urged the Kazakhs to refuse President Khatami's offer to visit Kazakhstan.[54] Although the Kazakh authorities have not completely yielded to these U.S. pressures, clearly they are aware that they cannot totally ignore America's sensitivities, as the following statement by Sanat Khushkumbayev, the first deputy director of the Kazakhstan Institute of Strategic Studies, illustrates. Reportedly, he told *Tehran Times* that "Kazakhstan will definitely need to consider the opinions of 'outsiders' like the U.S. and the EU before beefing up its connections with Iran."[55]

As a sign of improved relations, President Ahmadinejad visited Kazakhstan in April 2009 and was warmly received by the president.[56] However, when the four Caspian littoral states decided to meet in September 2009, Ahmadinejad was not invited. Some sources speculated that this might have been in reaction to the controversial nature of Iran's presidential elections.[57]

Because of its small size and lack of resources, Kyrgyzstan has been of less interest to Iran. Nevertheless, Iran has been interested in expanded relations with it. As with Kazakhstan, there are no major irritants in Iranian-Kyrgyz relations, with the possible exception of the Islamic factor. Kyrgyzstan has faced an Islamist threat in the South, where the majority consists of ethnic Uzbeks who are affected by developments in Uzbekistan and Tajikistan. At times, Kyrgyzstan has blamed Iran for their activity. This claim, however, is not very credible, because most of these Islamists are influenced by Wahhabi teachings and the Taliban philosophy, rather than by Iranian-style revolutionary Islam. *+ a competition - world-wide bet, Saudi + Iran?*

Since 2008, even Armenia, which has had the closest relations with Iran, has began somewhat to shift its position and to improve ties with both Israel and Turkey. In fact, in October 2009 Turkey and Armenia signed an agreement to normalize relations. Some sources reported that Israel had mediated in this regard. Other factors, especially the economic advantage of better relation with Turkey, played important roles in this shift. But long-standing U.S. pressure on Armenia not to pursue close relations with Iran but rather to improve relations with Turkey has been an important factor. In particular, while Armenia is concerned about a possible American attack on Iran, it clearly does not want to be left out in the cold should such an attack take place.

Initially, Georgia, too, was eager to have better ties with Iran. This desire was quite natural because in many areas, notably energy, Iran could potentially be a good partner for Georgia. In fact, on some occasions, notably 2006 when the Russian pipeline was damaged and gas supplies were disrupted, Iran pumped more gas to Georgia through the Azerbaijani pipeline.[58] Moreover, there are no territorial, ethnic, or any other disputes between Iran and Georgia to mar bilateral relations. Although some bad memories of Safavid rule in Georgia remain, by and large the number of Georgians who have a good memory of Iran and Iranian cultural influence, including that of ancient Iran, is considerable.

The main barrier to better Iranian-Georgian ties has been U.S. and Israeli opposition.[59] At one point, Georgian president Eduard Shevardnadze tried to mediate between Iran and the United States, hoping that improved U.S.-Iranian relations would eliminate U.S. opposition to expanded Georgian-Iranian ties.[60] However, soon realizing the complex nature of U.S.-Iranian estrangement, he abandoned this scheme. Later Georgia adopted a pro-Western policy, seeking to become a member of NATO. This pro-Western tilt became more accentuated following Georgia's so-called Rose Revolution and the coming to power of Mikhail Sakashvili. Yet the two countries have retained diplomatic ties, and Sakashvili visited Iran in 2004.[61]

Many Georgian experts and scholars have also argued that a strategic partnership with the United States should not exclude reasonable relations with Iran.[62] Iran's noncommittal stance on the Ossetian conflict between Russia and Georgia and its arguing that this type of issue should be handled through peaceful means were also appreciated by Tbilisi. However, it is unlikely that Georgia will be able to achieve the near impossible goal of good relations with Iran and a strategic partnership with Israel and the United States, unless there is a breakthrough in U.S.-Iranian relations.

In summary, because of its inability adequately to adjust to new systemic realities, Iran, despite its constructive policy, has failed to achieve its goals in Central Asia and the Caucasus, including membership in such organizations as the SCO. It has also been overlooked in schemes proposed for resolving security problems in the Caucasus, such as the Turkish proposal offered following the Russo-Georgian crisis over South Ossetia in 2008.

Absent significant change in Iran's foreign policy in a realistic direction and an end of its quarrel with the West, its position in the region will further suffer.

CHAPTER 9

Iran and the Arab World: Between Conflict and Accommodation

Iran and the Arab world have had a long and turbulent history of interaction; the Arabs and Iranians have deeply influenced each other's cultural evolution and have helped shape the Islamic civilization. The legacy of Arab-Iranian historical interaction still colors the two peoples' perceptions of each other and exerts a significant and largely negative influence on their contemporary relations. Broadly speaking, Arab-Iranian relations have historically been characterized by competition, deep-rooted mutual suspicions and misgivings, and expedient cooperation or at times only mutual accommodation.

Since the establishment of an Islamic government in Iran with a revolutionary ideology the competitive and conflictual aspects of Arab-Iranian relations have been enhanced by two factors: the Arab states' fear of revolutionary contagion; and their temptation to profit from Iran's postrevolutionary instability and to realize long-held territorial and other ambitions toward Iran. Iraq's invasion of Iran in September 1980 resulted from the combined effect of these factors, as did the Arab states' all-out support to Iraq during the eight-year war.[1]

Since the end of the war in August 1988, followed by the Soviet demise, Arab-Iranian relations have gone through several stages. During this period, much like the first decade of the Islamic regime and, indeed, the Pahlavi era, Arab-Iranian relations have been uneven in the sense that Iran has had good or reasonable relations with some Arab states, and strained or hostile relations with others.

This continuity in the underlying pattern of Arab-Iranian relations, despite a fundamental shift in the pattern of Iran's enmities and friendships in the Arab world in the postrevolution period, reflects the enduring influence of certain basic determinants of Arab-Iranian relations.

DETERMINANTS OF ARAB-IRANIAN RELATIONS

The following are the most important determinants of Arab-Iranian relations:

1. *Ethnic and Sectarian Differences and Cultural Competition*

Since the Arab-Islamic conquest of Iran in 642 c.e., ethnic and religious differences have provided a background of tension to Arab-Iranian relations. The following factors have been responsible for this phenomenon:

• Despite Islamization, and a long period of Arab rule, Iran was not linguistically or culturally Arabized, and by the 10th century c.e. it experienced a linguistic, cultural, and political revival, characterized by a rediscovery of its pre-Islamic history and traditions.

• Iranians had a tremendous role in the development of Islamic civilization, and the Arabs borrowed heavily from pre-Islamic Iran's political and administrative systems and its philosophical and scientific heritage. This Iranian role, although largely unrecognized by the Arabs, is, nevertheless, highly resented by them and has led to a long-standing cultural competition between the two peoples.[2]

• Following Iran's nearly complete Shiiazation in the 16th century, sectarian differences became another source of tension in Arab-Iranian relations. This has become particularly important after the Islamic Revolution and especially since the U.S. invasion of Iraq in 2003 and the fall of the Sunni-dominated government of Saddam Hussein.

• The Iranian regime's efforts to portray the Islamic Revolution as a transsectarian movement has led the Arab states to emphasize its Persian-Shia character and hence its inapplicability to the Sunni Arabs. Historically, because of the religious composition of the Persian Gulf Arab states, sectarian differences have had a significant impact on Iran's relations with these countries (see table 9.1).

2. *Geographic, Demographic, and Resource Disparities*

In the case of the Persian Gulf Arab states, disparities in size, population, and resource base have been a cause of tension in relations with Iran, which is the largest,

Table 9.1   Sectarian Division in the Persian Gulf

Country	Sunni % of Population	Shia % of Population
Bahrain	20 to 35%	65 to 80%
Iran	3 to 3.5%	96 to 97%
Iraq	35 to 40%	60 to 65%
Kuwait	65 to 70%	30 to 35%
Oman	92%	7%
Qatar	95%	13%
Saudi Arabia	75 to 80%	20 to 25%
UAE	67%	16%

Source: Author's calculation from figures obtained from the *CIA World Fact Book* and other estimates.

most populous and resource-rich (except for oil) country in the region. The low level of indigenous population of smaller Gulf states and the presence of substantial Iranian minorities in them enhances their anxiety regarding Iran. At times, non-Persian Gulf Arab states, such as Egypt, with their own interests in the Gulf Arab states, have portrayed the Iranian minorities as a danger to the Persian Gulf's so-called Arab character. Yet neither the Gulf Arabs nor other Arab states view the Pakistani or Indian immigrants as a threat to the Gulf's Arab character, although their numbers are larger than the Iranian minorities. In the past, some Arab regimes, such as Nasser's Egypt, had likened Iranian migration to the Gulf states to the early Jewish immigrants to Israel.[3]

After the Islamic Revolution, these minorities have been viewed as a potential source of Shia subversion (see table 9.2).

3. Competing Nationalisms and Territorial Disputes

Since the early 1930s, the rise of modern nationalism in Iran and the Arab world, with its ethnocentric character and political dimension, has been another source of tension in Arab-Iranian relations. Arab nationalism is no longer as strong as it was throughout the 1950s, 1960s, and 1970s and, to a lesser extent, the 1980s.[4]

Table 9.2 Iranian Minorities in the Persian Gulf Arab States

Country	Total Population	Nonnational	Percentage Iranian
Bahrain	708,573	235,108	8*
Iraq	27,499,559	None	n.a.
Kuwait	2,505,559	1,291,354	4
Oman	3,311,460	577,293	1
Qatar	824,789	—*	10
Saudi Arabia	28,146,656	5,576,076	0**
UAE	4,621,399	3,781,409*	10–15***

Source: CIA World Fact Book, 2008.

*The number of 8 percent for Bahrainis of Iranian origin seems somewhat conservative, especially if it is kept in mind that many Bahraini nationals are of Iranian origin.[1]
**There are however, a number of prominent Iranian origin families in Saudi Arabia.
***The *CIA World Fact Book* does not specify the percentage of Iranians in the country's total population and only mentions the same percentage that it did a decade earlier for combined other Arab and Iranian, at 23 percent of the population. However, in the last decade the number of Iranians living in the UAE, especially in Dubai, has increased. The figure cited is the author's conservative estimate.

[1]David Holden, *Farewell to Arabia* (London: Faber and Faber, 1966).

Nevertheless, some of its ethos is still powerful and affects the Arab countries' political positions, especially toward non-Arab states.

From Iran's perspective, what the late Professor Majid Khaduri has called Arab nationalism's "irredentist" and "romantic" dimensions have been particularly ominous. The irredentist dimension is reflected in the Arab claims to Iran's Khuzestan Province and to the three Persian Gulf islands—Abu Musa and the Greater and Lesser Tunbs, as well as in the Arab campaign to change the historic name of the Persian Gulf into the Arab [or Arabian] Gulf.

Since the 1930s, Iran, too, has tried to reassert its position in the Persian Gulf and prevent further territorial losses, albeit without much success. In 1971, Iran gave up its claim to Bahrain under British and American pressure. However, for the following reasons, Iran's anger at Bahrain's loss still simmers:

+ Bahrain's gradual separation from Iran was part and parcel of the overall British policy of reducing Iran's presence in the Persian Gulf and in the approaches to India.

+ The decision to give up Iran's claim to the island was taken without national consultation and hence was considered a sellout by the Shah.

+ After independence, Bahrain has become a vassal of Saudi Arabia.

Furthermore, Iran's giving up of Bahrain made the formation of the UAE possible and, despite earlier promises, the Shah failed to get a clear acceptance of Iran's rights toward the three Persian Gulf islands, either by Britain or by the newly formed United Arab Emirates. Now, the UAE is calling the islands "occupied territories." Additionally, despite an eight-year war, Iran has not obtained Iraq's agreement to the equal division of the Shat-al-Arab (Arvand Rud). Ironically, even Arab states friendly to Iran have always supported these irredentist claims, thus betraying the influence of Arab nationalist ethos.

Because the Islamic regime initially adopted an antinationalist discourse, Arab states hoped that Iran would give up the islands and accept a change in the name of the Persian Gulf. But nationalist sentiments remained strong in Iran and, added to security concerns, ensured continuity in Iran's policy regarding these issues.

4. Ideological Differences and Diverging Pattern of Alliances

Ideological differences and diverging patterns of alliances of Iran and Arab states have also deeply influenced the character of their relations. In general, Iran has always had good or reasonable relations with those Arab countries with which it shared similar ideology and allies. Before the revolution, Iran had good relations with pro-Western Arab states, including Saudi Arabia, while its relations with pro-Soviet radical Arab countries were tense.

The Islamic regime's animosity toward the conservative Arab regimes largely derives from their association with the West, rather than their practice of what the Iranian regime has branded "American Islam." By contrast, Iran has overlooked anti-Islamic policies of those Arab countries, such as Syria, with which it has had many ideological and political affinities.

In the post-Soviet period, Iran has tried to pursue a nonideological policy toward Arab states and even has naïvely tried to delink its bilateral relations with them from their alliance with the United States. However, Arab states have not been receptive to this Iranian ploy, partly because of concern over U.S. reaction.

ideology more important then religion?

5. Competing Power Ambitions

But Assad has Shia roots

Competing power ambitions between Iran and some Arab countries, especially in terms of regional supremacy in the Persian Gulf and influence in the Arab and Islamic worlds, have also impacted their relations in pre- and postrevolution periods.

Iran's main Arab competitors have been Saudi Arabia, Egypt, Syria, and Saddam-era Iraq. In the prerevolution era, Saudi Arabia competed with Iran in the Persian Gulf and South Asia, especially in regard to Pakistan and Afghanistan. In the 1970s, Saudi Arabia undermined the Shah in order to make itself the favored U.S. ally. After the revolution, Saudi-Iranian competition was expanded to the rest of the Islamic world and acquired intense sectarian and ideological dimensions. /// ✗

Iran and Saddam's Iraq also competed for regional power. Iraq's invasion of Iran in September 1980 was not, as some Western and Arab commentators and scholars have maintained, motivated mainly by fear of revolutionary contagion. Rather, Saddam used Iran's postrevolution instability to establish its domination in the region and hence in the Arab world. This interpretation was validated by Saddam's invasion of Kuwait, in 1991. Even after Saddam's departure, Iranian-Iraqi relations have not been free of competition.

Egypt, with brief intervals, has also seen Iran as a competitor. An interesting aspect of Arab-Iranian power competition is the Arabs' view of any Iranian presence in the Middle East as illegitimate, whereas they do not seem to have the same sensitivity to a Turkish presence. This sensitivity is partly due to sectarian differences and cultural competition.

6. Iran and Intra-Arab Politics

From the early 1950s, Cold War dynamics, the rise of ideas—such as Arab nationalism, Pan-Arabism and Arab socialism—and the emergence of revolutionary regimes in the Arab world led to increased interaction, both within the Arab world and between it and non-Arab regional states, especially Iran. Consequently, the character and ideology of Arab political systems and that of Iran and, hence their external behavior, acquired greater importance for both Iran and Arab states, thus making Iran a factor in intra-Arab politics and balance of power.

Before the revolution, Iran strengthened the position of pro-Western governments, while its own security was undermined by radical Arab states. After the revolution, the situation became more complex, because the Iranian regime, while virulently anti-West, was not exactly pro-Soviet. Furthermore, Iran's ideology of revolutionary Islam potentially threatened both conservative and leftist Arab regimes, because it cast itself as an alternative to both Western liberal capitalism and socialism in its different versions. Furthermore, although Iran's ethnic and sectarian peculiarities, later coupled with the Islamic regime's poor economic performance, limited its appeal to the Arab masses, its defiance of the great powers and its discourse of Islamic unity made it appealing to some Arabs, thus making Iran an even more important factor in intra-Arab politics and generating complaints by conservative Arab regimes that Iran was interfering in Arab affairs.

7. The Israel-Palestine Factor

Arab-Iranian relations have been strongly affected by Iran's position toward the Palestinian-Israeli conflict, Iran's position vis-à-vis Israel, and the Middle East peace process. Before the revolution, Arab states, especially those with left-leaning governments, accused Iran of having secret relations with Israel. True, Iran did have secret dealings with Israel, but, unlike Turkey, it never officially recognized Israel. Nevertheless, although Turkey established full diplomatic relations and, in 1998, a full-fledged strategic alliance with Israel, it never attracted the same hostility as Iran has done. Arab states have never branded Turkey, together with Israel, as an enemy of the Arabs, whereas Jordan's Crown Prince Hassan in the 1980s wrote that Arabs have two enemies, Iran in the East and Israel in the West.

Ironically, in the mid-1970s, when the Shah adopted a more balanced policy toward the Arab-Israeli conflict, improved relations with the PLO, and criticized Israel's occupation of Arab lands, he became a target of Israel's anger and animosity. According to some sources, this change in the Shah's policy, coupled with Iran's growing economic and political power, led Israel to generate a campaign against the Shah in the U.S. Congress, exemplified by congressional opposition to U.S. arms sales to Iran, and it encouraged pro-Israel media in the United States to criticize the Shah and promote Khomeini.[5] Others go further and claim that Israel played a major role in bringing the Shah down.[6]

Ironically, the Islamic regime's support for the Palestinian cause has not been enough to blunt the influence of other factors, as illustrated by the PLO's and Arafat's support to Iraq during the Iran-Iraq War. And since 1992, Iran's support for the Palestinians has become a source of conflict among Iran, conservative Arab regimes, and the Palestinian Authority. Furthermore, Israel has made Iran the focus of its hostility and has tried to use Arab concerns over Iran to forge an Arab-Israel coalition against it.

8. The Post-Soviet International Order: Impact on Arab-Iranian Relations

Post-Soviet systemic changes, plus the consequences of the 1991 Iraq War, negatively affected Arab-Iranian relations. The elimination of the Soviet threat, coupled with the more extensive and official U.S. military presence in the Persian Gulf, emboldened the Arab states and made them less willing to accommodate Iran. Meanwhile, changes in Russia's foreign policy outlook, from one based on ideology to one determined exclusively by national interests, has meant that it would not sacrifice its interests in the Arab world for Iran's sake.

ARAB-IRANIAN RELATIONS IN THE 1980s: SAUDI ARABIA AND OTHER GCC STATES

In analyzing Iran's relations with the Gulf Cooperation Council (GCC) members, the following points should be noted:

+ Despite their adoption of common official positions, the views and policies of GCC member states on many issues, including relations with Iran, often differ. Historically, the character of Iran's relations with individual GCC member states have differed.
+ Because of differences in their size, population, and resources, the power aspirations of individual GCC states have also differed. Thus, countries like Qatar, Kuwait, Oman, and Bahrain do not aspire to regional leadership, and hence are not excessively competitive with Iran, unlike Saudi Arabia, which seeks regional and Arab leadership.
+ GCC member states are divided by border disputes and dynastic and/or tribal rivalries.[7]
+ Smaller GCC states favor a balance of power among the three larger states—Iran, Saudi Arabia, and Iraq.
+ Ethnic and sectarian characteristics of individual GCC states and their history with Iran have impacted the nature of their relations with Iran. Countries with large Shia populations and substantial Iranian-origin minorities, but with Sunni leaderships, such as Kuwait and Bahrain, have been more wary of Iran. In Bahrain's case, Iran's historic claim to the island has made it particularly sensitive about Iran.

Consequently, those GCC states either more competitive with Iran or feeling threatened by it have had strained relations with it and have favored its exclusion from regional security arrangements. Meanwhile, historically Iran has had good relations with Oman and, since 1995, with Qatar.[8] However, ultimately, the shape of Iranian-GCC relations has been determined by changing ideological orientations and the pattern of alliances and enmities.

During the 1980s, the following factors most affected Iran's relations with Saudi Arabia and the GCC states. Some of these factors are still influencing Iranian-Gulf Arab relations.

Iran's Revolutionary Threat

Saudi Arabia and other Persian Gulf Arab states viewed as an existential threat Iran's Islamic universalist pretensions and its revolutionary and antimonarchy discourse, a discourse influenced by left-leaning Third Worldist views that considered Arab reaction, together with imperialism and international Zionism, as forming a triangle of evil. The Islamic regime's desire to export its revolution further enhanced these anxieties.[9] In Saudi Arabia's case, the concentration of its Shia minority in the oil-rich eastern province exacerbated fears of ideological contamination.[10]

Iranian officials' calling Saudi Arabia's and other Persian Gulf states' leaders clients of the West and anti-Islamic, plus the activities of some clerical figures in Kuwait and Bahrain, enhanced these fears.[11] Two such figures were Hojat ul Islams Hadi Modaresi in Bahrain and Abbas Mohri in Kuwait. Eventually both were expelled from these countries.

Saudi Arabia was also concerned that Iran's new Islamic identity and its abandonment of Persian-centric nationalism could make it a more serious rival for the leadership of the Islamic world.[12] *more powerful*

Iran's defeat in the war with Iraq, the Islamic regime's poor economic and political performance, and the ethnic and sectarian differences between the Iranians and the Arabs have seriously eroded Iran's ideological appeal and hence its threat to regional states. Nevertheless, Iran's championing of Arab and Islamic causes, especially that of the Palestinians, while conservative Arab regimes have been inactive on these fronts, still provides Iran a degree of appeal and influence with segments of the region's population.

Hence it is universalist with the people

HAJJ PILGRIMAGE: OPPORTUNITY TO EXPORT ISLAMIC REVOLUTION

The Islamic regime has used the annual Hajj pilgrimage to spread its revolutionary message, to attack so-called American Islam, and to propagate its anti-U.S. and anti-Israeli views by staging political rallies and protests. Iran has justified these activities on the ground that the Prophet's main purpose in instituting the Hajj was to provide an opportunity for Muslims to become acquainted with one another's views, to discuss challenges facing Muslims worldwide, and to find ways to meet these challenges. Otherwise, no purpose would be served by Muslims gathering in the same place at the same time every year.

Saudi Arabia and other conservative Arabs do not agree with Iran's interpretation of the purpose behind the Hajj and view the Iranian pilgrims' activities as sabotage. Consequently, since the 1980s, Iranian pilgrims' activities and Saudi treatment of them have become a particularly thorny issue in Saudi-Iranian relations. Throughout the 1980s, Saudi Arabia periodically expelled many Iranian pilgrims and limited the number of Iranians allowed to perform the Hajj to 100,000. There was a brief period of détente in 1985, after Iran removed the radical Hujat ul Islam Khoeiniha from the leadership of the Hajj.[13] However, this détente was short-lived, and conflicts over Hajj ceremonies resumed.

In July 1987, during Hajj demonstrations, 275 Iranians, plus 84 Saudis and 42 other pilgrims, died in clashes with the Saudi police, thus unleashing verbal attacks from Iranian officials, mass demonstrations in Iranian cities, and the ransacking of

is a rival bec. it has universalist ambit.

why does it support the palestinian' if its aim is to promote Shiism?

the Saudi embassy in Tehran in August 1987.[14] In retaliation, during a meeting of the foreign ministers of the Arab League, Saudi Arabia accused Iran of terrorism and of wanting to take power in Saudi Arabia. Finally, in 1988, it broke diplomatic relations with Iran. The question of Iranian pilgrims and Saudi treatment of them is still a major source of tension in their relations.

IRANIAN SUBVERSION IN PERSIAN GULF ARAB STATES AND ARAB SUPPORT FOR THE IRANIAN OPPOSITION

During the 1980s, Iran was accused of bombings and assassinations in Kuwait, which led to the expulsion of large numbers of Iranians from Kuwait and of supporting the Islamic Front for the Liberation of Bahrain.

Most likely, Iran was behind some of these incidents because it both wanted to export its revolution and to punish those Gulf states, especially Kuwait, for supporting Iraq. Yet the Gulf states exaggerated Iran's role, attributed all their political problems to Iranian instigation, and overlooked other potential sources of subversion.

For example, Iran was blamed for the 1985 assassination attempt on the life of the emir of Kuwait, although there were reports that Syria or even Iraq might have been the culprit. In Syria's case, resentment over the stoppage of financial aid, and in Iraq's case warning against any slackening of support, could have provided convincing motives. However, because of considerations of intra-Arab politics, these possibilities were not mentioned by Kuwait.

Meanwhile, Saudi Arabia and some other Gulf states supported a number of Iranian opposition groups, including the Mujahedin-e-Khalq, based in Iraq, and some royalist opposition figures.

THE IRAN-IRAQ WAR

Iraq's invasion of Iran and all-out Arab support for Iraq adversely affected Iranian–Gulf Arab relations and, indeed, Iranian-Arab relations across the board.[15]

A discussion of the causes of the war, its evolution, and its termination are beyond the scope of the present work. Suffice it to say that the main impetus behind the Iraqi invasion was a combination of long-held irredentist claims, quest for domination on Iraq's part, fear of revolutionary contagion, Iran's internal weakness, and Iraqi miscalculation about the reaction of Iran's ethnic Arab minority.

During the early part of the war, fear was the main reason for the Gulf Arabs' support for Iraq. A victorious Iran would have pushed for the overthrow of conservative Arab regimes. By the end of 1986, however, it had become clear that Iran could not win the war. Yet the Gulf Arabs' attitude toward Iran stiffened, and their policy shifted from containing Iran to solving the Iran problem once and for all. Kuwait's request that the United States reflag its tankers was part of this strategy.

However, during the 1980s, Iran's relations were not bad with all Gulf Arab states. The UAE, despite the islands disputes, did not assist Iraq financially, and, because of its lucrative re-export trade with Iran, Dubai was branded a traitor to the Arab cause by Iraq. Oman and Qatar also retained reasonable relations with Iran.

IRAN'S INTERNAL DIVISIONS AND MIXED SIGNALS

During this period, ideological and other intra-regime differences, plus deficiencies in the Iranian foreign policy-making structure, resulted in a confused and contradictory Iranian policy toward the Gulf states, with adverse consequences for bilateral relations. Thus while Iranian officials claimed that they wanted normal and friendly relations with the Gulf Arab states, other organizations continued their ideological propaganda and, at times, even subversion in these countries, and influential clerics and sometimes officials made disparaging remarks about Gulf Arab leaders.

THE CEASE-FIRE OF AUGUST 1988 AND THE FIRST GULF WAR

The Islamic regime had characterized the war with Iraq as a battle between evil and righteousness (*Haq va Batel*), and since Iran was on the side of righteousness, it believed that it would emerge victorious. Yet this expectation was not realized and in 1988 Iran faced the unenviable choice of either continuing a losing war and risking the loss of part of Iranian territory or agreeing to a cease-fire. For once, caution prevailed and Ayatullah Khomeini, as he put it, drank "the poisoned chalice" and signed the August 1988 cease-fire.[16]

The cease-fire eliminated the major cause of friction in Iranian-Gulf relations. This factor, plus Iran's expressed determination to improve relations with the Gulf states and, especially, to expand economic ties as part of its economic revitalization efforts, led to better Iranian-Gulf relations. One of the first states to normalize relations and resume diplomatic ties was Kuwait. Its initiative was quite natural because Iraq had emerged as the strongest power in the region and was behaving in an overconfident manner, leading the Gulf states to revert to their traditional policy of balancing Iran and Iraq.

However, for the following reasons, Iran's relations with Saudi Arabia remained tense:

+ Saudi Arabia's greater regional weight.
+ Its intense anti-Shia tendencies.
+ The Hajj controversy.
+ Saudi Arabia's power ambitions.

The passing of Ayatullah Khomeini in June 1989 and the coming to power of Hashemi Rafsanjani, which ushered in a period of more pragmatic foreign policy, despite the persistence of intra-regime ideological differences and power struggles, further helped improve Iranian-Gulf relations.

IRAQ'S INVASION OF KUWAIT

Saddam Hussein's invasion of Kuwait in August 1990 demonstrated the mistake made by the Gulf Arab states in unconditionally supporting Saddam Hussein. It also provided Iran with an opportunity dramatically to improve its relations with the Gulf states and obtain significant advantages from them and from the United States and Europe, by joining the anti-Saddam coalition.[17]

However, the continued influence of revolutionary ideology with its anti-American tendencies, along with deep divisions within Iranian leadership, prevented it from grasping this opportunity. Quite the contrary, as noted earlier, Iraq's action presented Iran with a serious dilemma and unleashed a sharp debate that pitted Iranian pragmatists and radicals against one another.[18] The latter, notably Ayatullah Sadeq Khalkhali, called for Iran to join Iraq in an anti-imperialist coalition. But given Iran's recent history with Iraq, this was unacceptable, and Iran was saved from potential retaliatory measures by the anti-Saddam coalition.

However, because of the radicals' influence, Iran was not able to take advantage of this opportunity, and, in a pattern of behavior that has since continued, chose a halfway policy. It opted for neutrality, which served the interests of the coalition and the Gulf states, without gaining any benefits for itself. After victory over Iraq, the United States and the Gulf states forgot the benefits of Iran's neutrality, hardened their attitude toward it, and adopted a policy of its containment and exclusion from discussions on regional security arrangements. The Gulf states, emboldened by Iraq's weakened state and greater U.S. military presence, rebuffed Iran's offers of better ties.

POST-SOVIET PERIOD: THE RAFSANJANI PRESIDENCY, 1989–1997

The soviets didn't have competing ideologies

What is need is more time for Iran to develop consistency

As part of its pragmatic diplomacy aimed at reintegrating Iran in the international community and acknowledging that Iran's aggressive rhetoric had unnecessarily alienated other countries, including its neighbors in the Persian Gulf, President Rafsanjani was determined to improve political relations with the Gulf states and expand economic ties with them.

However, several factors made the pursuit of this policy difficult: *The Qs is whether the retreat is tactical or strategic.*

- Systemic changes produced by the Soviet collapse.

- Developments within the Middle East following the Gulf War, notably new hopes raised for the resolution of the Arab-Israeli conflict, pursuant to the Madrid Conference of October 1991.

+ The PLO-Israel Oslo peace agreement of 1993.

+ The lack of interest by Gulf Arab states in rapprochement with Iran because of these developments.

Rafsanjani's overture to the Gulf states was also undermined by the radicals' activities, including the committing of terrorist acts within and without Iran. One such incident was the Khobar Towers bombing in June 1996, which killed and wounded a number of American military personnel stationed in Saudi Arabia. This incident was blamed on Iran and the supposedly Iran-supported Saudi Hizbullah. However, the Saudis initially did not pursue the Iran angle, thus avoiding a showdown with Iran. But in 1998, they declared that Iran was responsible for the attack.[19] Ten years later, however, former U.S. officials argued that the culprit was al Qaeda.[20]

Iran's relations with Bahrain also suffered during this period, partly because of agitations among Bahraini Shias, for which Iran was held responsible. Sensing the shifting geopolitical winds, the UAE, too, adopted a stiff position toward Iran and asked that the Gulf states not improve relations with Iran until the issue of the disputed islands was settled.

In April and August 1992, two incidents provided the occasion for the UAE to reopen the whole issue of the islands and take it to the UN. In April 1992, Iranian authorities on the island of Abu Musa expelled 100 foreigners working for the UAE on charges of lacking Iranian visas and espionage; and in August 1992, they refused to allow foreigners lacking an Iranian visa and turned back a UAE vessel. However, while refusing to compromise on the issue of its sovereignty over the islands, Iran tried to soothe the UAE's anger by offering bilateral negotiation to resolve differences and to prevent future incidents. But the UAE was implacable. Some Arab states, notably Egypt, supported the UAE, and Radio Cairo compared Iran's actions to Iraq's invasion of Kuwait. So did the Western media. The *New York Times* wrote that: "Abu Musa is the largest of the three islands *belonging to the Emirates occupied* [emphasis added] by Iranian troops in 1971," thus implying that they belong to the UAE. The fact, however, is that, for Sheikh Zaid "[the] choice of 1992 to make an issue out of Abu Musa was dictated more by the circumstances in the region than by Iranian actions. The Iranians had been militarizing the island throughout the eighties, during the Iran-Iraq War, and he did not make an issue of it. He did not make an issue of it during the Kuwait crisis of 1990–91. He waited until all that was over, when he had the support of the international community, he made an issue of it."[21]

KHATAMI PRESIDENCY, 1997–2005: UNMET EXPECTATIONS

The victory of Seyyed Muhammad Khatami in Iran's presidential elections of 1997 ushered in a new era in Iran's foreign policy. As noted earlier, the underlying principles of Khatami's foreign policy were dialogue and reduction of tensions. For the following reasons, Khatami's regional overtures were initially received more favorably by the Gulf states than had been the case with Rafsanjani's advances:

+ Khatami won on a platform of domestic liberalization and opening to the outside world.

+ The West's response to Khatami's initiatives was more positive.

+ The painstaking efforts of Rafsanjani and his foreign minister, Ali Akbar Velayati, had already eased some of the tensions in Iranian-Gulf relations.

+ The Arabs' early hopes of an Arab-Israeli peace and expanded Arab-Israeli economic and political cooperation had been dissipated by Yitzhak Rabin's assassination and the coming to power of the Likud party.

+ The growing strategic cooperation between Turkey and Israel had alarmed the Arabs.

+ The fall in oil prices; and

+ The assumption of the day-to-day management of Saudi affairs by Prince Abdullah, the crown prince, who was more interested in improving relations with Muslim countries.

IRAN HOSTS THE OIC SUMMIT

The first sign of improved Iranian-Gulf relations was the holding of the Organization of Islamic Conference's (OIC) Summit in Tehran on December 9, 1997, with the participation of the Saudi crown prince.[22] During his trip, Prince Abdullah met with Ayatullah Khamenei, thus indicating Khamenei's approval of Khatami's policy of outreach to Saudi Arabia and Iran's abandonment of its negative view of the Kingdom.

The momentum toward better Iranian-Gulf relations was maintained by former president Rafsanjani's visit to Saudi Arabia and Bahrain in February 1998. The trip lasted 10 days and included a visit to the Shia-inhabited Eastern province. This was a very unusual event and reflected the changing Saudi attitude toward Iran. However, Rafsanjani's trip was marred by disparaging remarks made by a Saudi cleric about the Shias during Rafsanjani's visit to the Prophet's mosque in Medina. Some in Iran demanded that he return home immediately. Rafsanjani, however, completed his trip in Saudi Arabia and went to Bahrain.

This trip was followed by Khatami's visiting the Kingdom in May 1999 and by the Supreme Leader's expression of a desire for stronger ties with Saudi Arabia.[23] Prince Abdullah reciprocated by inviting Khamenei to visit the Kingdom.[24] Contacts also accelerated between economic and defense officials of the two countries. The Saudi defense minister, Prince Sultan Bin Abdul Aziz, visited Tehran in May 1999, and Iran's minister of defense, Admiral Shamkhani, visited Saudi Arabia in April 2000.[25] The two sides also discussed the signing of a security agreement.

Nevertheless, Saudi Arabia remained suspicious of Iran, and important figures, such as Prince Sultan, the defense minister, and Prince Naïf, minister of interior, did not favor better ties with Iran. Thus, when there was talk of a security agreement, Naïf pointed out that the security pact under discussion was about fighting terrorism and drug trafficking and not a defense pact.[26] Others, meanwhile, stressed that it would take time to establish trust between the two countries.

Iran also pursued security and defense cooperation with other Gulf states, notably Qatar and Oman. With Qatar, there was talk of having military attachés in the two countries' embassies,[27] and in July 1998, 31 officers belonging to different GCC states, studying at Oman's military academy and staff headquarters, visited Iran for a week.[28]

Iran's relations with other Gulf states, with the exception of the UAE, also improved, and a number of Gulf leaders, including Kuwait's heir-apparent and the emir of Qatar, visited Iran, as did Bahrain's foreign minister. Following the latter's visit, Iran and Bahrain agreed to exchange ambassadors.[29] These events were followed by Khatami's visit to Qatar and Oman in May 1999.

The UAE was unhappy about the improvement in Iranian-Gulf relations. It maintained that the Gulf states should not improve ties with Iran before the islands issue was resolved, presumably in the UAE's favor.[30] The UAE also rejected Iran's offers for bilateral talks to resolve differences. However, there were exchanges between the two countries. President Khatami sent a special envoy to the UAE in August 2001,[31] and the latter's foreign minister, Sheikh Hamed Bin Zayed Al Nahyan, visited Iran in May 2002.[32]

TERRORIST ATTACKS OF 9/11 AND THE AFGHANISTAN AND IRAQ WARS: IMPACT ON IRANIAN-GULF RELATIONS

The terrorist attacks of 9/11 and the Afghan and Iraq Wars interrupted the trend of improving Iranian-Gulf relations because of changes that they produced in U.S. policy toward the region and Iran. Especially important was the initial U.S. determination to change the Middle East's political map by eliminating governments deemed unacceptable to the United States.

Because of close U.S.-Gulf relations, the hardening of the U.S. position on Iran halted the warming trend in Iranian-Gulf relations. The coming to power of a Shia-dominant government in Iraq also contributed to the deterioration of Iranian-Gulf relations by intensifying the Gulf states' fears of Iranian influence, the enhancement of Shia political consciousness, and the possible emergence of a so-called Shia crescent.

THE AHMADINEJAD PRESIDENCY

President Ahmadinejad had declared that the principal goal of Iran's domestic and foreign policies was the restoration of the values of the first decade of the revolution. However, this did not mean the revival of all policies of the early days of the Islamic regime, such as the aggressive export of revolutionary ideology, which had strained Iranian-Gulf relations. On the contrary, on regional issues Ahmadinejad pursued the conciliatory policies of his predecessors. It was other aspects of Iran's foreign policy under Ahmadinejad, notably the assumption of a more aggressive tone toward Israel and a more uncompromising stand on the Palestinian conflict, that adversely affected Iranian-Gulf relations.

Despite a much less congenial atmosphere, Ahmadinejad's government demonstrated great eagerness to expand relations with Gulf Arab states. For example, Iran made a number of proposals for the creation of a security system in the Persian Gulf, including an agency to deal with regional security issues, and an economic cooperation council. Iran also urged expanded bilateral economic and other ties with the Gulf states.

Iran made these proposals during a landmark visit by Ahmadinejad to Qatar in 2007, during which he attended the annual GCC summit meeting.[33] In the same year, Ahmadinejad also visited other Gulf states—Kuwait, Bahrain, Oman, and the UAE—during a major tour of the GCC members. In Oman, he signed agreements on oil and gas cooperation.[34] However, Ahmadinejad's most important visit was to Saudi Arabia. He went there in December 2007 during the Hajj pilgrimage at the invitation of King Abdullah, which was an unusual event.[35]

Two other motives were behind Ahmadinejad's charm offensive in the Persian Gulf:

+ To deflect Gulf states' fears of Iran's nuclear program and to discourage them from cooperating with the United States in case of a military attack on Iran.

+ To reassure them about Iran's intentions in Iraq.

Iran also tried to ease Saudi Arabia's concerns regarding events in Iraq and Lebanon. Saudi Arabia had been supporting Iraq's Sunnis, including some insurgents. In Lebanon, too, Saudi Arabia had tried to check Hizbullah's influence by supporting Sunni groups, including some extremist elements. Meanwhile, Iran had supported the Shias, both in Iraq and in Lebanon. Ahmadinejad sent a message to Saudi Arabia and proposed that the two countries cooperate in stabilizing Iraq and Lebanon.[36] However, these advances did not succeed and, due to the following factors, by December 2008, Iranian-Gulf relations had become highly strained:

+ The Israeli attack on Gaza in December 2008, in retaliation to missile attacks by Hamas on Israeli targets.

+ Iran's uncompromising support for the Palestinians.

+ Arab silence on Gaza.

+ Growing popular criticism in the Arab world of the Arab governments' approach toward events in Gaza.[37]

The Gulf and other Arab governments accused Iran of interfering in intra-Arab affairs and declared that Iran should not interfere in Palestine and Lebanon. To show their unhappiness, many Arab governments indicated that they would not attend an Arab Summit to be held in Doha if Qatar invited Iran to participate as an observer.[38]

Arab reaction was also caused by Ahmadinejad's popularity among Arab masses because of his stand on the Palestinian issue, as well as the popularity of the Lebanese Shia leader, Sheikh Hassan Nasrullah, which was due to his resistance during the Israeli war on Lebanon in 2006.[39] Gulf and other Arab states interpreted Iran's policies as part of a plan to dominate the Arab world.

Regional dynamics and the fundamental causes of Iranian-Gulf tensions were behind the latest worsening of their relations. However, U.S. policy greatly contributed to the worsening of Iranian-Gulf relations, especially former U.S. secretary of state Condoleezza Rice's strategy of building an anti-Shia coalition, focused on Iran, in order to try jump-starting the Arab-Israeli peace process.[40] U.S. policy, especially the consideration of a military attack on Iran, also emboldened some Gulf Arab states, especially the UAE, but also Saudi Arabia, to harden their attitude toward Iran and, at least privately in discussions with the United States and Israel, to support a military strike on Iran. Iranian media even reported that the Saudi foreign minister, Prince Saud Al Faisal, in discussions with Israeli authorities, had indicated that Gulf Arabs preferred Israel to Iran. Israel's foreign minister Tzipi Livni also made similar comments.[41]

Iran became worried about the state of its relations with the Gulf Arabs, especially after Saudi Arabia's foreign minister, during a meeting of Arab League foreign ministers in March 2009, said that Arab states must confront Iran's ambitions in the Arab world.[42] To defuse tensions, Iran's foreign minister, Manouchehr Muttaki, visited Saudi Arabia and was received by King Abdullah. This gesture indicated Saudi willingness to reduce tensions, while also pointing to long-standing differences of opinion within the Saudi leadership on relations with Iran. Muttaki also paid visits to Bahrain and the UAE.[43] Nevertheless, the downward spiral of Iranian-Gulf relations continued.

Relations with Saudi Arabia became particularly strained as the Saudi authorities ratcheted up their concern over Iran's threat and lobbied countries like China and Russia to join in anti-Iran sanctions. The Saudis also seemed to favor U.S. military strike on Iran as they indicated that sanctions were a long term deterrent and could not deal with Iran's immediate threat. Prince Saud Al Faisal said, "sanctions are long term solution. They may work, we can't judge. But we see the issue in the shorter term may be because we are closer to the threat so we may need an immediate resolution rather than a gradual resolution."[44] Considering that Faisal was making this statement during a joint press conference with the visiting U.S. Secretary of State Clinton, indicated that the Saudis had become emboldened by the hardening of the Obama administration's Iran policy.

The media speculated that the United States and Saudi Arabia might have discussed military option against Iran.[45] In the past, Iranian media had reported that the Saudis had told Israel that they would allow the use of their airspace if Israel were to attack Iran.

Iran's main complaints regarding relations with Saudi Arabia, although not raised officially, but widely discussed in Iranian media, have been

- Saudi Wahhabi proselytizing among Iran's Sunni minorities. Iranian media have reported that Saudi Arabia, in cooperation with the United States and Britain, has sent 4,000 Wahhabi fighters, trained in Chechnya, to Iran. Moreover, they have claimed that the Saudi embassy in Tehran has rented a house where it organizes Friday prayer meetings for Iran's Wahhabis;[46]

+ support for separatist/terrorist groups, such as the Sunni Jundullah in Baluchistan;

+ the mistreatment of Iranian Hajj pilgrims.

Comments by Iran's former speaker of parliament, Ali Akbar Nateq Nouri, in January 2009, criticizing the Shah for giving up, created a storm not only in Iranian-Bahrain but also in Iran Gulf relations.[47] In retaliation, Bahrain stopped negotiations over the sale of Iranian gas to Bahrain and banned Iranian nationals from entering its territory.[48] The GCC demanded that the Iranian government condemn Nateq Nouri's statement.[49] The Iranian government dissociated itself from these comments. Nateq Nouri, too, said that his statement was not meant to resurrect Iran's claim, but to demonstrate the subservient nature of the Shah's foreign policy. The Iranian media, however, noted that the Arab overreaction to Nouri's statement was a ploy to distract from the Gaza crisis and Arab silence.[50]

Tensions were finally eased when Iran's minister of interior visited Bahrain and the Bahraini foreign minister came to Tehran.[51]

The only bright spots have been Iran's relationship with Oman and Qatar. In June 2009, it was reported that Sultan Qabus would visit Iran. However, following post-election turmoil in Iran, his trip was postponed until August. In August, accompanied by a large and high-level delegation, he visited Iran and was received warmly.[52] Among the issues discussed were a security agreement, about which the two countries had been negotiating for three years, and Oman's desire to import natural gas from Iran and invest in the Kish gas field near Kish Island.[53] According to some reports, Oman could invest up to $12 billion for the exploitation of this field.[54]

As sign of better relations, in February 2010 Qatar's Crown Prince Sheikh Tamim bin Hamad Al Thani visited Tehran, and on February 24, 2010 Iran's minister of defense visited Qatar.[55] During this trip the two sides signed what has been variously characterized as a "defense agreement,"[56] or a "security protocol."[57] In March 2010, Iran's minister of interior visited Qatar for the signing of the security agreement. The agreement covers areas of cooperation against terrorism, drug and human trafficking, money laundering, and other criminal activities.[58]

IRAN'S RELATIONS WITH THE ARAB EAST: EGYPT, SYRIA, LEBANON, JORDAN, THE PALESTINIANS, AND IRAQ

The basic determinants of Arab-Iranian relations discussed earlier have also shaped the character of Iran's ties with the countries of the Arab East in pre- and postrevolution periods. During the Pahlavi regime, Iran had good relations with pro-Western Arab governments, while its ties with left-leaning radical governments, like those of Egypt and Syria, were strained. Arab nationalists, in particular, saw Iran as a major obstacle to the achievement of their goals. In different periods, Egypt, Syria, and Iraq also saw Iran as a rival for regional influence.

Under Egypt's president Anwar Sadat, Iranian-Egyptian relations vastly improved and the two countries almost became allies.[59] By contrast, the coming to power of a revolutionary regime in Iraq, starting in 1958, turned a friendly relationship into acute hostility. Despite the Shah's efforts to improve relations with Syria in the mid-1970s, Syrian-Iranian relations remained hostile.

IRAN'S RELATIONSHIP WITH THE ARAB EAST IN THE 1980S

By dramatically altering Iran's political system, ideology, and worldview, the Islamic Revolution reversed the pattern of its regional ties: Egypt under Sadat and Hosni Mubarak became enemies, while Syria became a friend.

The following were principal causes of worsening Egyptian-Iranian relations:

- Egypt's fear of revolutionary contagion, especially in light of the growing appeal of Islamist groups in Egypt. Brotherhood?
- Iran's opposition to the Camp David agreement and the Egyptian-Israeli Peace Treaty.[60]
- Egypt's close relations with the United States.
- Sadat's decision to offer refuge to the Shah.
- Iran's naming of a street after Sadat's assassin, Khalid Al Islambuli.
- Egypt's all-out support to Iraq during its war with Iran.

By contrast, for the following reasons Iran and Syria grew closer:

- A shared view on Iraq and Syria's support for Iran in the Iran-Iraq War.
- Similar worldviews: Syria had close relations with the USSR and strained ties to the United States.
- Similar positions on the Arab-Israeli conflict, as Syria was part of the Arab rejectionist front opposed to peace with Israel.
- Similarity of faith between Iran's Shias and Syria's ruling Alawites, and Iran's help in getting them acceptance as mainstream Shias.
- Iran's pragmatic approach toward Syria's Islamist movement, illustrated by its silence in the face of their massacre in Hama in 1981.

However, Syrian-Iranian relations were not free of tension during the 1980s. Syria's secular Ba'athist regime was suspicious of Iran's Islamist ideology, and, after the 1982 Israeli invasion of Lebanon, the two became competitors for influence in Lebanon.[61]

Relations with Iraq during the 1980s were dominated by the war.

The Post-Soviet Era: The Rafsanjani Years

The Rafsanjani government, in pursuit of its pragmatic foreign policy, reached out to Egypt through Syrian and Jordanian mediation. As early as January 1990, Iran communicated to Egypt its desire to cooperate in a number of agricultural areas and to increase the capital of the joint Egyptian-Iranian bank (Bank Misr-Iran).[62] Iran also expressed its willingness to release 100 Egyptian military personnel who had been captured while fighting on Iraq's side in the Gulf War.

However, the following factors prevented any breakthrough:

+ Iran's position on the Camp David Accords and the Egyptian-Israeli peace.[63]
+ Mubarak's strong dislike of the Islamic regime.
+ Egypt's strong reservations regarding Iran's reintegration into the international community because this would have undermined Egypt's value to the West and hindered its ambitions in the Persian Gulf.
+ Egypt's insistence—rightly—that Iran rename the street named after Sadat's assassin.
+ Systemic changes produced by the Gulf War (1990–1991) and the Soviet collapse. After the end of the Gulf war, Egypt was anxious to play a more important military and political role in the Persian Gulf and marketed itself as a counterweight to Iran. Iran responded to this by saying that Egypt's ambition to have a role in the Persian Gulf would be like Iran's wanting to help guard the security of the Suez Canal.[64]
+ The opposition of the regime's radical elements to Rafsanjani's policy of détente with the outside world.

Nevertheless, the two countries' officials remained in contact. For instance, during the Non-Aligned Movement's foreign ministers meeting in Cairo in 1994, Ali Akbar Velayati, Iran's foreign minister, met Hosni Mubarak. However, a real breakthrough eluded the two sides.[65] Even Syrian foreign minister's mediation efforts failed.[66]

Egypt and Iran blamed each other for this lack of success. Velayati complained that Egypt was setting preconditions for improved relations.[67] This was partly true. Egypt insisted that Iran stop supporting terror and Egypt's Islamists, and change the name of the street named after Sadat's assassin. Mubarak, meanwhile, has claimed that he was "about to appoint an Ambassador to Tehran" but that he changed his mind when he heard a statement made by Velayati in response to the question "how can Iran set up relations with a country that signed a peace treaty with Israel?" Velayati's response was that "relations would be kept at a cultural representation level." "*When I* [Mubarak] *heard that I scrapped everything*" [emphasis added].[68]

Iran's contradictory statements and actions, reflecting the divided nature of its leadership, played an important role in its worsening relations with pro-Western Arab governments. However, factors noted earlier were equally significant in this trend.

Khatami Presidency:
Almost-Restored Relations

President Khatami's diplomatic style and discourse, plus improved prospects for U.S.-Iranian ties, created a better atmosphere for Iranian-Egyptian reconciliation.

However, Egypt showed no eagerness for better ties. Despite reports that Egypt was warming up to Iran's new leadership,[69] President Hosni Mubarak did not attend the OIC summit in Tehran.[70] He was invited to attend in May 1997 by the outgoing President Rafsanjani.[71]

During the Khatami presidency, too, initiatives for better relations came from Iran. In an interview with the Qatari daily *Al Sharq* in December 2000, Khatami called Egypt "the gate of Arabs" and added that Iran was taking "swift steps" to improve ties.[72] Then in 2001, during a telephone conversation, Mubarak congratulated Khatami on the latter's reelection.[73] Finally, in December 2003, the two met in Geneva in the margins of the UN-sponsored World Summit on the Information Society.[74] Prospects for the resumption of diplomatic relations between the two countries further improved after Iran changed the name of the street named after Sadat's assassin to "Intifada," leading to reports of a planned Mubarak visit to Tehran in early 2004.[75] The VOA even reported that Egypt might send an ambassador to Tehran before Mubarak's visit.[76]

Efforts at normalization came to a halt when the Egyptian security agency accused an Iranian diplomat of trying to recruit a spy "to perform doubtful operations in Egypt, including coordinating with Shiite groups and planning explosions in Egypt and Saudi Arabia."[77] This about-face on Egypt's part is interesting. Of course, the diplomat might have been guilty as charged. But given Iran's new attitude to such operations under Khatami, Egypt's reaction looks suspect. A more likely explanation is that, for other reasons, Egypt changed its mind and used this argument to justify the change of policy. The following factors could have contributed to this change of heart on Egypt's part:

+ Changed regional conditions.
+ Concern over the so-called Shia threat and Iranian influence in Iraq.
+ The U.S. policy of regime change in Iran and its isolation.
+ Possible U.S. pressure on Egypt not to normalize relations with Iran.[78]
+ Israeli opposition to the improvement in Egyptian-Iranian relations before a change in Iran's attitude toward Israel and the Arab-Israeli conflict. This development would have amounted to what a commentary called the "Nightmare Alliance," because it would have shifted the balance of power in the Middle East against Israel.[79]

Perhaps more important was Egypt's deep suspicion of Iran's motives for seeking better ties. Some in Egypt commented that Iran wanted better relations with Egypt because they argued that creating the hope for a Shi'ite crescent requires neutralizing

Egypt by establishing economic relations with it, "which would prevent Egypt from intervening with the Iranian plans in the future."

THE AHMADINEJAD PRESIDENCY:
EGYPT REBUFFS IRAN AGAIN

Ahmadinejad's more confrontational and combative style of diplomacy did not apply to relations with the Arabs, and he went even further than Khatami in befriending Arab governments. Arab states, however, were not responsive to him, arguing that Iran wanted to dominate the Middle East and that therefore accommodating it would appear as validating Iran's ambitions.

During the first two years of the Ahmadinejad presidency, official relations with Egypt were stagnant. Egyptian papers, including the semi-official *Al Ahram*, accused Iran of being behind the assassination in 2005 of the former Egyptian ambassador in Iraq, Ihab al Sharif, and the attacks by the Justice and Equality Movement in Omdurman in Sudan. Sudan dismissed this accusation, and the Algerian paper, *Sawt al Ahrar*, questioned how Egypt could accuse Iran now, when in 2005 Egyptian and American officials said that Abu Mussab Al Zarqawi and Al Qaeda were behind the assassination.[80]

Nevertheless, in May 2007, Ahmadinejad declared that Iran was ready to open an embassy in Cairo if Egypt would reciprocate.[81] Following this statement, during 2007–2008, there were a number of visits between mid-level and high-ranking Iranian and Egyptian officials.[82] In December 2007–January 2008, the secretary of Iran's National Security Council, Ali Larijani, visited Cairo and met with top officials and religious leaders, including the intelligence minister, Omar Suleiman, and the head of Al Azhar, Sheikh Muhammad Seyed Tantawi. Larijani offered the sale of Iranian wheat and help in the development of Egypt's nuclear program.[83] In January 2008, Ahmadinejad telephoned Mubarak to discuss the situation in Gaza, thus indicating Iran's willingness to cooperate with Egypt on regional matters.[84] In May 2008, the speaker of Iran's parliament, Gholam Ali Haddad Adel, who was in Cairo for the meeting of the parliament speakers of the OIC member states, met with President Mubarak.[85]

However, because of the aforementioned factors, plus Iran's unfulfilled promises, Egypt's response to Iranian overtures was even more cautious than during Khatami's presidency. An especially sour item was the case of the street named after Al Islambuli. Although Iran had changed the name of the street, it had not removed the street signs and a huge mural of Al Islambuli. In an interview with Al Arabiyya TV, Egypt's foreign minister, Ahmad Abul Gheit, said that if Iran removed tributes to Islambuli "90% of the problem [would be solved], and then we can discuss the form of our future relations."[86] Meanwhile, conflicting signals from Egypt indicated some difference of opinion within the Egyptian leadership on how to deal with Iran. The foreign ministry appeared more forthcoming. But statements by President Mubarak, such as that Arab Shias are more loyal to Iran, did not help matters. Meanwhile, Iran's inability to satisfy Egypt's demands regarding Al Islambuli indicated the influence of early revolutionary sentiments.

However, the real reasons for lack of progress were

+ deep differences in worldview;

+ intense rivalry for regional influence;

+ differences of opinion regarding the value and necessity of restoring ties.[87]

[handwritten margin note: C'ld be ethnic — but also religious & ideological]

Nevertheless, Egypt made some positive gestures, including opposing the use of military power to solve Iran's nuclear issue.[88]

THE BATTLE OF THE MOVIES AND CRISIS IN GAZA

Egyptian-Iranian relations further deteriorated in July 2008, following the making of an anti-Sadat movie by an independent organization in Iran. In it, Sadat was characterized as a traitor. Egypt retaliated by deciding to make an anti-Khomeini film.[89] The Iranian government tried to distance itself from the movie, saying that it did not reflect official views. But this would not placate Egypt. It cancelled a football match with Iran, and its foreign minister did not attend the NAM foreign ministers' meeting in Tehran. Moreover, there was a barrage of criticism against Iran by Egyptian commentators and experts, who gave Iran's nuclear program an ethnic and sectarian tinge, calling it "the Shi'ite bomb."[90]

The outbreak of the Gaza crisis in 2008–2009, accusations that Egypt acquiesced and even cooperated with Israel, plus competing efforts of Iran and Egypt to resolve the crisis, further strained ties. In particular, Iran's sending of envoys to Arab countries and urging them to unite and help the Palestinians irritated Egypt.[91] Iran also convened an international conference in support of the Palestinians in Tehran, while Egypt gathered Arab and Western leaders in Sharm al-Sheikh on the same theme but with different objectives.[92]

The 2009 killing of a pregnant Egyptian woman resident in Germany, Merve Al Shirbini, with Iran's championing of her cause while Egypt reacted coolly, became another bone of contention, further dimming prospects of reconciliation.

SYRIA

Since the Islamic Revolution, and especially after Syria sided with Iran during its war with Iraq, the two countries have developed a relationship that they often characterize as strategic.[93] However, Syrian-Iranian relations in the last 30 years have neither been free of tension and competition nor balanced in terms of costs and benefits; they have been more advantageous to Syria.

Initially, Syrian-Iranian relations developed as a result of the commonality of their worldviews, positions on the Palestinian question, and on many other international issues. The following factors further contributed to Syria's desire for friendship with Iran:

- The minority-based character of the Syrian regime. Syria is a predominantly Sunni country, ruled by minority Alawites who are not considered true Muslims by the Sunnis.[94] By contrast, the Shias have a more tolerant attitude toward the Alawites.

- Ideological rivalry and competition for the leadership of the Arab world between the Syrian and Iraqi Ba'athist regimes.

- The Syrian desire to offset the impact of the 1979 Egyptian-Israeli Peace Treaty. When the Iranian Revolution occurred, Syria was feeling exposed to Israeli military threat and saw in alliance with Iran a way to rectify the imbalance created by the treaty. As Patrick Seale has noted: "Syria saw Iran as the natural counterweight to Egypt as much as King Faisal had done in the 1960s."[95]

- Economic advantages in the form of supply of oil on favorable terms, investment, and revenue from Iranian tourists.

In the late 1990s and 2000s, Iran's investment in Syria picked up, and, according to a report in *Al Ahram Weekly*, at the end of 2008 stood at $3 billion. Iran has been involved in a variety of agricultural and industrial projects in Syria, including a car factory and a cement plant.[96] There are also plans to build an oil refinery in Hama and to export Iran's natural gas to Syria through Turkey.

For Iran, relations with Syria have been important, first as a means to deflect the perception that its war with Iraq was a war against all Arabs and, since the end of the war, to ease its regional and international isolation.

SYRIAN-IRANIAN RELATIONS: THE 1980S

During the 1980s, Syrian-Iranian relations were dominated by the dynamics of the Iran-Iraq War. After the establishment of an Iranian presence in Lebanon following the Israeli invasion of 1982, developments in Lebanon also deeply affected their relations.

Syria was worried about the potential impact of an Iraqi victory on the intra-Arab balance. Therefore, its support for Iran was intended to prevent a massive shift of power in Iraq's favor, although it did not want Iran to emerge victorious either. What Syria wanted was the toppling of Saddam Hussein and his replacement by a pro-Syrian Ba'athist regime. Had Iran succeeded in removing Saddam Hussein, most likely the Syrian-Iranian alliance would have degenerated into a fierce competition over Iraq's political future.[97]

Consequently, Syria calibrated its policy based on the two antagonists' fortunes in the war, while also nurturing its Arab ties, even if this meant irritating Iran. Thus in 1986, despite Iran's objections, it participated in the OIC Summit in Kuwait as well as the Amman Summit, which formalized the Arab alliance against Iran.[98] At times, Syria even indicated that it might be persuaded to stop supporting Iran, thus leading King Hussein of Jordan, on several occasions, to try to mediate between Syria and Iraq.

Throughout the 1980s, competition for influence in Lebanon was another source of tension in Syrian-Iranian relations. Since the 1970s, Iran had been instrumental in the awakening of Lebanon's marginalized Shia population, including the creation of Afwaj al Muqawama al Lubnaiya (AMAL). After the Israeli invasion of Lebanon in 1982, Iran expanded its presence in Lebanon and helped establish Hizbullah.

For most of the 1980s, Syria used Iran to counter Israeli and Western influence. However, it was uneasy about Iranian influence in Lebanon, partly because Syria has long considered Lebanon to be part of Greater Syria or, failing that, under Syrian influence. However, when Iran, with the establishment of Hizbullah, seemed to emerge as a rival, Syria moved swiftly to undermine Iran's influence. Thus when the Iran-Iraq War ended in August 1988, leaving Iran weakened, Syria moved to curtail Iran's influence. It supported AMAL against Hizbullah, which was supported by Iran, in the intra-Shia infighting, which broke out in Lebanon during 1988–1990, triggered by AMAL's attacks on Hizbullah in South Lebanon.[99]

According to many observers, the intra-Shia infighting was caused by Syria's and Iran's competing objectives in Lebanon. They argue that, since AMAL was completely dependent on Syria for arms and supplies "it must have been given the go-ahead [to attack Hizbullah] by Damascus."[100] Shortly afterward, Syria moved to stabilize Lebanon under its own influence and to gain Arab endorsement for Syria's role. This was done by the signing of the Taif agreement in 1989 in Saudi Arabia without Iran's participation. Ultimately, the two countries reached an understanding in this regard, although Iran felt embittered by Syria's position. According to a former Iranian ambassador to Damascus, Muhammad Hassan Akhtari, the understanding was reached after long discussions.[101]

Post-Soviet Period

Iraq's attack on Kuwait in August 1990 once more enhanced Iran's importance for Syria, again largely because of concern over the potential impact of Iran's stand on the intra-Arab balance of power. Syria was anxious to secure Iran's participation in the anti-Iraq coalition or at least its neutrality in the conflict, leading Hafez Al Assad to pay his first visit to Tehran in 1990. Rafsanjani returned the visit in 1991.

Soon after, however, regional changes, triggered by Iraq's defeat and the Soviet demise, generated new disagreements between Syria and Iran, notably regarding Arab-Israeli peacemaking. Unlike Iran's ideologically determined and uncompromising approach toward the Palestinian issue, since 1991 Syria's position has become steadily more pragmatic. Syria's main goal has been to regain its lost territory. Consequently, it has been open to discussion with Israel in various contexts. Thus Syria participated in the Madrid Peace Conference in October 1992, and it has since been open to negotiations with Israel, even if it meant forsaking Palestinian interests, as Egypt had done. This Syrian attitude was criticized by Iran's vice president in 1991; he charged that "Syria seemed to be mainly concerned with the Golan Heights."[102]

Therefore, most likely, if Israel returned the Golan Heights and resolved a few other territorial issues, Syria would relinquish its links to Iran. This view is supported by Basher Al Assad's comment when asked why Syria had relations with Iran and North Korea: "Well, I have no choice. I have to have some friends."[103]

This calculation has also been behind Western and Arab efforts since at least 2006 to separate Syria from Iran in order further to isolate the latter.[104] However, Israel has not been willing to satisfy Syria's demands. Nor, without some advance on the Palestinian front, would Syria be able to embrace Israel, following a peace agreement, as the latter wants. Moreover, in case of their estrangement, Iran could manipulate groups like Hamas and the Islamic Jihad, which are present in Syria, to undermine the government in Damascus.

Because of these differences, between 1988 and 1997, Syrian-Iranian relations remained strained. By 1997, the dissipation of hopes for Middle East peace generated by the Madrid Conference and the Oslo process, plus the Turkish-Israeli strategic partnership, which had undermined Syria's position, led Syria again to turn to Iran, thus leading to Hafez Al Assad's second visit to Iran in 1997, followed by Khatami's visit to Syria in 1999.[105]

The events of 9/11, the U.S. war on terror, the U.S. invasion of Afghanistan and Iraq, and the U.S. policy of regime change in Syria and Iran, plus Syria's leadership transition, further cemented their relations. Iran supported Basher Al Assad, who initially had faced some challenges, thus resulting in frequent high-level visits.[106] Basher Al Assad and Muhammad Khatami visited each other's capitals in 2003. During Ahmadinejad's presidency, Assad visited Iran in 2003, 2005, 2007, and 2009, while Ahmadinejad visited Damascus in 2006 and 2008.[107] Ahmadenijad's last visit to Syria was in February 2010.

Throughout their 30-year cooperation, Syria has not sacrificed its Arab connection for Iran's sake. It has always supported Arab positions in their disputes with Iran, including the islands dispute with the UAE, albeit less stridently. It has also used its relations with Iran to get financial assistance from Arab states and has enhanced its value for Arab states as an intermediary between them and Iran.

During 2008 and 2009, Assad has tried to play the same role vis-à-vis the West. In summer 2009, Assad played a role in gaining the release of a French academic who was imprisoned in Iran on charges of spying, for which Assad was thanked by the French foreign minister. Nevertheless, Syria has argued against any military attack on Iran.[108]

During the latter part of 2009 and early 2010, as part of its policy of squeezing Iran, the United States decided on exchange of Ambassadors with Syria and appointed Robert Ford as its ambassador to Damascus.[109] Although talk of the exchange of ambassadors had been going since summer 2009, the appointment of an Ambassador caused panic in Tehran and led to Ahmadinejad's aforementioned trip to Damascus. Sheik Nasrullah of Lebanon also participated in the meeting, thus supposedly demonstrating the unity of Iran-Syria-Hizbullah axis.[110]

However, if Israel were to offer Syria the Golan Heights and satisfy its other demands, and the United States offer it aid and other incentives, Syria will abandon Iran.

What so far has prevented Syria form doing so is its lack of confidence that Israel will return the Golan and the preconditions set by the United States. For example, the

U.S. Secretary of State Clinton listed what Syria should do for better relations with the United States as the following: "greater cooperation with respect to Iran; the end to interference in Lebanon and the transport and provision of weapons to Hizbollah; a resumption of the Israeli-Syrian track on the peace process . . . and generally to move away form relationship with Iran which is so deeply troubling to the region as well as to the United States."[111]

LEBANON

Iran's ties to Lebanon date to pre-Islamic times, although the deep religious links between Iran and Lebanon's Shia community date only to the early 16th century.[112] The Shia Safavids lured to Iran Shia scholars from Lebanon's Jabal Amil.[113] These relations continued in the following centuries under the Qajar and Pahlavi dynasties.[114] After the Second World War, Iran's relations with Lebanon became increasingly affected by Cold War dynamics and their impact on intra-Arab politics and on Arab-Iranian relations.

For most of its postindependence life, Lebanon was a Christian-dominated and pro-Western country. Consequently, its relations with Iran, another pro-Western regional state, were good, although there were areas of tension between the two, caused by activities of Iranian opposition in Lebanon, especially after the PLO set up camps there, following its expulsion from Jordan by King Hussein in 1970.[115]

The Shia connection also cemented Iran's ties to Lebanon, as the Shah financially assisted Shia institutions in Lebanon and, initially, even helped Musa Sadr. Meanwhile, Lebanese ambassadors to Iran often belonged to the country's prominent Shia families. After the establishment of the PLO there, the dramatic disruption of Lebanon's political life, finally leading to a bloody Civil War (1975–1990), fundamentally altered the character of its relations with Iran.

Lebanon and the Opposition to the Shah: Foundation for Postrevolution Relations

Since the early 1960s, radical Arab countries and movements both financially and otherwise supported the Shah's Islamist, leftist and Islamo-leftist opponents, and members of these groups were trained in the PLO camps in Lebanon. Some of them, like Mustapha Chamran, who was largely responsible for the creation of the ideologically motivated Revolutionary Guards, played important roles in the revolution and attained high positions in the Islamic government, and some other Iranian opposition figures were trained in AMAL camps.

Yet Iran's relations with Lebanon would not have developed as they did, had it not been for the Israeli invasion of 1982 and the ensuing struggle to determine Lebanon's future, both among various Lebanese factions and regional states. Certainly, Iran would not have been able to introduce its Revolutionary Guards there and try to wean over Lebanon's disaffected, but increasingly politically conscious, Shia population, eventually helping establish Hizbullah.[116]

The underprivileged conditions of the Lebanese Shias, especially those who, because of Israeli-PLO conflict in the South, had been forced into Beirut and Baalbek, helped Iran's claims that it was fighting for the rights of the oppressed. Iran was also helped by Syria, which was worried about the potential geopolitical shifts that the victory of Falangists in Lebanon, possibly leading to a Lebanese-Israeli peace treaty, would have produced. As it turned out, Israel failed to achieve its goals, and in 1984 President Amin Gemayel rescinded the treaty that Lebanon had signed with Israel in order to pave the way for a national unity government.

During the first decade of the revolution, Iran's relations with Lebanon's Shias remained complex and were sometimes conflictual. In particular, Iran's revolutionary and uncompromising positions, both on Lebanon's future and on the Palestinian issue, strained its relations with the more pragmatic AMAL and its leader, Nabih Beri. Even within Hizbullah, there were differences of opinion about Iran's role. These factors, plus Syria's dominant role in Lebanon during the 1980s and early 1990s, limited Iran's influence there.

Diplomatic relations between Iran and Lebanon were cut after the revolution and were only restored in 1984, when a national unity government came to power. Iran's identification with Lebanon's Shias also soured its relations with the Sunnis and the leftist and Arab nationalist groups that supported Iraq in the war with Iran.

POST-SOVIET PERIOD: THE RAFSANJANI YEARS

By the late 1980s, Iran's influence in Lebanon had faded and Syria had emerged as the dominant influence there. Yet Lebanon remained important to Iran because of the continued problem of remaining Western hostages. This problem complicated Rafsanjani's efforts to focus on domestic reconstruction and rapprochement with the West. Therefore, Rafsanjani tried hard to gain the hostages' release, with mixed success. This failure was partly due to the fact that, contrary to Western belief, Iran did not have total control over the hostage takers.

The effects of the systemic consequences of the first Gulf War and the Soviet demise on Syria and on Lebanon's internal dynamics, including moving Hizbullah toward transformation into a mainstream political party, also negatively affected Iran's position there.[117] By contrast, Iran's relations with Lebanon's government improved when Lebanon's prime minister, Omar Karami, welcomed Iran's new policy of "openness and support," and this led to the visit of Iran's vice president, Attaollah Mohajerani, to Beirut in December 1991.[118]

However, Israel's continued occupation of South Lebanon, the activities of the Israeli-sponsored South Lebanon Army (SLA), and the fading of a Middle East peace deal again propelled Hizbullah, and hence Iran, into a major force, and between 1994 and 2000, when Israel finally unilaterally withdrew its forces from Lebanon, Hizbullah became the main group challenging Israel's presence there.

During this period, Hizbullah periodically shelled northern Israel, at times eliciting a harsh response from Tel Aviv, such as the 1995 Operation Grapes of Wrath, as well as straining official Iranian-Lebanese relations. However, Iranian officials denied any "coolness" in bilateral relations.[119] By early 1997, relations improved after President Rafsanjani met Prime Minister Rafiq Hariri on the margins of the OIC meeting in Islamabad and invited him to visit Tehran. The visit took place during Khatami's presidency.[120]

THE KHATAMI PRESIDENCY

State-to-state relations between Iran and Lebanon benefited from Khatami's policy of reduction of tensions and led to Prime Minister Hariri's visit to Tehran in October 1997, the first such visit since the 1979 revolution. During this visit, he met the Supreme Leader, Ayatullah Khamenei, and offered to help improve Arab-Iranian ties and mediate between Iran and the United States.[121] Hariri again visited Tehran in June 2001, ostensibly to congratulate Khatami on his reelection to the presidency, and Khatami returned the visit in 2003. He was warmly received, especially by Lebanon's Shia population.[122]

Israel's withdrawal from South Lebanon in 2000, for which Hizbullah largely took credit, along with the diminished Iranian-Syrian conflict over Lebanon and influence over Hizbullah, facilitated Iranian-Lebanese rapprochement. Soon, however, international and regional events changed Lebanon's internal politics, and hence the character of its relations with Iran.

THE CEDAR REVOLUTION, SYRIAN WITHDRAWAL, HARIRI ASSASSINATION, ISRAELI ATTACKS, AND FEARS OF SHIA REVIVAL

Some analysts have maintained that the U.S. invasion of Iraq in March 2003 was part of a larger plan to reshape the greater Middle East's political map through regime change in Iran and Syria and the elimination of their influence from Lebanon.[123] In support of their views, they point to the passing of a bill by the U.S. Congress in June 2003, entitled the Syrian Accountability and Lebanese Sovereignty Restoration Act, which strengthened sanctions on Syria and called for the withdrawal of its troops from Lebanon.

Then in February 2005, Lebanon's prime minister, Rafiq Hariri, was assassinated. Syrian intelligence was accused of the assassination.[124] Hariri's assassination generated intense resentment over Syria's military presence and against Hizbullah and its other patron, Iran, among large numbers of Lebanon's Christians, Druze, and Sunni populations, finally culminating in the so-called Cedar Revolution. The revolution's goals were to depose the pro-Syrian president, Emil Lahoud, and to eliminate Syrian and Iranian influence. The revolution was supported by Arab countries concerned about the emergence of a potential Shia crescent and by the West.

In July 2006, Israel attacked Lebanon in retaliation for Hizbullah's abduction of two Israeli soldiers. However, some observers have claimed that Israel had planned to attack Lebanon before their abduction.[125] Whether the attack was planned before or was triggered by the abduction, Israel saw this provocation as an opportunity "to generate a political process in which the Lebanese army could achieve monopoly over the use of force in Lebanon." Israel also calculated that it "could encourage Lebanon to become a regular state and that the Israeli army could crush Hezbollah's Lebanese state within a state."[126]

Despite massive air attacks, Hizbullah showed great resilience and finally forced Israel to accept a cease-fire. Many Lebanese and Arabs blamed Hizbullah and its patrons, Iran and Syria, for Lebanon's suffering. Nevertheless, among Arab populations, Hizbullah's leader, Sheikh Hassan Nasrullah, despite being Shia, became a hero. Iran's prestige in Lebanon also received a boost.[127]

However, Lebanon's problems did not cease with the end of Israeli attacks and it plunged into turmoil, caused by disagreements between the Siniora government, supported by the Druze and the Sunnis and led by Saad Hariri, and an opposition formed mainly by Hizbullah and some Christians, led by General Aoun. The situation further deteriorated when the Sunni Salafist group, Fatah Al Islam, attacked the Palestinian refugee camp, Al Nahar Al Bared, and became engaged in fighting with the Alawi community in Tripoli. Opinions have varied on the origins of these attacks and those responsible for them. Some Western and Arab analysts believe that this was a strategy agreed on by the Siniora government, Saad Hariri, Saudi Arabia, and the United States, in order to undermine Hizbullah and to eliminate Iranian and Syrian influence, not only in Lebanon but in the entire region.[128] Others blame Syria.[129]

These groups' activities and Lebanon's crisis finally aroused the anxiety of all concerned and led to Arab, especially Saudi, mediation in which Iran indirectly participated. This resulted in the Doha Agreement of August 2008. After this crisis, Hizbullah strengthened its position, increased its representation in the government, and gained greater political legitimacy.[130] Following its ally's victory, Iran's prestige in Lebanon also received a boost. Hizbullah's victory seemed to vindicate the more hard-line policy of Iran's president Ahmadinejad on the Palestinian conflict.

Following the election of Lebanon's new president, General Michel Suleiman, Iran's relations with Lebanon's government also improved, and President Suleiman visited Tehran on November 24, 2008. During his trip, the Lebanese president asked that Iran provide Lebanon with small arms, and the two sides signed a defense agreement.[131] During visits by other Lebanese officials to Tehran, the two sides discussed ways to expand bilateral economic and trade relations.[132]

Iran, trying to show that it supported Lebanon's unity and territorial integrity and was open to friendship with all groups, said that it would welcome a visit by Lebanese prime minister Fuad Siniora. However, the trip did not take place.[133] And when Hizbullah and its allies failed to win in Lebanon's parliamentary elections of June 2009, Iran, although disappointed, declared that it respected the will of the Lebanese people.

Since the formation of a national unity government in Lebanon under the premiership of Saad Hariri in November 2009, Iran has continued to court the Lebanese government.[134] However, so far despite maintaining a friendly tone toward Tehran, in practice the new Lebanese leadership has remained cool vis-à-vis Iran. For example Hariri has visited Saudi Arabia, France, Egypt, and even Syria, and yet, despite rumors of an impending visit to Tehran, as of April 2010 he had not traveled to Iran.[135] This shows that Iran has lost part of its influence in Lebanon which never has been as much as either claimed by the West or by the Iranian leadership.

JORDAN

After the Islamic Revolution, the Pahlavi era's close Iranian-Jordanian relationship ended. When Jordan unconditionally supported Iraq in the Iran-Iraq War, the two countries broke diplomatic relations. Throughout the 1980s, King Hussein retained a special place in Iran's demonology, and he was referred to as "Shah Hussein" because of his U.S. ties and his past secret dealings with Israel.

During the Rafsanjani presidency, relations somewhat improved, indicated by the visit of Iran's vice president, Attaollah Mohajerani, to Jordan on December 21, 1991, which culminated in the resumption of diplomatic relations.[136] However, during most of the 1990s, relations remained limited, partly because of Jordan's signing a peace treaty with Israel in 1994, although contacts between the two countries' academic institutions increased.[137]

At the beginning of Khatami's presidency, Jordan indicated its interest in better ties by sending Crown Prince Hassan to the 1997 OIC summit in Tehran. Iran showed its goodwill by returning two Jordanian prisoners captured during the Iran-Iraq War.[138] This was followed by invitations extended by King Abdullah to President Khatami and by Khatami to Abdullah for him to visit Iran, and also by the visit of Iran's foreign minister, Kamal Kharazi, to Amman in June 1999.[139] However, because of the two countries' diametrically opposed ideologies and policies, especially regarding the Palestinian issue, there was no rapid improvement in relations. Jordan complained about the Iranian embassy's activities and curtailed its freedom of action.

In 1999, after King Abdullah called Iran a security threat to the region, Tehran cancelled a delegation to King Hussein's funeral, and King Abdullah postponed his trip to Tehran that had been scheduled to take place in 2000. The visit finally took place in 2003, after the U.S. invasion of Iraq.

Developments in Iraq, the influx of large numbers of Iraqi Shia refugees into Amman, the growing influence of Hizbullah, and Ahmadinejad's confrontational and uncompromising stand on the Palestinian issue caused further deterioration of relations. Finally, together with Egypt and Saudi Arabia, Jordan formed the Arab triumvirate ready to join the U.S.-inspired Sunni coalition against Iran. However, this time a total rupture in diplomatic relations was avoided.

IRAQ: ETERNAL RIVAL OR A POTENTIAL ALLY?

Since the conquest of Babylon by Cyrus the Great in 550 b.c., an Iranian ethnic and cultural presence has existed in Iraq. During the Sassanid period, most of present-day

Iraq was part of Iran. The remains of Iran's famed capital, Madain, and the famous Taq-e Kasra are located in today's Iraq. Even after the Arab conquest, Iran's cultural influence was deeply felt in the region, especially under the Abbasid Caliphs. Between the 16th and 18th centuries, Iran and the Ottomans competed for influence in present-day Iraq. By the 19th century, both empires' weakness and the encroachment of European powers led to a modus vivendi between them, and their frontiers remained largely peaceful.

Following Iran's Shiiazation under the Safavids, not only did Iranian kings do much to embellish and enlarge Shia shrines in Iraq, but a large number of Iranians settled near the holy shrines, and close personal and professional relations developed between Iran's and Iraq's Shia religious centers.[140] After the breakup of the Ottoman Empire, the British carved up Iraq by combining diverse territories, including some which had been a matter of dispute between Iran and the Ottomans. They also established a regime for the Shat Al Arab (Arvand Rud), which favored Iraq. This has become a bone of contention between the two states ever since.

While Iraq was ruled by the Hashemite dynasty and both countries were pro-West, these disputes did not prevent good relations between them. When both countries joined the Baghdad Pact (later CENTO) in 1954, efforts to resolve disputes were intensified and showed some promise of success. The revolution of 1958, led by Abdul Karim Qasim, followed by the Ba'athist revolutions of 1968 and 1972, changed Iraq from a pro-Western monarchy into a pro-Soviet socialist and Arab nationalist republic. These developments led Iranian-Iraqi relations to become poisonous. The two engaged in subversive activities against one another. Iran helped Iraq's Kurdish insurgents, while Iraq supported the anti-Shah opposition and created separatist movements in Iran's Khuzestan Province. But in 1975, Iraq wearied of the Kurdish conflict and signed the Algiers agreement, which established the sharing of the Shat Al Arab along the *thalweg*.

Iran in exchange stopped supporting the Kurdish insurgency.

IRANIAN-IRAQI RELATIONS IN THE 1980S

The Iranian Revolution simultaneously provided Iraq with an opportunity to revenge the Shah's policies and generated strong fears of revolutionary contagion, especially in light of Iraq's large and persecuted Shia population. The result was Iraq's invasion of Iran in September 1980 and the ensuing war that dominated the two states' relations. A discussion of the evolution of the war is beyond the scope of this book. Suffice it to say that it deeply affected Arab-Iranian relations, regional and international politics, and Iran's internal evolution. Its legacy is still casting a shadow over Iran's relations with Iraq and other Arab states.

Not Saddam's desire for conquest?

POST-SOVIET PERIOD

The cease-fire of 1988 left a significant portion of Iran's territory under Iraqi occupation, and it was not followed by a permanent peace treaty. Therefore, Iran's main preoccupation between August 1988 and August 1990, when Iraq invaded Kuwait and unilaterally pulled out of Iranian territory, was the implementation of the provisions of UN Security Council Resolution 598, Iraq's withdrawal from its territory, and the signing of a peace treaty. Despite various UN-sponsored negotiations, Iran failed to achieve these goals, partly because Iraq wanted to leverage its near-victory over Iran into gaining more advantageous terms, especially regarding the Shat Al Arab. The West's, especially America's, view of Iraq as their new regional partner and as an instrument to contain Iran was another factor.[141]

When Iraq decided to attack Kuwait, ostensibly "to improve its economic and strategic position in the Persian Gulf," it initiated contacts with Iran, beginning with an exchange of letters between President Rafsanjani and Saddam Hussein. However, for most of the 1990s, Iraq did not agree to the Algiers formula on the Shat Al Arab. It also made hostile comments at the 1990 Arab Summit against Iran, leading Rafsanjani to say that "the resolution of the Baghdad Summit discouraged us in our assumption that the Iraqis are serious in the establishment of peace."[142] It was only after the invasion of Kuwait that Saddam Hussein accepted all of Iran's conditions, including the validity of the 1975 Algiers Agreement as the basis for discussions on the Shat Al Arab, plus withdrawal of Iraqi forces from Iran in two weeks.[143]

As discussed earlier, Iraq's invasion of Kuwait posed serious dilemmas for Iran and led it to adopt a neutral position in the war, although it did condemn Iraq's invasion.[144]

After the war, the United States adopted a policy of containing both Iraq and Iran. However, being the subject of U.S. containment did not bring the two together, and their mutual misgivings persisted.[145] Nevertheless, Iran condemned sanctions on Iraq and opposed the creation of a Kurdish enclave, fearing the impact on its own Kurdish population, and the periodic U.S. air strikes on Iraq. Iran's main concern was that such acts could create a precedent that could apply to Iran as happened in 1996, when the United States imposed sanctions on Iran.

There was a brief thaw in relations after Khatami came to power and a number of prisoners were exchanged. However, the fundamental issues and the question of a peace treaty remained unresolved.

For the following reasons, Iran, despite all it had suffered at Saddam Hussein's hands, opposed the U.S. attack on Iraq:

+ A unilateral U.S. attack on Iraq would set a precedent for a similar attack on Iran.

+ Iraq under Saddam was weak and isolated, whereas a post-Saddam pro-U.S. government in Iraq could become a formidable foe for Iran.

+ Many circles in the United States, Israel, and Europe were indicating that Iran was next on the list for regime change.

Post-Saddam Period

Events in Iraq did not develop according either to U.S. expectations or to Iran's hopes. Conventional wisdom holds that Iran has been the principal winner of Saddam

Hussein's removal and Iraq's ensuing weakening. The reality, however, is different. Although Iran might have gotten some short-term benefits, in the long run, Saddam's removal and the forging of a close military and political alliance between Iraq and the United States could prove highly threatening to Iran's security, especially if U.S.-Iranian hostility continues. Already, because of the massive U.S. military presence in Iraq and increased U.S. naval presence in the Persian Gulf, Iran's security environment has significantly deteriorated.

During the first few years of the war, the risk of a military encounter between Iran and the United States increased, as the United States accused Iran of destabilizing Iraq. Even after the drawdown of American troops, for some time 50,000 U.S. military personnel will remain in Iraq. Naturally, in any future Iranian-Iraqi disagreement, the United States will favor its ally by, among other things, helping it to improve its relative power position vis-à-vis Iran. It has already been reported that Iraq intends to buy sophisticated U.S. aircraft.

Additionally, because of the following factors, Iran's involvement in Iraq's domestic politics, by virtue of its long-standing connections with its Shia population and political groups, entails long-term risks:

+ The divided character of Iraq's Shia groups;
+ Rivalries among prominent Shi'a clerical families;
+ Enhanced Sunni hostility toward Iran.

These factors mean that Iran is incapable of imposing its will on competing Iraqi factions and would be blamed by all. The experience of postinvasion Iraq supports this view. During this period, some prominent Shia politicians, including the fiery Muqtada Al-Sadr, have criticized Iran for its role in Iraq.[146] One Iraqi prime minister, Ibrahim Ja'afari, was removed partly because he favored close Iranian-Iraqi relations. The Kurds were particularly opposed to him because, as reported "their [Kurds] challenge to Mr. Ja'afari [is] part of a struggle over the country's future between two bigger players: the United States and Iran."[147]

Nor can Iran be sure of the Shias' loyalty, because once the Shias consolidated their position in Iraq, they would act according to their own interests and ambitions and not in fulfillment of Iran's political designs. Similarly, the idea that a Shia-dominated Iraq would not compete with Iran for regional influence or would be more forthcoming on issues such as the Shat Al Arab is equally naïve. Already, Jalal Talebani and his foreign minister, Hoshyar Zibari, have indicated that Iraq does not accept the Algiers Agreement,[148] while Iran insists on its validity.[149] There were also skirmishes between the security forces of the two countries when the Iraqis began oil exploitation in a disputed field. The two sides seem to have agreed on joint exploitation of the fields.[150]

On issues like the disputed islands, Iraq's Shia-dominated government has sided with the UAE. The Iraqi Shias' attitude toward Iran could grow even cooler if Sunni Arab governments stopped undermining them by supporting the Sunnis' claim to continued domination of Iraq and even helping Sunni insurgents.

The future shape of the Iraqi government, especially the balance of power between the Shias and the Sunnis, will also affect relations with Iran. At time, the United States has favored the Sunnis, especially when Zalmay Khalilzad was ambassador there, and it has even favored the rehabilitation of the Ba'athists and their inclusion in government.[151] At one point, the United States was suspected of wanting to replace Nouri al Maliki, Iraq's prime minister. Any such shift of power in the Sunnis' favor would adversely affect relations with Iran since, as put by Iraq's Sunni defense minister Hazim Sha'alan in July 2004, they view Iran as "the number one enemy of [their] country" [emphasis added.] Reportedly he was rebuked for saying this by the then Iraqi interim prime minister, Iyad Alavi.[152] More recently, the Iraqi government has complained of the agreements signed by the United States and Turkey with the Sunni insurgents.[153] In the run up to the March 7, 2010 elections, disputes emerged between the United States and the Maliki government over the latter's de-Ba'athification policies, and the Iraqis accused the United States of wanting to bring the Ba'athists back to power via elections. The narrow election victory of the electoral bloc led by Iyad Alawi and supported by the U.S., Saudi Arabia, and reportedly Turkey, gives some credence to these claims.

Despite persistent misgivings about Iran and long-term challenges, postwar conditions have forced Iraq to be receptive to Iran's offers of cooperation. On the political front, Iran has insisted on maintaining Iraq's territorial integrity and supported the official government. It has also offered economic and other help. Reportedly, trade between Iran and Iraq has been flourishing and is expected to reach $5 billion by the end of 2009. According to some reports, Iran supplied 48 percent of Iraq's total imports in 2006.[154] Among other projects, Iran has signed contracts to build a rail link between Basra and Khoramshahr and two power plants.

Presidential and other high-level visits have been frequent between the two countries. Ibrahim Ja'afari first visited Iran in July 2005.[155] Jalal Talebani has visited Iran six times since becoming president, the last time in March 2010 to take part in the celebration of the Iranian and Kurdis new year, Now Rouz, and Nouri Al Maliki, the current prime minister, visited Iran three times between 2006 and 2009. Reportedly, during his last visit Maliki's main purpose was to allay Iranian fears of close Iraqi-U.S. relations, the signing of the security agreement, and the possibility that the United States might use Iraq to launch military strikes against Iran.[156] In 2008, Ahmadinejad made a controversial visit to Baghdad.

The pilgrimage to holy places of Iran and Iraq has resumed. Nearly two million Iranians visit holy places in Iraq every year and constitute an important source of revenue for Iraq. However, Iranian pilgrims have been the target of bombings, as have been major Shia shrines, notably the blast that destroyed the shrines of Imam Hadi and Hassan Askari in Samara. There has also been progress on the question of remaining prisoners of war and the missing-in-action (MIAs). Iraq's dismantling of Camp Ashraf and its decision to expel the MEK from Iraq could help bilateral relations.[157] However, Iraq might not be able to do so because of external pressure, especially in case of a U.S.-Iranian military confrontation. Other unresolved thorny issues are war reparations by Iraq, demarcation of borders, and the settling of the Shat Al Arab issue.

The character of the government that finally emerges following the March 2010 elections, especially the balance of power between the pro- and anti-Iran elements, would also have a significant impact on whether Iran-Iraq relations evolve in a more cooperative direction or return to the competitive and conflictual pattern of the past.

IRAN AND THE PALESTINIAN GROUPS

Palestinian groups, notably the PLO, had close contacts with groups opposing the Shah and trained their members in camps in Lebanon. These groups' animosity toward Iran derived partly from Iran's secret relations with Israel and partly from diverging ideologies and pattern of alliances: Iran was pro-West while the PLO was pro-Soviet. The Shah's efforts in 1974 to reach a modus vivendi with the PLO, by adopting a more pro-Palestinian posture, did not succeed. Consequently, the Islamic Revolution was enthusiastically embraced by the Palestinians, and the PLO leader, Yassir Arafat, in a visit to Tehran in February 1979, said:

> We consider ourselves an extension of our brother Iranians. They have given to us *and we have given to them*. However, we will never match what they have given to us. This Revolution has created a new era in the area . . . [emphasis added].[158]

Iranian-PLO amity was short-lived. It ended when the PLO, in accordance with its Arab nationalist ethos, supported Iraq in the war. Arafat tried to mediate between Iran and Iraq, but he failed because of his lack of credibility in Tehran. Iran's refusal to settle its differences with Iraq aroused the Palestinians' resentment of Iran because they believed that the war was deflecting attention from the struggle against Israel. However, difficulties with the PLO did not lessen Iran's support for the Palestinian cause; the Islamic regime adopted an uncompromising attitude on the Palestinian issue, and it established Jerusalem (Al Quds) Day, during which Iranians demonstrate in support of the Palestinians.

Post-Soviet Period

After the Soviet collapse, the PLO's position, like that of all of the Soviet Union's Arab allies, was eroded. This factor, coupled with Israel's greater willingness to make peace with the Palestinians as part of its new Arab Option strategy, convinced the PLO to reach an accommodation with Israel, which ultimately culminated in the signing of the Oslo Agreement in 1993.

The PLO's new policy deepened its estrangement from Iran because it continued to view Israel as illegitimate. However, from 1994 onward, Iranian leaders, from Rafsanjani to Ahmadinejad, despite the latter's hostile statements on Israel, have said that Iran would accept the Palestinians' decisions. Notwithstanding this position, throughout the 1990s, Iran forged strong ties with such Palestinian groups as the Islamic Jihad (formed in 1979) and Hamas, formed in 1987, both of which oppose accommodation with Israel until the Palestinians' rights are restored.[159]

Yet Iran was not behind the formation of Hamas. Even Israeli sources, which claim that Hamas is Iran's client, admit that during the 1990s "Iran found it more worthwhile to invest in Hizbullah located in post-Taif Lebanon than in Hamas."[160] Nevertheless, the U.S. policy of dual containment and the growing entente between Israel and the Arab countries led Iran to look to radical Palestinian movements as a defensive means and a potential bargaining chip in its relations with the West, Israel, and Arab states because, as noted by the Iranian analyst, Saeed Leylaz, "Iran's strategic goals are based on its perception that the United States is a threat to its survival."[161] This link between the Western attitude toward Iran and the latter's courting of radical groups is illustrated by the fact that relations between Hamas and Iran grew closer as the possibility of a U.S. or Israeli military action against Iran increased. Reportedly, in 2005, a Hamas leader promised Iran to step up attacks against Israel if it attacked Iran.[162]

FADING OF PEACE HOPES AND HAMAS ELECTORAL VICTORY

The fading hopes of an Arab-Israeli peace after the assassination of Yitzhak Rabin, the Palestinian Intifada of 2000, and Arafat's death under suspicious circumstances in 2004 undermined the PLO and enhanced Hamas's standing among the Palestinians. When in January 2006 Hamas won the parliamentary elections in the Palestinian territories, it became a more appealing partner for Iran, which was under increasing threat of military attack by the United States, Israel, or both.

Under Ahmadinejad, Iran's relations with Hamas and the Islamic Jihad intensified, with frequent visits by their leaders to Iran, and the holding of various conferences by Iran on the Palestinian problem, often coinciding with conferences and meetings held by Western and pro-Western Arab states on the same subject.

Yet Iran neither controls Hamas nor provides the bulk of its financial and military needs. Rather, public and private Gulf Arab sources account for most of Hamas' finances. Iran does provide some weapons, but the amount is unclear. The London Economist, in an article entitled "Hamas' Links with Iran May be Hazier than They First Seem," noted that "Hamas leaders live in Damascus not Tehran, and they are Sunni and not Shi'a."[163]

Turkish prime minister Recep Tayyip Erdogan echoed the same sentiment when he said that Hamas is not Iran's client. Hamas' alliance with Iran is one of convenience and results from its lack of recognition by Western countries and adequate support from Arab states. Any time Arab states, like Saudi Arabia and Egypt, have shown any willingness to deal with Hamas, it has jumped at the opportunity. It is important to note that after victory in the 2006 parliamentary elections, Khalid Mashal, the Hamas leader, first visited Riyadh and not Tehran. Moreover, Hamas has taken positions that have been against Iran's wishes, such as participating in the 2006 elections, and they, unlike Iran, have never taken hostile positions against Arab countries, including those which have signed peace treaties with Israel.[164] In short, if the Arab states treat Hamas better, it will abandon Iran as did the PLO.

THE MAGHREB COUNTRIES

Iran's relations with the Maghreb countries, too, have been determined by the factors which have shaped its relations with other Arab states, notably diverging ideologies and pattern of alliances; fear of revolutionary contagion; and Iran's alleged support for the Maghreb countries' Islamist groups.

IRANIAN-LIBYAN RELATIONS: SUBJECT TO GADHAFI'S CHANGING MOODS

Mu'ammar Gadhafi's and Ayatullah Khomeini's ideas regarding Islam's role in managing contemporary Muslim societies and politics were diametrically opposed, while their worldviews are fairly close, with both having a dislike of the West, Israel, and the conservative Arab regimes. This commonality of views is observable in their joint communiqués, issued at the end of the visit of the speaker of the Iranian Parliament, Ayatullah Rafsanjani, to Libya in 1985. In it, they confirmed their stand against *"Zionism, U.S. imperialism and hireling reactionaries"* [emphasis added].[165]

It was because of this common outlook that Libya initially supported Iran in its war with Iraq and provided it with military aid.[166] During Rafsanjani's 1985 visit to Libya, Gadhafi expressed regret that Iraq had imposed a war on Iran and urged Iran not to hold all Arabs responsible. He added that reactionary Arab forces were trying to turn the war into an Arab-Persian war because that is "something which is in line with America-Israeli plan," whereas in reality this [Iran-Iraq War] is "a war between revolution and reactionaries."[167] In exchange, Iran supported Libya in its confrontation with the United States in 1986 and may have helped its oil industry.

In September 1987, and only two month after the visit of the Libyan foreign minister to Tehran, during which he reiterated Libya's support for Iran, Gadhafi shifted his support to Iraq and all but declared Iran to be responsible for starting the war. Reportedly, reverses suffered by Libya in Africa and Gadhafi's need to regain acceptance by the Arab world were behind this shift of position. However, this sudden shift also showed the fragile nature of any Arab-Iranian cooperation.[168]

Post-Soviet Period

As a close Soviet ally, Libya was negatively affected by the USSR's collapse. Events in the Middle East, such as the first Gulf War, followed by a reactivation of the Arab-Israeli peace process, coupled with Libya's own foreign policy reverses in Africa and the Middle East, led Gadhafi to strike a more moderate and reconciliatory tone. Libya patched up relations with Egypt and expelled the Abu Nidal group.[169]

These shifts in Libya's policies led to a further cooling of its relations with Iran. However, Iran under Rafsanjani was determined to improve its global ties and did not react strongly to these changes. Consequently, for the rest of the 1990s, Iranian-Libyan relations remained limited but not hostile. Official contacts continued, and Libya sought Iran's help in establishing relations with the Central Asian countries.[170]

Under Khatami, relations took a turn for the better and, in 1999, Iran's foreign minister visited Libya and delivered a message from the Iranian president to Gadhafi. He again visited Libya in December 2002.[171] The two sides also signed a number of agreements on cooperation in various economic fields.[172] In January 2006, Iran's vice president visited Tripoli, and in July 2006, during the OAU meeting in Gambia, Ahmadinejad met with Gadhafi.[173]

Since 2003, when Gadhafi abandoned Libya's nuclear ambitions, Libya has made contradictory statements on Iran. At times, he has warned that if Iran does not abandon its nuclear ambitions it will suffer "Iraq's fate," while at other times he has told the Arabs that it is not in their interest to alienate Iran, because they "have no escape from Iran," which is "a neighbor and a Muslim brother."[174] He has also condemned efforts to ignite the Sunni-Shia conflict and has called for the restoration of the Shia Fatimid Caliphate in North Africa.[175] Nevertheless, Libya voted for UN sanctions against Iran, although it criticized aspects of the UN Security Council's resolution.[176]

In summary, despite ups and downs, Iranian-Libyan relations have remained basically good, although under the impact of external events, combined with domestic reverses in both countries, they have lost the revolutionary intensity of the 1980s.

ALGERIA, TUNISIA AND MOROCCO: EFFORTS AT COOPERATION AND PERSISTING SUSPICIONS

As with other pro-West Arab states, after the Islamic Revolution Iran's friendly relations with Morocco and Tunisia suffered. With Morocco, it was Iran that broke diplomatic relations in 1981, because of King Hassan's decision to offer asylum to the Shah. Tunisia broke relations with Iran in 1987, claiming that it was fomenting Islamic radicalism there. However, reportedly, the Tunisian government had "heightened a purported threat from abroad to justify its hostility to most forms of dissent at home."[177]

Because of the Algerian government's Third Worldist leanings, throughout the 1980s Iran's relations with Algeria remained good, and Algeria played a key role in resolving the American hostage issue. But the outbreak of a civil war in Algeria in 1992 between the Islamist opposition and the government led to the severing of diplomatic relations with Iran, as Algeria accused Iran of supporting its Islamist opposition.[178]

Post-Soviet Period

Under Khatami, Iran tried to repair ties with the Maghreb countries and sent a number of emissaries to Maghreb states. Iran's vice president, Hassan Habibi, visited

Tunisia in April 2001, followed by a visit by its foreign minister, Kamal Kharazi, in June 2003.[179] Kharazi visited Morocco in May 2004.[180]

Iran's charm offensive was fairly successful in Algeria and Tunisia,[181] while relations with Morocco experienced only mild improvement, followed by a new crisis and the severing of diplomatic relations by Morocco in 2009 on the pretext that Iran was spreading Shiism in Morocco, and also in response to the statement of an ex-Iranian official regarding Bahrain.[182]

Improved relations with Algeria were due to the fact that Algeria, unlike Morocco, is not close to the United States and Israel. This improved state of relations is reflected in the visits of Iran's presidents Khatami and Ahmadinejad to Algeria in October 2004 and in July 2007, respectively,[183] and by the visit of the Algerian president to Iran in October 2003 and August 2008.[184] These visits have resulted in the signing of a number of economic and cultural agreements.[185] Cooperation might extend to the defense area, as indicated by the visit of the Iranian defense minister to Algeria in April 2005.[186] Both Algeria and Tunisia have supported Iran's right to peaceful nuclear energy.[187]

According to one Tunisian professor, Tunisia has at times used the threat of closer relations with Iran to gain economic advantages from the West.[188]

However, mistrust of Iran remains even in Algeria and more so in Tunisia. They also disagree on key issues, such as the Arab-Israeli conflict. This mistrust of Iran and dislike of aspects of its domestic policies were evident in some of the commentary in the Algerian press, especially the French language press, following Ahmadinejad's visits there. For instance, *L'Expression* talked about a culture of intolerance in Iran, and others accused Iran of wanting to penetrate Algerian markets.[189] Pro-government publications like *Al Moujahid* were supportive of the visit. In an article entitled "Trust and Peace," it wrote that Algeria and Iran are "two Muslim countries which could put all their weight on the international scene at the political, cultural and especially energy levels."[190]

ASSESSING IRAN'S POLICY IN THE ARAB WORLD

Despite serious efforts at courting its Arab neighbors and other key Arab states, and putting up with some humiliating behavior on their part, as well as pursuing an essentially pragmatic policy toward the Arab world, in the post-Soviet period Iran has failed to ease their hostility and to obtain their cooperation. On the contrary, some aspects of Iran's regional foreign policy, especially its uncompromising stand on the Arab-Israeli conflict, instead of advancing Muslim unity and reconciling the Arabs to Iran, have brought the Arabs and the Israelis closer together. Worse, Iran's position has not even helped the Palestinians to gain their rights.

Iran's estrangement from the West has further enabled the Arab states to score points against it on such symbolically important questions as the name of the Persian Gulf. Today, elements of the U.S. Defense Department and the U.S. military, in their official communications, refer to the Arabian Gulf instead of the historic name of the Persian Gulf, and the United States and other Western countries are more sympathetic to the UAE's position on the question of the three disputed islands. Iran's hostile relations with the West have also put it at a disadvantageous position vis-à-vis even its Arab friends, such as Syria. It has been using Iran as a bargaining chip to obtain concessions from the West.

The failure of Iran's Arab diplomacy has been primarily due to

- the same factors that have also been responsible for the failure of its strategy in other regions—namely, its lack of full appreciation of post-Soviet systemic changes and its inability to adjust to them. For instance, Iran has not realized that Gulf Arabs will not sacrifice their relations with the United States for Iran's sake, even in the absence of any other factors. It is interesting to note that Iran's success in improving ties with Gulf Arabs has taken place during periods when Iranian-West relations have been experiencing periods of relative thaw. Iran has also not fully appreciated that given their security vulnerabilities the Gulf Arabs need Western protection and would not forego it. Nor would they accept Iran's protection;

- Iran's inability to understand that it cannot simultaneously pursue revolutionary objectives seen as threatening by Arab states and friendly state-to-state relations. For example, it is naïve to believe that Iran could improve relations with Egypt while hailing Sadat's assassin as a hero and attacking the Camp David Accords;

- underestimating the limiting impact of ethnic and sectarian factors, as demonstrated by the fact that Iran's protestations of Islamic unity have been viewed with suspicion by Arab states.

Total amity between Iran and the Arab world under any Iranian regime is impossible. However, a more nuanced and less ideologically determined Iranian approach to relations with Arab countries, coupled with more realistic Iranian behavior internationally, would have succeeded in reducing Arab-Iranian tensions, improved prospects for cooperation, and better protected Iran's interests.

CHAPTER 10

Iran's Relations with Africa and Latin America: Seeking Economic Advantage or Anti-Imperialist Coalition?

The Islamic government of Iran has always seen itself as the champion of all deprived and downtrodden masses and not only those of the Muslim world. In addition to Islamic principles, this aspect of Iran's self-image has been shaped by ideas popular in the Third World during the 1960s and the 1970s. The following are some of the more important of these ideas:

- The need to reform the international economic system and make it more equitable.[1]
- The necessity to promote Third World countries' individual and collective economic self-sufficiency.
- The necessity to promote intra-Third World economic and other cooperation within the framework of South-South relations.

This aspect of the Iranian regime's self-image and worldview to a great extent explains the Islamic Republic's policy of expanding its political and economic relations with African and Latin American countries, especially those with anti-Western positions. This is why, during the first decade of the revolution, Iran developed friendly relations with Cuba and later with the Nicaragua of Daniel Ortega, and expanded its diplomatic representation in Africa.[2]

However, even during the Shah's rule, Iran championed Third World causes, sometimes to the point of irritating its Western allies, and expanded its relations with developing countries.[3] Moreover, both before and after the revolution, important practical reasons have motivated Iran's approach to relations with developing countries. Under the Shah, Iran's policy toward the Third World was influenced by its view of its future needs for raw materials and export markets as it pursued a policy of rapid industrialization.[4] During the first decade of the revolution, the spread of revolutionary ideology was an added objective of Iran's Third World diplomacy.

RELATIONS WITH AFRICA

Iranians have been familiar with at least parts of Africa since ancient times. The Achaemenid emperor Cambyses conquered Egypt in 524 B.C.E, and the Persians ruled Egypt for 200 years. Darius reached the Red Sea.[5]

In the Islamic era, Iran's connection with Africa was focused on its eastern coast. In fact, "long before the Gulf oil boom, sailors and traders from Iran sailed down to East Africa with the North-East monsoons in their magnificent wood hulled ships, gorgeously sculpted from stem to stern. Mogadishu in Somalia; Bagamayo, Kilwa and Zanzibar in Tanzania; and Beira in Mozambique were their ports of call."[6] Some of them settled there and are today represented by Zanzibar's "Shirazis," or the descendants of a group of Iranians from Shiraz who went there 800 years ago.[7]

In modern times, Africa became a focus of Iranian diplomacy in the 1950s, 1960s, and 1970s. During the 1950s and 1960s, Iran's efforts were concentrated on the anti-colonial movement, partly because of its own experience with colonial powers. At this time, Iran was active in the United Nation's Special Committee on Decolonization. In recognition of Iran's contribution, its representative to the UN was chosen to present the UNGA Resolution 1560 on decolonization to the General Assembly.

By the late 1960s, growing security concerns, resulting from increased Soviet inroads in parts of Africa, notably the Horn, intensified Iran's interest in the continent. The Shah's government, which was concerned both about Iran's encirclement by the USSR and the safety of maritime oil-export routes, sought to counter Soviet inroads by providing assistance, including in some cases military, to moderate African countries.[8] During this period, however, Iran's growing ties with South Africa's apartheid regime, coupled with its limited financial resources, handicapped its African diplomacy. Nevertheless, by 1976, Iran had established diplomatic relations with 31 African countries.

POSTREVOLUTION PERIOD

During the first decade of the Islamic regime, the following factors enhanced Iran's interest in Africa:

+ Iran's growing difficulties with traditional trade and economic partners in Europe and Asia.
+ The need to harness support from Third World countries in its war with Iraq.
+ Interest in Africa's large Muslim populations as potential converts to Iran's Islamic ideology.

An early act of Iran's Islamic regime was the severing of diplomatic relations with South Africa and the granting of unconditional support to the African National Congress (ANC). This act significantly improved Iran's image in Africa and in the Third

World in general. According to some African sources, the Islamic regime's image in the continent also benefited from its defiant attitude toward the United States.[9]

During this decade, Iran increased the number of its embassies in Africa, promoted diplomatic visits, and provided some help to a number of African countries. The most prominent Iranian visitor to Africa was its then-president Ayatullah Ali Khamenei; he toured the continent in 1986. Toward the end of the 1980s, Iran tried to market some of its manufacturing goods, including military hardware, on the continent.[10]

The results of Iran's African diplomacy during the 1980s were mixed. On the political front, Iran failed to gain the full support of African nations in its war with Iraq. Moreover, its activities to spread its revolutionary ideology created serious strains in its relations with key African Muslim states, such as Senegal, and led to the rupture of diplomatic ties with Dakar in 1984. Senegal justified its decision on the basis that the personnel of the Iranian embassy in Dakar "were involved in activities that violate international norms." The embassy personnel were involved in "fundamentalist propaganda in Senegalese Muslim associations."[11]

Meanwhile, because of Iran's Shia character, its ideological appeal in Africa remained limited, although its efforts to promote its ideology have led to accusations of wanting to convert African Muslims to Shiism.[12] Nevertheless, in some parts of Africa, notably Nigeria, Iran's Islamic Revolution increased the appeal of Shia Islam. Prior to the 1980s, there were no Shias in Nigeria, whereas now Nigeria has approximately 3.5 million Shias. Some sources put their number even higher. Nigeria's Shias are concentrated in Kano and Sokoto states. The most prominent Shia cleric is Sheikh Ibrahim Zakzavi, who reportedly has spent considerable time in Iran (see table 10.1).[13]

Table 10.1   Shia Population in Selected African Countries

Country	Shia Population
Ghana	1,188,000
Tanzania	1,095,000 (a large % are Ismaili)
Kenya	560,000
Senegal	549,000
Ivory Coast	436,800
Niger	407,400
Nigeria	3,500,000
Ethiopia	387,000
Uganda	301,280

Source: Nation Master Encyclopedia.[1]

[1]http://www.nationmaster.com/encyclopedia/Shi'a-population.

THE POST-SOVIET PERIOD: IRANIAN-AFRICAN RELATIONS
DURING THE RAFSANJANI AND KHATAMI PRESIDENCIES

From 1989 until 1995, Iran's main foreign policy preoccupations were the improvement of relations with the West; adjusting to the new Russia; and expanding relations
with Asia, including the newly independent republics of Central Asia, plus the Caucasus. Consequently, relations with developing, including African countries, were no
longer a priority of Iranian diplomacy.

The change in the focus of Iranian diplomacy during the post-Soviet era reflected
both Iran's economic needs and the changes triggered by the Soviet collapse. Relations
with the Third World, including African countries, also suffered because of domestic
criticisms of the government's Third World focus in the 1980s as ineffective. The only
African country with which Iran expanded its relations in the late 1980s and early
1990s was Sudan.

The Sudan-Iran rapprochement was the result of coming to power of an Islamically oriented government in Sudan in 1990, following a coup d'état by General Omar
Al Bashir. The coup was supported by the National Islamic Front (NIF) of Hassan
Al Turabi. He was a supporter of Muslim unity, easing of Sunni-Shia tensions, and
an admirer of the Ayatullah Khomeini. Moreover, during the 1990s, Sudan became
the refuge of a number of Islamic and other extremist groups, some of which had affiliations with Iran. All these factors contributed to improved Sudan-Iran relations.[14]
In December 1991, President Rafsanjani, accompanied by a large delegation, visited
Sudan. Since then, Western and Arab sources have claimed that Iran has been training
Sudanese military forces and using its presence there to gather intelligence and spread
extremist ideologies.[15]

However, relations with the rest of Africa were not completely neglected, and diplomatic exchanges, including high-level visits, continued. Between 1988 and 1994, a
number of African leaders, notably Tanzania's president Ali Hassan Mwinye (June
1989), Zimbabwe's president Robert Mugabe, Kenya's president Daniel arap Moi
(December 1989), and Uganda's president Yoweni Mueveni (March 1991), visited
Iran, as did Nelson Mandela, head of the African National Congress (ANC).[16]

By 1996, Iran's westward policy had hit serious snags, especially with the imposition of trade sanctions by the United States, thus leading Iran to revitalize its relations
with developing countries, including those in Africa. This renewed interest in Africa
was manifested in President Rafsanjani's tour of six African countries (Kenya, Uganda,
Sudan, Zimbabwe, Tanzania, and South Africa) in fall 1996.

Rafsanjani was warmly received in South Africa, Including by President Nelson Mandela. Iran had established diplomatic relations with South Africa in 1994. This warm
welcome was despite warnings from the United States that Rafsanjani's visit should
not signal closer relations between Iran and South Africa.[17] The scope of Rafsanjani's visit was somewhat limited. For instance, he did not visit Cape Town to speak
in the parliament, partly because the city at the time had been the site of anticrime
ferment within the Muslim community, some of whom reportedly had pro-Iran sympathies. Nor were any agreements signed during this trip. Nevertheless, South Africa

expressed the hope that its trade gap with Iran, largely the result of South Africa's oil imports from Iran, would narrow in the future.[18] A Joint Economic Commission was also created between the two countries. Over the next decade, trade and investment between Iran and South Africa expanded. According to the South African minister of foreign affairs, Nkosazana Dlamini Zuma, speaking at the eighth joint session of the Iranian–South African economic commission in December 2004, the amount of South African investment in Iran had reached $1.5 billion and Iranian investment in South Africa was at $150 million.[19]

During the presidency of Muhammad Khatami, Iranian-African relations continued to expand, with the focus shifting to specific projects and areas of economic and industrial cooperation. Early in his presidency, Khatami hosted the prime minister of Kenya, Daniel Arap Moi, in December 1998.[20]

Iranian-African relations received a boost when Khatami toured seven African countries—Nigeria, Senegal, Mali, Benin, Sierra Leone, Zimbabwe, and Uganda—in January 2005. On this trip, Khatami emphasized economic cooperation and exploring ways in which Iran's private sector could become engaged in Africa's development.[21] Khatami's visit to Senegal signaled the end of the period of coolness in bilateral relations. In March 2005, Iran's foreign minister, Kamal Kharazi, visited Ghana. During this trip, Iran signed an agreement giving Ghana $1.5 million in aid for budgetary support.[22]

Before his African tour, President Khatami had paid a visit to Sudan in October 2004. He was warmly received and the visit was characterized as a "landmark" in the two countries' relations.[23] Sudan's warm reception was partly due to the fact that, by that time, because of events in Darfur it had come under severe international pressure and, like Iran, it felt isolated.

AHMADINEJAD PRESIDENCY: RETURN TO EARLY PRIORITIES

Upon assuming the presidency in 2005, Mahmud Ahmadinejad declared that his principal goal was a return to the values and principles of the early years of the revolution in Iran's domestic and foreign policies. In foreign policy, this meant greater attention to the expansion of relations with developing countries. However, other factors, notably growing Western pressure, including the imposition of economic sanctions because of Iran's nuclear program, also contributed to this shift of policy.

To counter Western pressures, Iran needed Third World, including African, countries' sympathy for its positions and their cooperation at the IAEA and the UNSC. Hence, the Ahmadinejad government's cultivation of ties with Africa. Meanwhile, rising oil prices improved Iran's financial conditions and made it a more attractive partner for African countries. An important result of Iran's new Africa focus was that it was granted observer status at the Organization of African Unity (OAU), and Ahmadinejad attended the seventh OAU summit held in Banjul, the capital of Gambia, in July 2006.[24]

Ahmadinejad's other important African visit was to Senegal on the occasion of the 11th summit meeting of the Organization of the Islamic Conference in March 2008.[25] Before, in June 2006, the Senegalese president, Abdoulaye Wade, had visited Tehran. He visited Tehran two more times, the last time in October 2009.[26] Economic ties between Iran and Senegal also expanded, and Iran became involved in a number of projects there, including a car factory which produces the Samand, made by Iran Khodro with a production capacity of 10,000 vehicles annually. Iranian sources covered 60 percent of the cost of production, the Senegalese government 20 percent, and the rest was covered by the Senegalese private sector.[27] Iran expressed its readiness to help Senegal set up tractor factories and to build rail and road systems. It requested that the Senegalese government provide it with land for the setting up of a permanent commercial center in Dakar.[28]

Under President Ahmadinejad, relations with Sudan also grew closer. In April 2006, Sudan's president, Omar Al Bashir, visited Iran,[29] and in February 2007, Ahmadinejad returned his visit.[30] Iran has tried to expand economic relations with Sudan, by setting up a car assembly factory, and helping with other projects. However, the implementation of cooperation agreements has been slow. In March 2008, during the visit to Sudan by Iran's minister of defense, Mustafa Muhammad Najjar, the two countries signed an agreement on military cooperation.[31]

Beginning in 2007, Iran has tried to create a long-term framework for its relations with African states and, as a first step, has suggested the holding of an Iranian-African conference. The African Union has also been looking into prospects and modalities of an enhanced Africa-Iran partnership. To explore these possibilities, in March 2008 a delegation from the African Union Commission visited Tehran.[32]

Other countries in Africa with which Iran has tried to expand ties include: Gambia, whose president visited Iran in December 2006;[33] Tanzania, whose foreign minister visited Iran in October 2008;[34] Zimbabwe, Gabon, Djibouti, and Malawi, whose presidents visited Iran in September 2006 and May 2008, respectively;[35] plus Mali and Eritrea. In March 2009, Iran's foreign minister visited Mali, where Iran is helping build the Kanai dam and has established a clinic in Bamako. During his trip, Foreign Minister Muttaki expressed Iran's willingness to help Mali in the fields of energy—especially new types—agriculture, water, and the building of factories to produce tractors and other agricultural machinery.[36]

In February 2009, Ahmadinejad went on an African tour. It took him to Djibouti, Kenya, and Comoro. In Djibouti, he signed five economic cooperation agreements and declared the granting of a credit line to Djibouti.[37] During his Kenya visit, Ahmadinejad was accompanied by a large delegation, including private businessmen. Iran and Kenya have reasonable trade relations, and Iran is a key market for Kenya's tea. During this trip, a number of agreements were signed, which reportedly could increase the volume of bilateral trade to $500 million by 2010. Other agreements related to the establishment of a direct air link between Tehran and Kenya, the setting up of a shipping line between Mombasa in Kenya and Bandar Abbas in Iran, the establishment of an Iranian trade center in Nairobi, and the protection of Iranian investors in Kenya. Kenyan media also reported that Kenya might ask Iran to help it built a nuclear-powered

Table 10.2   Iran's Trade with Selected African Countries in 2008 in Million Euros

Country	Iran's Exports	Iran's Imports
Kenya	43.9	—
South Africa	3,014.3	197.7
Sudan	40.0	—
Tanzania	10.4	—

Source: European Commission.

electricity plant. Reportedly, an Iranian private company is already building a hydro-electric power plant north of Nairobi and a gas power plant near Mombasa.[38] As can be seen from table 10.2, Iran's only major trading partner in Africa is South Africa.

ASSESSING IRAN'S AFRICAN DIPLOMACY

Iran's African diplomacy has only partially succeeded in achieving Iran's objectives. In the economic area, despite some inroads into African markets, the level of trade and investment between Iran and Africa has remained limited. Only South Africa has a substantial level of trade and investment ($1 billion) in Iran.

Factors similar to those responsible for the poor results of Iran's diplomacy in Central Asia have also limited the results of its African policy. The following are the most important of these factors:

- Iran's limited financial, economic, and technological resources.
- Iran's domestic needs for consumption and investment.
- Africa's massive need for investment and export markets.

For most African countries, Iran is only attractive as a potential source of economic aid and investment. Iran has not been able to satisfy the Africans' expectations of itself in any substantial way and is unlikely to do so in the foreseeable future. This particular feature of Iranian-African relations is a reflection of the limits of the so-called South-South cooperation, because of the South's lack of capital and technology.

Politically, Iran's gains have been meager, as African countries, while mostly supporting Iran's right to peaceful nuclear technology, have voted cautiously in international organizations. For example, even South Africa, arguably the African country friendliest to Iran, abstained during the voting in the IAEA on whether to refer Iran's nuclear dossier to the UN Security Council.

In Muslim Africa, Iran's Shia character has handicapped it. For example, even in Sudan, many accuse Iran of promoting Shiism and thus oppose close relations with it.[39] Should there be a change of government in Sudan, all of Iran's investment could come to naught. Meanwhile, Iran is being criticized by other African countries for supporting the Sudanese government, despite its handling of the Darfur problem. Articles skeptical of closer ties with Iran have also appeared in Kenya and Malawi.[40] A main theme of these articles is that close relations with a country which has an international reputation as being repressive is not beneficial to African states. Moreover, as seen in the following quote, the belligerent and anti-Western tone of Iranian diplomacy is not always welcomed in Africa. Rose Wanjiku wrote that "President Mahmoud Ahmadinejad is coming to Kenya this month . . . The visit will definitely ruffle feathers because of the Iranians' standing with countries we consider friends . . . Hopefully he won't be repeating his disbelief in the Holocaust or berating U.S. president George Bush, his successor Barack Obama, or Britain."[41]

The controversial nature of Iran's 2009 presidential elections and the arrests that followed mass protests would certainly tarnish Iran's image among African nations.

In sum, if Iran had moderated the tone of its overall diplomacy, liberalized domestically and thus improved its global image, and responded wisely to post-Soviet systemic changes, its chances of improving its relations with Africa would have been enhanced.

IRAN'S RELATIONS WITH LATIN AMERICA

Because of geographic distance, cultural differences, the lack of significant common interests, and absence of conflicts, Iran's relations with Latin America were late in developing. The only exception was Venezuela, where the two countries' interest in gaining greater control over their oil resources had led to some contacts and a degree of cooperation between them in the late 1940s. Iran and Venezuela were also among the founding members of the Organization of Oil Exporting Countries (OPEC) in 1962.

During the 1970s, Iran expanded its presence in Latin America by establishing diplomatic relations with Brazil, Argentina, Mexico, and Venezuela. In 1975, in line with its National Independent Policy, Iran established diplomatic relations with Cuba. Iran's motive was to dissuade Fidel Castro from helping the regime's leftist opposition. Relations were broken shortly afterward when, during a trip to Moscow, Fidel Castro met with the leaders of Iran's outlawed Communist Party. However, even before this meeting, Iran had realized that Cuba was continuing to help the Iranian opposition through its Middle East allies.[42]

POSTREVOLUTION PERIOD: THE FIRST DECADE

Iran's revolutionary ideology has been strongly influenced by both militant Third Worldism and leftist ideologies, both of which have also been influential in Latin America, and have thus created a certain bond between the Islamic regime and leftist Latin American countries. Consequently, the Islamic regime in the 1980s expanded its relations with leftist Latin American countries, such as Cuba and the Sandinista government in Nicaragua. The strong anti-American tendencies of all three countries and their sense of being revolutions under siege facilitated their cooperation.[43] Iran helped Nicaragua by providing it with oil on credit terms, and Daniel Ortega was met by Ayatullah Khomeini during his visit to Iran. Cuba established a significant presence in Iran during the early years of the revolution and, according to some reports, helped train the Revolutionary Guards. However, during the Iran-Iraq War, Cuba's close ties with Iraq became a source of strain in relations with Iran.

During the 1980s, Iran, because of its economic needs and Western pressures, also reached out to major Latin American countries like Brazil and Argentina.

THE POST-SOVIET PERIOD

Because of its other priorities noted earlier, between 1989 and 2005 Iran pursued a less activist diplomacy. However, it continued to cultivate existing ties, as reflected in the visit of Mir Hussein Mussavi, Iran's former prime minister and an adviser to President Rafsanjani, to Uruguay in 1990.

During the Khatami presidency, Iran's approach toward Latin America became more activist and resulted in increased high-level visits between Iran and Latin American officials. In July 1999, Iran's first vice president visited Colombia, Cuba, and Venezuela.[44] In October 2000, Cuba's vice president paid a visit to Iran, and in May 2001, Fidel Castro visited Tehran.[45] He was followed by the Venezuelan president, Hugo Chavez.[46] In October 2000, Khatami had visited Cuba at the invitation of Fidel Castro.[47] Khatami first visited Venezuela in 2000 on the occasion of the Summit Meeting of OPEC countries. This was followed by Hugo Chavez's visit to Iran in 2004 and Khatami's official visit to Caracas in 2005, during which the foundation of more expanded Iranian-Venezuelan cooperation was laid.[48]

During his 2005 visit, Khatami inaugurated a tractor factory built with Iran's help, and the two countries signed a free trade agreement,[49] plus other agreements reportedly worth $1 billion dollars, including the setting up of a car factory and a $200 million cement plant.[50]

On the Venezuelan side, a closer Iranian-Venezuelan relationship was made possible by the coming to power of the leftist and anti-U.S. government of Hugo Chavez, bent on bringing about a so-called Bolivarian Revolution in Venezuela. For Iran, the West's cool response to its overtures and later, the adoption of a policy of pressure and isolation, were the main impetus behind its renewed focus on Latin America.

AHMADINEJAD PRESIDENCY: AN EMERGING IRANIAN-LATIN AMERICAN PARTNERSHIP?

Ahmadinejad's presidency was marked by a renewal of the way of thinking current during the first decade of the revolution, which emphasized the expansion of Iran's relations with like-minded governments of the Third World. His presidency also coincided with the emergence of left-leaning governments in Bolivia and Ecuador, and rising oil prices. Higher oil prices revived Third Worldist tendencies, such as reducing the developing world's dependence on the international economic system dominated by Western powers in Latin America, as illustrated by Hugo Chavez's launching of the Bolivarian Alternative (ALBA) in response to the U.S.-sponsored NAFTA (North American Free Trade Area).

Consequent to political shifts in Iran and in some Latin American countries, between 2006 and 2009 there was a flurry of high-level visits between Iranian and Latin American officials. Iranian-Venezuelan relations, particularly, became quite close, and Chavez referred to Ahmadinejad as his brother. He visited Iran seven times, the last time in September 2009,[51] and Ahmadinejad paid three visits to Caracas.[52] Ahmadinejad's last visit to Caracas was November 25, 2009. Reportedly the two sides came to agreements on various fields.[53] During this period, Iran and Venezuela declared that the goal of their relations was to end U.S. global hegemony, to create a multipolar world, and to establish a more just and equitable international system.[54]

When the U.S. Congress passed a resolution to sanction companies that exported gasoline to Iran, Venezuela declared that it would provide 20 percent of Iran's 40 percent need for imported gasoline. However, Iran felt that the price Venezuela wanted to charge was excessive. This led the Venezuelan ambassador in Tehran to argue that most of Iranian-Venezuelan economic agreements favored Iran.

Some commentators have seen a security dimension in Iran's approach to Latin America. According to them, the Bush administration's policy of regime change in Iran, including if need be by military means, prompted Iran to establish a presence in proximity to the United States. In this way, they argue, Iran hoped to be able to retaliate against America, including through a resort to terrorism, in case of a U.S. military attack on Iran. According to them: "When you have got Washington calling you evil, and there's a steady stream of reports from Washington about bombing campaigns, what would you do if you were an Iranian strategic planner? These guys have a record of using diplomats and diplomatic missions as a mechanism for terrorism, so why wouldn't they be making that calculation now?" (see table 10.3).[55]

With the election of Daniel Ortega to the Nicaraguan presidency in January 2007, Iran and Nicaragua reestablished diplomatic ties, which had been severed in 1990, following Ortega's ouster from power. To show Iran's friendship, Ahmadinejad visited Nicaragua in January 2007 to congratulate Ortega on his election to the presidency.[56] During this trip, Iran and Nicaragua signed an agreement addressing Nicaragua's development problems, including questions related to dam-building, housing, agricultural, industrialization, and energy. They also discussed the building of factories to produce cars, trucks, bicycles, and motorcycles for the regional market.[57] Additionally, Iran and Venezuela agreed to build a deepwater port at Monkey Point on Nicaragua's Caribbean shore at the cost of $350 billion.[58]

In 2009, the U.S. secretary of state, Hillary Clinton, said that the Obama administration will counter Iran's presence in Latin America.[59] As a sign of Iran's mischievous plans in Latin America, she referred to the building of a huge Iranian embassy in

Table 10.3   Commercial Relations between Iran and Venezuela

Area	Project
Agriculture and food industry	Factory for producing Tractors (Ven Iran Tractor Co.); 6 plants to produce dairy products; 160 refrigerators for supermarkets; 10 plants to process corn
Auto-industry	Car factory "Venirauto," producing Samand LG and SAIPA 141
Construction	Cement factory; building 1700 houses in 4 Venezuelan cities
Finance	Two bi-national funds, each for $200 million
Gas, oil, and petrochemicals	Various projects, in the Faja Petrolifera del Orinoco
International air travel	Agreements between CONVIASA and Iran Air for passenger and Cargo
Naval industry	Construction of 4 shipyards to produce ships for oil industry (Tankers)
Plastic industry	Bloque Cardon II of the Rafael Urandaneta project to build 100 plastic injection machines

Venezuela has signed 150 agreements with Iran.

Source: Embassy of the Bolivarian Republic of Venezuela in Tehran, February 2007.[2]

[2]http://www.emveniran.gob.ve.

Managua, and said "you can imagine what that is for." However, it later transpired that there were no such plans.[60]

Iran also developed close relations with Bolivia and Ecuador. These countries' interest in Iran is mainly economic and financial, as they seek its help in their development projects. Ahmadinejad visited Bolivia and Ecuador in January 2007 and established diplomatic relations between them and Iran. The Bolivian president, Evo Morales, called Ahmadinejad's visit historic.[61] During his trip, Ahmadinejad promised that Iran will invest $1 billion to help Bolivia develop its natural gas reserves and minerals, produce more electricity, and fund agricultural and construction projects. There has also been speculation that Iran is interested in Bolivia's uranium resources.[62] Morales made a return visit to Iran in September 2008.[63] Ahmadinejad again visited Bolivia in November 2009 during his Latin American tour. In January 2007, Ahmadinejad also visited Ecuador and participated in the inauguration ceremony of its new president, Rafael Correa. Correa made a return visit to Tehran in December 2008 and signed 12 agreements. He was hopeful that the agreements would be implemented; he said that he was sure the agreements would not remain on paper only.[64]

The Ahmadinejad government, however, had more difficulty in strengthening relations with nonleftist, or moderately leftist, governments in Latin America, such as Brazil, which, given its level of economic and technological development and international weight, is more important in terms of meeting Iran's economic and political needs. For example, Ahmadinejad had wanted to visit Brazil during his Latin American tour in 2007. But reportedly, President Lula da Silva had declined to see him, on the pretext that his and Ahmadinejad's schedules were in conflict.[65] Most likely, Brazil's president had not wanted to be associated with Ahmadinejad's anti-American policies. Israel's lobbying might also have influenced Brazil's decision. Nevertheless, Iran pursued closer ties with Brazil. Despite the problem of Ahmadinejad's visit, Brazil, too, remained interested in expanding economic ties with Iran. As a sign of this interest the Brazilian foreign minister, Celso Amorim, visited Tehran in November 2008. During this trip, he said that Tehran and Brazil could upgrade their ties beyond commercial exchanges to include scientific, industrial, technological, and cultural cooperation as well.[66] Brazil has already invested in Iran's Tusan oil field in the Persian Gulf[67] and may invest in the exploration of its Caspian region.[68] In response, Iran's foreign minister stated that Iran attaches priority to relations with Brazil.[69] More importantly, Brazil has supported Iran's right to develop peaceful nuclear energy at the UN, and President Lula has rejected U.S. calls for Brazil to shun Iran.[70] Brazil's president met Ahmadinejad at the UN General Assembly meeting in September 2009 and invited him to visit Brazil in November, and indicated that he would visit Iran in 2010. Iran's efforts to cultivate Brazil finally paid off and Ahmadinejad visited Brazil in November 2009. Following this visit, Brazil has consistently argued that Iran should not be backed into a corner. Despite personal lobbying by Secretary Clinton, as of spring 2010 Brazil had resisted American pressures to join in sanctioning Iran.[71]

Meanwhile, relations with Argentina remained tense over the 1994 bombing incident of a Jewish community center in Buenos Aires, which killed 86 people and injured 200. Two years earlier an attack had been made on the Israeli Embassy. Argentine prosecutors, as well as the United States and Israel, have blamed Hizbullah and some senior Iranian officials and members of Iran's diplomatic mission in Argentina as having been the masterminds behind the attacks. They asked Interpol to issue arrest warrants for a number of Iranian officials. Iran denies these charges.

Iran also established relations with Paraguay, and the advisor to Iran's president attended the inauguration ceremony of Paraguay's new left-leaning president, Fernando Lugo Mendez, in August 2008.[72] Reportedly, Iran was the only Asian country to have been invited to these ceremonies. Following the election of a leftist politician and a former member of the guerrilla group Tupamaros to the presidency of Uruguay, Iran tried to cultivate its links with that country. It sent its Minister of Cooperatives to attend his inauguration. In response, the new president Jose Mujicas reportedly said that his country "intends to bolster its cooperation with Iran."[73] However, the United States, whose secretary of state met the new president just before his inauguration is certain to discourage such moves.[74]

Table 10.4   Iran's Trade with Selected Latin American Countries
in 2008 in Million Euros

Country	Iran's Exports	Iran's Imports
Argentina	None	301.6
Brazil	11.4	1,525.9
Chile	0.9	46.9
Cuba	None	108.7
Mexico	38.3	18.1
Venezuela	35.2	15.6

Source: European Commission.

ASSESSING IRAN'S LATIN AMERICAN DIPLOMACY

Iran's Latin American diplomacy, too, has been only partially successful. Economically, countries with which Iran has developed the closest relations are not in a position to help Iran. Rather, the interest of impoverished countries such as Nicaragua, Bolivia, Ecuador, and Paraguay in Iran is to get its help for their own development. Countries like Brazil, which can be a more rational economic partner for Iran, have, while expanding trade relations, been somewhat hesitant in advancing other economic and political relations because of concern over U.S. reaction, although this might be changing. The trade volume between Iran and Latin America indicates the limited success of Iran's economic diplomacy in Latin America (see table 10.4). Politically, too, while some Latin American countries, notably Venezuela, voted against sending Iran's nuclear dossier to the UN, and some supported its efforts to gain a nonpermanent seat in the UN Security Council, Iran ultimately lost in both cases. Moreover, many of the current Latin American governments with which Iran has good relations face strong opposition at home and could be replaced in future elections. These opposition groups oppose close ties with Iran.[75]

In Iran itself, many remain highly skeptical of the usefulness of its Third Worldist diplomacy, and some categorically oppose it. They argue that the money spent on Latin American countries should be spent on those Iranians who need help. According to one author, "The news on the Iranian government's so-called kindness diplomacy seems unending to the ears of the bewildered Iranian citizen who has to deal with power blackouts and unavailability of free medical care."[76] Additionally, the expansion of Iranian-Latin American relations during the Ahmadinejad presidency was largely due to higher oil prices and cannot be sustained when oil prices are low or falling. Also, the excessively ideological tone of Iran's Latin diplomacy has alienated the more moderate Latin American countries.

Conclusions

Since the advent of the Islamic Revolution in February 1979, Iran's foreign policy has been subjected to two contradictory influences and has been largely determined by their interaction. These influences have been the Islamic Republic's ideology, including its worldview and self-image, shaped by a particular interpretation of Islam and a left-leaning Third-Worldism; and the requirements of dealing with an outside world and an international system resistant to Iran's efforts to realize its revolutionary goals.

The phenomenon of systemic resistance to revolutionary movements bent on challenging the system has not been limited to Iran's case. Rather, historically all revolutionary movements have been subject to such resistance. What has been different in Iran's case has been the Islamic regime's persistence in pursuing certain ideological goals despite tremendous damage done to the country's national interests and the well-being of its people. This is not to suggest that the Islamic Republic has not adjusted to the requirements of international life. On the contrary, fairly early on after the revolution, the Islamic regime had to abandon some of its more unrealistic ideological principles, such as pursuing "people-to-people" rather than "state-to-state" relations. However, the Islamic government has been slow in doing so and only after suffering considerable damage, as best illustrated by its eight-year war with Iraq.

Moreover, the Islamic government has been most reluctant to abandon those aspects of its ideology most damaging to Iran's national interests, notably its excessively antagonistic posture on Israel and Arab-Israeli relations, which has gone beyond the position of even radical Arab regimes, and its unwillingness to deal with the United States in an open manner and in accordance with the rules of international diplomacy.

The Islamic government's inability to shed this damaging ideological baggage has, in turn, resulted from two factors: the ideological rather than national and democratic basis of its legitimacy, of which resistance to great-power pressure and support for Islamic causes are two essential components; and the fragmented nature of the ruling elite along ideological and power lines, and the elites' manipulation of these fundamental ideological principles of the regime for their own interests.

As amply demonstrated in the course of this study, the negative fallout of the regime's fragmented nature and the manipulation of ideology by rival groups and individuals in their struggle for power has been most strongly felt in the case of Iran's relations with the Western world and, especially, the United States.

The character of the international political system, dominated by East-West rivalry, provided a degree of protection to Iran during the first decade of the Islamic Revolution. But this situation drastically changed after the Soviet Union's disintegration and resulted in the worsening of Iran's geopolitical predicament. Yet, as has been shown in this study, Iran has failed fully to appreciate the dimensions of systemic change and the negative consequences for itself. This lack of understanding of the new systemic dynamics has led Iran to pursue unrealistic policies, be it trying to create a multipolar international system or to forge an anti-American bloc with countries which, while not inordinately fond of America, do not share Iran's view or at any rate have a more pragmatic approach toward the United States. The end result has been that Iran has approached nearly all of its partners, ranging from Russia to Pakistan, Turkmenistan, and the Arab states, from a position of weakness, thus enabling them to manipulate Iran's estrangement from major international players to their advantage, while Iran has been incapable of retaliating against them.

Iran's unrealistic foreign policy and the regime's unwillingness or, more seriously, inability to shed its ideological baggage, without undermining its legitimacy and even raison d'être, have also seriously undermined the country's security by encouraging key players to destabilize it. They have done this by imposing economic sanctions and manipulating Iran's vulnerabilities, including ethnic and religious cleavages and economic discontent, to destabilize and perhaps even cause it to disintegrate. The involvement of Western and Gulf Arab countries and Pakistan with Iran's ethnic and religious minorities, notably those in Baluchistan and Kurdistan, best illustrates this situation.

The Islamic government's unrealistic foreign policy has also seriously set back the country's economic development and has worsened its people's living conditions. Today, despite vast energy reserves, other natural resources, and a fairly well-educated workforce, Iran lags far behind Turkey in terms of economic and industrial development.

In addition to being unrealistic, at times during the last two decades Iran's diplomacy has been excessively concessionary and naïve. Iran's mishandling of diplomacy following the invasion Afghanistan, during the Khatami presidency, plus the Ahmadinejad presidency's approach toward postinvasion Iraq, are examples of this failure. In Iraq, Iran has succeeded in earning both Western and Arab blame for Iraq's problems, while Sunni Arab countries, including Iran's so-called strategic ally, Syria, have financed the Iraqi insurgency, which is Sunni and Ba'athist, and provided it with fighters and passage to Iraq.

Iran's diplomacy has also been naïve in the sense that it has thought that it could pursue normal state-to-state relations while also pursuing revolutionary goals. Iran's efforts to normalize relations with Egypt while glorifying Sadat's assassin amply demonstrate this Iranian naïveté.

Worse, Iran has failed to win over those constituencies—Arab and Islamic—for whose sake it has sacrificed so much in terms of its own national interests. In the Arab world, Iran's pro-Arab and anti-Israel rhetoric and policy have failed to eliminate anti-Persian sentiments, and in the Arab world and other Muslim countries, Iran's rhetoric of Islamic unity has not changed their perception of its being a heretic Shia entity. Even Iraqi Shias are not enamored of the Iranians. Thus while Turkish prime minister Recep Tayyip Erdogan's outburst against Israeli president Shimon Peres at the 2009 Davos Conference made him a hero in Arab eyes, most view Iran's pro-Arab statements as undue interference in Arab affairs. Finally, Iran has managed to unite against itself traditional enemies, such as the Arabs and the Israelis, and to make itself vulnerable to a destructive military attack, which potentially could signal the end of its 3,000-year existence as a nation.

If, so far, Iran has escaped a fate worse than that which it has suffered since the revolution, that has not been because of its skillful diplomacy but rather the ineptness of American policies, such as supporting Saddam Hussein and the Taliban, as well as mishandling of the Afghan and Iraq wars.

In theory, Iran could change these aspects of its foreign policy. However, given the role of ideology in the Islamic regime's definition of its legitimacy and the manipulation of foreign policy–related issues in intra-regime rivalries, to make such drastic change, without at least finding a face-saving way of doing so, would be very difficult. The growing ideological cleavage in Iran in general—and not merely within the regime, as demonstrated by the 2009 presidential elections and its repercussions—could make this task even more difficult.

Iran's dilemma is that of all governments whose legitimacy is based on ideology namely: how to stay in power while shedding a destructive ideology since ideology justifies the political elite's claim to power.

Yet without fundamental changes in its foreign policy orientation, Iran would even more dangerously undermine its security and well-being. What allows for some cautious optimism that Iran might make such a change is the fact that, at least once, the regime did finally accept the inevitable, when in 1988 the Ayatullah Khomeini drank from the poisoned chalice and accepted a cease-fire with Saddam's Iraq.

Moreover, the Iranian regime might realize that its unrealistic foreign policy, coupled with that policy's adverse consequences, is becoming a threat to its survival rather than a factor of strength. The United States might also realize that its Iran policy since the Iran-contra debacle has not served either American interests or those of its allies and lead it to pursue true engagement with Iran with the goal of reaching either a broad agreement or a modus vivendi. Iran's ship of state is headed toward troubled waters and needs a competent skipper to get it to safe shores.

Notes

INTRODUCTION

1. The only time that small states impact the evolution of the international system is when, in one way or another, they engage the interest of the key players.

2. An important case in modern times of less powerful states trying to change the nature of the international system, especially in its economic dimensions, was the efforts of the Third World countries during the 1970s in the context of the call for a New International Economic Order (NIEO), later followed by the call for a new international information order.

3. This situation prevailed during the Cold War.

4. Since the mid-19th century, a major aspect of Iran's foreign policy had been desperate efforts to enlist the assistance of a third great power in Iran in order to balance the overwhelming influence of Britain and Russia. Shireen T. Hunter, *Iran and the World: Continuity in a Revolutionary Decade* (Bloomington: Indiana University Press, 1990), pp. 21–26.

5. Since neither Russia nor Britain could totally dominate Iran, their strategy was to keep it alive but very weak.

6. For example, had it not been for the onset of the Cold War and intensified U.S. interest in Iran, the Soviet army may not have withdrawn from Iranian territory it had occupied during the Second World War. Similarly, fear of Soviet reaction inhibited the United States from using military means against Iran after the Islamic Revolution of 1979, despite serious Iranian provocations, including the holding of American diplomats hostage.

7. For example, Iraq's attack on Kuwait in 1991 forced the United States to change its attitude toward Baghdad. Iraq, before that time, had been considered the new pillar of U.S. policy in the Persian Gulf. Similarly, it was the Taliban's (and their protégé Osama Bin Laden's) attacks on U.S. embassies in Nairobi and Dar es Salaam in 1998 and then in the United States itself in 2001 that led the United States to try to eliminate them, a new policy which helped Iran. The U.S. military invasion of Iraq and the difficulties that it created also somewhat limited its ability to put military pressure on Iran.

8. Hans Morgenthau, *Politics among Nations: Struggle for Power and Peace* (New York: Alfred A. Knopf, 1985). This remains an excellent representative of the realist school.

9. Alexander Wendt, *Social Theory of International Politics* (Cambridge: Cambridge University Press, 1999).

10. Kenneth N. Waltz, *Theory of International Politics* (Reading, MA: Addison Wesley Publishing Company, 1979).

11. Margot Light, "Foreign Policy Analysis," in *Contemporary International Relations: A Guide to Theory*, ed. A.J.R. Groom and Margot Light (London: Pinter Publishers, 1994), p. 94.

CHAPTER 1

1. There is a difference between hegemony and dominance, although often these two terms are used interchangeably. Hegemony is based partly on influence over others because other states believe that the hegemon is acting more or less in the interests of, if not all, at least most of the other states, and hence they follow its lead. Domination, by contrast, relies far more heavily on coercion, including the use of military power. Thus, it has been argued that U.S. hegemony over the free world during the Cold War was at least partially based on "its capacity to mobilize consent and cooperation internationally, by acting in such a way as to make it at least plausible to others the claim that Washington was acting in the general interest, even when it was really putting narrow American interests first." Giovanni Arrighi, "Hegemony Unraveling," *New Left Review* 32 (March/April 2005).

2. At the time of the Soviet Union's collapse, economically China was in a weaker position than it is today. Even today, militarily China is no match for the combined military power of the West.

3. However, the failure of market-driven reforms in a number of developing countries, notably in Latin America, has led to a renewed popularity for a more state-centered and socialist form of economic and social development in such countries as Venezuela and Bolivia.

4. Francis Fukuyama, *The End of History and the Last Man* (New York: Harper Perennial, 1993).

5. Samuel P. Huntington, "The Lonely Superpower," *Foreign Affairs* 78, no. 3 (March/April 1999): 35.

6. Ibid., pp. 35–36.

7. China's censorship of the Internet and the U.S. arms sales to Taiwan were some of the reasons for rising U.S.-China tension starting in early 2010. Chris McGrael and Robbie Johnson, "Hilary Clinton Critisizes Beijing Over Internet Censorship," *The Guardian*, January 21, 2010; Riz Rozoff, "U.S.-China Military Tensions grow," *Center for Strategic Analysis*, January 20, 2010.

8. Ibid., p. 36.

9. William Kristol and Robert Kagan, "Toward a Neo-Reaganite Foreign Policy," *Foreign Affairs* 75, no. 4 (July/August 1996).

10. Robert Jervis, "The Remaking of a Unipolar World," *Washington Quarterly* 29, no. 3 (Summer 2006): 8.

11. Excerpts from 1992 draft "Defense Planning Guidance," available at: http://www.pbs.org/wgbh/pages/frontline/shows/iraq/etc/wolf.html.

12. The term "backlash states" was applied by Anthony Lake, U.S. national security advisor during the first term of President Bill Clinton. Anthony Lake, "Confronting Backlash States," *Foreign Affairs* 73, no. 2 (March/April 1994).

13. The principal architect of the strategy of dual containment was Martin Indyk. He had complained that the administration of George H. W. Bush had not used the strategic advantage

it gained following the victory in the first Gulf War to reshape the Middle East. The strategy of dual containment was supposed to remedy this neglect. Martin Indyk, "Watershed in the Middle East," *Foreign Affairs* 1, no. 1 (1992).

14. Alvin Z. Rubinstein, Albina Shayevich, and Boris Zlotnikov, *The Clinton Foreign Policy Reader: Presidential Speeches with Commentary* (Armonk, NY: M. E. Sharpe, 2000), p. 6.

15. See the text of the 1993 speech by Anthony Lake in Rubinstein et al., *The Clinton Foreign Policy Reader*, Op. cit., p. 25.

16. Condoleezza Rice, "Promoting the National Interest," *Foreign Affairs* 79, no. 1 (January/February 2000): 47.

17. Ibid.

18. Sarah O'Connor, "Neo-Conservatives as Wilsonians?" *International Affairs Journal at UCDAVIS* 2, no. 2 (Winter 2006), available at: http://davisaiaj.com/content/view/112/86. The author convincingly argues that Wilson's ideals and the way he proposed to pursue them are completely different from those of the neoconservatives. She especially points to Wilson's disdain of power politics and his desire to see a more law-based international system, which sharply contrasts with the neoconservatives' views.

19. Even the Bush administration, however, tried to gain endorsement of its politics by NATO, other allies, and the UN, albeit with mixed results.

20. Michael J. Glennon, "The New Interventionism: The Search for a Just International Law," *Foreign Affairs* 78, no. 3 (May/June 1999).

21. The only exception was NATO. However, even NATO has had to find new missions in order to remain relevant.

22. Of course, during the Cold War, ideological differences and diverging attitudes toward the two competing camps caused tensions among regional countries, which otherwise did not have major conflictual issues, or they exacerbated such conflicts.

23. See chapter 3 on U.S.-Iran relations.

24. Samuel P. Huntington, "The Clash of Civilizations," *Foreign Affairs* 72, no. 3 (Summer 1993).

25. Madeleine Albright, *The Mighty and the Almighty: Reflections on Power, God and World Affairs* (New York: HarperCollins, 2006); Douglas Johnston and Cynthia Sampson, eds. *Religion: The Missing Dimension of Statecraft* (New York: Oxford University Press, 1994).

26. In the 1990s, with few exceptions, as in the case of France because of the Algerian civil war, Western countries were not even targeted by extremist nonstate Muslim actors. Rather, because of the war in Chechnya, Russia suffered more from terrorism perpetrated by Muslim extremists. Shireen Hunter, *Islam in Russia: The Politics of Identity and Security* (Armonk, NY: M. E. Sharpe, 2004).

27. Charles Feldman and Stan Wilson, "Ex-CIA Director: U.S. Faces 'World War IV,'" CNN.com/us (April 2003), available at: http://www.cnn.com/2003/US/o4/03/sprj.irq.woolsey.world.war. Robert Kagan and William Kristol also wrote in the *Weekly Standard*, the neoconservative publication, that military action in Afghanistan was just the beginning of a conflict that may last a hundred years.

28. The inventor of the phrase "axis of evil" was David Frum, a speechwriter for President Bush. The text of the 2002 State of the Union address is available at: http://www.washingtonpost.com/wp-srv/onpolitics/transcripts/sou012902.htm.

29. For details, see Gary Dorrien, "Benevolent Global Hegemony: William Kristol and the Politics of American Empire," available at: http://www.logosjournal.com/dorrien.htm.

30. William Kristol and Robert Kagan, "Wanted: Osama Bin Laden and Saddam Hussein," *Weekly Standard*, October 1, 2001.

31. The text of President Bush's speech is available at: http://www.Whitehouse.gov/news/releases/2003/11/20031106–2html. See also Jeremy Sharp, "The Broader Middle East and North Africa Initiative: An Overview," *Congressional Research Service Report for Congress*, February 15, 2005.

32. Russia, which had been facing an Islamic insurgency in Chechnya and terrorist attacks in Moscow and other major cities especially in the North Caucasus, felt vindicated.

33. As of February 2010, the number of U.S. dead in Iraq was 4,379 and the number of U.S. dead in the Afghan war stood at 1,000.

34. Scott Wilson, "Hamas Sweeps Palestinian Elections, Complicating Peace Efforts in Mideast," *Washington Post*, January 27, 2006.

35. Max Boot, "The Case for American Empire," *Weekly Standard*, October 15, 2001.

36. "Don't Let Iran Cause World War Three Warns George Bush," *Daily Mail*, October 18, 2007, available at: http://www.dailymail.co.uk/pages/lives/articles/news/news.html?in_article_id=488178&i.

37. Matt Spelatnik and Tabassum Zakaria, "Bush Says Iran Threat to World Security," Reuters, January 13, 2008, available at: http://www.reuters.com/articleprint?articleId=USL13511 75520080113.

38. Steve Yuhas, "Iran & Nazi Germany: Predictable Outcome," *Conservative Voice*, March 4, 2007, available at: http://www.theconservativevoice.com/article/23180.html.

39. In a speech delivered at the National Defense University, President Bush stated that "the need for missile defense in Europe is real and I believe it is urgent. Iran is pursuing the technology that could be used to produce nuclear weapons and ballistic missiles of increasing range that could deliver them." "Bush Says Missile Shield 'Urgently Needed' to Counter Iranian Threat," Wikinews, October 24, 2007, available at: http://en.wikinews.org/wiki/Bush-says_missile_shield_%22urgently%22_needed_to-co.

40. Gregory Kunadze, "Russia Pursues New Foreign Policy," *Daily Yomiuri*, March 14, 2000.

41. See Julie M. Rahm, "Russia, China, India: A New Strategic Triangle for a New Cold War," *Parameters* (U.S. Army War College Quarterly) 31, no. 4 (Winter 2001); and Aleksey Chichkin, "An 'Asian Entente' Could Become a Reality," *Rossiskaya Gazeta*, May 12, 1997. Chichkin stated that "elements of a new world order are starting to take shape in Asia. They are being created in relations among three great powers—Russia, China, and Iran."

42. The communiqué issued at the end of Jacques Chirac's visit to China in 1997 said: "Both parties have decided to engage in reinforced cooperation, to foster the march toward multi-polarity, to create wealth and well being, on the basis of respecting plurality and independence . . . and to oppose any attempt at domination in international affairs." "China, France Sign Joint Declaration," *Beijing Review* 40, no. 22, June 2–8, 1997, available at: http://www.dawning.iist.unu.edu.edu/china/bjreview/95.jun/97–22–7.html. Russia and China also emphasized the point that countries should be free to chose their own economic, social, and political system without outside interference. "Text of PRC-Russia Statement Released," Xinhua Domestic Service, April 25, 1996.

43. "Russia Pushes Regional Alliance," *Toronto Star*, December 22, 1998; also "Wooing Delhi," *Financial Times*, December 23, 1998.

44. Quote in "Iran Talks of Bid for New Alliances," *New York Times*, September 26, 1993.

45. "Iran: Nabavi on U.S.-Iran Relations," Foreign Broadcasting Information Service, FBIS/NES-98065 (Foreign Broadcasting Information Service, Near East and South Asia), March 6, 1998.

46. "Yeltsin Champions 'Multipolar World,'" Interfax, *Daily News Bulletin* (Moscow), February 7, 1998.

47. Peter Rodman, "The World's Resentment: Anti-Americanism as a Global Phenomenon," *National Interest*, no. 60 (Summer 2000): 33.

48. Lukin made this comment at a conference in Moscow on May 28, 2002.

49. See Joshua Eisman, Eric Heginbotham, and Derek Mitchell, eds., *China and the Developing World* (Armonk, NY: M. E. Sharpe, 2007).

50. Declan Walsh, "Taliban Reaches beyond Swat Valley in Pakistan," *Guardian*, April 25, 2009.

51. Spencer Ackerman, "Obama Announces 30K More Troops for Afghanistan," *Washington Independent*, December 1, 2009, available at: http://www.washingtonindependent.com/69301/obama-announces-30k-more-troops-for-afghanistan.

52. Rajiv Chandrasekaran, "U.S. Launches Major Surge against Taliban in Afghanistan," *Washington Post*, February 13, 2010.

53. Amir Shah and Deb Riechmann, "Taliban Attack in Kabul; Insurgents not Crippled," *Washington Times*, February 27, 2010.

54. On June 30, 2009, U.S. military forces began withdrawing form major Iraqi cities. Steven Lee Myers and Marc Santora, "Premier Casting U.S. Military Withdrawal as Iraq Victory," *New York Times*, June 26, 2009. The text of the Iraq-U.S. security agreement is available at: www.mnf-iraq.com/images/CGS_Messages/security_agreementpdf.

55. Financially, U.S. operations in Iraq, estimated initially at $50–$60 billion, had topped $706 billion as of February 2010 and was expected to rise. Professor Joseph E. Stiglitz has estimated the long-term cost of the war at $4 trillion, and the Congressional Budget office at $1 trillion to $2 trillion. David M. Herzenhorn, "Estimates of Iraq War Cost Not Close to Ballpark," *New York Times*, March 19, 2009. The cost of Afghan operations stood at more than $222 billion by July 2009 and was also expected to rise. To this must also be added the expenses of operations in Pakistan.

56. Text of speech available at: http://www.state.gov/secretary/rm/2009a/july/12607htm.

57. Arnold Wolfers, *Alliance Policy in the Cold War* (Baltimore: Johns Hopkins Press, 1966).

58. Niall Ferguson, "America: The Fragile Empire," *Los Angeles Times*, February 28, 2010.

CHAPTER 2

1. F. S. Northedge, "The Nature of Foreign Policy," in F. S. Northedge, ed., *The Foreign Policies of the Powers* (London: Faber and Faber, 1968), p. 10. Also see: James N. Roseneau, *Linkage Politics: Essays on the Convergence of National and International Systems* (New York: The Free Press, 1969).

2. For example, until the scientific and technical revolutions in weaponry and massive human migratory movements, island nations like Japan and Britain and those surrounded by vast oceans like the United States historically have been far less vulnerable to external attacks than other nations without such protective shields.

3. Greek armies destroyed Iran's Achaemenid-era historic and cultural sites, including Persepolis. Arab armies destroyed Iran's main cultural centers, including the world famous university of Jundi Shapur, located in present-day Ahwaz in Khuzestan, as well as many books and records. Mongols similarly destroyed large cities such as Nishabur in present-day Khorasan, including its vast library. According to Professor Charles Issawi, even during the Safavid renaissance Iran did not achieve the level of economic prosperity it had prior to the Mongol invasion.

Charles Issawi, ed., *The Economic History of Iran: 1800–1914* (Chicago, IL: University of Chicago Press, 1971), p. 9.

4. Ibid., p. 16.

5. On the issue of modernization and Iran's national identity debate, see: Shireen T. Hunter, "Islamic Reformist Discourse in Iran: Proponents and Prospects," in *Reformist Voices of Islam: Mediating Islam And Modernity*, ed. Shireen T. Hunter (Armonk, NY: M. E. Sharpe, 2009), pp. 33–97.

6. This process began in earnest after the end of the Iran-Iraq War. All Iranian leaders have visited Persepolis and many of them refer to Iran's achievements before Islam, although they continue to emphasize the post-Islamic period.

7. Ada Bozeman, "Iran, U.S. Foreign Policy and the Tradition of Persian Statecraft," *Orbis*, Summer 1979.

8. Said Nafisi, *Tarikh e Siyassi va Ejtemaie Iran* [Iran's political and social history], (Tehran: Intesharat e Bonyad, 1335 [1958]), pp. 100–21.

9. Daniel L. Byman and Kenneth J. Pollack, "Let Us Now Praise Great Men: Bringing the Statesman Back," *International Security* 25, no. 4 (2001): 109.

10. Margaret G. Hermann, Charles F. Hermann, and Joe D. Hagan, "How Decision Units Shape Foreign Policy Behavior," in *New Directions in the Study of Foreign Policy*, ed. Charles F. Hermann, Charles W. Kegley Jr., and James N. Roseneau (Boston: Allen and Unwin, 1987), p. 314.

11. According to James Roseneau, leaders serve as a bridge between the public and the official. Through their words and actions they shape public attitudes. James N. Roseneau, *National Leadership and Foreign Policy: A Case Study in the Mobilization of Public Support* (Princeton, NJ: Princeton University Press, 1963), p. 17.

12. See: Richard C. Snyder, H. W. Bruck, and Burton Sapin, "Decision-Making Approach to the Study of International Politics," in *Foreign Policy Decision-Making: An Approach to the Study of International Politics*, ed. Richard C. Snyder, H. W. Bruck, and Burton Sapin (Glencoe, IL: The Free Press of Glencoe, 1963); Graham T. Allison and Phillip D. Zelikow, *Essence of Decision: Explaining the Cuban Missile Crisis*, 2nd ed. (New York: Addison Wesley Longman, 1999); and Graham T. Allison and Morton H. Halperin, "Bureaucratic Politics: A Paradigm and Some Policy Implications," in *Theory and Policy in International Relations*, ed. Raymond E. Tanter and Richard H. Ullman (Princeton, NJ: Princeton University Press, 1972).

13. Hans J. Morgenthau, *Politics among Nations* (New York: Alfred A. Knopf, 1985), p. 92.

14. Scott Burchill et al., eds., *Theories of International Relations*, 3rd ed. (Basingstoke, Hampshire, UK: Macmillan, 2005).

15. Zbigniew Brzezinski, *Ideology and Power in Soviet Politics* (Westport, CT: Greenwood Press, 1976), pp. 4–5.

16. Two interlinked examples of this phenomenon were Josef Stalin's moderating of communist propaganda and elevating of nationalism following the 1941 Nazi invasion of the Soviet Union, coupled with Winston Churchill's embrace of an alliance with that communist state: "If Hitler invaded hell I would make at least a favorable reference to the devil in the House of Commons."

17. This saying was used as a slogan by the reformist candidates during the 2009 presidential elections.

18. See: "Imam Khomeini Donbal–e- Islam-e-Nowandish boudanded" [Imam Khomeini favored reformist Islam], available at: http://www.noandish.com/com.php?id=16299.

19. The English text of the revised constitution (1989) is available at: http://www.iranonline.com/iran/iran-info/Government/constitution-9–1.html.

20. Ibid.

21. Ayatullah Taleghani was the most senior leftist cleric at the time of the revolution. Ayatullah Murtaza Mutahari is the more traditional and anti-left representative. Shireen Hunter, ed., *Reformist Voices of Islam: Mediating Islam and Modernity* (Armonk, NY: M. E. Sharpe, 2008), pp. 43–48.

22. Ibid., pp. 50–56.

23. Ibid., Also: Ervand Abrahamian, "The Guerrilla Movements in Iran, 1963–1977," *MERIP Report*, no. 86 (March/April 1980): 3–21.

24. See: Seyed Mohamad Ali Taghavi, *The Flourishing of Islamic Reformism in Iran (1941–61)* (London/New York: Routledge Curzon, 2005), p. 122.

25. Ibid., pp. 62–111.

26. A case in point is the abortive efforts at U.S.-Iran reconciliation in the context of the ill-fated Iran-Contra affair.

27. Shireen T. Hunter, *Reformist Voices of Islam*, pp. 68–84.

28. For details, see: Shireen T. Hunter, *Iran and the World: Continuity in a Revolutionary Decade* (Bloomington: Indiana University Press, 1990), pp. 28–29.

29. Quoted in Foreign Broadcasting Information Service (FBIS), *South Asia*, July 24, 1984, pp. 1–4. (This publication is no longer published.)

30. Reported in the *Washington Post*, November 27, 1986.

31. Chamran, who was educated in the United States and, according to some sources, held U.S. citizenship, was one of the founders of the Lebanese Shia movement, Amal. Prior to embracing militant Islamism, he was a Communist. He died in combat during the Iran-Iraq War.

32. For details, see: Farhang Rajaei, *Islamic Values and Worldview: Khomeini on Man, the State, and International Politics* (New York: University Press of America, 1983), pp. 45–46.

33. *Keyhan*, January 16, 1982.

34. A good example of this kind of rivalry is that between Supreme Leader Khamenei and Ayatullah Rafsanjani during the latter's presidency. The same situation prevailed with Khatami. An example of the politics of revenge is the vicious attacks of the left-wing of the reformist movement against Rafsanjani, which ultimately undermined reform efforts and helped bring the conservatives to power. Akbar Ganji was particularly virulent in his attacks against Rafsanjani. In the last few years, conservatives have launched a campaign to try discrediting Muhammad Khatami. These rivalries are not limited to ideologically opposing camps but also affect those who are ideologically in agreement.

35. This tendency may disappear as a consequence of controversy over Iran's 2009 presidential elections and Khamenei's determination to impose his will on others.

36. See: Shireen T. Hunter, *Iran after Khomeini* (Washington, DC: Center for Strategic and Strategic Studies, and New York: Praeger Publishers, 1992), pp. 24–33.

CHAPTER 3

1. The permanent members of the United National Security Council, plus Germany. The high representative for the EU's Common Foreign and Security Policy, Javier Solana, also takes part in 5+1 deliberations.

2. "Iranian Speaker Blasts West for Seeking 'Chicanery' on Nuclear Deal," *Xinhua*, October 25, 2009 available at: http://news.xinhuanet.com/english/2009=10/25/content_12319226.htm.

3. Robert F. Worth, "Iran Hints at Change to Plan to Ship Enriched Uranium," *New York Times*, October 28, 2009.

4. Mahmoud Foroughi, "Iran's Foreign Policy Towards the United States," in *Iran in the 1980s*, ed. Abbas Amirie and Hamilton A. Twitchell (Tehran: Institute for International and Economic Studies, 1978), p. 393.

5. Abraham Yeselon, *United States-Persian Diplomatic Relations, 1883–1921* (New Brunswick, NJ: Rutgers University Press, 1956), p. 22.

6. *Washington Post*, January 4, 1989.

7. "Saudi Arabia Human Rights Abuses in the Name of Fighting Terrorism," Amnesty International, July 22, 1998, available at: http://www.amnesty.org/en/news-and-updates/report-saudi-arabia-human-rights-abuses-na. The site has other extensive reports on the subject.

8. For example, between 1953 and 1961, Iran received $548.1 million in economic loans and $506 million in military aid, while India received $2,407.5 billion in economic aid, Pakistan $1,418.7 million in economic aid and $508.2 million in military aid. Even Nasser's Egypt received $302 million in economic aid. Source: U.S. Senate Foreign Relations Committee, *U.S. Overseas Loans and Grants*, (CONG-R-0105).

9. There were some mob attacks on the U.S. embassy in Tehran, but these were instigated by the leftist forces. Cheryl Benard and Zalmay Khalilzad, *The Government of God: Iran's Islamic Republic* (New York: Columbia University Press, 1984), pp. 160–61.

10. In addition to the Cottam book, see: Gary Sick, *All Fall Down: The United States' Tragic Encounter with Iran* (New York: Random House, 1985) and James Bill, *The Eagle and the Lion: The Tragedy of U.S.-Iran Relations* (New Haven, CT: Yale University Press, 1988).

11. One of these actions was a Senate resolution condemning the killing of a number of Shah-era personalities, including a prominent Jewish businessman with close links to Israel. Some religious figures and circles interpreted the Senate resolution as proof of what they saw as collusion between U.S. imperialism and international Zionism. According to the late Richard Cottam, the U.S. Department of State was against this Senate action, arguing that it would set back the process of normalization. Richard Cottam, *Iran and the United States* (Pittsburgh, PA: The University of Pittsburgh Press, 1988), p. 209.

12. Ibid.

13. According to some sources, some Iranian officials had complained to the U.S. embassy about the Palestinians' penetration of Iran. Benard and Khalilzad, *The Government of God*, p. 161.

14. The text of the speech is available at: www.jimmycarterlibrary.gov/documents/.

15. See Gary Sick, *The October Surprise: America's Hostages in Iran and the Election of Ronald Reagan* (New York: Times Books, 1991).

16. Kenneth R. Timmerman, *The Death Lobby: How the West Armed Iraq* (New York: Houghton Mifflin, 1991). Also, Howard Teischer, *Twin Pillars of Desert Storm: America's Flawed Vision in the Middle East from Nixon to Bush* (New York: William Morrow and Company, 1993).

17. Said Aburish claims a meeting took place between Saddam and U.S. intelligence officers as early as 1979 in Amman, during which he discussed his plans for attacking Iran. Said K. Aburish, *The Politics of Revenge* (New York: Bloomsbury, 2000).

18. Top Secret "Talking Point," on 1981 trip to the Middle East. See Robert Parry, "The Consortium: Saddam's 'Green Light,'" available at: http://www.consortiumnews.com/archive/xfile5.html.

19. Barry M. Lando, *A Web of Deceit* (New York: Other Press, 2007).

20. Text of address of Secretary Haig at the Chicago Council of Foreign Relations, in *American–Arab Affairs*, no. 1 (Summer 1982): 191–96.

21. The text of the memorandum on U.S.-Israel strategic cooperation is available at: www. mfa.gov.il. . ./U.S.-Israel+Memorandum+of+Understanding.htm.

22. Michael Dobbs, "U.S. Had Key Role in Iraq Buildup," *Washington Post*, December 30, 2002, and Patrick E. Taylor, "Officers Say U.S. Aided Iraq in War Despite Use of Gas," *New York Times*, August 18, 2002.

23. See Ayatullah Khomeini's statement to the clergy as reported in Foreign Broadcasting Information Service/South Asia (FBIS/SA), October 6, 1983.

24. Based on personal interview in the late 1988 with a former member of the National Security Council.

25. Based on personal interview with a former official of the Reagan administration in 1988.

26. Eric Hoogland, "Factions Behind U.S. Policy in the Gulf," *Middle East Report* 18, no. 2 (March/April 1988).

27. For details, see among others: Ann Wore, *Lives, Lies and the Iran-Contra Affair* (London and New York: I. B. Tauris, 1991).

28. *Washington Post*, November 27, 1986.

29. For arguments in favor of reflagging and their critique, see: Shireen T. Hunter, *Iran and the World*, pp. 68–69.

30. Ibid., p. 70.

31. Ibid., pp. 70–71.

32. Joseph Trento and Susan Trento, "The United States and Iran: Part VII: A Tragic Mistake, A Cover–up and Escalation," August 18, 1998, available at: http://www.storiesthatmatter. org/20090818243/NSNS-Stories/the=united-states-and-iran-p.

33. Shireen T. Hunter, *Iran and the World*, pp. 71–72.

34. This Iranian willingness to be forthcoming if the United States helped it with the full implementation of UNSC Resolution 598 was confirmed in a discussion in the early 1990s the author had with a senior official of the U.S. Department of State.

35. This is reflected in the Department of State's effort to stop the passage of a resolution by the House of Representatives, condemning Iraq's use of chemical weapons. Finally, the bill was watered down to the point of making it meaningless.

36. George Bush, Inaugural Address, Friday, January 20, 1989, available at: http://www. bartleby.com/124/pres63.html.

37. "Daily on U.S. Spies, Algiers Accord Violations," FBIS/NESA, May 3, 1989.

38. "Iran Broke CIA Spy Ring, U.S. Says," *New York Times*, August 8, 1989.

39. "U.S.: Diplomatic Ball is in Tehran's Court," *Christian Science Monitor*, June 13, 1989.

40. "U.S. Sees Long Process in Hostage Negotiations," *Washington Post*, August 7, 1989.

41. "Hashemi Rafsanjani 'Ready to Help' in Lebanon," FBIS/ME/SA, August 4, 1989.

42. Syria, which was competing with Iran for influence in Lebanon, did not want Iran to get the credit for the hostages' release. Moreover, Syria wanted to obtain concessions from the United States, as illustrated by the Syrian foreign minister's comment to the UN mediator, Marrack Goulding, that a solution to the crisis "depended on a change in American policies in the area." "Syrian Help on Hostages Has a Price," *Christian Science Monitor*, August 11, 1989.

43. Giandomenico Picco, *Man without A Gun* (New York: Times Books, 1999), p. 113.

44. Ibid., pp. 113–14.

45. Ibid., p. 115.

46. Barbara Slavin, *Bitter Friends, Bosom Enemies* (New York: St. Martin's Press, 2007), pp. 180–81.

47. The 17 members of Al Dawa were accused of orchestrating bombings in Kuwait in 1983.

48. Some observers have said that the United States encouraged Iraq to attack Kuwait because it wanted to go to war with it as part of a long-term plan to gain control of the Persian Gulf's oil and gas. See Linda Diebel, "Was Saddam Set Up for the Kill?" *Toronto Star*, March 10, 1991.

49. Mary Curtius, "Finding Friends in the Foe's Foes," *Boston Globe*, September 11, 1990.

50. Davies H. Lockwood, "Holy War Would be Suicide," *Sunday Herald*, January 27, 1991.

51. Ibid.

52. Ed Blanche, "Iran Claims Neutrality in Gulf War, But Nervous of Iraq," Associated Press, June 29, 1991.

53. "Baker Warns Sanction-Busters," *Sunday Herald*, September 16, 1990.

54. Giandomenico Picco, *Man without A Gun*, pp. 5–6.

55. President Bush, in an interview with NBC Nightly News on February 2, 1991, said that new order means that "the U.S. has a new credibility. What we say goes." Available at: http://www.counterpunch.org/cohen1228.html.

56. Thomas L. Friedman, "U.S. to Counter Iran in Central Asia," *New York Times*, February 6, 1992.

57. Martin Indyk, "Watershed in the Middle East," *Foreign Affairs* 71, no. 1 (1992).

58. The text of Indyk's speech to WINEP can be found on the proceedings of the Soref Symposium, *Challenges to U.S. Interests in the Middle East*, May 18–19, 1993, available at: http://www.thewashingtoninstitute.org/print.php?template=C04&CID=197.

59. Anthony Lake, "Confronting Backlash States," *Foreign Affairs* 73, no. 2 (1994).

60. For details on these points, see chapter 1.

61. *Challenges to U.S. Interests in the Middle East*, Loc.cit.

62. For example, one of the reasons the United States acquiesced in or perhaps even encouraged the creation of the Taliban by Pakistan was that it saw them as a means of blocking Iran in Central Asia. In fact, General Naseerullah Babur is reported to have made this point.

63. "Argentina Still Lacks Evidence in Bombing," *New York Times*, March 23, 1992, also "Bombers Away," available at: http://judaism.about.co/library/2_history/bl_buenosaires_dhtm. It says that a report entitled "The Trail That Menem Fears," leads to a Syrian connection to the bombings.

64. Batsheva Tsur, "Peres: Israel Almost Certain of Identity of Terrorists behind Buenos Aires Embassy Bombing: Iran and Hizbullah were Responsible," *Jerusalem Post*, March 18, 1993.

65. Douglas Jehl, "3 leaders Angered by New Terrorist Attacks," *New York Times*, July 27, 1994.

66. Barbara Slavin, *Bitter Friends, Bosom Enemies*, p. 182.

67. Text of Warren Christopher's speech, entitled "Maintaining the Momentum for Peace in the Middle East," October 24, 1994, available at: http://findarticles.com/p/articles/mi_m1584/is_n43_v5/ai_15979902/.

68. Agis Salpukas, "Iran Signs Oil Deal With Conoco; First Since 1980 Break With U.S.," *New York Times*, March 7, 1995.

69. "Why Didn't Conoco See This Coming?" *Business Week*, March 27, 1995.

70. Ibid.

71. *Journal of Commerce*, July 5, 1995.

72. Colin MacKinnon, "Clinton's Executive Order," *Washington Report on Middle East Affairs* (July/August 1995). Also, by the same author, "U.S. Slowly Changes Sanctions Policy," *Washington Report on Middle East Affairs* (October/November 1999).

73. Kenneth Katzman, "The Iran Sanctions Act," *CRS Report for Congress*, updated August 26, 2008.

74. "Case Studies in Sanctions and Terrorism, Case 84–1, U.S. v. Iran, Chronology of Key Events," Peterson Institute for International Economics, available at: http://www.iie.com/research/topics/sanctions/iran.pdf.

75. "Conoco Secures $10 billion UAE Deal," Gulfnews.com, February 15, 2008.

76. Youssef M. Ibrahim, "Saudi Rebels are Main Suspects in June Bombing of a U.S. Base," *New York Times*, August 15, 1996.

77. Perry interview is available at: http://www.upi.com/Security_Terrorism/Briefing/2007/06/perry_us_eyediran_attack_after_bombing//7045.

78. The text of Gareth Porter's article is available at: http://original.antiwar.com/2009/06/24.us-officials-leaked-falsestory-blaming-iran-for-khbar-attack/.

79. Ibid.

80. Elaine Sciolino, "Seeking to Open a Door to U.S., Iranian Proposes Cultural Ties," *New York Times*, January 8, 1998.

81. Kenneth M. Pollock, *The Persian Puzzle* (New York: Random, House, 2004), p. 315.

82. Transcript of the Amanpour interview with Khatami, January 7, 1998, available at: http://www.cnn.com/WORLD/9801/07/iran/.

83. Trita Parsi, *Treacherous Alliances: The Secret Dealings of Israel, Iran and the United States* (New Haven, CT and London: Yale University Press, 2007), pp. 212–14.

84. Paul Findley, "Cool Clinton Response to Khatami Initiative Shows Israel–Inspired Dual Containment Policy Not Yet Dead," *Washington Report on Middle East Affairs* (April 1998).

85. Kenneth M. Pollack, *The Persian Puzzle*, p. 323.

86. Ibid., p. 323.

87. One such person is Michael Rubin. See his "Iran's 'Dialogue of Civilizations': A First-Hand Account," *The Middle East Quarterly* (March 2000).

88. For background on student movements in Iran and the 1998 riots, see: Ali Akbar Mahdi, "Wake up Call: The Student Protests of July 1999," *The Iranian*, July 3, 2000, available at: http://Iranian.com/Opinion/2000/July/Students/index.html.

89. The author was told by someone close to the reformist camp that some of them tried to reach a deal with Rafsanjani's supporters through the wee hours of the night for the upcoming parliamentary elections but were thwarted by the left wing of the reformist movement.

90. Text of the letter is available at: http://www.newamericancentury.org/iraqclintonletter.htm.

91. Quote in Gareth Porter, "Pentagon Targeted Iran for Regime Change after 9/11," May 5, 2008, available at: http://www.ipsnews.net/news.asp?idnews=42241.

92. See: BBC Monitoring, Middle East, September 11, 2001.

93. Reported in *Daily Telegraph* (London), September 17, 2001.

94. Barbara Slavin, *Bitter Friends, Bosom Enemies*, p. 194.

95. James Dobbins, "How to Talk to Iran," *Washington Post*, July 22, 2007.

96. Barnett R. Rubin, "The U.S. and Iran in Afghanistan: Policy Gone Awry," *Audit of the Conventional Wisdom*, October 2008, available at: web.mit.edu/csi/asw.html.

97. James Dobbins, *After the Taliban: Nation Building in Afghanistan* (Dulles, VA: Potomac Books, 2008), p.

98. Slavin quotes Powell's chief of staff Lawrence Wilkerson on this subject. See *Bitter Friends, Bosom Enemies*, p. 196.

99. Sasan Fayazmanash, *The United States and Iran: Sanctions, Wars and the Policy of Dual Containment* (London and New York: Routledge, 2008), pp. 108–9.

100. Ibid., p. 106.

101. Barnett R. Rubin, "The U.S. and Iran in Afghanistan: Policy Gone Awry."

102. Ibid.

103. January 6, 1998. *Jerusalem Post* report quoted in Sasan Fayazmanesh, *Iran and the United States*, p. 110.

104. Rolf Tophoven, "Intel Agencies Say Saudis Funded Karine A," *Die Welt*, January 31, 2002, available at: http://www.freepublic.com/focus/fr/619226/posts.

105. Brian Whitaker, "The Strange Affair of Karine A," *Guardian*, January 21, 2002. Also, Graham Usher, "The Karine-A Affair," *Al Ahram Weekly*, January 10–16, 2002, available at: http://weekly.aharam.org.eg/2002/568/rel.htm.

106. For a detailed account, see: Sasan Fayazmanash, *The United States and Iran Sanctions, Wars and the Policy of Dual Containment*, pp. 111–12.

107. Charles D. Smith, "The 'Do More' Chorus in Washington," *Middle East Report*, April 15, 2002, available at: http//www.merip.org/mero/mero041502.html.

108. In a strange twist, the ship's previous owner said that it could not recognize it from the television images and photographs. David Osler and Nigel Lowry, "'Phantom' Twist in Karine A Mystery," *Lloyd's List*, January 10, 2002, available at: http://www.lloydslist.com/11/news/phantom-twist-in-Karine-a-mystery/1008971598877.htm.

109. According to Bush advisor David Frum, "The Karine A incident finished Arafat in Bush's eyes." Quoted in Sassan Fayazmanash, *The United States and Iran*, p. 113.

110. Robert Satloff, "Karine-A: The Strategic Implications of Iranian-Palestinian Collusion," The Washington Institute for Near East Policy: *Policy Watch*, no. 593 (January 15, 1998).

111. Text of the speech available at: www.americanrhetoric.com/speeches/stateofthe union2002.htm.

112. Barbara Slavin, *Bitter Friends, Bosom Enemies*, pp. 203–4.

113. For the full text of the letter, see: Trita Parsi, *Treacherous Alliance*, Appendices A and B, pp. 341–43.

114. Tom Regan, "Cheney Rejected Iran's Offer of Concessions in 2003," *Christian Science Monitor*, January 18, 1998.

115. "Flynt Leverett on Sec. Rice Misleading Congress in Reuters," New America Foundation, February 14, 1998. (Flynt Leverett was a member of the NSC at the time.)

116. Steven R. Weisman, "Iran Turns Down American Offer of Relief Mission," *New York Times*, January 3, 1998.

117. Afshin Molavi, "U.S. Humanitarian Response to Iran Earthquake Sparks New Debate on Relations," *Washington Report on Middle East Affairs* (March 2004).

118. "U.S. Quake Teams Split Iranian Leadership," Foxnews.com, January 3, 2004, available at: http://origin.foxnews.com/primter_friendly_story/0,3566,10722,00.html.

119. "Undeniably Offensive," *Guardian*, December 13, 2006.

120. John Ward Anderson, "Cartoons of Prophet Met with Outrage," *Washington Post*, January 31, 2001.

121. Ewen MacAskill and Chris McGreal, "Israel Should be Wiped Off the Map, Says Iran's President," *Guardian*, October 27, 2005, and Arash Norouzi, "Iran's President Did Not Say 'Israel Must Be Wiped Off the Map,'" *Information Clearing House*, January 18, 2007, at: http://www.informationclearinghouse.info/article16218.htm.

122. Gholam Reza Afkhami, ed., *Barnameh e Energy e Atomi e Iran, Talshha va Taneshha: Mosahebeh ba Akbar e Etemad, Nakhostin Raeis e Sazman e Energy e Iran* [Iran's atomic energy

program: Efforts and tensions: Interview with Akbar Etemad, the first director of Iran's atomic energy organization], Washington DC, Foundation of Iranian Studies, 1997.

123. Ibid.

124. EURODIF stands for European Gaseous Diffusion Uranium Enrichment Consortium, a subsidiary of the French company Areva. It was formed in 1973 by France, Belgium, Italy, Spain, and Sweden. In 1974, Iran lent $1 billion to the company, plus $180 million in 1977. In 1975, Sweden sold its 10 percent share to Iran. After the Islamic Revolution, Iran demanded a refund and withdrew from EURODIF. Some Iranians believe that this was part of deal between Bazargan and the French even before the revolution, in order to undermine Iran's nuclear program. However, there is no way to substantiate these claims.

125. Some analysts have attributed Russia's hesitation to signing the agreement with Iran to U.S. and Israeli pressures. See: *The United States and Iran*, pp. 127–28. This may have played a role, but the evolution of Russia's foreign policy concepts had a greater impact. See chapter on Russia-Iran Relations.

126. See: *The Scotsman*, December 14, 2002.

127. See chapter on Iran-Europe relations.

128. Report of the IAEA Director General, available at: http://www.payvandnews.com/news/09/aug/1262.html.

129. Ibid.

130. Barbara Slavin, *Bitter Friends, Bosom Enemies*, p. 216.

131. The full text is available at: http://www.finalcall.com/artman/publish/printer_2607.ahtml.

132. "Obama Could Send message to Iran With . . . a Message to Iran," *U.S. News and World Report*, May 1, 2009.

133.

134. Ewen MacAskill, "U.S. Plans to Station Diplomats in Iran for First Time Since 1979," *Guardian*, July 17, 2008.

135. "Iranian Downgrades Importance of Opening U.S. Diplomatic Mission," *Arab-American*, December 24, 2008, available at: http://www.arabicnews.com/ansub/Daily/Day/081224/2008122422.html.

136. Barbara Slavin, *Bitter Friends, Bosom Enemies*, p. 217.

137. Ibid., p. 223.

138. "Human Rights Abuses in the MKO Camps," Human Rights Watch, May 2005, available at: http://hrw.org/background/mena/iran0505/4.htm.

139. Khalilzad, a Sunni and a former supporter of the Taliban, was viewed as biased against the Shias and was known among them as Mullah Omar or Abu Omar. Edward Wong and Abdul Razzaq Al Saieidi, "The Struggle For Iraq: U.S. Envoy Says He Had Meetings with Iraq Rebels," *New York Times*, March 26, 2006.

140. Kathleen Ridolfo, "Samara Bombing Set Off Year of Violence," Radio Free Europe/Radio Liberty (RFE/RL), February 12, 1998.

141. Simon Freeman, "Iran Leader Backs Talks with U.S. on Iraq," *Times* (London), March 22, 2006.

142. "Iran May Consider Higher Level Contacts with U.S. on Iraq," Foreign Ministry of the Islamic Republic of Iran, July 25, 1998, available at: http://web-srv.mfa/ir/output/English/documents/doc903htm.

143. Peter Symonds, "Iranian Diplomat Kidnapped in Baghdad: Another U.S. Provocation?" *Global Research*, February 11, 2007. Also Robin Wright and Nancy Trejos, "U.S. troops Raid 2 Iranian Targets in Iraq, Detain 5 People," *Washington Post*, January 12, 2007.

144. "Arrests Violated Law," *Sky News*, January 12, 2008.

145. "Seymour Hirsh, "U.S. Training Jondollah and MKE for Bombing Preparation," Campaign Against Sanctions and Military Intervention in Iran (CASMI), July 8, 1998; and Peter Symonds, "Washington's Proxy War inside Kurdish Iran," *World Socialist Web site*, September 20, 2007.

146. Anne Flaherty, "General sees Iraq-Iran Link, Says Ahmad Chalabi Keeping Sunnis at Bay," philly.com, February 17, 2010, available at: http://www.printthis.clickability.com/pt/cpt?action=cp&title=General+sees+Iraq-Iran+lin.

147. Jim Loney, "Biden Visits Iraq Amid Election Row," Reuters, January 23, 2010, available at: http://www.reuters.com/assets/rpint?aid=USTRE60MOLV20100123; see also "Clinton 'Heartened' by Iraq Move to Reinstate Candidates," *Agence France Press*, February 5, 2010, available at: http://www.google.com/hostednews/afp/article/ALeqM5hx5VqjEMTpbn4AmpFrs1cZHc.

148. The text of speech is available at: www.npr.org/templates/story/story.php?storyId=91150432.

149. Ibid.

150. Ibid.

151. See: "Translation of Ahmadinejad's Letter," *Washington Post*, November 6, 2008, available at: http://www.washingtonpost.com/wp-dyn/content/article/2008/11/06/AR2008110603030.html.

152. Barbara Slavin, "Obama Sends Iran New Year's Greetings," *Washington Times*, March 20, 2009.

153. Khamenei said, "You change, our behavior will change," thus in the clearest way accepting the principle of reciprocity. See Zahra Hosseinian and Fredrik Dahl, "Iran to U.S.: 'You change, our behavior will change,'" Reuters, March 21, 2009, available at: http://www.reuters.com/article/newsMaps/idUSDAH12844520090321.

154. Larijani said that Iran's problems with the United States are not emotional ones to be solved with soothing words. "Moshgel Iran ba Amrica Atefi Nist" (Iran's problem with the U.S. has nothing to do with sentiment). Mehr News Agency, March 26, 2009.

155. David Morgan, "Clinton Says U.S. Could 'Totally Obliterate' Iran," Reuters, April 22, 2008, available at: http://www.reuters.com/article/print?articleId=USN2224332720080422.

156. Mark Landler, "Iran Looms Over Clinton's Middle East Trip," *New York Times*, March 5, 1998.

157. "Gates Seeking to Reassure Gulf Allies on Outreach to Iran," *USA Today*, May 4, 2009.

158. "Peres: We Will Attack Ahmadinejad Militarily" [Ahmadinejad ra Mord e Hamleh e Nezami Gharar khahim Dad], *Entekhab News*, April 13, 2009.

159. James Hider, "Leon Panetta's Mission to Stop Israel Bombing Iranian Nuclear Plant," *Times* (London) May 15, 2009.

160. "Lieberman: Bombing Iran Not Israel's Intent" *Huffington Post*, June 3, 2009.

161. Flynt Leverett and Hillary Mann Leverett, "Have We Already Lost Iran?" *New York Times*, May 24, 2009.

162. Nathan Guttman, "Congress Gives Obama Deadline for Dealing with Iran," *Jewish Daily Forward*, July 29, 2009.

163. Peter Beaumont, "Iran Jails U.S. Journalist Roxanna Saberi as Spy," *Observer*, April 19, 2009. Also, Nahid Siamdoust, "Roxanna Saberi: Out of Iranian Prison, Into a Soap Opera," *Time*, May 12, 2009, available at: http://www.time.com/time/printout/0,8816,1897440,00.html.

164. Warren P. Strobel, "In Shift, Obama Administration will Join Iran Nuclear Talks," *Mc-Clatchy Newspapers*, April 8, 2009, available at: http://www.mcclatchydc.co/world/v-print/story/65771.html.

165. See various issues of newspapers and news sites like VOAnews.com, BBC News, Press TV, and Pavvand News for accounts of the events.

166. "Western Nations Deny Iranian Claims of Inciting Violence" VOAnews.com, June 22, 2009, available at: http://www.voanews.com/english/archive/2009–06/2009–06-22-voa43.cfm?moddate=2009.

167. David Gollust, "U.S. Rescinds 4th of July Invitations to Iranian Diplomats," VOA news.com, June 25, 2009, available at: http://www.payvand.com/news/09/jun/1275.html.

168. Middle East Media Research Institute, June 30, 2009, available at:http://www.memri.org/bin/articles.cgi?Page=archives&Area=sd&ID=SP242509.

169. "Obama Eshtebahat e Bush ra tekrar Nakond" [Obama should not repeat Bush's mistakes], Mehr News Agency, June 26, 2009.

170. Julian Borger, "Iran Nuclear Plant: Miliband Refuses to Rule Out Military Action," *Guardian*, September 26, 2009.

171. James Blitz, Daniel Dombey, and Najmeh Bozorgmehr, "Iran's N-Plant Condemned," *Financial Times*, September 26, 2009. Also Alan Cowell and Nazila Fathi, "Iran Test-Fires Missiles That Put Israel in Range," *New York Times*, September 29, 2009.

172. "A Nuclear Debate Brews: Is Iran Designing Warheads?" *New York Times*, September 29, 2009.

173. Gary Milhollin and Valerie Lincy, "Lifting Iran's Nuclear Veil," *New York Times*, September 30, 2009.

174. Glenn Kessler, "Iran, Major Powers Reach Agreement on Series of Points," *Washington Post*, October 2, 2009.

175. "Swiss Confirm Visit to U.S. Hikers Held in Iran," Reuters Alert Net, September 29, 2009.

176. Glenn Kessler, "U.S. Helping Iran Get Uranium," *Washington Post*, October 11, 2009.

177. "Iran Reminds IAEA of West's Broken Promises," Press TV, March 1 2010.

178. Japan reportedly made this offer during a visit by Ali Larijani, the Speaker of Iran's parliament to Japan in February 2010. "Iran 'to Study Japan Offer to Enrich Uranium,'" RESS TV, February 25, 2010.

179. "Iran Should Pay for Nuclear Fuel and Reject Swap Deal: Rohani," *Tehran Times*, February 2010, available at: http://www.tehrantimes.com/NCms/2007.asp?code=214739.

180. "Elam Amadeghi Iran Baraye Mobadeleh 400 Kilogeram Uranium dar Kish" [Iran ready to swap 400 kilograms of uranium in Kish], IRNA, December 12, 2009.

181. "Zohrehvand: Mobadeleh Soukht Neshan Dahandeh e Enetaf e Diplomacy e Hasteeh Iran Ast" [Zoherehvand: Swap proposal indicates the flexibility of Iran's nuclear diplomacy], IRNA, February 3, 2010.

182. "Iran Khastar Hosour Bazrasan e Agance Dar Frayand e Ghanisazi 20 Dar sad Shod" [Iran requests the presence of IAEA inspector in its 20% enrichment], Fars News Agency, February 8, 2010.

183. "McCain: Bayad ba Tashvigh e Anasor e Dakheli Az Barandazi Hokoumat e Iran Hemayat Konim" [McCain: We must support regime change in Iran by encouraging internal elements], as reported by Fars News Agency, September 30, 2009. Also Robert Kagan, "Forget the Nukes: The Most Fruitful Target Is Iran's Weakening Regime," *Washington Post*, September 30, 2009.

184. "Israel Endorses Iran Nuclear Plan," BBC News, October 30, 2009.

185. Matt Sugrue, "Administration Asks Congress to Delay Sanctions," National Iranian American Council, October 7, 2009, available at: http://www.niacouncil.org/index.php?option=com_content&task=view&id=1514&Itemid=2.

186. "U.S. Warns Iran not to Build Bomb," BBC News, February 14, 2010.

187. "Obama Says World Moving Fast on Iranian Sanctions," Reuters, February 9, 2010, available at: http://www.reuters.com/assets/print?aid=USLDE61705120100209.

188. Mohammed A. Salih, "U.S. steps Up Sanctions Diplomacy against Iran," Antiwar.com, February 15, 2010, available at: http://original.antiwar.com/salih/2010/02/15us-steps-up-sanctions/print; see also Heather Maher, "Clinton Hopes to Change Brazil's Mind on Iran Sanctions," Radio Free Europe/Radio Liberty (RFE/RL) March 3, 2010, reprinted at: http://www.pavand.com/news/10mar/1024.html.

189. MJ Rosenberg, "Senate Passes AIPAC's Iran Sanctions Bill in Five Minutes," *World News Daily,* Information Clearing House, February 9, 2010, available at: http://information-clearinghouse.info/article24622.htm.

190. The IAEA report, *GOV/2010/10,* p. 9. Available at: www.iaea.org.

191. The IAEA report, *GOV/209/74,* p. 6. Available at: www.iaea.org.

192. "The IAEA Report on Iran 'Reopened Already Closed Issues,'" Press TV, March 3, 2010; see also "NAM Critizises Amano Over Report," hamsayeh.net, March 1, 2010, available at: http://www.hamsayeh.net/hamsayehnet_iran-international%20news970.htm.

193. Jason Ditz, "Israel FM Calls for U.S. to Adopt 'Cuba Style Embargo on Iran," antiwar.com, March 2, 2010, available at: http://news.antiwar.com/2010/03/02/israeli-fm-calls-for-us-to-adopt-cuba-style-embargo-on-iran.

194. Mark Landler, "Iran Policy now more in Sync with Clinton's View," *New York Times,* February 17, 2010.

195. "Admiral Mark Mullen Seemed Particularly Aware of the Potential Consequences of a War with Iran. U.S. Warns against Military Attack on Iran," Press TV, January 7, 2010.

CHAPTER 4

1. In fact, the word "barbarian" was coined by the Greeks for Persians because they had beards and also could not speak Greek.

2. The latest example of such movies is the film *The Three Hundred,* which is highly derogatory to the Iranians. See: Breffni O'Rourke, "Iran: Film on Ancient Persian-Greek Battle Angers Iranians," RFE/RL, 21 March 2007, at http://www.rferl.org/content/article/1075411.html.

3. Iran in ancient times was the main conduit to Europe not only of Chinese silk but also of culture.

4. The Greeks considered Zoroaster a demigod. The word "magic" means "wisdom of the magi." See: Yves Bonnefoy, *Asian Mythologies,* translated under the supervision of Wendy Doniger (Chicago, IL: University of Chicago Press, 1993), p. 160.

5. Cyril Elgood, "Jundi Shapur—A Sassanian University," *Proceedings of the Royal Society of Medicine* 32 (November 2, 1938).

6. Norman Cohen, *Cosmos, Chaos and the World to Come: The Ancient Roots of Apocalyptic Faith* (New Haven, CT: Yale University Press, 2001).

7. J. H. Iliffe, "Persia and the Ancient World," in *The Legacy of Persia,* ed. A. J. Arberry (Oxford: Clarendon Press, 1953), p. 1.

8. Quoted in C. Elgood, "Persian Science" in *The Legacy of Persia,* ed. A. J. Arberry, p. 292.

9. "Talash Baraye Arab Danestan Mashahir e Irani/Bitavajohi rasaneh Beh BBC" [Efforts to portray Iranian luminaries as Arab/The lack of attention of the media (Iranian media) to BBC (reporting)], Mehr News Agency, May 8, 2009.

10. Dennis Wright, *The English Among the Persians* (London: William Heinemann, 1977), pp. 1–4.

11. Charles Issawi, ed. *The Economic History of Iran: 1800–1914* (Chicago, IL: University of Chicago Press, 1971), p. 16.

12. The letter of Scheel to Lord Palmerston written in on August 4, 1850, quoted in Fereydoun Adamiyat, *Andisheh Taraqi va Kokoumat e Qanoon, Asr e Sepahsalar* [*The idea of progress and the rule of law: The era of Sepahsalar*] (Tehran: Entesharat e Kharazmi, 1351 [1973]), pp. 338–39.

13. Hooshang Nahavandian in his book, *The Last Shah of Iran*, says that Count Alexandre de Marenches, the head of the French Intelligence Services, wrote in his memoirs that he "had been present at a meeting, where one of the questions raised was 'how do we get rid of the Shah, and with whom shall we replace him?'" Quoted in "Why and How the Shah of Iran was Overthrown: Two Excerpt Passages from the Last Shah of Iran," *Studien Von Zeitfragen*, 2009, available at: http://www.studien-von zeitfragen.de.Eurasian/Shah_of-Iran/Shah_of-iran.html.

14. For details see: Shireen T. Hunter, *Iran and the World: Continuity in a Revolutionary Decade* (Bloomington: Indiana University Press, 1990), p. 144.

15. Ibid., p. 143.

16. Ibid.

17. Ibid., pp. 154–56.

18. The issue of EURODIF and Iran's contribution to it was one of these problems. See: Ibid., pp. 148–54.

19. Ibid., pp. 145–48.

20. Christopher Rundle, "Iran-United Kingdom Relations since the Revolution: Opening Doors" in *Iran's Foreign Policy: From Khatami to Ahmadinejad*, ed. Anoushirvan Ehteshami and Mahjoob Zweiri (Reading, England: Ithaca Press, 2008), p. 94.

21. A former foreign minister of a major European country told the author that he had developed a formula that would have resolved the Rushdie issue long before 1998, but the British blocked it.

22. For a detailed account of these issues see: Seyyed Hossein Moussavian, *Iranian-European Relations: Challenges and Opportunities* (London: Routledge, 2008), pp. 94–123.

23. "Habibi Holds News Conference; Says 'Several' European Leaders to Visit Iran Soon," BBC Summary of World Broadcasts, July 10, 1991.

24. Julian Nundy, "Mitterrand to Make Official Visit to Iran," *Independent*, July 4, 1991.

25. Alan Riding, "Iran's Premier in Stormy Time Found Slain Near Paris," *New York Times*, August 9, 1991 and Julian Nundy, "Bakhtiar Allegations Threaten Mitterrand Visit," *Independent*, September 23, 1991.

26. Other incidents related to the activities of Iranian dissidents had earlier caused tensions in Iran-German relations. A case in point was the arrest of the Iranian writer and dissident Faraj Sarkouhi at the house of the German cultural counselor in Tehran.

27. For details, see: Ronen Bergman, *The Secret War with Iran: The 30-Year Clandestine Struggle against the World's Most Dangerous Terror* (New York: Free Press, 2008).

28. One individual, Saied Emami, who later was accused of masterminding what came to be known as Chain Murders carried out in Iran itself over a number of years against prominent journalists, intellectuals, and political activists, was said to have been responsible for the Mykonos assassinations. According to some Iranian sources, he seems to have had an adventurous

history. His real name allegedly was Daniyal Ghavami and he had worked for the shah-era intelligence organization, SAVAK. Some in Iran have accused him of working for the Israeli intelligence organization, MOSSAD, as part of a plan of undermining the Iranian regime and possibly causing instability in the country. Supposedly, Saied Hajarian, himself an official of the intelligence apparatus, had wanted Ghavami out of the Ministry of Information. See: "Who Was Daniyal Ghavami?" *Persicus Maximus*, September 5, 2008, available at: http://persicus-maximus.blogspot.com/2008/09/who-was-daniyal-ghavami.html.

The Iranian reformist writer and prominent dissident in a series of articles in 1998 accused Rafsanjani and the chief of Iran's intelligence, Fallahian, as those really responsible for these acts. Conservative, and even some reformist, elements such as the advisor to the presidential candidate Mehdi Karrubi, meanwhile, have accused the radicals-turned-reformists, such as Saied Hajarian, as masterminds of these acts. See: "Moshavver e Karrubi: Hajarian Teorissian e qatlhaye Zanjireie Ast" [Karrubi's advisor: Hajarian is the theoretician of chain murders], *Entekhab News*, May 13, 2009, available at: http://www.entekhabnews.com/portal/index.php?news+4495&print.

29. For example, the Arabic language *Al Hayat* published in London in its April 15, 1997, issue that "ex–president Abolhassan Bani Sadr has a record of activity against the regime and cannot be considered a just or reliable witness."

30. Seyyed Hossein Moussavian, *Iranian-European Relations*, pp. 97–123.

31. "Espania Nemitavand Dar Moghabel Iran Mostaghel Amal Kond" [Spain can not act independently toward Iran], Interview with Spanish analyst Luciano Zakara, *Iranian Diplomacy*, April 7, 2009.

32. For the text of the treaty see: www.eurotreaties.com/maastrichtec.pdf.

33. According to Christopher Rundle, Iranians complained of British "double standards vis-à-vis Iran on the one hand and the Gulf monarchies on the other." "Iran-United Kingdom Relations since the Revolutions."

34. Seyyed Hossein Mousavian, *Iran's Relations with Europe*, pp. 207–8.

35. "United Nations Report 1997," no. 114, pp. 2–4.

36. Seyyed Hossein Moussavian, *Iran's Relations with Europe*, p. 209.

37. Even Iranian sources have admitted that this statement contributed to the guilty verdict in the Mykonos affair, which led to the break in Iran-EU diplomatic relations. Seyyed Hossein Mousavian, *Iran's Relations with Europe*, p. 97.

38. According to the Belgian government, the United States alerted them to the existence of the consignment. Reportedly, when the ship arrived in Hamburg, the consignment was removed. According to Iran's ambassador in Germany, a German official told him that "the Americans even knew the name of the individual who had transferred this cargo to the ship in the Iranian port of Bandar Abbas." Also the MKO in its newsletter published photographs and particulars of this consignment, which raises the question of how they obtained this information. Ibid., pp. 116–17.

39. Fawas Gerges, "Washington's Misguided Iran Policy," *Survival* 38, no. 103 (Winter 1996): 8.

40. RFE/RL, *Iran Report* 2, no. 11 (March 15, 1998).

41. "News Headlines on Mond 20 September 1999-Iran-Autra president," *News and Reports*, available at: http://former.president.ir/Khatami/eng/croninews/1378/7806/780629/780629.htm.

42. On Aznar's visit and the background to Iran-Spain relations and agreements signed during Aznar's trip, see: M. R. Khoshgou, "Iran's Relations with Spain," available at: http://www.iranexportsmagazine.com/Archive/mag%2073/cover%2073.htm.

43. Anne Penketh, "Straw Will Visit Tehran to Forge Unlikely Alliance." *Independent*, September 22, 2001.

44. "Timeline: UK-Iran relations," BBC News, March 23, 2007.

45. "News Headlines on Mon 10 July 2000, Khatami-Meeting-Berlin," *News and Reports*, available at: http://former.president.ir/Khatami/eng/cronicnews/1379/7904/790420/794020.htm.

46. Quoted in Shahriar Sabet-Saeidi, "Iranian–European Relations: A Strategic Partnership?" in *Iran's Foreign Policy: From Khatami to Ahmadinejad*, ed. Anoushirvan Ehteshami and Mahjoob Zweiri, p. 65.

47. This led to the cancellation of the state dinner that King Juan Carlos was to hold in Khatami's honor. A similar situation arose when Khatami went to France in 2005. On Spain, see: "Iran And Spain Agreed on No Wine, No Scarf Compromise," Iran Press Service, October 22, 2002.

48. Justin Huggler, "Jews Accused of Spying are Pawns in Iran Power Struggle," *Independent*, June 4, 2000.

49. General Affairs and External Relations Council, 2,518th Council Meeting.

50. "EU Envoy Warns Iran," BBC News, August 30, 2003, available at: http://news.bbc.co.uk/1/world/middleeast/3190319.stm.

51. Seyyed Hossein Mousavian, *Iran–Europe Relations*, pp. 157–58.

52. Ibid., pp. 158–59.

53. Text of the Brussels Agreement obtained by the author.

54. "Larijani Az Posht e Parde e Mozakerat e Hasteei Sokhan Goft" [Larijani spoke of the behind the scene aspects of nuclear negotiations], Islamic Republic News Agency (IRNA), May 5, 2009, available at: http://www.irna.ir/View/Fullstory/Tools/Printversion/?newsId=471116.

55. Seyyed Hossein Mousavian, *Iranian-European Relations*, pp. 168–70.

56. Seyyed Hossein Mousavian, *Iranian-European Relations*, p. 180.

57. Based on the author's conversations in Brussels in July 2009.

58. Seyyed Hossein Mousavian, *Iranian-European Relations*, pp. 181–82.

59. Russo-British rivalry in the 19th century had prevented Iran form building a railroad. Iran's Western allies also did not help it to build a steel mill. The first Iranian steel mill was built in 1965 with Soviet help.

60. "Larijani: Iran-EU Nuclear Talks Near Unity of View," China.or.cn, April 27, 2007.

61. Charles Bremmer, "Sarkozy Talks of Bombing if Iran Gets Nuclear Arms," *Times* (London), August 28, 2007, http://www.timesonline.co.uk/tol/news/world/europe/article2237190.ece?print=yes&randnu.

62. Alex Spilius and Tim Butcher, "Prepare for War with Iran, Says French Minister," Telegraph.co.uk, September 18, 2007.

63. "Solana Beh Larijani: Motaesfam Kharabkaran kar e Khodeshan ra kardanded" [Solana to Larijani: I am sorry the saboteurs did their work], *Aftab News*, May 5, 2009, available at: http://www.aftabnews.ir/prtguq.ak97w4prra.html.

64. "Miliband to speak out over Iran," BBC News, November 23, 2008.

65. Kaveh L. Afrasiabi, "Europe Out of Step with U.S. over Iran," *Asia Times*, March 26, 2009, available at: http://www.atimes.com/atimes/printN.html.

66. Dominic Kennedy, "Report Reveals Iran Seized British Sailors in Disputed Waters," *Times* (London), April 17, 2008. The sailors were released.

67. Britain denies Iran bomb claim," BBC News, October 16, 2005.

68. "Iran's Oil Minister to Visit Germany for Gas Talks," Mathaba.Net, May 5, 2009, available at: http://www.mathaba.net/0_index.shtml?x=620158.

69. "Sarkozy Urges Tougher Iran Sanctions, Warn French Firms," Haatez.com, September 24, 2007. The head of Total, Christophe de Margerie, criticized this policy. "Enteghad Shadid Total Az Feshar e Paris bar Tehran" [Total's strong criticism of Paris' pressure on Tehran], *Entekhab News*, February 23, 2009.

70. Elizabeth Adams and Benoit Faucon, "Statoil Hydro Halts Investments in Iran in Current Climate," Dow Jones Newswires, October 30, 2009, available at: http://www.rigzone.com/news/article.asp?a_id=81977.

71. "Russia, Ukraine Dispute Leaves European Nations without Gas," Foxnews.com, January 6, 2009.

72. "Merkel Thinks Iran Wants to Destroy Israel," Press TV, January 20, 2009; "Germany Turns Back on Traders with Iran," Press TV, January 26, 2009.

73. "Iran, Switzerland Sign Gas Export Deal," *Mining Top News*, March 19, 2008; "Iran Signs Gas Deal with Austria's OMV," Fars News Agency, April 22, 2007.

74. "Mozakerat Khosousi e Mottaki va Hamtay Bellarusy/Efteteahe Khat e Dovom e Samand" [Mottaki's private talks with his Belarusian counterpart/the inauguration of the second line of Samand], Mehr News Agency, November 12, 2008; "Ravand Matloub e Hamkari Nafti e Tehran-Minsk" [Satisfactory progress of Tehran-Minsk oil cooperation], Mehr News Agency, November 12, 2008.

75. "Rahkarhaye e Towseh Iran va Belarus Barresi Shod" [The ways to expand Iran-Belarus development studied], IRNA, February 2010.

76. "Rasahaneh ye Hamegani e Lahestan az Ehyay e Commissione e moshtarak e do keshvar Estegbal Kardand" [The polish mass media welcome the restoration of joint economic commission between the two countries], IRNA, January 12, 2008.

77. "EU Nations Criticize Iran Election, Concerned Over Protests," Associated Press, June 14, 2009.

78. The text of the communiqué is available at: http://www.esteri.it/MAE/IT/Sala_Stampa/ArchivioNotizie/Approfondimenti/2009/06/200.

79. "Ehzar e Safir e Englis dar Tehran beh Vezarat e Kharejeh" [The British ambassador in Tehran is called to the foreign ministry], Iran Students News Agency (ISNA), June 16, 2009.

80. Jeanne Wellman, "Arrests Raise Ire of U.K.," *Wall Street Journal*, June 29, 2009, and "U.K. Expels Two Iranian Diplomats," BBC News, June 23, 2009.

81. "UK Fury as Staff Arrested in Iran," BBC News, June 28, 2009, available at: http://news.bbc.co.uk/2hi/middle_east/8122871.stm.

82. In general, despite an overall improvement in Franco-American relations, Presidents Obama and Sarkozy have disagreed on a number of issues and Sarkozy has accused president Obama of "naïveté," Christopher Dickey, "Sarkozy's Obama Obsession," *Newsweek*, October 5, 2009.

83. "Azm e Majles Dar Kahesh Ravabet Ba Englis Ghati Ast" [Parliament is determined to downgrade relations with England], Fars News Agency, February 9, 2010.

84. Monavar Khalaj, "Italy Arrests Iranian Journalist over alleged Arms Smuggling," FT.com, March 5, 2010, available at: http://.ft.com/cms/s/bc480114-27f6-11df-9598-00144feabdc0.

85. "Iran Summons Germany Envoy over PJAK," upi.com, March 10, 2010, available at: http://www.upi.com/Top_News/Special/2010/03/10/Iran-summons-Germany-envoy-over.

86. "Italy Rejects Partaking in Iran Satellite Project," Press TV, November 11, 2009.

87. "Porrouyi e Modir Amel e Total: Iran ravabetesh ra be Israel behbood bakhshahd ta Sarmayeh Gozari Konim" [The audacity of Total's director general: Iran should improve its relations with Israel if it wants us to invest there], *Entekhab News*, July 11, 2008.

CHAPTER 5

1. See: R. K. Ramazani, *The Foreign Policy of Iran: A Developing Nation in World Affairs, 1500–1941* (Charlottesville: University Press of Virginia), 1966.

2. Muhammad Taghi Bahar, *Tarikh e Ahzab e Siasi* [The history of political parties] (Tehran: 1323 [1945]), vol. 1, p. 27.

3. Sepehr Zabih, *The Communist Movement in Iran* (Berkeley: University of California Press, 1966), pp. 13–45.

4. This treaty was part of Lenin's policy of normalizing the Bolshevik government's external relations.

5. Sepehr Zabih and Shahram Chubin, *The Foreign Relations of Iran: A Developing State in a Zone of Great Power Conflict* (Berkeley: University of California Press, 1974).

6. Ali Reza Nobari, ed., *Iran Erupts* (Stanford, CA: Iran-America Documentation Group, Stanford University, 1978), pp. 238.

7. Leonid Medvedko, "Islam and Liberation Revolution," *New Times*, no. 43, (October 1979): 18–21.

8. Shireen T. Hunter, *Iran and the World*, pp. 83–93.

9. Shevardnadze's visit was for the purpose of delivering Mikhail Gorbachev's response to the letter sent by the Ayatollah Khomeini to Gorbachev in January 1989. In this letter, Khomeini invited Gorbachev to study the Koran.

10. Iran prevented the inflow of refugees into its territory but set up tents and other facilities for them within the borders of the Republic of Azerbaijan.

11. There is one important exception to this rule: namely, Russia's stance toward Georgia's separatist republics of Abkhazia and South Ossetia.

12. This situation might change if the positive trend in U.S.-Russia relations under President Obama continues.

13. Alexander Dallin, "New Thinking on Foreign Policy," in *New Thinking in Soviet Politics*, ed. Archie Brown (New York: St. Martin's Press,1992), p. 75. Others have mentioned the impact of the Afghan war.

14. Since the time of Peter the Great and his modernization process, Russia has been torn between two poles in terms of its identity and external orientation. One pole has been Europe and the other has been the idea of Russian uniqueness as a Eurasian country encompassing both Europe and Asia and bridging the civilizational divide between the two. See: Shireen T. Hunter, *Islam in Russia: The Politics of Identity and Security* (Armonk, NY: M. E. Sharpe, 2004), pp. 127–91.

15. Alexander Rahr, "'Atlanticists' versus 'Eurasians' in Russian Foreign Policy," REF/RL *Research Report* 1, no. 22 (May 29, 1992): 19.

16. See Shireen T. Hunter, *Islam in Russia*, p. 293.

17. "B. N. Yeltsin's Press Conference in the UN," *Rossiskaya Gazeta*, February 3, 1992, printed in *Current Digest of Post-Soviet Press* 44, no. 5 (February 1992): 12.

18. Andranik Mingranyan noted that the Euro-Atlanticists had replaced Soviet ideology with another dogmatic ideology, according to which "following the elimination of the CPSU and the Marxist-Leninist ideology, a complete unity of goals and values exist between the U.S. and the West and Russia." Andranik Mingranyan, "Russia and the Near Abroad," *Nevazisimaya Gazeta*, January 12, 1994, reprinted in the *Current Digest of the Post-Soviet Press* 46, no. 6, 9 (March 1994).

19. Sergei Stankevich, one-time state counselor to Yeltsin, argued that "Russia's foreign policy must provide for goals and tasks elevated above opportunistic pragmatism." He argued that

Russia could become "the conciliator, Russia connecting, Russia combining; . . . a country imbibing West and East, North and South, unique and exclusively capable of harmonious combination of many different principles of a symphonic harmony." Sergei Stankevich, "Russia in Search of Itself," *National Interest* (Summer 1992): 57.

20. Quoted in Mohiaddin Mesbahi, "Russian Foreign Policy and Security in Central Asia and the Caucasus," *Central Asia Survey* 12, no. 2 (1993).

21. Igor Torbakov, "The 'Statists' and the Ideology of Russian Imperial Nationalism," RFE-RL *Research Report* 1, no. 11 (December 1992): 10–16.

22. Alexei Malashenko, "Rossiia I Islam" [Russia and Islam], *Nezavisimaya Gazeta*, February 22, 1992.

23. Dugin's philosophy is based on the idea that geography determines the character of civilizations. According to Dugin, since ancient times there have been two kinds of civilizations, those of the "Continent." or land–based, and "Islands." In their ultimate form, they represent two types of empire *tellurokratia* (continental) and *talsssokratiya* (island). The earliest example of such an empire is Carthage, but the British Empire and what Dugin considers its successor, the United States, best represent this type of empire. According to him, the island civilization's ideology, "Atlanticism," is based on instability, rootlessness, and materialism, whereas a continental empire, whose ideology is "Eurasianism," is an integrative, spiritual, and nonexploitative civilization. See: Wayne Allensworth, *The Russian Question: Nationalism, Modernization, and Post-Soviet Russia* (Lanham, MD: Rowman and Littlefield, 1998), p. 259.

24. Alexander Dugin, *Islam protiv Islama* [Islam against Islam], February 15, 2000, available at: http://www.arctogaia.com/public/du7.htm.

25. See chapter 1.

26. Shireen T. Hunter, *Iran and the World*, p. 94. During Rafsanjani's trip, Gorbachev said that "we explicitly declare that our country supports your anti-imperialist revolution," and he added that "we [the USSR] are ready to go as far as Iran is ready to meet us." "Rafsanjani Meets Gorbachev," *Middle East Economic Digest* 3, no. 25, (June 30, 1989): 23.

27. During a visit to Turkey in 1992, Kozyrev expressed Russia's fear of Central Asia's Islamization. Ma Kism Yusin, "Tehran Declares 'Great Battle' for Influence in Central Asia. Russia, the U.S., and Turkey Seek to Prevent Iran from Winning that Battle," *Izvestia*, February 7, 1992, reproduced in the *Current Digest of the Post-Soviet Press* 44, no. 6 (March 11, 1992).

28. Yuri Fedorov, "Interest Groups and Russia's foreign policy," *International Affairs* 44, no. 6. (1998): 173–83.

29. Andarnik Migranian, "Real and Illusory Guidelines in Foreign Policy," *Rossiskaya Gazeta*, August 4, 1992, reproduced in the *Current Digest of Post-Soviet Press* 44, no. 32. (September 9, 1992).

30. Kozyrev interview with *TASS* reproduced in the FBIS-SOV-92–118, June 18, 1992.

31. Vladimir Putin made this point in an article he wrote in the *New York Times*, titled "Why We Must Act," and he drew parallels with what Russia was doing in Chechnya and past U.S. antiterrorist acts. *New York Times*, November 14, 2001.

32. It was only in 2001 that Yevgeny Primakov, former Russian foreign and prime minister, admitted that the "Iran-Russia alliance has been instrumental in the Caucasian region and in bringing peace to Tajikistan." "Iran: Russians See Khatami's Moscow Visit as Big Event," IRNA, March 11, 2001.

33. "Interior Minister Kulikov Thanks Iran for 'Circumspect Position' on Chechnya," Interfax, *Daily News Bulletin*, December 20, 1997, from BBC Summary of World Broadcasts, December 20, 1997.

34. Natalya Hmelik, "Russia's Special Relationship with Iran's Mullahs," *Global Politician*, available at: http://www.globalpolitician.com/print.asp?id=1690, accessed September 28, 2009.

35. Ibid. Also, see Lionel Beehner, "Russia-Iran Arms Trade," Council on Foreign Relations, November 1, 2001, available at: http://www.cfr.org/publications/11869/russianiran_arms_trade.html.

36. *The Foreign Policy Concept of the Russian Federation, Approved by the President of the Russian Federation V. Putin,* June 28, 2000, available at: http://www.fas.org/nuke/guide/russia/doctrine/econcept.htm.

37. Maxim Gribov, "Khatami Receives Guests from Moscow," *Nezavisimaya Gazeta*, December 2, 2000, in the *Current Digest of the Post-Soviet Press* 52, no. 49 (December 2, 2000).

38. Quoted in Simon Saradzhan, "Visiting Khatami to Deal for Arms," *Moscow Times*, March 12, 2001.

39. Robert O. Freedman, "Russian Policy toward the Middle East Under Putin: The Impact of 9/11 and the War in Iraq," *Alternatives: Turkish Journal of International Affairs* 2, no. 2. (Summer 2003), available at: http://www.alternativesjournal.net/volume2/number2/putin.htm.

40. "Russia Finishes Division of Caspian Sea with Azerbaijan," *Izvestia*, June 7, 2002, reproduced in *Russian Oil and Gas Report*, June 10, 2002, and "Focus: Russia and Kazakhstan Agree on Offshore Boundary," *Petroleum Economics* 25 (June 2002).

41. "Iran and Russia Sign Joint Communiqués on Caspian Sea, Tajikistan," *Voice of the Islamic Republic of Iran*, July 19, 1998, in the BBC Summary of World Broadcasts, July 20, 1998.

42. A. I. Gousher, "k novomu etapu Rossisko-Iranskikh Otnoshenii" [Toward a new stage of Russian-Iranian relations], *Evrazisky Vestnik* [Eurasian Herald], January 9, 2001.

43. "Iran Criticizes Russia's Military Exercises in Caspian," IRNA, January 11, 2001, in BBC Monitoring, January 11, 2001.

44. Ahmad Majidyar, "Russo-Iranian Relations from Iran's Perspective," *Iran Tracker*, May 20, 2009, available at: http://www.irantracker.org/analysis/russo-iranian-relations-irans-perspective.

45. John Cherian, "The Bushehr Conundrum," *Frontline*, August 17, 2002, available at: http://www.thehindu.com/fline/f11917/19170530.htm.

46. Mark N. Katz, "Putin and Ahmadinejad," *United Press International*, August 13, 2006, available at: http://www.spacewar.com/reports/Putin_and_Ahmadinejad_999html.

47. David E. Sanger and William J. Broad, "Bush and Putin Want Iran to Treat Uranium in Russia," *New York Times*, November 19, 2005.

48. Ibid. Ali Larijani, secretary of Iran's National Security Council, went to Moscow to dissuade Russia from voting for the referral to the UNSC.

49. "Putin to Visit Iran despite Reports on Assassination Threat," *Xinhua*, October 15, 2007.

50. Adrian Bloomfield, "Israel to Press Russia Not to Sell Air Defences to Iran," *Daily Telegraph*, October 6, 2008, and Rory McCarthy, "Netanyahu Visits Moscow in Secret to Obstruct Iran Missile Sale," *Guardian*, September 11, 2009.

51. "The Bushehr Payment Dispute: Moscow Signals the Limits of Its Support for Iran," *WMD Insights*, May 2007, available at: http://www.wmdinsights.com/115/115RU1_Bushehr Payment.htm.

52. "Russia's Medvedev Won't Rule Out Iran Sanctions," RFE/RL, September 15, 2009.

53. Robert Mackey, "For Iran's Opposition 'Death to Russia' Is the New 'Death to America,'" *New York Times* News Blog, July 20, 2009, available at: http://thelede.blogs.nytimes.com.

54. "Election Winner Ahmadinejad Visiting Moscow for SCO," available at: http://www.russiansentry.com/?area=postView&id=1236.

55. Sophie Hradach and mark Heinrich, "Russia Says it may Consider Iran Sanctions," Reuters, March 6, 2010.

56. "Moscow dismayed by Iran's reaction to nuclear proposals," *Rianovosti*, January 27, 2010, available at: http://en.iran/russia/20100127/157698234-print.html.

57. "Iran Gives Russian Pilots Two Months to Leave: Report," Reuters, March 6, 2010, reprinted in Yahoo! News at: http://news.yahoo.com/s/nm/20100306/w1_nm/us_iran_russia-pilots_1/print.

CHAPTER 6

1. "Iran Proposes Setting Up 'Asian Union,'" Press TV, October 15, 2009.

2. Relations between Iran and China go back to the pre-Islamic period. The earliest record of these relations dates back to 115 B.C. Relations between China under the Tang dynasty and Sassanid China were particularly extensive.

3. Some of Iranian-Indian cultural links derive from the impact of Aryan tribes, which settled in both countries. Sanskrit and Avestan Persian are quite close. Interaction between the two countries was particularly intense during the Sassanid period. In the Islamic era, Persianized Moguls expanded Persian culture in India, as best reflected in the Taj Mahal.

4. Amir Taheri, "Policies of Iran in the Persian Gulf Region," in *The Persian Gulf and Indian Ocean in International Politics*, ed. in Abbas Amirie (Tehran: Institute for International and Political Studies, 1975), p. 262.

5. Shireen T. Hunter, *Iran and the World: Continuity in a Revolutionary Decade* (Bloomington: Indiana University Press, 1990), pp. 158–62.

6. On Rafsanjani and Khamenei trips, see: "Tehran Views Hashemi-Rafsanjani's PRC Visit," Foreign Broadcasting Information Service (FBIS) South Asia, July 5, 1985, and "Trade, Cultural Exchanges," FBIS NES, May 9, 1989.

7. Muhammad Reza Nazari, "Ayandeh e diplomacy e sharqi: barrasi e–sayr e monasebat Iran va Chin" [The future of eastern diplomacy: A review of Iran-China relations], *Aftab News*, May/June 2008, available at: http://www.aftabnews.ir/pretexv8jh8nvi.82hzbgb994b.j.html.

8. For details of China's military assistance to Iran, see: "China's Missile Exports and Assistance to Iran," NTI (Nuclear Threat Initiative), available at: http://nuclearthreatinitiative.org/db/china/miranpos.htm.

9. "China, One of our Real Friends, Rafsanjani," *Keyhan*, August 20, 1988.

10. The Shah had proposed the formation of an Asian Common Market, which some commentators believed was a prelude to a defensive cooperation system, perhaps in response to the USSR's proposal for an Asian Collective Security pact. Dieter Brown, "The Implications of India's Nuclear Policy for the Region," in *The Persian Gulf and the Indian Ocean in International Politics*, ed. Abbas Amirie, p. 210.

11. Bhabani Sen Gupta, "View From India," in Ibid., p. 183.

12. See: Shireen T. Hunter, *Iran and the World*, pp. 132–33.

13. R. A. Karanjia, *The Mind of a Monarch* (London: George Allen and Unwin, 1977).

14. In 1984, Iran's foreign minister, Ali Akbar Velayati, stated that "India is one of the few Third World countries which has achieved a high level of self-sufficiency and in many respects resembles our country, its experiences in various scientific, technical and agricultural areas can be communicated to us." FBIS/NES, December 4, 1984.

15. "Iran: Are China's Muslims Worthy of Islamic Republic's Support?" *Los Angeles Times*, July 12, 2009.

16. For example, Leslie H. Gelb in an opinion piece in the *New York Times* suggested such an idea.

17. On Sino-Israeli relations, see: "Israel and China Mark 15 Years of Diplomatic Relations," Israel Ministry of Foreign Affairs, January 24, 2007, available at: http://www.mfa.govil/MF/ MFA+events/Around+the+world/Israel+and+China+_mark+. Also on Israeli-Chinese military ties, see P. R. Kumarasawami, "At What Cost Israel-China Ties?" *Middle East Quarterly* 13, no. 2, (Spring 2006).

18. These have included visits by Iranian presidents—Rafsanjani (September 1992), Khatami (June 2000), and Ahmadinejad (2006)—and visits by Chinese president Yang Shang-kun (October 1991), State Council Chairman Hu Jianto (January 2000), and President Jiang Zamin (April 2002), plus visits by foreign and defense ministers of the two countries.

19. See: "Ghardad e 2 milliard dollari towsehe e meydan e nafti Yadavaran emza shod" [The 2 billion dollar agreement for Yadavaran was signed], *Fars News*, September 12, 2007.

20. "Iran's Major Oil Customers," *Tehran Times*, August 19, 2009, available at: http://www. tehrantimes.com/Index_view.asp?code=201312.

21. Muhammad Sahimi, "Why Russia & China Love Iran's Hardliners," *Tehran Bureau*, August 5, 2009, available at: http://tehranbureau.com/russia-china-irans-violent-crackdown/.

22. John Calalbrese, "China and Iran: Mismatched Partners," Occasional Paper, Jamestown Foundation, August 2006, available at: http://www.jamestown.org.

23. "Iran-China Seeking to Boost Trade to $50 billion," Fars News Agency, May 11, 2009.

24. "Arab Countries Become Major Sources of China's Oil Imports," China.org.cn, January 19, 2006.

25. Bates Gill, "Chinese Arms Exports to Iran," *MERIA* (Middle East Review of International Affairs) 2, no. 2. (May 1998).

26. See: "China's Missile Exports and Assistance to Iran," NTI.

27. Ibid.

28. "His Majesty King Abdullah to Visit China," Embassy of the Peoples Republic of China in the Kingdom of Saudi Arabia, January 19, 2006, at: http://www.chinaembassy.org/sa/eng/ xnyfgk/t231866.htm.

29. "President Hu Jianto to Visit Saudi Arabia," SURSIS (Saudi-U.S. Relations Information Service), February 5, 2006.

30. Geof Dyer, "Israel Presses China over Iran Sanctions," *Financial Times*, March 4, 2010.

31. Ibid.

32. Satish Kumar, "India between America and Russia: Need to Tilt Towards U.S.," *Journal of World Affairs*, January 16, 2001.

33. "U.S.-India Sign Defense, Nuclear Deals," VOANews.com, July 20, 2009.

34. The North-South corridor is to some degree a response to the U.S.-sponsored East-West energy and transportation corridor. "Russia and Iran Promote 'North-South' Transportation Corridor," *Analyst*, April 16, 2001, available at: http://www.cacianalyst.org?q=node/639/ print. Also, "Russia to Hold North-South Transport Corridor Rally," Press TV, August 13, 2009. Since the trilateral agreement was reached in 2001, 11 other countries, including Syria and Bulgaria, have joined it.

35. "PM's Oman-Qatar Visit to Boost Investment, Energy Security," November 8, 2008, at: http://www.thaindian.com/newsportal/sports/pms-oman-qatar-visit-to-boost-investment-en.

36. Report of "A Round Table Discussion on Engaging Iran: Opportunities and Challenges for India," available at: http://www.idsa.in/reports/RTEngagingIran060809html.

37. "India-Iran Broaden Prospects for Trade," IRNA, October 17, 2008.

38. "Iran's Major Oil Customers, Energy Partners," *Tehran Times*, August 19, 2009.

39. "Ghardad e dah milliard dollaribargh miyan e Iran, Hend va Pakistan nehayee mishavad" [The 10 billion dollar electricity contract among Iran, India, and Pakistan will be finalized], IRNA, August 24, 2008.

40. For the background, see: David Temple, "The Iran-Pakistan-India Pipeline: The Intersection of Energy And Politics," Institute of Peace and Conflict Studies, New Delhi, India, April 2007, available at: www.ipcs.org.

41. Glenn Kessler, "India Nuclear Deal May Face Hard Sell: Rice Set to Defend Landmark Accord," *Washington Post*, April 3, 2006.

42. P. R. Kumaraswamy, "India's Persian Problems," *Strategic Insight*, July 2008, available at: http://www.ccc.nps.navy.mil/si/2008/jul/kumaraswamyjul08.asp.

43. During a visit to India in 2003, Ariel Sharon, the Israeli prime minister, expressed Israel's concerns regarding warming Indo-Iranian relations. P. R. Kumaraswamy, "Indo-Iranian Ties: The Israeli Dimension," in R. Hathaway et al., "The Strategic Partnership between India and Iran," A Program Special Report, Washington, DC, The Woodrow Wilson Center for International Scholars, no. 120.

44. "India Refashions Itself as Global Military Power," *DNA-Daily News & Analysis*, September 22, 2008, available at: http://www.dnaindia.com/dnaprint.asp?newsid=1192345.

45. See: Pramit Mitra and Vibhuti Hate, "Iran-India Relations: Changing the Tone?" *CSIS South Asia Monitor* no. 29, March 8, 2009.

46. For historic background on Iranian-Japanese relations, see: Shireen T. Hunter, *Iran and the World*, pp. 157–58.

47. Sarah Noorbakhsh, "Although Under Pressure from U.S. to Sanction Iran, Japan Has Upheld Steady Ties with the Controversial Nation," *Japan Inc*, November 4, 2008.

48. "Asefi Predicts Khatami Visit to Japan to be a Turning Point," *Payvand News*, October 30, 2000, available at: http://www.netative.com/news/00/oct/1156.html.

49. Richard Hanson, "Japan, Iran Sign Major Oil Deal, U.S. Dismayed," *Asia Times*, 2004, available at: http://www.atimes.com/atimes/printN.html.

50. Hissane Masaki, "Japan's Energy Drive Stalls over Iran," *Asia Times Online*, 2006, available at: http://www.atimes.co/atimes/printN.html.

51. "Iranian-Japanese Relations," *The J@pan.Inc Newsletter* no. 474, July 16, 2008, available at http://www.japaninc.com/jin474.

52. "Japan Imposes Sanctions on Iran," Gulfnews.com, February 16, 2007, available at: http://gulfnews.com/indepth/irancrisis/World_reaction/10104728.html.

53. Gideon Rachman, "Why Japan is Edging Closer to China," *The Financial Times*, March 9, 2010. The article attributes the comment to Japan's foreign minister Katsuya Okada.

54. "Siyasat e japon as sabr va Entezar beh taamol Dar Parvandeh hasteh e Iran Rasideh Ast" [Japan's policy toward Iran's nuclear dossier has shifted from waiting to cooperation], Fars News Agency, March 8, 2010.

55. "Iran's Larijani to Start Five Days Tour of Japan" *Payvand News*, February 20, 2010, available at: http://www.payvandnews.com/news/10/feb/1200.html.

56. "Iran's Larijani Pays Visit to Nagasaki," *The Japan Times*, February 28, 2010, available at: http://search.japantimes.co.jp/print.nn20100228a6.html.

57. "Japan Voices Readiness to Help Resolve Iran's Nuclear Dossier," Nam News Network, February 25, 2010, available at: http://news.brunei.fm/2010/02/25/japan-voices-readiness-to-help-resolve-irans-nuclear-doss.

58. "Japan's 2010 Iran crude imports set to hit 17-year low," REUTERS, March 30, 2010 at: http://reuters.com/articleprint?articleId=INTOE62P01E20100330; "China Imports Less Iranian Oil, Despite Jump in Demand," RFE/RL March 22, 2010.

59. David Camroux, "State Responses to Islamic Resurgence in Malaysia: Accommodation, Co-Option, and Confrontation," *Asian Survey* 36, no. 9 (September 1996): 866.

60. According to some sources, on June 26, 1996, Malaysia's then foreign minister and current prime minister, Abdullah Badawi, said that "the government's move to check Shi'ism's influence in the country is purely a domestic issue and not an international one . . . There are many opportunities for us to cooperate with Iran . . .," quoted in Adam Indikt and Tzvi Fleischer, "Rafsanjani's Iran Pushes into Asia: Wolf among Asia's Tigers," *The Australia/Israel Review* 22, no. 3 (March 1997), available at: http://www.join.org.au/aijac/97–03–1/iran-2htm.

61. "Iran's President Thanks Indonesia for Not Supporting UN Resolution," VOA News, March 11, 2008.

62. On Khatami's visit, see: "News Headlines in Tue 23 July," *News and Reports*, available at: http://former.president.ir/Khatami/eng/cronicnews/1381/810501/810501.htm.

63. The first project under this agreement is a three-dimensional animation film on Salah Eddin Ayubbi, jointly produced by Iran and Malaysia. "News Headlines in Wed July 24," *News and Reports*, available at: http://former.preisdent.ir/Khatami/eng/cronicnews/1381/8105/810502/810502.htm.

64. See the text of Prime Minister Badawi's keynote address to the Malaysia-Iran Business Forum, available at: http://www.pmo.gov.my/WebNotesApp/Abdullah.nsf/75b3202912e2d4f6482570c400031. The volume of Iranian-Malaysian trade was, according some U.S. sources, at U.S. $224 million in 2000 and around $765 million in 2005. See: Bruce Vaughn and Michael Martin, "Malaysia: Political, Security, Economic, and Trade Issues Considered," Congressional Research Service, February 13, 2007, p. 2.

65. See the text of the speech of the Malaysian foreign minister, "The Sixth Joint Commission Meeting between Malaysia and the Islamic Republic of Iran 21–23 November 2006," available at: http://www.kln.govmy?m_id=25&vid=384.

66. "News Headlines in Tue 23 July," *News and Reports*, July 25, 2002, available at: http://former.president.ir/Khatami/eng/cronicnews/1381/8105/1810501/810501.htm.

67. Faisal Aziz, "UPDATE3-Malaysia's Petronas Still Assessing Iran Pars Project," Reuters, July 15, 2008, available at: http://www.reuters.com/articlePrint?articleId=USSP160914200807115.

68. "ONGC Eyes 27% Stake in Tide Water Oil," *Business Standard*, October 11, 2008, available at: http://www.business-standard.com/India/storypage.phb?autono=212539. According to this report, ONGC, an Indian company, may pick up Petronas's share.

69. Zahra Hosseinian, "UPDATE2-Iran, Malaysia's SKS Sign Major Gas Deal," Reuters, December 26, 2006, available at: http://uk.reuters.com/articlePrint?articleId=UKDAH62707620071226.

70. "Malaysia Stands by Iran Gas Deal," BBC News, February 2, 2007, available at: http://nesvote.bb.co.uk/mpapps/pagetools/print/news.bbc.co.uk/2hi/business/6323401.s.

71. On the role of Islam in determining Indonesia's foreign policy, see: Leo Suryadinata, "Islam and Suharto's Foreign Policy: Indonesia, the Middle East, and Bosnia," *Asian Survey* 35, no. 3 (March 1995).

72. See: Donald K. Emmerson, "Invisible Indonesia," *Foreign Affairs* 66, no. 2 (Winter 1987/1988).

73. For example, in an interview with the *Indonesia Times* in July 1984, Iran's then foreign minister, Ali Akbar Velayati, said that "interference in the internal affairs of other countries is contrary to the Islamic Republic of Iran's foreign policy and its constitution. We therefore refrain from interfering in other countries' internal affairs. All accusations against Iran so far had their

sources from the imperialists and Zionists and are intentionally launched to discredit Iran." Reproduced in *FBIS/SA*, June 18, 2004.

74. Adam Indikt and Tzvi Fleischer, "Rafsanjani's Iran Pushes into Asia: Wolf Among Asia's Tigers."

75. Indonesia has had reasonable relations with Israel. See "Indonesia, Israel Sign First Business Pact," *Kabar-Indonesia*, June 29, 2006, available at: http://www.kabar-irian.com/pipermail/kabar-indonesia/2006-june/007959.html.

76. Paulo Gorjao, "Why Indonesia Should Influence Iran," *Asia Times*, March 2, 2004, available at: http://www.kabar-irian.com/pipermail/kabar-indonesia/2004-March/ooo68.html. For background and details see: John Saltford, "United Nations Involvement with the Act of Self-Determination in West Irian (Indonesia West New Guinea) 1968 to 1969," Angelfire.com, 2000, available at: http://angelfire.com/journals/issues/irian/html.

77. Ibid.

78. On Ahmadinejad's visit, see: Breffni O'Rourke, "Iran: Ahmadinejad Seeks Support in Indonesia as Nuclear Crisis Sharpens," *Radio Free Europe/Radio Liberty*, May 10, 2006, available at: http://www.globalsecurity.org/wmd/library/news/iran/2006/iran-060510-rfer101.htm. On the visit of Indonesian president to Iran, see: "Indonesia's President Makes Landmark Visit to Iran," March 13, 2008, available at: http://kbri-beirut.org/index.php?option=com_content7task=view&id=119Itemid=99999.

79. "Indonesia Backs Iran on Nuclear Ambitions," NewsMax.com Wires, May 8, 2006, available at: http://archive.newsmax.com/archives/articles/2006/5/8/124822.ahtml. Also see "Indonesia Offers Iran Mediation," BBC News, May 10, 2006, available at: http://newsvote.bbc.co.uk/mpapps/pagetools/print/news.bbc.co.uk/2hi/asia-pacific/47567.

80. "Indonesia Keen to Invest in Iran's Oil, Gas Sector," Freerealtime.com, September 10, 2008, available at: http://quotes.freerealtime.com/dl/frt/N?art=C2008091000254u4585&SA=Latest%20News.

81. "Iran, Indonesia Agreed to Build Oil Refinery in Banten," Antara News Agency, March 12, 2008, available at: http://www.indonesiaottowa.org/information/details.php?type=news_copy&id=5266; "Iran and Indonesia Consider Nuclear Energy Cooperation," AsiaNews.it, November 12, 2006.

82. The author met with members of Thailand's Iranian community. Diplomatic relations existed between the kingdom of Siam and Safavid Iran since the 17th century c.e. See: "Iran's Relations with the Countries under the Purview of the Seventh Political Department," Ministry of Foreign Affairs, Tehran, 1976 (in Persian), pp. 19–24. Also: "Perspectives from Abroad by Thai Ambassadors: H. E. Kriangsak Kittichaisaree, Thai Ambassador to the Islamic Republic of Iran Challenged to Lead the Re-Invigoration of Trade and Cultural Ties," Embassy of Thailand, Tehran, February 2008, available at: http://64.233.169.104/research?q=cache"VYZd_QY5iXOJ:www.thaiembassy-tehran.org/abo.

83. "Thailand Moves to Expand Cooperation With Iran," *Inside Thailand*, September 2004, available at: http://Thailand.prd.go.th/print.php?id=321&type=inside.

84. "Iran-South Korea Cooperation," *News and Reports*, August 11, 2001, available at: http://former.president.ir/Khatami/eng/cronicnews/1380/8005/800520htm.

85. "South Korea Tries to Solace Furious Iran," IRNA, November 29, 2003, available at: http://www.globalsecurity.org/wmd/library/news/iran/2003/iran-o31129-irnao2.htm.

86. Paul Hughes and Parisa Hafezi, "Iran Bans U.K.-South Korea Trade Over Atomic Issue-Sources," *Iran Focus*, October 19, 2005, available at: http://forthefreedomofiran.blogspot.com/2005/10/iran-bans-uk-south-korea-trade-over.html.

87. "Trade Talks With S. Korea," *Iran Daily*, February 23, 2005, available at: http://www.iran-dily.com/1383/2220/html/economy.htm.

88. "Iran and South Korea Sign $500 million LNG contract," *Payvand's Iran News*, February 7, 2007, available at: http://www.payvand.com/news/07/feb/1091.html.

89. "Iran, South Korea Establish Joint Investment Committee," IRNA, October 14, 2008, available at: http://www2.irna.ir/en/news/view/line-18/0704073329154110htm.

90. "Ghardad gazi jadid 2 milliard euroei ba Kore e Jonoubi emza mishavad" [New two billion euro contract to be signed with South Korea], Mehr News Agency, October 12, 2009.

91. "IRS, S. Korea Oil Companies to Sign Agreement," October 13, 2009, available at: http://www.iranembassy.pk/en/economic/eco-news/373-korea-oil.htm?tmpl=component?p.

92. SAARC was established in 1985. Its members are: India, Nepal, Bangladesh, Maldives, Bhutan, Sri Lanka, and Pakistan. http://www.mapsofworld.com/saarc-member-countries.htm.

93. ASEAN was established in 1967 by Indonesia, Malaysia, Thailand, Singapore, and the Philippines. Over the next two decades, Brunei Darussalam, Cambodia, Vietnam, Laos, and Myanmar joined the organization.

94. "Reous barnamehaye siesta khareji dowlat e nohom elam shod: Harkat dar jadeh tashkil etehadiehe Asia" [The major points of the 10th government's foreign policy are declared: Movement toward creation of an Asian union], Fars News Agency, August 26, 2009.

CHAPTER 7

1. The signing of the Saadabad Treaty in 1937 by Iran, Turkey, and Afghanistan was largely prompted by their fear of the new Soviet regime.

2. These concerns were not totally unfounded. In fact, even before the Soviet Union's collapse, with the improvement in U.S.-Soviet relations questions were raised in America about the wisdom of providing large amounts of aid to countries like Turkey and Pakistan. For example, in 1987, a number of members of the U.S. Congress argued that U.S. economic and financial assistance to certain countries, such as Turkey, which no longer were strategically important to the United States, should be reduced or altogether eliminated.

3. Quoted in Ejaz Haider, "Pakistan's Afghan Policy and Its Fallouts," *Central Asia Monitor*, no. 5 (1998): 3.

4. Zia became president in 1978, but the actual takeover under martial law government was in October 1977.

5. The founder of the Jama'at-i-Islami was Maulana Abul Ala Maududi.

6. The PPP's slogan was "Islam is our faith, Democracy is our policy, Socialism is our economics, All power to the people."

7. General Zia ul Haq played an important role in the Black September events in Jordan in 1970.

8. The Saudis pursued a similar policy in Afghanistan, such as replacing Hanafi schools with Wahhabi-style schools. Olivier Roy, *Islam and Resistance in Afghanistan* (Cambridge: Cambridge University Press, 1990).

9. The main Shia movement in Pakistan was the Tahrik e Nefaz e Fiqh e Jafaria. The movement later divided into a political party open to non-Shias named Tehrik Jafria and a religious movement, Tahrik e Nefaz e Fiqh e Jafria (Movement for the Implementation of Jafari Fiqh). For details, see: Zahid Hussain, *The Struggle with Militant Islam* (London: I. B. Tauris), 2007.

10. Mariam Abou Zahab, "The Regional Dimensions of Sectarian Conflicts in Pakistan," in *Pakistan: Nationalism without a Nation*, ed. Christopher Jaffrelot (New York: Zed Books, 2002).

11. Zia Sarhadi, "Turning Pakistan into a Sectarian Battleground," *Muslim Media*, February 1–15, 1998, available at: http://www.mulsimmedia.com/ARCHIVES/world/pakisect.htm.

12. Iranian authorities criticized Pakistan for not providing adequate security for its diplomats. See: "Iran Criticizes Pakistan over Abduction," Press TV, November 16, 2008.

13. Five suspects were detained, but as of November 2009 the captured Iranian diplomat had not been released.

14. Even the U.S. secretary of state pressured Pakistan to respond swiftly to the attacks and to capture those behind them. Following these pressures, Pakistan put a leading figure affiliated with the Lahkar-e-Taiba under house arrest and imprisoned other extremists. "Pakistan Moves on Mumbai Accused," BBC News, December 12, 2008, available at: http://newsvote.bbc.co.uk/mpapps/pagetools/rpint/news.bbc.co.uk/2hi/south_asia/77780.

15. RCD was created by Iran, Turkey, and Pakistan following the dismantling of CENTO (Central Treaty Organization), itself a successor to the Baghdad Pact after its inefficiency became clear during the 1965 Indo-Pak War.

16. In 1972, Iran and Afghanistan signed an agreement resolving this issue. However, the coup d'état that soon followed rendered the implementation of the agreement impossible.

17. In an interview with the Indian journalist, R. A. Karanjia, the Shah stated that his ultimate purpose in expanding Iran's relations with India, Pakistan, and Afghanistan was to bring about "a renascent Aryan brotherhood of Iran, India, and Afghanistan" in order "to hold high the torch of a glorious, humanitarian and moralistic civilization." R. A. Karanjia, *The Mind of a Monarch* (London: George Allen & Unwin, 1977), p. 236.

18. By the mid-1960s, Pakistan had become a refuge for Islamist students in Afghanistan agitating against the government. These students included Ahmad Shah Masud and Gulbudin Hekmatyar, who later became leaders of the anti-Soviet resistance.

19. Barnett R. Rubin, *The Search for Peace in Afghanistan* (New Haven, CT: Yale University Press, 1995).

20. Shireen T. Hunter, "In Afghan Act II, Let U.S. be Wary of Friends Aims," *Los Angeles Times*, April 3, 1989.

21. Anwar-ul Haq Ahady, "Saudi Arabia, Iran, and the Conflict In Afghanistan," in *Fundamentalism Reborn*, ed. William Maley (New York: New York University Press), p. 121.

22. In January 1992, then U.S. secretary of state James Baker traveled to Central Asia with the purpose of telling the newly independent countries that the United States looked askance at close relations between them and Iran. Thomas Friedman, "U.S. to Counter Iran in Central Asia," *New York Times*, February 6, 1992.

23. "Iran Mourns Diplomats Murdered by the Taliban," *Salam Iran*, September 11, 1998, available at: http://www.salamiran.org/events/Afghan_crisis/.

24. "Taliban Threatens Retaliation if Iran Strikes," CNN.com, September 15, 1998.

25. See the chapter on U.S.-Iran relations.

26. "Elimination of Taliban Helps Iranian-Pakistani Relations Improve," Iran Press Service, November 30, 2001.

27. Ismail Khan was brought to Kabul and given a minor government position.

28. "Karzai Says Pakistan behind Indian Embassy Bombing," *Christian Today*, July 14, 2008, available at: http://www.christiantoday.com/articledir/print.htm?id=20507.

29. Among these terrorist acts was the attack on a bus carrying Iranian revolutionary guards, killing 11 of them; the kidnapping of Iranian policemen in Saravan; the kidnapping of Iranian

soldiers in June 2008; and other acts. See: "Iran Urges Pakistan to Help Free Kidnapped Police," *International Herald Tribune*, October 6, 2008, and Golnaz Esfandiari, "Iran: Group Releases Turks, Still Holding Soldiers Hostage," RFE/RL, January 17, 2006. In December 2008, Iranian authorities reported that the Rigi group had killed the 16 kidnapped soldiers. "Iran: Police Killer Terrorists backed by U.S. UK," Fars News Agency, December 14, 2008, available at: http://English.farsnews.com/printable.php?nn=8709241652.

30. "Iranian Commanders Assassinated," BBC News, October 18, 2009.

31. Speaking to the UAE-based TV Al Arabiyya, Rigi claimed that he is fighting for the rights of Iran's Sunnis. "Iran Sunni Rebels Say Willing to Talk to Tehran," Reuters, August 7, 2008, available at: http://www.alertnet.org/thenews/newsdesk/L779234.htm.

32. "Iran's Interior Minister in Pakistan over Jundullah," Press TV, October 23, 2009.

33. "Ghol e hamkari Pakistan Baraye Bazdasht va Tahvil e'Abdulmalek Rigi,' beh Iran" [Pakistan promises cooperation in the arrest and delivery of Abdulmalek Rigi to Iran], Fars News Agency, October 23, 2009.

34. "Iran va Pakistan Tavafoghnameh e Jamee aminyati emza mikonand" [Iran and Pakistan will sign comprehensive security agreement], Fars News Agency, October 24, 2009.

35. "Pakistan Releases Iran Revolutionary Guards," *Times* (London), October 27, 2009.

36. "Ghol e hamkari Pakistan Baraye Bazdasht va Tahvil e'Abdulmalek Rigi,' beh Iran" [Pakistan promises cooperation in the arrest and delivery of Abdulmalek Rigi to Iran], Fars News Agency, October 23, 2009.

37. Richard Esposito and Brian Ross, "Pakistan May Turn Over U.S. 'Spies' to Iran," ABC News, May 23, 2008, available at: http://abcnews.go.com/print?id=4913927. Iranian authorities also claimed that they had documents indicating that Britain was also helping the group.

38. "Raeis Jomhuri e Pakistan Chaharshanbeh Ayande beh Iran Miayad" [Pakistan's president arrives in Tehran next Wednesday], Fars News Agency, March 6, 2009.

39. "Iran Summit to Resolve Regional Problems," Press TV, May 24, 2009, and "Iran, Pakistan Sign Gas Deal," IRNA, May 24, 2009.

40. "Pakistan's Parliament Speaker to Visit Iran," *Tehran Times*, February 2, 2010, available at: http://www.tehrantimes.com/NCms/2007.asp?code=213518.

41. "Iran Captures Sunni Insurgent Leader Abdolmalek Rigi," *Guardian*, February 23, 2010.

42. "Pakistan Hands over 2nd Rigi Brother to Iran," *The Dawn*, February 23, 2010, available at: http://thedawn.com.pk/2010/Pakistan-hands-over-2nd-rigi-brother-to-iran.

43. "Ahmadinejad Calls U.S. Bluff on Counterterrorism," Press TV, March 10, 2010.

44. The majority of the Afghan population is part of the Indo-Iranian family. Persian historically was the language of literature and learning. It was only in the 1940s and 1950s that efforts to turn Pashtu into the country's official language and develop it began. Today, Afghanistan's Tajik, and Hazara population, as well as educated Pashtuns, speak Persian.

45. For example, the Afghans claim that Afghanistan was the true "Iran" (the land of the Aryans), which they call Arianna. They also claim as their own such iconic Iranian literary figures as Firdowsi, the author of the epic "Book of Kings," who is credited with resurrecting Iran's pre-Islamic history.

46. Ahmad Shah Masud, the legendary Afghan military leader and defense minister in the Rabbani government, had tried to convince the West that, although Tajik, he is not pro-Iran.

47. Shireen T. Hunter. "The Afghan Civil War: Implications for Central Asian Stability," in *Energy and Conflict in Central Asia and the Caucasus*, ed. Rajan Menon and Robert Ebel (Oxford: Rowan and Littlefield, 2000).

48. Barnett R. Rubin, "U.S. Policy in Afghanistan," *Muslim Politics Report*, no. 11, (January/February 1997): 6.

49. On the U.S. elimination of pro-Iran Afghan personalities, see: Thomas H. Johnson, "Ismail Khan, Herat, and Iranian Influence," *Strategic Insights* 3, no. 7 (July 7, 2004).

50. See the text of the speech of Iran's representative to the UN General Assembly on November 29, 2005, available at: http://www.iran-un.org/statements/generalasembly/sessions59/27.htm.

51. For details of some of these projects see: Bill Varner, "Iran Building Influence in Afghanistan," *Seattle Times*, July 19, 2008.

52. "Afghan-Iranian Highway Opens," BBC News, January 27, 2005.

53. "Bush and Karzai differ over Iran," *International Herald Tribune*, August 7, 2007.

54. Nazila Fathi, "A Nation Challenged: Diplomacy; In Tehran Visit, Karzai Appeals to Iran, U.S. to Make Up," *New York Times*, February 25, 2002. Also "Iranian President Visits Afghanistan with Offers of Aid," available at: http://www.buzzle.com/editorials/8-13-2002-24396.asp.

55. "Iranian President Kicks Off Regional Tour with First Afghan Visit," RFE/RL, August 14, 2007.

56. Julian Borger, "Britain to Hamid Karzai: Start Afghanistan Peace Talks Now," *Guardian*, March 10, 2010.

57. "Iran-U.S. Spar over Afghanistan," CBC News, March 10, 2010 available at: http://license.icopyright.net/user/viewFreeUse.act?fuid=NzQoMTK5Mw%3D%3D. Gates said Iran is "playing a double game" in offering aid to Afghanistan while undermining NATO efforts in the country by aiding Taliban-led insurgents.

58. "Iran Attacks U.S. over Afghanistan," BBC News, March 10, 2010, available at: http://newsvote.bbc.co.uk/mpapps/pagetools/print/news.bbc.co.uk/2/hi/south_asia/855908.

59. "Zarourat e Gostaresh e Hamkari haye Ghazei Beine Iran va Afghanistan" [The necessity of expanding judiciary cooperation between Iran and Afghanistan], Mehr News, March 10, 2010, available at: http://mehrnews.com/fa/Newsprint.aspx?NewsID=1049612.

60. "Kimia Sanati, Afghan Refugees: Pawns in Standoff with the West," InterPress Service News Agency, May 15, 2007, available at: http://ipsnews.net/print.asp?idnews+37727.

61. Ibid.

62. "Iran Deporting Afghan Refugees" RFE/RL, April 27, 2007. Also "Afghans Protest Iran Deportations," RFE/RL, May 1, 2007.

63. Walliullah Rahmani, "Iran's Decision to Expel Refugees May Destabilize Western Afghanistan," *Jamestown Foundation, Terrorism Focus* 4, no. 13 (May 8, 2007).

64. Richard O'Regan, "Afghan Immigrants Find Refuge in Oil-rich Iran," Worldfocus, October 19, 2009, available at: http://worldfocus.org/blog/2009/10/19/afghan-immigrants-find-refuge-in-oil-rich-iran/78.

65. The best example of this situation is Iran's Azerbaijan Province. From a purely ethnic point of view, its population is more Iranian than Turk, as seen from their physical attributes. However, because of linguistic Turkification, many of these people identify themselves as Turks. For a discussion of the process of linguistic change in Azerbaijan and its identity related implications, see: Shireen T. Hunter, "Greater Azerbaijan: Myth or Reality," in *Le Caucasse Post-Sovietique: La transition dans le conflict*, ed. M. R. Djalili (Brussels: Bruylant, 1995).

66. Part of the reason for the popularity of pan-Turkism in the late Ottoman period was the loss of the empire's European possessions and severe erosion of its influence in Muslim parts of the empire because of European encroachments and the rise of Arab nationalism, leading the Ottomans to look for both a new basis of political identity and legitimacy besides the concept of "Ottomanism," and for new areas of influence in Turkic or Turkic-speaking areas, which included parts of Iran.

67. The more nationalist Turks are particularly concerned about the fate of the so-called Turks.

68. Suha Bulakbasi, "Turkey Copes with Revolutionary Iran," *Journal of South Asian and Middle Eastern Studies* 13, nos. 1 and 2 (1989): 95.

69. Ibid.

70. Robert Olson, *Turkey-Iran Relations, 1979–2004: Revolution, Ideology, War, Coups and Geopolitics* (Costa Mesa, CA: Mazda Publishers, 2004), p. 1.

71. Fuat Ali Borovali, "Turkish Insurgencies, the Gulf War, and Turkey's Changing Role," *Conflict Quarterly* 7, no. 4 (Fall 1985): 41.

72. "Turkish Trade Rises Despite Press Raw," *The Middle East Economic Digest* 31, no. 25 (June 20, 1987): 12–13.

73. Hugh Pope, "Pointing Fingers at Iran," *Middle East International,* no. 443 (February 5,1993).

74. Hugh Pope, "Conflict over Killings," *Middle East International,* no. 444 (February 19, 1993).

75. For details, see: Robert Olson, *Turkey's Relations with Iran, Syria, Israel and Russia, 1991–2000* (Costa Mesa, CA: Mazda Publishers, 2001), pp. 30–32.

76. Ibid., pp. 51–52.

77. Robert Olson, *Turkey-Iran Relations, 1979–2004: Revolution, Ideology, War, Coups and Geopolitics,* pp. 56–60.

78. Ibid., pp. 63–64.

79. The AKP is closely linked with the Gullen movement, whose leader, Fetullah Gullen, has anti-Shia sentiments. See: Bulent Aras, "Turkish Islam's Modern Face," *The Middle East Journal* 53, no. 4 (Autumn 1999).

80. "Iranians Flee to Turkey and Dream of U.S.," *New York Times,* May 26, 1987.

81. Quoted in Suha Bulakbasi, "Turkey Copes with Revolutionary Iran," pp. 103–4.

82. Turkish politicians, notably Tansu Çiller, used this tactic frequently.

83. For a list of these groups, see: Shireen T. Hunter, *Current History* 89, no. 549 (October 1990), and Shireen T. Hunter, *Central Asia since Independence* (Westport, CT: Praeger, 1996).

84. I first used the term "Islamic Iron Curtain" in an article "The Emergence of Soviet Muslims: Impact on the Middle East," *Middle East Insight,* May 1992.

85. Quoted in Sami Kohen, "Contacts with Central Asian States: A Foundation for Pan-Turkism," *The Washington Report on Middle East Affairs* (August/September 1992).

86. Ibid.

87. When Iran's mediation efforts failed, Suleiman Demirel, the Turkish prime minister, said that this should teach the Azerbaijanis that they should not run to Iran to solve their problems.

88. Robert Olson, *Turkey-Iran Relations, 1979–2004,* pp. 117–18. The leader of the Iranian Azerbaijani separatist movement, Mahmud Ali Chehreganli, was received in Turkey.

89. "Paper Views Common Interests with Israel," *Miliyat,* November 7, 1994, reproduced in FBIS/WEU, 94–240, November 15, 1994.

90. On the various dimensions of the Turkish-Israeli alliance, see: Daniel Pipes, "A New Axis: The Emerging Turkish-Israeli Alliance," *National Interest* (Winter 1997–1998), available at: http://www.merforum.org/article/pipes/293.

91. For details, see: Neil Ford, "Modernists v. Mullahs Row Holds Back Progress," *The Middle East,* (August/September 2004) available at: http://findarticles.com/p/articles/mi_2742/is_348/ai_n25095063/print?tag=artBody;coll. Also: "A Humiliated Khatami Cancels Visit To Turkey," Iran Press Service, September 2004, available at: http://www.iran-press-service.com/ips/articles-2004/September/majles-cabinet-26904-print.

92. Marco Villa, "Israel Criticizes Turkey for Planned Ahmadinejad Visit," instablogs, November 23, 2008, available at: http://marcovilla.instablogs.com/entry/Israel–criticizes-turkey-for planned-Ahmadinejad-visit/.

93. "Syria's Assad Meets Erdogan as Turkey Mediates for Mideast Peace," *The Journal of Turkish Weekly*, August 6, 2008, available at: http://www.turkishweekly.net/news/5831/Syria-s-assad-meets-erdogan-as-turkey-mediates.

94. "Turkey to Mediate between Afghanistan, Pakistan," *World Bulletin*, available at: http://www.worldbulletin.net/news_print.php/id=28349.

95. Dan Bilefsky, "Intentions of Turkey Worry West," *New York Times*, October 28, 2009.

96. Ibid.

97. Arzou Dilmaghani, trans., "Turkey and Neo-Ottomanist Policies," *Iranian Diplomacy*, October 26, 2009. Also Arzou Dilmaghani, "Turkey's Policy is More Toward the West than Iran: Turkey in Search a Bigger Role," *Iranian Diplomacy*, October 16, 2009.

98. Simon Tisdal, "Israel is in Denial over Turkish Rage," *Guardian*, October 22, 2009.

99. "U.S. Backs Turkey Ties with Syria, Lebanon to Offset Iran," World Tribune.com, May 19, 2009. According to the article, Turkey is planning a major arms sale to Lebanon.

100. "From 1993 to 1995, Ankara was willing to use its support of the KDPI as a lever to prevent Iran from supporting the PKK." Olson, *Turkey-Iran Relations, 1979–2004*, p. 12. (KDPI stand for the Kurdish Democratic Party of Iran.)

101. Turkey, Iran, and Syria often met to emphasize the importance of maintaining Iraq's territorial integrity, which they saw as being potentially endangered as a result of the creation of the Kurdish zone after the first Gulf War and the establishment of a No Fly Zone. After the U.S. invasion of Iraq, too, Iran and Turkey have insisted on maintaining Iraq's territorial integrity. However, in contrast to Iran, Turkey does not favor a Shia-dominated government in Iraq.

102. Yalman Onaran, "Defying U.S. Sanctions, Turkish Premier Visits Iran," Associated Press, August 10, 1996, and "Turkey Signs 20 Billion Dollar Gas Deal With Iran," Deutsche Presse-Agentur, August 12, 1996.

103. "Rafsanjani and Demirel to Meet in Turkey Next Week," Deutsche-Presse Agentur, December 12, 1996.

104. Gagendra Singh, "Turkey & Iran Coming Closer," *South Asia Analysis Group*, paper no. 1077, August 3, 2004, available at: http://www.southasiaanalysis.org/%5Cpaper1077.html.

105. "Erdogan: U.S., Europe Unfair on Iran Rights," Press TV, October 26, 2009.

106. See Erdogan's interview with IRNA, available at: http://www.irna.ir/View/Fullstory/Tools/PrintVersion/?NewsId=758955.

107. "Political Tensions Mount in Turkey over Alleged Coup Plot," AFP (Agence France Presse), February 18, 2010, available at: http://www.google.com/hostednews/afp/article/ALeqM5jN9U0ccvln4alOEDloW3QyOti5zg.

108. "U.S. Stepping up Pressure on Turkey to Back Iran Sanctions," *Dow Jones*, February 24, 2010, reprinted in *Zawya*, available at: http://www.zawya.com/printstory.cfm?storyid=ZW20100224000095&1=090356100224.

CHAPTER 8

1. Iran's immediate neighbors in Central Asia are Turkmenistan, which has a 992-kilometer-long land border with Iran and Kazakhstan, which shares the Caspian Sea with

Iran. In the Caucasus, Iran has land and sea borders with Azerbaijan and land borders with Armenia.

2. The Republic of Georgia has access to the Black Sea.

3. Daniel Pipes, "Turkic Peoples and Persian Cultures," *Middle East Insight* 10, no. 1 (1994).

4. For a list of these organizations, see: Shahrbanou Tadjbakhsh, "The Tajik Spring of 1992," *Central Asia Monitor*, no. 2, 1993.

5. Iran was a competitor to Russia in terms of energy, especially gas resources, and a more efficient and economic export route for these regions' energy resources.

6. Some scholars, however, pointed out early on that neither Iran nor Turkey will emerge as the leading influence in the post-Soviet space. See: Shireen T. Hunter, "The Muslim Republics of the Former Soviet Union: Policy Challenges for the United States," *Washington Quarterly* 15, no. 2 (Summer 1992).

7. Iran has not received enough credit for its role in ending the Tajik conflict, and the Russians have claimed most of the credit.

8. Shireen T. Hunter, *The Transcaucasus in Transition: Nation-Building and Conflict* (Washington, DC: Center For Strategic and International Studies, 1994), p. 107.

9. ECO is a revived and renamed version of RCD (Regional Cooperation for Development), with Turkey, Iran, and Pakistan, and was created in 1984 at Iran's initiative.

10. Russia and China, the two most important members of the SCO, as well as some Central Asian countries, such as Uzbekistan, oppose Iran's full membership. This opposition partly derives from concern that expanding the membership of SCO will dilute its original character. SCO members are also concerned that Iran may want to turn the organization into an anti-Western institution, something that they do not want.

11. Even Iranians living abroad began to establish contact with these two countries.

12. After Velayati's visit, a number of Central Asian officials visited Iran. See, for instance, Shahmohammadi, "Relations between Iran and Uzbekistan: a Chronology," *Tehran Times*, October 21, 1993, available at: http://www.lexisnexis.com/us/Inacademic/delivery/printDoc. do?fromC.

13. For a history of the term "Azerbaijan," see: Shireen T. Hunter, "Greater Azerbaijan: Myth or Reality," in *Le Caucasse Post-Sivietique: La Transition Dans Le Conflict*, ed. M. R. Djalili (Brussels: Bruylant, 1995), pp. 121–22.

14. Bruce Pannier, "Turkmenistan/Iran: Good Relations Take Turn for the Worse," RFE/RL, January 15, 2008, available at: http://www.rferl.org/.

15. Ibid.

16. "Safir e Turkmenistan beh vezarat kharejeh ehzar shod" [Ambassador of Turkmenistan summoned to the foreign ministry], *Aftab News*, June 5, 2009, available at: http://www.aftab-news.ir/prtclipq4.2bq4i8laa2.html.

17. Some of the problems related to working out a new legal regime for the Caspian derived from the difficulties involved in its definition. Caspian Sea is in reality a lake and thus not subject to the International Law of the Sea. For a discussion of these issues and various options for dividing the resources of the Caspian, see, among others: S. Vinogradov and P. Wouters, "The Caspian Sea: Quest for a New Legal Regime," *Leiden Journal of International Law*, no. 9 (1996): 87–98. Also, Barbara Janusz, "The Caspian Sea: Legal Status and Regime Problems," *Briefing Paper* 5, no. 2, London: Chatham House, August 2005.

18. Bahamn Aghai Diba, "The Legal Regime of the Caspian Sea & Recent Incident between Azerbaijan and Iran," text of speech delivered at the Middle East Institute, September 19, 2001, available at: http://www.gasandoil.com/speeches/the_legal_regime_of the_caspian _sea_02–01–02.

19. See: Mahir Iskenderov and Tim Wall, "Caspian Sea Disputes Flare, Raising Doubts About Oil and Gas Exploration," Eurasianet.org, July 31, 2001, available at: http://www.eurasianet.org/departments/insights/articles/eav0730101.shtml.

20. Since the independence of the former Soviet republics, there has been a major campaign of historic revisionism and falsification of Iran's and Azerbaijan's history by Azerbaijani, and also unfortunately by some Western scholars. The most outrageous of these revisionist readings is the suggestion, first promoted by the Azerbaijani poet, Bakhtiar Vahhabzadeh, that Iran and Russia, in a conspiracy, divided a nonexistent unified Azerbaijan into two sections. This claim does not take into account that Iran fought two wars with Russia, in 1804–1813 and 1824–1828, and lost its Transcaucasian possessions, including what is now the Republic of Azerbaijan, as a result of these wars.

21. "Iranian-Central Asian Rail Link Opened," Iran Railways Archive, available at: http://www.msedv.at/rai/archive.html.

22. "3-way Railroad Plan Will Go Ahead," Rail page, Australia and New Zealand, November 29, 2007, available at: http://www.railpage.com.au/f-p1173715.htm.

23. "Negahi beh Ahmiat e Rah Ahan e Iran-Turkmenistan-Kazakhstan" [A look at the importance of Iran-Turkmenistan-Kazakhstan railroad], IRNA, May 5, 2009.

24. C. Raja Mohan, "India and Afghan Railroads," The Hindu, February 20, 2003.

25. "Tehran Welcomes ECO Train," Tehran Times, August 24, 2009.

26. "Erdogan-Ahmadinejad Agree to Build Iran-Turkey Railroad," Hay Azg, September 28, 2007, available at: http://www.hayazg.com/news/index.php?nid=3293&ct=)&year=2007&month=097day=2.

27. "New Railroad to Link Iran, Russia" Press TV, July 15, 2008, available at: http://www.presstv.ir/pop/print.aspx?id=63816.

28. Haroutiun Khacatrian, "Armenia and Iran Agree on New Communications Projects," Central Asia-Caucasus Institute Analyst, January 14, 2009, available at: http://www.caciaanalyst.org/?q=node/5016.

29. "Russia Backing Iran-Armenia Rail Link," Iran Daily, November 10, 2008.

30. Emil Danielyan, "Armenia Deepens Ties with Embattled Iran," Eurasia Insight, July 7, 2006, available at: http://www.eurasianet.org.

31. Saeed Vosoughi and Tajmohammad Shahmansori, "Cooperation between Iran and Central Asian Countries in Rail and Road Transportation: Opportunities," paper presented to the Isfahan Conference, November 2008.

32. "Vazir Energye ye Tajikistan Naghash Iran dar towseh e Eghtesadi Keshvarash ra mohem khand" [Tajikistan's minister of energy considers Iran's role in his country's development important], IRNA, October 22, 2008.

33. "Mojahaz Tarine Bimarstan e Ghalb e Asia e Markazi dar Dushanbe Eftetah Mishavad" [The best cardiology hospital to open in Dushanbe], Fars News Agency, September 6, 2009.

34. "Russia Wants Exclusive Control of Caspian Oil and gas," Iranian Diplomacy, September 4, 2009.

35. "Iran to Begin Gas Exports to Armenia," Press TV, October 7, 2008.

36. "Iran Dar Tarh e Towseh e Meidan Gasi Turkmenistan Sarmayeh Gozari Mikond" [Iran will invest in Turkmen gas field], IRNA, January 28. 2009.

37. Quoted in Abbas Maleki, "Iran," in The New Silk Roads: Transport and Trade in Greater Central Asia (Washington, DC and Uppsala, Sweden: Central Asia and Caucasus Institute, 2007). The text is also available at: http://silkroadstudies.org/new/docs/publications/GCA/GCAPUB.06.pdf.

38. In summer 2009, Simon Peres visited Baku, "Azerbaijan, Sakou ye jasousi e Israel dar Iran" [Azerbaijan: Israel's spy station on Iran], *Aftab News*, May 4, 2009.

39. For an account of Iran-Azerbaijan relations during the presidency of Ayaz Mutalibov, Elçibe, y and the early Aliev periods, see: Shireen T. Hunter, *The Transcaucasus in Transition: Nation-Building and Conflict*, pp. 83–85 and 91–95.

40. Sebnum Arsu, "Turkish President Visits Armenia," *International Herald Tribune*, September 7. 2008. Also, "Armenia and Israel Throw Down a Gage to Iran and Turkey," Heyclub Forum.com, January 21, 2006.

41. Arif Yunus, "Azerbaijan-Between America and Iran," *Russia in Global Affairs*, no. 3. (July–September 2006), available at: http://eng.globalaffairs.ru/region-humanrights/num bers/16/1044.html.

42. Ibid.

43. Tariq Saeedi, "Gas Row and its Effect on Turkmenistan-Iran Relations," *News Central Asia*, January 16, 2008, available at: http://www.newscentralasia.net/print/211.html.

44. John C. K. Daly, "Turkmenistan Doubles Natural Gas Prices to Iran," *Eurasia Daily Monitor* 5, no. 81 (April 29, 2008), available at: http://www.jamestown.org/single/?no_cache=1&tx_ttnews%5Btt_news55D=33590. By February 2009, however, bilateral relations seemed to be on the mend and Turkmenistan's president visited Tehran. See: "Rais Jomhouri e Turkmenistan Vard e Iran Shod" [Turkmenistan's president arrived in Iran], IRNA, February 13, 2009.

45. Ali Mussavi Khalkhali, "The Inauguration of Israel's Embassy in Turkmenistan, and Iran's Strange Neglect," *Iranian Diplomacy*, June 7, 2009.

46. "Turkmen President in Iran to Discuss Energy," RFE/RL, April 14, 2009.

47. "Spokesman Elaborates on Ahmadinejad's Agenda in Turkmenistan, Tajikistan," Fars News Agency, January 3, 2010, available at: http://english.farsnews.com/printable. php?nm=8810131564. Also, for details of the projects see "Iran-Turkmenistan Set to Cement Ties, *Islami Dawet*, November 1, 2009, available at: http://www.islamidavet.com/english/tag/mohammad-reza-forqani.

48. "Central Asia: Awkward Friends," *Economist*, April 8, 1995, p. 7.

49. On Karimov's statement on endorsing U.S. trade sanctions on Iran, see: ". . . And Iran Embargo," *OMRI*, no. 88, May 5, 1995.

50. "Denies Backing U.S. Embargo," FBIS/NES-95-141, July 24, 1995.

51. Iranian papers reacted sharply to these comments. See: "Commentary Assails Peres' Remarks in Tashkent," FBIS/NES-96-134, July 13, 1994.

52. On the background to Andijan events and its unfolding, see, among others: Jim Nichol, "Unrest in Uzbekistan: Context and Implications," *Congressional Research Service* (CRS), June 8, 2005, available at: www.fas.org/sgp/crs/row/RS22161.pdf.

53. "Zholdasbekoy on Future Relations With Iran," in FBIS/Sov-25-120, June 22, 1995.

54. Ibragim Alibekov, "Khatami, In Kazakhstan, Asserts Iran as a Crucial Partner for Kazakhstan," *Eurasia Insight*, April 26, 2002, available at: http://www.eurasianet.org/departments/insight/articles/eav042602a_pr.shtml. Also see: Marat Yermukanov, "'American Threat' Looms Over Kazakh-Iranian Talks," *Central Asia-Caucasus Analyst*, October 20, 2004, available at: http://www.casianalyst.org/?q=node/2534.

55. Quoted in "Kazakhstan and Iran, sitting in a tree . . . but, you know, they are just friends," Registan.net, September 1, 2008, available at: http://www.registan.net/index.php/2008/9/01/kazakhstan-iran/.

56. "Ahmadinejad Az Jahesh dar Ravabet e Iran va Kazakhstan khabar dad" [Ahmadinejad tells of jump in Iran-Kazakhstan relations], Mehr News Agency, April 6, 2009, available at http://www.mehrnews.com/fa/NewsPrint.aspx?NewsID=855775.

57. "The Analysis of the Central Asian Media of Ahmadinejad's Absence from the Caspian Meeting," *Iranian Diplomacy*, September 4, 2009.

58. Giorgi Sepashvili and Tea Gularidze, "Deal with Iran to Partially Ease Gas Shortage," *Civil Georgia*, January 28, 2006.

59. "Israeli Foreign Minister Raises Georgian-Iranian Ties," *Civil Georgia*, October 23, 2007, available at: http://www.Civil.ge.eng/_print.php?id=16083. Reportedly, Tzipi Livni, then Israel's foreign minister, told her counterpart of the "problematic view that Israel has of the ongoing dialogues between Georgia and Iran."

60. See for details: Shireen T. Hunter, *The Transcaucasus in Transition*, p. 138.

61. On the Sakashvili visit, see: "Khatami Urges Efforts to Establish Regional Peace," News Headlines July 7, 2004, P.I.R.I News Archive.

62. Nino Khutsidze, "Pundits Say More Pragmatism Needed in Ties with Iran," *Civil Georgia*, January 20, 2007.

CHAPTER 9

1. Only Syria and Libya supported Iran.

2. This fact has led some scholars, such as Ada Bozeman to refer to the phenomenon of Iran's conquest of Islam.

3. Shahram Chubin and Sepehr Zabih, *The Foreign Policy of Iran: A Developing State in a Zone of Great Power Rivalry* (Berkeley: University of California Press, 1974), p. 148.

4. The last gasp of Arab nationalism as a political ideology was Saddam Hussein's attack on Kuwait in 1991.

5. Samuel Rogov, *The Iranian Triangle: The Untold Story of Israel's Role in Iran-Contra Affair* (New York: The Free Press, 1988).

6. Quoted in Behrouz Souresrafil, *Khomeini and Israel* (Wellington, NZ: CC Press, 1989), pp. 33–34.

7. Among these disputes are that between Bahrain and Qatar over Hawar Island, which nearly caused a war in 1986. However, this dispute was sent to the International Court of Arbitration and is currently dormant. Another dispute is between Saudi Arabia and the UAE over the oasis of Buraimi. This dispute was supposedly resolved in the early 1970s. But reportedly the UAE raised it again in 2005. In addition there are tribal and dynastic tensions among GCC member states, such as that between Bahrain's Al Khalifa ruling family and the Al-Thani of Qatar. Also, smaller Gulf states do not like Saudi Arabia's claim to the leadership of the GCC. See, among others: "Border Disputes Erupt between Saudi Arabia, UAE; Riyadh Denies," *Arab-American*, February 23, 2005. Also Turki al Hamad, "Will the Gulf Monarchies Work Together?" *Middle East Quarterly* (March 1997), available at: http:www.mefo rum.org/340/will-gulf-monarchies-work-together.

8. Since 1995, Qatar has adopted a policy of reaching out to all regional countries and to international actors and of playing the role of mediator for the resolution of regional disputes. Relations with Iran have benefited from this policy.

9. Ayatullah Khomeini has said that "it does not take sword to export this [revolutionary Islam] ideology. The export of ideas by force is no export." Quote in Henner Furtig, *Iran's Rivalry with Saudi Arabia between the Gulf Wars* (Reading, England: Ithaca Press, 2002), p. 33.

10. Some disturbances by the Shia occurred in late 1979, when the Shia of Qatif, in defiance of the government's ban, gathered to observe the anniversary of Ashura, the martyrdom of the third Shia Imam.

11. Some authors have claimed that Iran embarked on a widespread anti-Saudi campaign in the Arab world and among Muslim communities in the West. S. M. Badeeb, *Saudi-Iranian Relations, 1932–1982* (London: Echoes, 1993), p. 91.

12. Saudi Arabia, however, did try (and with some success) to argue that because Iran was non-Arab and Shia, its ideology had no place in the Sunni majority Arab world.

13. On Saudi-Iranian relations in this period, see: Shireen T. Hunter, *Iran and the World*, pp. 119–22.

14. According to the Saudi foreign minister following the seizure of the Kaaba, a message from Ayatullah Khomeini was to be read, followed by a further uprising in the Shia-inhabited province of Al Hasa. The Saudis foiled this plot, thanks to information provided by a Saudi intelligent officer in Tehran. Quoted in S. Holly, *Conflict in the Gulf: Economic and Maritime Implications of the Iran-Iraq War* (Colchester, UK: Lloyds of London Press, 1988), p. 16.

15. In 1986, when Iran seemed to be winning the war, the Saudis engaged in a policy of over-production of their oil in order financially to cripple Iran. Iran criticized the Saudis for having dealt "a severe blow to OPEC by glutting the oil market" and being "guilty of the greatest treason ever committed against the oppressed and deprived countries." Other oil producers, including non-OPEC members such as Egypt, were also unhappy about Saudi policy. "Besharati Blames Saudi Arabia for Oil Market Glut," FBIS/SA, June 30, 1986.

16. For the text of Khomeini's message to the Revolutionary Guards on the acceptance of the cease-fire, see: Muhammad Doroudian, *Az Aghaz Ta Payan: Seyri Dar Jang e Iran Va Eragh* [From the beginning to the end: A survey of the Iran-Iraq War], (Tehran: Pajman Publishers, no date, pp. 206–7).

17. The United States was even willing to establish diplomatic relations with Iran, and Israeli Prime Minister Yitzhak Rabin said that the United States should forget its disagreement with Iran and reach out to it.

18. For these debates, see: Bahman Bakhtiari, "Revolutionary Iran's Persian Gulf Policy: The Quest for Regional Supremacy," in Hooshang Amirahmadi and Nader Entessar, eds., *Iran and the Arab World* (New York: St. Martin's Press, 1993), p. 85.

19. Philip Shenon, "23 U.S. Troops Die in Truck Bombing in Saudi Base," *New York Times*, June 26, 1996. Some sources have claimed that the United States, which was trying to improve relations with Iran, encouraged the Saudis not to pursue the affair. See: "Former FBI Director: Clinton Undermined Saudi Bombing Probe," CNN.com, October 10, 2005.

20. See the chapter on U.S.-Iranian relations.

21. William A. Rugh, "Past, Present and Future Leadership," in "Symposium: A Century in Thirty Years: Shaykh Zayed and the United Arab Emirates," *Middle East Policy* 6, no. 4 (June 1999): 31.

22. "Three Monarchs to Attend Islamic Summit in Tehran," Deutsche Presse-Agentur, November 25, 1997, obtained through: http://wwwlexisnexis.com/us/Inacademic.

23. "Iranian President Starts Landmark Visit to Saudi Arabia," Deutsche Presse-Agentur, May 15, 1999.

24. "Khamenei Says Tehran Wants Stronger Ties with Saudi Arabia," BBC Summary of World Broadcasts, December 11, 1997.

25. "Iran's Defence Minister in Landmark Visit to Saudi Arabia," Deutsche Presse-Agentur, April 24, 2000.

26. "Saudi Interior Minister on Yemen Treaty, Security Pact with Iran," FBIS/NESA 1999–050, June 11, 2000.

27. "Qatar to Expand Military Cooperation with Iran," Deutsche Presse-Agentur, July 18, 2000.

28. "Military Officers from Oman, Other Gulf States Begin Visit," IRNA, July 12, 1998.

29. See: Shireen T. Hunter, "Outlook for Iranian-Gulf Relations: Greater Cooperation of Risk of Renewed Conflict," in *Iran, Iraq and the Arab Gulf States*, ed. Joseph A. Kechichian (New York: Palgrave, 2001), pp. 429–30.

30. Douglas Jehl, "Overtures from Iran Ignites Bitter Debate among Arab States," *New York Times*, June 9, 1999.

31. "Iranian President Khatami's Special Envoy Arrives in the UAE," IRNA, August 6, 2001.

32. "UAE Foreign Minister Leaves after Talks on Regional Security," IRNA, May 28, 2002.

33. "Roundup: Iranian President Seeks for Cooperation with Gulf Arab Nations," Xinhua General News Service, December 4, 2007.

34. Kate Dourian, "Iran and Oman Sign Oil, Gas Cooperation Agreement," *Platts Oilgram News*, May 18, 2007.

35. "Ahmadinejad Invited to Hajj in Saudi: Iran Ambassador," Agence France Presse, December 12, 2007, and Donna Abu Nasr, "Ahmadinejad Visits Saudis Amid Tensions," Associated Press, March 3, 2007.

36. Saudi foreign minister Saud Al Faisal said that Iran had approached his country to "cooperate in averting strife between Sunnis and Shiites in Iraq and Lebanon." Abdullah Shihri, "Saudi Arabia-Iran Cooperating on Crises," Associated Press, January 31, 2007.

37. Sherine Bahaa, "Criminals vs. Cowards," *Al Ahram Weekly*, January 2009, available at: http://weekly.ahram.org.eg/print/2009/928/re42.htm.

38. "Amr Moussa: Az Iran Baraye Hozur Dar Conferane Doha Dawat Nashodeh Ast" [Amr Moussa: Iran has not been invited to the Doha Conference], *Entekhab News*, March 17, 2009, available at: http://ww.entekhab.org/portal/index.php?news=1750&print.

39. "Ahmadinejad: Shi'a Folk Hero of Arab World," *Los Angeles Time*, September 24, 2007, and Dan Murphy, "In War's Dust, a New Arab 'Lion' Emerges; Hizbullah's Nasrallah is Hailed as a Regional Hero," *Christian Science Monitor*, August 29, 2006.

40. Muriel Mirak-Weisbach, "Why Condi's Anti-Shi'ite Alliance Won't Work," *EIR International*, November 17, 2006, pp. 48–50.

41. "Didar e Maharamaneh e Saud Faisal ba Maghamat e Israeli: Shoma ra beh Iran Tarjih Midahim" [Saud Al Faisal's secret meeting with Israeli officials: We prefer you to Iran], *Entekhab News*, March 5, 2009.

42. "Arabs Must Unite to Confront a Nuclear Iran, Saudi FM Says," Haaretz.com, March 3, 2009.

43. "Iran to Saudis: Don't Forsake Muslim Unity," Press TV, March 16, 2009. Also "Iran to Ensure Security of PG States," Press TV, March 17, 2009.

44. "Saudi Doubts Over Iran Sanctions," BBCNEWS, February 16, 2010, available at: http://newsvote.bbc.co.uk/mpapps/pagetools/print/news.bbc.co.uk/2/hi/middle-east/851730.

45. Ibid.

46. "Chahar Hezar Wahhabi vared e Iran Shodand" [Four thousand Wahhabis entered Iran], *Entekhab News*, February 19, 2009 at: http:www.entekhab.org/portal/index.php?news=504&print; and "Namaz e Jomeh e Wahhabioun Dar Tehran Kojast?" [Where are the Wahhabis Friday prayers in Tehran?], *Entekhab News*, February 22, 2009.

47. "Iran Cleric's Claim Angers Bahrain," *Los Angeles Times*, February 22, 2009.

48. "Bahrain Stops Gas Talks with Iran," Press TV, February 19, 2009, and "Bahrain Warned Against Anti-Iran Drive," Press TV, February 23, 2009.

49. "Iran-GCC Dispute Simmers," Press TV, February 24, 2009.

50. Muhammad Farazmand, "Ijad e yek noghteh e Jadid barkhord ba Iran" [The creation of another point of conflict with Iran], *Iranian Diplomacy*, February 27, 2009.

51. "Iran Moves to Ease Tensions with Bahrain," Press TV, February 23, 2009, and "Bahrain Foreign Minister: Bahrain Wants the Strengthening and Expansion of Relations with Iran," Mehr News Agency, February 26, 2009.

52. "Sultan Qaboos Visits Iran to Cement Relations," *Kuwait News*, August 5, 2009.

53. "Iranian, Omani Leaders Hold Talks in Tehran," *Tehran Times*, August 5, 2009.

54. "Iran: Oman to Fund $12 bn Kish Gas Project," September 2008, available at: http:www.highbeam.com/doc/1G1=18512963.html.

55. "Iranian DM to Visit Qatar Wednesday," Fars News Agency, February 22, 2010, available at: http://english.farsnews.com/printable.php?nn=8812031540.

56. Edward Yeranian, "Iran Signs Cooperation Pact with Gulf Neighbor Qatar," VOA News. com, February 24, 2010, available at: http://www.printthis.clickability.com/pt/cpt?action=cp& title=Iran+Sgns+Cooperation+pac.

57. "Iranian DM to Visit Qatar Wednesday."

58. "Iranian Interior Minister: Qatar-Iran Ties 'Intimate and Good,'" *Qatar News Agency*, March 9, 2010, available at: http://www.qnaol.net/QNAEn/Ne3ws_bulletin/News/Pages/10-03-09-1932_111_0066.aspx.

59. Efforts to reduce tensions between Iran and Egypt had started before Nasser's death. By 1974 the two countries had resumed diplomatic relations.

60. Because of the peace treaty with Israel, Egypt was expelled from the Arab League and the headquarters of the League were transferred from Cairo to Tunis. Sadat's own foreign minister, Ismail Fahmy, was among the opponents of Sadat's trip to Jerusalem and the subsequent peace treaty, and he resigned in 1977 in protest. For his views on the subject, see: Ismail Fahmy, *Negotiating for Peace in the Middle East* (Cairo: American University of Cairo Press, 1983).

61. Shireen T. Hunter, "Syria and Iran: From Hostility to Political Alliance," in *Iran And the Arab World*, ed. Hooshang Amirahmadi and Nader Entessar (New York: Palgrave Macmillan, 1993).

62. William Millward, "Egypt and Iran: Regional Rivals at Diplomatic Odds," *Commentary No. 22*, Canadian Security Intelligence Service, May 1992, available at: http://www.csis-scrs.gc.ca/pblctns/commntr/cm22-eng.asp.

63. The statement by Iran's deputy foreign minister "that Iran would be pleased to restore relations with an Egypt that had withdrawn from the Camp David agreement" illustrates the constraining impact of this factor on any potential thaw in Egyptian-Iranian relations.

64. *Tehran Times*, June 29, 1991.

65. "Velayati Rejects Criticism on His Visit to Cairo," Xinhua News Agency, June 9, 1994, accessed through: http://www.lexixnexis.com/us/Inacademic. Also, Safa Haeri, "Press Attacks Rafsanjani," *Independent*, June 10, 1994.

66. "Mubarak Meets Syrian Foreign Minister for Talks on Iran," Agence France Presse, July 4, 1996.

67. "Mubarak Calls on Iran to Break with Terrorism Ahead of Rapprochement," Agence France Presse, October 22, 1997. Other preconditions included the issue of the three disputed islands, which Iran considers a bilateral issue with the UAE, plus the problem of Khalid Al Islambuli.

68. Quoted in ibid.

69. "Egypt Warms toward New Iran President," *United Press International*, May 28, 1997.

70. "Mubarak to Stay Away from OIC Summit in Tehran," Agence France Presse, November 12, 1997.

71. "Mubarak Receives the Iranian Foreign Minister," Deutsche Presse-Agentur, May 6, 1997.

72. "Iran: President Khatami Reportedly Describes Egypt as 'Gate of Arabs,'" IRNA, December 20, 2000.

73. "Iran: Egypt's Mubarak Sends Congratulatory Message to Khatami," IRNA, June 12, 2001.

74. "Iranian and Egyptian Presidents Hold Landmark Meeting, Call for Better Ties," IRNA, December 3, 2003, and "Egyptian Press: Mubarak-Khatami Summit 'Historic and Crucial' Turning Point" IRNA, December 14, 2003.

75. "Iran Renames Khaled Eslambuli Street in Tehran to Intifadah," ILNA, January 6, 2006. In exchange, Egypt changed the street named after the Pahlavis to Dr. Mussadiq. Also, "Iran Street Name Change 'Very Positive' Egypt's Foreign Minister," MENA (Middle East News Agency), June 6, 2004.

76. Roger LaMotte, "Egypt-Iran Relations Reach New High With Mubarak's Planned Visit to Tehran," January 4, 2004, reprinted in *Payvand's Iran News*, available at: http://www.payvand.com/news/04/jan/1033.html.

77. Abdel Fattah Mady, "Iranian-Egyptian Relations Between Past and Present," *Islam*, February 20, 2008, available at: http://www.islamonline.net.servelet/Satellite?c=Article_C&cid=1203515457342&pagenam.

78. "Egypt-USA 'Special Relations' Reportedly Problem for Iran-Egypt Ties," *Hayat e Now*, December 20, 2000.

79. Brad Macdonald, "A Nightmare Alliance," *Trumpet*, March 2008, available at: http://www.thetrumpet.com/print.pjp?q=4754.0102.0.

80. Jennie Mathews, "Sudan Dismisses Egypt's Claim of Iran Role in Rebel Attack," Agence France Presse, May 27, 2007, and "Algerian Daily Dismisses Anti-Iran News in Egyptian Daily," IRNA, January 31, 2007.

81. "Ahmadinejad: Iran Ready to Reopen Embassy in Cairo at Earliest Term," *Deutsche Presse-Agentur*, December 26, 2007.

82. "Egyptian and Iranian Officials Hold Talks," Deutsche Presse-Agentur, September 18, 2007. The Iranian official was Abbas Araqchi, the deputy foreign minister.

83. "Ranking Iranian Official in Rare Egypt Visit Probes Normalizing Relations," *Deutsche Presse-Agentur*, December 26, 2007.

84. "Iran's Ahmadinejad Telephones Egyptian President Over Gaza," *Deutsche Presse-Agentur*, January 23, 2003.

85. "Rapprochement," *Iran Daily*, February 7, 2008, available at: http://ww.iran-daily.com/1386/html1/dotcoms.htm.

86. "Removal of a Single Mural Could Solve 90% of Egyptian–Iranian Problem," *National Post*, May 19, 2007.

87. For example, an Egyptian expert at the Al Ahram Center, Diaa Rashwan, was reported to believe that renewing ties with Iran would be in Egypt's interest, while Hala Mustapha, another expert, noting Egypt's dependence on the United States, considered this an imprudent act. In Egypt, Samah Abdullah, an Egyptian journalist writing in *Al Ahram*, the semiofficial daily, argued that Arabs should unite against Iran. Quoted in A. Savyon, Y. Mansharof, L. Azuri, "Iran's Attempts to Renew Relations with Egypt," *MEMRI*, no. 426, March 12, 2008. And Gamal Essam El-Din, "Iranian Rapprochement," *Al Ahram Weekly*, May/June 2008, available at: http://weekly.ahram.org.eg/print/2008/882/eg4.htm. In Iran, clearly the revolutionary purists considered establishment of ties as betrayal of the revolution's ideals. See: Kaveh L. Afrasiabi, "Iran and Egypt Point to a New Order," *Asia Times*, June 5, 2007.

88. "Egypt Rejects Armed Strike Against Iran," Associated Press/*Jerusalem Post*, September 19, 2007.

89. "Iran's Film on President Anwar Sadat the 'Assassination of a Pharaoh,'" *Now Public*, July 6, 2008, available at: http://www.nowpublic.com/world/irans-film-president-anwar-sadat-assassination-pharaoh, and Moustafa Suleiman, "Egypt Hits Back at Iran with Anti-Khomeini Movie," Al Arabiya.net, July 15, 2008. The name of the Egyptian movie is "Imam of Blood."

90. Quoted in K. L. Afrasiabi, "Iran and Egypt Pointing to a New Order," *Asia Times*, June 5, 2009.

91. "Iran's Ahmadinejad Presses Egypt on Gaza Stance," Reuters, January 10, 2009.

92. Ali Akbar Dareini, "Iran Hosts Pro-Hamas Gathering to Back Militant Group, Counter Gaza Meeting in Egypt," Associated Press, March 5, 2009, and "Egypt Hosts Gaza Summit after Ceasefire Declared," *Manila Times*, January 19, 2009.

93. For the background of Syrian-Iranian relations, see: Shireen T. Hunter, "Iran and Syria: From Hostility to Limited Alliance."

94. The number of Alawites is estimated between 15 to 20 percent of Syria's population. Another 10 percent of the population is Twelver Shia and the rest Sunni.

95. Patrick Seale, *Assad: The Struggle for the Middle East* (Berkeley: University of California Press, 1988), p. 353.

96. Bassel Oudat, "Friends in Need," *Al Ahram Weekly*, no. 926, December 18–24, 2008.

97. Shireen T. Hunter, "Iran and Syria: From Hostility to Limited Alliance," p. 209.

98. Ibid.

99. Mohammad Salam, "Iran Seeks To Rescue Its Ally in Lebanon," Associated Press, January 14, 1989.

100. Charles van der Leuw and John Bulloch, "Syria-Iran Conflict behind AMAL Attacks; Lebanon," *Sydney Morning Herald*, January 14, 1989.

101. "Former Iranian Envoy to Syria Discusses Role in Founding Hezbollah," *Al Sharq al Awsat*, May 14, 2008, BBC Monitoring-Middle East, accessed through Lexis-Nexis.

102. Quoted in *The Middle East Today*, no. 70, August 1991.

103. Quoted in Mohammad Tabaar, "Analysis: Breaking the Syria-Iran Alliance," BBC News, August 26, 2006.

104. For diverging views on whether such a strategy would succeed, see: Bassel Oudat, "Iran and Syria: How Strong is Their Alliance," *Al Ahram Weekly*, 2008.

105. "Syrian President in Tehran on Unexpected Visit," Xinhua News Agency, August 1, 1997, "Khatami Due in Syria on Thursday," IRNA, October 6, 2004. This was his third trip to Syria after his 1999 visit.

106. Michael Slackman, "Wary of U.S. Syria and Iran Strengthen Ties," *New York Times*, June 25, 2006, and Sami Moubayad, "Syria's One True Friend-Iran," *Asia Times*, 12 July, 2006.

107. Among others, see: "Syrian President Hold Talks with Iranian Counterpart, Other Officials," BBC Monitoring Middle-East, February 17, 2007, and "Ahmadinejad Visits Syria," *Guardian*, January 19, 2006.

108. Ian Black, "Middle East: Grave Mistake to Attack Iran, Warns Syria," *Guardian*, July 15, 2008.

109. "U.S. to Send Ambassador to Syria," VOA NEWS.com, March 9, 2010, available at: http://www.printthis.clickability.com/pt/cpt?action=cpt&title=U.S.+To+Send+Ambassador. Also, on the connection between U.S. overtures to Syria and pressure on Iran, see: Andrew J. Tabler, "The Hand Extended to Syria Is also Extended as a Blow to Iran," *The Independent*, February 18, 2010.

110. "Hezbollah Chief Meets Ahmadinejad in Damascus," Channelnesasia.com, February 27, 2010, available at: http://www.channelnewsasia.com/stories/afp_world/print/1040162/1/.html.

111. Quoted in "U.S. To Send Ambassador To Syria."

112. The first contact between what is now Iran and Lebanon took place in the Achaemenid period, when Persia ruled the Phoenician coast between 539 to 332 B.C. Josette Elayi, *Economie des cites phenicienne sou l'empire perse* (Naples: Istituto Universitario Orientale), p. 77.

113. Albert Hourani, "From Jabal Amil to Persia," in *Distant Relations: Iran and Lebanon in the Last 500 Years,* ed. H. E. Chehabi (London: I.B. Tauris, 2006), pp. 51–61.

114. See: H. E. Chehabi and Hassan I. Mneimneh, "Five Centuries of Lebanese-Iranian Encounters," in ibid., pp. 9–28.

115. Ibid., pp. 25–29.

116. Nassif Hitti, "Lebanon in Iran's Foreign Policy: Opportunities and Constraints," in Amirahmadi and Entessar, eds., p. 182.

117. Augustus Richard Norton, "Hizbullah: From Radicalism to Pragmatism," *Middle East Policy* 5, no. 4 (January 1998).

118. "Karami Sees New Iranian Policy of 'Openness' and 'Support,'" Radio Lebanon, September 11, 1991, BBC Summary of World Broadcasts, and "Iran's Vice President in Lebanon," Xinhua General News Service, December 26, 1991.

119. Douglas Davis, "Syria, Lebanon Upset at Secret Iranian Aid to Hizbullah," *Jerusalem Post,* January 14, 1996. Reportedly, when Iranian foreign minister Ali Akbar Velayati visited, Lebanon's president Elias Hrawi refused to meet with him. Ibid. Also, "Iran-Hizbollah; Iranian Official Says No 'Coolness' between Lebanon and Iran," *Al-Sharq Al Awsat,* May 12, 1996, BBC Summary of World Broadcasts.

120. "Lebanese Prime Minister Meets Iranian President in Islamabad," Radio Lebanon, March 23, 1997, BBC Summary of World Broadcasts.

121. "Hariri Ends Iran Visit with Khamenei Meeting," Associated Press Worldstream, October 28, 1997, and "Hariri Says Lebanon Ready to Help Improve Iran-Arab Ties," IRNA, October 25, 1997.

122. Hussein Darkoob, "Khatami Receives Triumphant Welcome on First Visit to Lebanon by an Iranian President," Associated Press, May 12, 2003.

123. Stephen Zunes, "The United States and Lebanon: A Meddlesome History," *Foreign Policy In Focus (FPIF) Policy Report,* April 26, 2006.

124. For a more skeptical view of Syrian involvement see: Naseer H. Aruri, "Remapping the Middle East: The Politics of Hariri's Assassination," *Counterpunch,* February 22, 2005, available at: http://www.counterpunch.org/aruri02222005.html.

125. Efraim Inbar, "How Israel Bungled the Second Lebanon War," *Middle East Quarterly* (Summer 2007), available at: http://www.meforum.org/1686/how-israel-bungled-the-second-lebanon-war.

126. Ibid.

127. Dan Murphy and Sameh Naguib, "Hizbullah Winning over Arab Street," *Christian Science Monitor,* July 18, 2006.

128. In an interview with CNN, Seymour Hersh claimed that the United States, the Siniora government, and Saudi Arabia, through the intermediary of Prince Bandar, supported the militants. The text of the interview is available at: http://peoplesgeography.com/2007/05/23/hersh-lebanon-violence-us-saudi-lebanese-government. Also Chris Marsden, "Bush Administration Endorses Anti-Palestinian, Anti-Syrian Offensive in Lebanon, *Global Research,* May 27, 2007.

129. Rym Ghazal, "Lebanese Defense Minister Urges Caution on Alleging Syria-Fatah Al Islam Link," *Daily Star*, June 22, 2007.

130. Robert F. North and Nada Bakri, "Lebanon Agreement Shifts Power to Hezbollah," *International Herald Tribune*, May 21, 2008.

131. "Lebanese President Requests Medium Weapons from Iran," Xinhua News Agency, November 26, 2006.

132. "Faaliat e Sanati e Iran dar Lobnan Gostarash miyabad," [Iran's industrial activity to increase in Lebanon], IRNA, February 25, 2009.

133. "Iran/Lebanon Envoy Says Iran, Lebanon Planning Siniora Visit to Tehran," *Thai Press Reports*, December 10, 2008.

134. "Lebanon Forms National Unity Government with Hezbollah," Rianovosti, November 10, 2009, available at: http://en.iran.ru/world/20091110/156775719-print.html.

135. Mohammad Irani, "A Lebanese in Tehran," *Iran Diplomacy*, February 1, 2010, available at: http://www.irandiplomacy.ir/index.php?lang=en&Page=21&TypeId=12&ArticleId=687&Br. The author argues that before coming to Iran, Hariri must get the OK of all regional countries.

136. "Iranian Vice President Ends Visit to Lebanon; Arrives in Jordan," BBC Summary of World Broadcast, December 31, 1991.

137. Sana Abdallah, "Jordan to Host Arab-Iranian Dialogue," *United Press International*, October 17, 1995.

138. "Iran Frees Two Jordanian Prisoners," *Deutsche Presse-Agentur*, December 11, 1997.

139. Tareq Ayyoub, "Iranian Foreign Minister Arrives in Amman Today," *Jordan Times*, June 19, 1999.

140. Pierre Jean Luizard, "Iraniens D'Irak, direction religieuse chiite et Etat arabe Sunnite" [Iranians of Iraq: Shi'a religious leadership and Sunni Arab state], *Cahier D'Etude Sur La Mediterranee Orientale Et Le Monde Turco-Iranien*, available at: http://cemoti.revue.org/document139.html.

141. For details, see: Andrew T. Parasiliti, "Iran and Iraq: Changing Relations and Future Prospects," in *Iran and the Arab World*, pp. 225–26.

142. Quoted in ibid., p. 223.

143. Ibid.

144. Some have alleged that Iran allowed some food and other products to get to Iraq. George Lardner Jr., "U.S. Intelligence Reports Says Iran is Getting Food to Iraq," *Washington Post*, September 25, 1990.

145. Kenneth Pollack claims that Iran tried to convince Iraq to join it in an anti-U.S. alliance. *Persian Puzzle*, p. 278.

146. "Al-Arabiyya Discusses Iraq Government, Al Sadr Trend Criticism of Iran Role," BBC Monitoring Middle East, May 5, 2008. Also Alisha Ryu, "Iraqi Shiites Caution Government about Renewing Ties with Iran," VOAnews.com, July 16, 2005.

147. Joost Hilterman, "External Forces on Iraq's New Government," *Christian Science Monitor*, April 19, 2006.

148. "Iran Criticizes Iraq President for Comments on Algiers Accord," IRNA, December 25, 2007.

149. Mina Islam, "garardad e Algezireh beh ghovat e khod baghi ast'" [The Algiers Agreement remains in force], *Iranian Diplomacy*, March 10, 2009.

150. "Ezharat Yak Magham e motalee Siyassi Dar Khousous masael Marzi Iran va Eragh" [A knowledgeable political official talks about Iran-Iraq border issues], IRNA, July 20, 2009,

and "Iran, Iraq Adopt Three Methods to Invest in Joint Oilfields," Mehr News Agency, September 12, 2009.

151. Mariam Karouny, "Analysis-Iraqi Shi'ites Alarmed at U.S. détente with Sunnis," Reuters AlertNet, November 1, 2006. Also "Ayatollah Yaqubi Demands Khalilzad's Expulsion," *Informed Comment*, March 31, 2006, available at: http://juancole.com.

152. "Lebanese Speaker Criticizes Iraqi Defence Minister's Statement on Iran," IRNA, July 27, 2004.

153. Christopher Torchia, "U.S. Talks with Sunni Insurgents Anger Iraqis," *Washington Times*, July 25, 2009.

154. "Iran-Iraq Trade to Increase," *The Ground Truth in Iraq*, March 26, 2009.

155. "Iraqi PM Arrives in Tehran to Kick Off Historical Visit," *China View*, July 16, 2006.

156. Kimi Yoshino, "Iraqi Prime Minister Visits Iran: Maliki is Expected to Try to Alleviate Tehran's Concerns About U.S. Influence in His Nation" *Los Angeles Times*, January 4, 2009.

157. "Al Rabei: Ekhraje Monafeghin Az Eragh Ghatei Ast" [Al Rabei: Expulsion of MKO from Iraq is certain.], Mehr News Agency, September 14, 2009.

158. FBIS/SA, February 21, 1979.

159. For a brief introduction to Islamic Jihad and Hamas, see: "Who Are Islamic Jihad?" BBC News, June 9, 2003, and "Hamas," Council on Foreign Relations, January 7, 2009.

160. Hillel Frisch, "The Iran-Hamas Alliance: Threat and Folly," *Perspective Paper*, no. 28, Begin-Sadat Center for Strategic Studies, May 1, 2007.

161. Scheherezade Faramarzi, "Hamas-Iran Links Full of Contradictions, But Also Mutual Interest," Associated Press Worldstream, March 19, 2007, obtained through Lexis-Nexis.

162. Ibid.

163. "How Iran Fits In," *Economist*, January 17, 2009.

164. Scheherezade Faramarzi, "Hamas-Iran Links Full of Contradictions, But Also Mutual Interest,"

165. "Joint Libyan-Iranian Communiqué: Rafsanjani's Talks in Syria," BBC Summary of World Broadcasting, June 25, 1985.

166. "Libyan Foreign Minister Denies Arms Sale to Iran," FBIS/SA, August 8, 1985, and Elaine Sciolino, "U.S. and Soviet Protest to Libya Over Iran Mines," *New York Times*, September 11, 1987.

167. "Iran's Rafsanjani in Libya: Talks with Qadhafi," BBC Summary of World Broadcasts," June 24, 1985.

168. Robert Fisk, "Libya Switches to Iraqi Side in the Gulf Conflict," *Times* (London), September 11, 1987.

169. Pinhas Inbari, "Libya Signals New, Moderate Message," *Jerusalem Post*, April 9, 1993.

170. "Libyan Official Seeks Help in Establishing Ties with Central Asian Countries," IRNA, September 21, 1995.

171. "Iranian Foreign Minister Ends Three Day Visit to Libya," IRNA, February 15, 1999.

172. "Iran-Libya to Ink Cooperation Agreement in Tripoli," IRNA, June 28, 2003.

173. "Iran's Vice President Arrives in Libya," BBC Worldwide Monitoring, January 16, 2006, and "Qadhafi Receives the Iranian President," Arabic News.com, July 3, 2006.

174. Khaled Yacoub Oweis, "Gadhafi Says Arabs Should Not Alienate Iran," Reuters, March 29, 2009.

175. "In Overture to Iran, Qadhafi Declares North Africa Shi'ite and Calls for Establishment of New Fatimid State," *Jihad Watch*, April 6, 2007.

176. "Qadhafi: Iran May Suffer Iraq's Fate," *Jerusalem Post*, August 5, 2008, and Ibrahim O. A. Dabbashi, "Libya Disagreed With UN Sanctions Resolution on Iran But Voted For It,"

Campaign Against Sanctions and Military Intervention in Iran, March 4, 2008, available at: http://www.campaignirsn.or/casmii.

177. Alan Cowell, "Tunisia Accusing Iran, Cracks Down on Dissent," *New York Times*, June 22, 1987.

178. This Algerian claim, however, seems unsubstantiated. Given the ideological outlook and the Sunni character of the Algerian opposition, it is highly unlikely that they were influenced by Shia Iran. In fact, when the author was visiting Algeria in May 1990, she was told that the Saudis were helping them financially and were spreading Wahhabism there. It was only after the Algerian Islamists supported Iraq in the first Gulf War (1991) that Saudi Arabia stopped supporting them.

179. "Iranian VP Stresses Economic Cooperation with Tunisia," *People's Daily*, April 21, 2001, and "Iranian-Tunisian Foreign Ministers Hold a Joint Press Conference," Ministry of Foreign Affairs of Islamic Republic of Iran, June 29, 2003, available at: http://web-srv,mfa.gov.ir.

180. "Iranian Foreign Minister to Visit Morocco in May," BBC Worldwide Monitoring, May 6, 2004.

181. "Electricity Cooperation between Iran and Tunisia Expands," Ministry of Energy News Agency, February 25, 2008. Also "Tehran Hosting Iran-Tunisia Joint Economic Commission," *Zawya*, April 8, 2008.

182. Sarah Touhari, "Moroccan Officials Concerned over Iranian Religious Intervention," *Maghrebia*, March 19, 2009.

183. "Khatami Says *Détente* Iran-Algeria 'Common Stance,'" IRNA, October 19, 2004, and "Iranian President to Begin Two-Day State Visit to Algeria 6, August 07," BBC Worldwide Monitoring, July 30, 2007.

184. "Algeria: President Bouteflika Holds Talks with Iranian Supreme Leader," BBC Worldwide Monitoring, October 20, 2003, and "Mixed Reports on Algerian President's Visit to Iran," BBC Worldwide Monitoring, August 7, 2008.

185. "Ravabet e Iran va Algezireh vared Marhaleh e Jadidi Mishavad" [Iran-Algeria relations to enter a new phase], Mehr News Agency, November 17, 2008.

186. "Iran's Defense Minister Wraps Visit to Algeria," IRNA, April 4, 2005.

187. "Tunisian President Backs Iranian Nuclear Rights," Arabic News.com, July 16, 2007, and "Iranian President Praises Algeria's Support for Its Nuclear Policy," BBC Worldwide Monitoring, September 17, 2006.

188. Conversations with the author in summer 2009.

189. "Algerian Press Divided Over Purpose of Iranian President's Visit," BBC Worldwide Monitoring, August 7, 2007.

190. Ibid.

CHAPTER 10

1. Efforts to change the inequitable international economic system were carried out in the context of the so-called New International Economic Order. For Iran's position on the subject see: Shireen T. Hunter, *OPEC and the Third World: The Politics of Aid* (Bloomington: Indiana University Press, 1984).

2. Shireen T. Hunter, *Iran and the World: Continuity in a Revolutionary Decade* (Bloomington: Indiana University Press, 1990), pp. 166–67.

3. In particular, the shah's repeated comparison between the price of raw materials and finished products was irritating to the industrial nations, as was his hawkishness on oil prices.

4. Nick Cumming Bruce, "Need for Supply Sources Broadens World Outlook," *Middle East Economic Digest* 9, no. 14 (April 4, 1975). Also, according to Firouz Vakil, by 1975 "the strategy of export promotion had become a no-choice policy for Iran's long-term development strategy." Firouz Vakil, "Iran's Macroeconomic Problems: A 20-year Horizon," in *Iran: Past, Present and Future*, ed. Jane V. Jacqz (New York: Aspen Institute for Humanistic Studies, 1976), p. 89.

5. It is believed that Darius tried to build a canal linking the Red Sea and the Mediterranean, a sort of precursor to the Suez Canal.

6. "Frontier Identity," *Africa Events*, February 1986.

7. These immigrants from Iran have become totally assimilated in the local population and have lost all distinctive features.

8. In this period, Iran helped to shore up Sudan, helped Zaire during the Shaba uprising, and assisted Somalia and promised more help should Ethiopia attack. Senegal, meanwhile, was the recipient of Iran's economic aid.

9. The following quote illustrates this point: "Iran has something else to offer Africa especially those fighting the apartheid in South Africa. They once held Vietnam as their symbol. . . . But Vietnam had both the material and moral support of China, the Soviet Union and other Communist nations. The Iranian Revolution, however, only had its own internal resources in the shape of mass resistance against the U.S. hubris. In this sense, therefore, Iran stands out as a natural inspirer, whose revolutionary fire the oppressed people of South Africa should emulate." In "Frontier Identity," *Africa Event*, February 1986.

10. Iran took part in the International Arms and Safety Equipment exhibition in Gabon in 1989 and displayed its domestically made arms. For details, see: FBIS/NES, January 26, 1989.

11. "Senegal-Iran: Dakar Embassy Closed," *Africa Research Bulletin* 21, no. 2 (February 1984).

12. For example, Iran was accused of converting Kenyans to Shiism. See: Arye Oded, *Islam and Politics in Kenya* (Boulder, CO: L. Rienner, 2000).

13. The presence of Shias is deeply resented by the majority Sunnis, especially those with Wahhabi tendencies, and the community has been under attack. In 2007, the Shia community center and other buildings were demolished by government forces. "Kano Shi'as Under Wahabi Threat," September 27, 2005, available at: http://al-huda-al-khoei.org. Also, "Nigerian Shi'a Base Knocked Down," BBC News, August 1, 2007.

14. Youssef M. Ibrahim, "Cutting Back in Lebanon, Iran Is Shifting to Sudan," *New York Times*, December 13, 1991. Also, Osama Bin Laden lived in Sudan for a period of six years from 1991 to 1996.

15. Ibid.

16. "Tanzania: Agreement Reached on Aid from Iran during Visit by President Mwinye," BBC Summary of World Broadcasts, June 20, 1989; "Ugandan President's Visit to Iran," BBC Summary of World Broadcasts, March 7, 1991; and "Zimbabwe: President Mugabe Assesses his Visits to Iran and Kuwait," BBC Summary of World Broadcasts, February 10, 1993.

17. "Iranian President Arrives for State Visit in South Africa," Deutsche Presse-Agentur, September 12, 1996.

18. Ibid.

19. Shona Kohler, "Dlamini Zuma: 8th Joint Commission Between SA-Islamic Republic of Iran," Polity org.za, December 14, 2004, available at: http://www.polity.org.za/print-version/dlamini-zuma-8thjoint-commission-between-saisla.

20. "President Moi Says Relations with Iran Good," BBC Summary of World Broadcasts, December 1998.

21. "Iranian President Terms His 7-Nation African Tour as Fruitful," IRNA, January 22, 2005.

22. "Iranian Delegation Calls at Foreign Ministry," *Modern Ghana News*, March 30, 2004, available at: http://www.modernghana.com/news/52437/1/Iranian-delegation-calls-at-foreign-ministry.html.

23. "Sudan Says Visit by Iranian President a Landmark in Relations," *Sudan Tribune*, October 5, 2004, available at: http://www.sudantribune.com/spip.php?mot78&debut_article_un=40.

24. "Ahmadinejad Calls on Oppressed Nations to Get United," June 30, 2006, Presidency of the Islamic Republic of Iran, *PIRI News Archive*, available at: http://www.president.ir/eng/ Ahmadinejad/cronicnews/1385/04/09/index-e.htm.

25. "President Ahmadinejad Returns from Senegal Visit," IRNA, March 14, 2008.

26. "Chaharomin e Safar e Rais Jomhour e Senegal beh Tehran" [The fourth trip of Senegal's president to Tehran], Mehr News Agency, October 15, 2009.

27. "Kharkhaneh e Tolid e Khodroye Samand Iran Dar Senegal Eftetah Shod" [Samand factory inaugurated in Senegal], IRNA, December 5, 2008, available at: http://www4.irna. ir/View/Fullstory/Tools/Printversion/?NewsId=252613.

28. "Vazir Niroo: Eradeh siassi Iran bara ye towseh eye ravabat ba Senegal ast" [Minister of energy: Iran's political will is to expand relations with Senegal], IRNA, December 3, 2008.

29. "Sudanese President to Visit Iran Monday," *Sudan Tribune*, April 23, 2006.

30. Cathy Majtenyi, "Iran-Sudan Hold Talks in Khartoum," VOAnews.com, February 28, 2007.

31. "Sudan-Iran Sign Military Cooperation Agreement," *Sudan Tribune*, March 8, 2008.

32. "The African Union and the Iranian Government Officials Hold Exploratory Meeting on the Africa-Iran Forum in Tehran," African Union, Division of Communication and Information, March 8, 2008.

33. "Gambia Looks to Iran for Support," News.com, December 4, 2006.

34. "Iran to Build Cheap Houses for Tanzania," Press TV, October 20, 2008.

35. "Iran Prepared to Expand All-Out Cooperation with Africa," Fars News Agency, September 3, 2006. Also, "Malawian Leader's Visit to Open New Page in Relations—Mottaki," Ministry of Foreign Affairs of the Islamic Republic of Iran, April 14, 2008, available at: http://web-srv-mfa.gov.ir/out put/English/documents/doc10862.htm.

36. "Muttaki az amadeghi e Iran Baraye hamkari ba Mali dar hozeh e energihaye now khabar dad" [Muttaki declares Iran's readiness to cooperate with Mali in the field of new energy], Fars News Agency, March 24, 2009.

37. "Emza ye panj sand e hamkari bein e Jomhuri Islami Iran va Jomhuri e Djibouti" [The signing of five economic cooperation agreements between the Islamic Republic of Iran and the Republic of Djibouti], Fars News Agency, February 24, 2009.

38. Alisha Ryu, "Iranian President Visits Kenya, Seeks Closer Relations," *Payvand News*, February 25, 2005, available at: http://www.payvandnews.com/news/09/feb/1303.html; and "Jozeiyat e movafegatnamehaye emza shodeh dar Nairobi" [Details of agreements signed in Nairobi], IRNA, February 26, 2009.

39. "Iran Accused of Promoting Shi'itism in Sudan," *Sudan Tribune*, December 24, 2006. Also, "Sunni Islamist Have Accused Iran of Trying to Spread Its Brand of Shi'ite Islam in the East African Country," *Sudan Tribune*, December 24, 2006. Iran for its part accused the Wahhabis, aided by Saudi Arabia, of anti-Iran activities. "Sudanese Deserve, Desire Closer Bonds," *Iran Daily*, November 15, 2008. In this article, Iran's cultural attaché in Khartoum says that

Wahhabis have mobilized in the last few years through building mosques, schools, and so forth, and by promoting anti-Shia tendencies with some success.

40. Thom Chiumia, "Analysts Critique of Malawi-Iran Relations," April 17, 2008, available at: http://www.nyasatimes.com/features67.html. According to the article, "Political analysts sound a warning that Malawians should be fearful when the Mutharika administration forges ties with undemocratic, repressive and unaccountable governments like Iran."

41. Rose Wanjiku, "Nuclear Power Not the Answer to Energy Problems," *Standard*, February 2, 2009, available at: http://www.estandard.net/rpint.php?id=1144004163&cid=15.

42. Cuba had links with Libya and the PLO, both of which were actively involved in subversion against the shah's regime. See: Damien J. Fernandez, *Cuba's Foreign Policy in the Middle East* (Boulder, CO: Westview Press, 1988), p. 85.

43. The following comments by the Ayatullah Khomeini to the visiting Nicaraguan minister of education illustrate this aspect of Iranian-Latin American relations. Khomeini said: "As you say, your county is very similar to our country. But ours has more difficulty . . . we should all try to create unity among the oppressed, regardless of their ideology or creed." Keyhan, 12 May 1983.

44. "Iran: First Vice President Arrives in Columbia," BBC Monitoring Middle East, July 6, 1999.

45. "Cuba: Vice President Lage Begins Official Visit to Iran," BBC Monitoring Latin America, October 7, 2000.

46. "Iran: Foreign Ministry Spokesman Lauds Visits by Cuban, Venezuelan Leaders," BBC Monitoring Middle East, May 21, 2001.

47. "Cuba-Khatami Visit," *News and Reports, PIRI News Headlines*, October 1, 2000.

48. Pascal Fletcher, "Iran Leader's Venezuela Visit May Irk U.S.," swissinfo.ch, March 7, 2005.

49. "Iran Signs First Free Trade Agreement," Mehr News Agency, March 15, 2005, available at: http://www.bilaterals.org/article.php3?id_article=2540.

50. "Iran-Venezuela to Ink Agreements Worth Over Billion Dollars," *Payvand's Iran News*, March 11, 2004.

51. "Chavez Baraye Haftomin Bar Beh Tehran Safar Khahad Kard" [Chavez will travel to Tehran for the seventh time], Mehr News Agency, September 4, 2009.

52. Since becoming president in 1999, Chavez has visited Iran seven times. Five of these visits have been during Ahmadinejad's presidency (2005–2009).

53. "Iran Leader Pushed Venezuela Ties," BBC News, November 25, 2009, available at: http://newsvote.bbc.co.uk/mpapps/pagetools/print/news.bbc.co.uk/2/hi/middle_eat/837831.

54. Yusuf Fernandez, "Iran, Latin America Construct New World System," Press TV, September 7, 2008.

55. "Iran Making Push into Nicaragua," *My Sa*, December 18, 2007.

56. Dan Murphy, "Latin America Welcomes Ahmadinejad," *Christian Science Monitor*, September 28, 2007.

57. "Nicaragua and Iran Sign Deals," *All Business*, January 18, 2007, available at: http://www.allbusiness.com/Caribbean/4012053-1.html.

58. "Iran Making Push into Nicaragua," *My Sa*, December 18, 2007, available at: http://printthis.clickability.com/pt/cpt?action=cpt&title=iran+making+push+into=Ni.

59. Paul Richter, "Hillary Rodham Clinton Warns of Chinese, Iranian Influence in Latin America," Chicagotribune.com, May 3, 2009.

60. Anne Marie O'Connor and Mary Beth Sheridan, "Iran's Invisible Nicaragua Embassy," *Washington Post*, July 13, 2009.

61. "Iranian President Ahmadinejad Visits Bolivia, Strengthens Ties with Leftist Governments of South America," *Arizona Daily Star*, September 28, 2008.

62. "Iran Wants to 'Exploit' Bolivian Uranium," BBC Monitoring Middle East, September 22, 2008.

63. "Bolivian President Evo Morales to Visit Tehran Monday" ISNA (Iranian Students News Agency), August 30, 2008.

64. "Sefartkhaneh hay e Iran va Ecuador Eftetah miyabad" [Iran and Ecuador open embassies], *Iranian Diplomacy*, December 3, 2008, available at: http://www.irdiplomacy.ir/index.php?lang=fa&Page=24&TypeId=10&ArticleId=3347&B.

65. "Brazilian President Lula Unable to Meet Iranian President," BBC Monitoring Latin America, September 25, 2007.

66. "Amorim says Brazil-Iran Tiers Can Move Beyond Trade Exchanges," *Tehran Times*, November 3, 2008.

67. Carlos Malmud and Carlota Garcia Encina, "Outside Players in Latin America-Iran," *ARI*, no. 124, April 12, 2007, available at: http://www.realinstitutoelcano.org/wps/portal/rielcano_eng/Content?WCM_GLOBAL_CO.

68. "Petrobras to Decide this Month on Iran Oil Deal," Press TV, January 21, 2009.

69. "Brazil a Priority for Iran," Press TV, November 2, 2008.

70. Conor Foley, "No One's Backyard," *Guardian*, October 4, 2007.

71. "Lula Urge Iran Nuclear Solution," BBC News, November 23, 2009, available at: http://newsvote.bbc.co.uk/mpapps/pagetools/print.news.bbc.co.uk/2/hi-middle_east/837382.

72. "S. Hashemi Meets Chavez," *Iran Daily*, August 20, 2008.

73. "Uruguay Seeks Expanded Ties with Iran," Press TV, March 6, 2010.

74. "Clinton Meets Uruguay's New President," *Washington Times*, March 1, 2010.

75. "Bolivian Government Defends, Opposition Criticizes Iranian President's Visit," BBC Monitoring Latin America, September 27, 2007.

76. Morteza Kazemian, "Continuity of a Failed Diplomacy," *Iran Diplomacy*, October 21, 2008.

Selected Bibliography

BOOKS

Ajami, Fouad. *The Vanished Imam: Musa al Sadr and the Shia of Lebanon.* Ithaca, NY: Cornell University Press, 1986.

Amirahmadi, Hooshang, and Nader Entessar. *Iran and the Arab World.* New York: St. Martin's Press, 1993.

Amirie, Abbas, and Hamilton A. Twitchell, eds. *Iran in the 1980s.* Tehran: Institute for International and Economic Studies, 1978.

Arberry, A. J., ed. *The Legacy of Persia.* Oxford: Clarendon Press, 1953.

Bahar, Muhammad Taghi. *Tarikh e Ahzab e Siassi* [History of political parties]. Tehran: n.p. 1323 [1945].

Benard, Cheryl, and Zalmay Khalilzad. *The Government of God: Iran's Islamic Republic.* New York: Columbia University Press, 1984.

Bill, James. *The Eagle and the Lion: The Tragedy of U.S.-Iran Relations.* New Haven, CT: Yale University Press, 1988.

Brown, Archie, ed. *New Thinking in Soviet Politics.* New York: St. Martin's Press, 1992.

Chehabi, H. E., ed. *Distant Relations: Iran and Lebanon in the Last Five Years.* London: I. B. Tauris, 2006.

Dobbins, James. *After the Taliban: Nation Building in Afghanistan.* Dulles, VA: Potomac Books, 2008.

Ehteshami, Anoushirvan, and Mahjoob Zweiri, eds. *Iran's Foreign Policy: From Khatami to Ahmadinejad.* Reading, England: Ithaca Press, 2008.

Eisman, Joshua, Eric Heginbotham, and Derek Mitchell. *China and the Developing World.* Armonk, NY: M. E. Sharpe, 2007.

Fukuyama, Francis. *The End of History and the Last Man.* New York: Free Press, 1993.

Groom, A.J.R. and Margot Light, eds. *Contemporary International Relations: A Guide to Theory.* London: Printer Publishers, 1994.

Holden, David. *Farewell to Arabia.* London: Faber and Faber, 1966.

Hunter, Shireen T. *Central Asia since Independence.* Westport, CT: Praeger, 1996.

Hunter, Shireen T. *Iran and the World: Continuity in a Revolutionary Decade.* Bloomington: Indiana University Press, 1990.

Hunter, Shireen T. *Islam in Russia: The Politics of Identity and Security.* Armonk, NY: M. E. Sharpe, 2004.

Hunter, Shireen T. *OPEC and the Third World: The Politics of Aid.* Bloomington: Indiana University Press, 1984.

Hunter, Shireen T. *The Transcaucasus in Transition: Nation-Building and Conflict.* Washington, DC: Center for Strategic and International Studies, 1994.

Hunter, Shireen T., ed. *Reformist Voices of Islam: Mediating Islam and Modernity.* Armonk, NY: M. E. Sharpe, 2008.

Hussein, Zahid. *Frontline Pakistan.* New York: Columbia University Press, 2007.

Issawi, Charles, ed. *The Economic History of Iran: 1800–1914.* Chicago, IL: University of Chicago Press, 1971.

Jaffrelot, Christopher, ed. *Pakistan: Nationalism without a Nation.* New York: Zed Press, 2002.

Karanjia, R. A. *The Mind of a Monarch.* London: George Allen and Unwin, 1977.

Keshishian, Joseph P. *Iran, Iraq, and the Arab Gulf States.* New York: Palgrave, 2001.

Lando, Barry M. *A Web of Deceit: The History of Western Complicity in Iraq from Churchill to Kennedy to George W. Bush.* New York: Other Press, 2007.

Levinson, Jerome, and Juan De Onis. *The Alliance That Lost Its Way.* Chicago, IL: Quadrangle Books, 1972.

Maley, William, ed. *Fundamentalism Reborn? Afghanistan and the Taliban.* New York: New York University Press, 1998.

Menon, Rajan, and Robert Ebel. *Energy and Conflict in Central Asia and the Caucasus.* Oxford: Rowan and Littlefield, 2000.

Morgenthau, Hans J. *Politics among Nations: Struggle for Power and Peace.* New York: Alfred A. Knopf, 1985.

Moussavian, Seyyed Hossein. *Iran-Europe Relations: Challenges and Opportunities.* London: Routledge, 2008.

Olson, Robert. *Turkey-Iran Relations, 1979–2004: Revolution, Ideology, War, Coups and Geopolitics.* Costa Meza, CA: Mazda Publishers, 2004.

Olson, Robert. *Turkey's Relations with Iran, Syria, Israel and Russia.* Costa Mesa, CA: Mazda Publishers, 2001.

Parsi, Trita. *Treacherous Alliances: The Secret Dealings of Israel, Iran and the United States.* New Haven, CT: Yale University Press, 2007.

Picco, Giandomenico. *Man without A Gun.* New York: Times Books, 1999.

Pollack, Kenneth M. *The Persian Puzzle.* New York: Random House, 2004.

Ramazani, R. K. *The Foreign Policy of Iran: A Developing Nation in World Affairs, 1500–1941.* Charlottesville: University of Virginia Press, 1966.

Rogov, Samuel. *The Iranian Triangle: The Untold Story of Israel's Role in Iran-Contra Affair.* New York: The Free Press, 1988.

Rubin, Barnett R. *The Search for Peace in Afghanistan.* New Haven, CT: Yale University Press, 1995.

Seale, Patrick. *Assad: The Struggle for the Middle East.* Berkeley: University of California Press, 1988.

Sepehr, Zabih and Shahram Chubin. *The Foreign Relations of Iran: A Developing Nation in a Zone of Great Power Conflict.* Berkeley: University of California Press, 1974.

Sick, Gary. *All Fall Down: The United States' Tragic Encounter with Iran.* New York: Random House, 1985.

Sick, Gary. *The October Surprise: America's Hostages in Iran and the Election of Ronald Reagan.* New York: Times Books, 1991.

Slavin, Barbara. *Bitter Friends, Bosom Enemies.* New York: St. Martin's Press, 2007.

Souresrafil, Behrouz. *Khomeini and Israel.* Wellington, NZ: CC Press, 1989.

Timmerman, Kenneth R. *The Death Lobby: How the West Armed Iraq.* New York: Houghton Mifflin, 1991.

Waltz, Kenneth N. *Theory of International Relations.* Reading, MA: Addison Wesley Publishing Company, 1979.

Wendt, Alexander. *Social Theory of International Politics.* Cambridge: Cambridge University Press, 1999.

Wright, Dennis. *The English among the Persians.* London: William Heinemann, 1977.

Yeselon, Abraham. *United States-Persian Diplomatic Relations, 1833–1921.* New Brunswick, NJ: Rutgers University Press, 1956.

Zabih, Sepehr, *The Communist Movement in Iran.* Berkeley: University of California Press, 1966.

JOURNAL ARTICLES

Borovali, Fuat Ali. "Kurdish Insurgencies, the Gulf War, and Turkey's Changing Role." *Conflict Quarterly* 2, no. 4 (Fall 1985).

Bulakbashi, Suha. "Turkey Copes with Revolutionary Iran." *Journal of South Asian and Middle Eastern Studies* 13, nos. 1 and 2 (1989).

Freedman, Robert O. "Russian Policy toward the Middle East under Putin: The Impact of 9/11 and the War in Iraq." *Alternatives, Turkish Journal of International Affairs* 2, no. 2 (Summer 2003).

Gerges, Fawaz. "Washington's Misguided Iran Policy." *Survival* 38, no. 103 (Winter 1996).

Glennon, Michael J. "The New Interventionism: The Search for a Just International Law." *Foreign Affairs* 78, no. 3 (1991).

Haidar, Ejaz. "Pakistan's Afghan Policy and Its Fallouts." *Central Asia Monitor* no. 5 (1998).

Hoogland, Eric. "Factions behind US Policy in the Gulf." *Middle East Report* 18, no. 2 (March/April 1998).

Hunter, Shireen T. "Iran's Pragmatic Regional Policy." *Journal of International Affairs* (Columbia University) 56, no. 2 (Spring 2003).

Hunter, Shireen T. "Muslim Republics of the Former Soviet Union: Implications for the US." *Washington Quarterly* 15, no. 3 (Summer 1992).

Hunter, Shireen T. "Nationalist Movements in Soviet Asia." *Current History* 89, no. 549 (October 1990).

Huntington, Samuel. "The Clash of Civilizations." *Foreign Affairs* 72, no. 3 (Summer 1993).

Huntington, Samuel. "The Lonely Superpower." *Foreign Affairs* 78, no. 3 (March/April 1999).

Indyk, Martin. "Watershed in the Middle East." *Foreign Affairs* 71, no. 1 (1992).

Jervis, Robert. "The Remaking of a Unipolar World." *Washington Quarterly* (Summer 2006).

Lake, Anthony. "Confronting Backlash States." *Foreign Affairs* 73, no. 2 (1994).

Mesbahi, Moheiddin. "Russian Foreign Policy and Security in Central Asia and the Caucasus." *Central Asian Survey* 12, no. 2 (1993).

O'Connor, Sarah. "Neo-Conservatives as Wilsonians?" *International Affairs Journal at UCDAVIS* 2, no. 2 (Winter 2006).

Pipes, Daniel. "A New Axis: The Emerging Turkish–Israeli Alliance." *National Interest* (Winter 1997–1998).

Rahm, Julie M. "Russia, China, India: A New Strategic Triangle for a New Cold War." *Parameters* 31, no. 4 (2001).

Rice, Condoleezza. "Promoting the National Interest." *Foreign Affairs* 79, no. 1, 2000.

Rodman, Peter. "The World's Resentment: Anti-Americanism as a Global Phenomenon." *National Interest*, no. 60 (Summer 2000).

Rubin, Michael. "Iran's Dialogue of Civilization: A First Hand Account." *The Middle East Quarterly* (March 2000).

Index

About the Author

SHIREEN TAHMASSEB HUNTER is a visiting professor at the Prince Alwaleed Bin Talal Center for Muslim–Christian Understanding of the Georgetown University's Edmund A. Walsh School of Foreign Service. She has been associated with the ACMCU since 2005. Before that she was the director of Islam Program (1998–2005) and deputy director of Middle East Program (1983–1993) at the Center for Strategic and International Studies (CSIS), and senior visiting fellow at the Center for European Policy Studies, Brussels (1994–1998). From 1966 to 1978 she was a member of the Iranian Foreign Service.

She is the author and editor of 14 books and 7 monographs, including *Iran and the World: Continuity in a Revolutionary Decade* (1990) and *Iran after Khomeini* (1992). She has contributed to 40 volumes and published 50 journal articles. Her latest publications include: *Reformist Voices of Islam: Mediating Islam and Modernity* (2008), *Modernization, Democracy and Islam* (Praeger, 2005), *Islam in Russia: The Politics of Identity and Security,* (2004), *Islam: Europe's Second Religion* (Praeger, 2002), and *The Future of Islam and the West: Clash of Civilizations or Peaceful Coexistence* (Praeger, 1998). Some of her books have been translated into Arabic and Persian.

She has widely lectured in the United States, Europe, the Middle East, Caucasus, Central Asia, and the Russian Federation, and regularly contributes to the media.

Cooperation 58

cultural + Social exchanges 54

pragmatism link to nationalism 56